Overview

Introduction

I. Writing Games with Lingo
1. Creating Games with Director and Lingo
2. An Introduction to Games

II. Puzzle Games
3. Matching Game
4. Memory Game
5. Jigsaw Puzzle
6. Sliding Puzzle
7. Falling Blocks Puzzle

III. Arcade Games
8. Falling Objects
9. Shooting Gallery
10. Sprite Invaders
11. Space Rocks
12. Paddle Bricks

IV. Word Games
13. Trivia Game
14. Cryptogram
15. Hangman
16. Word Search
17. Crossword Puzzle

IV. Card Games
18. Video Poker
19. Blackjack
20. Solitaire

V. Adventure and Strategy Games
21. Adventure Game
22. Maze Game
23. Strategy Game

VI. Multiplayer Games
24. High Score Boards
25. Multiplayer Game

Appendixes
A. Useful Lingo Index
B. Useful Internet Resources

Index

Contents

Introduction 1

I. **Writing Games with Lingo**

  1. **Creating Games with Director
      and Lingo** **11**
      Games and Macromedia Director 12
        Director's Strengths 12
        Director's Weaknesses 13
      Game Lingo 13
        Programming Step by Step 14
        One-Frame Movies 15
        Object-Oriented Thinking 15
        Using Behaviors 16
        Lists 17
      Making Games 18
        Game Screens 18
        Planning and Preparation 22
        Where to Start 22
        Finishing the Game 23
        Troubleshooting and Debugging 23
        User Testing 24
        Distribution 25

  2. **An Introduction to Games** **27**
      From *Senet* to *Space War* 28
        The Evolution of Board Games 28
        War and Role-Playing Games 29
      From *Space War* to *Pong* 30
      From *Pong* to *Pac-Man* 30
      The Video Game Comes Home 32
      Games Invade Computers 33
      Games and Macromedia Director 33
      Further Reading 34

II. **Puzzle Games** **37**

  3. **Matching Game** **39**
      Game Overview 40
        Close Enough for a Match 40
        Correct Matches 41

	Locking Sprites into Place	42
	Game Over	43
	Special Effects	43
	Making the Game	44
	Putting It All Together	51
	Game Variations	51
	Making a Longer Game	51
	Keeping Score	51
	Timing the Player	52
	Creative Screen Layout	53
	Randomness	53

4. Memory Game **55**

Game Overview	56
Shuffling the Deck	57
Time for Pause	57
The Hidden Picture	57
The Cards	58
Game Over	58
Special Effects	59
Making the Game	59
Putting It All Together	65
Game Variations	66
Keeping Score	66
Adding a Timer	67
Two-Player Game	69

5. Jigsaw Puzzle **71**

Game Overview	72
Dragging	72
Creating Puzzle Pieces	73
Random Placement	74
Payoff	74
Special Effects	74
Making the Game	75
The Frame Behavior	75
The Sprite Behavior	77
Putting It All Together	84
Game Variations	84
Looking at the Box	85
Different Puzzle Shapes	86

6.   Sliding Puzzle **87**
  Game Overview 88
    Puzzle Pieces 88
    The Sliding Motion 89
    Detecting Game Over 89
    Special Effects 89
  Making the Game 90
    Frame Behavior 90
    The Sprite Behavior 95
  Putting It All Together 96
  Game Variations 97
    Rectangular Pieces 97
    Sliding Number Puzzles 97

7.   Falling Blocks Puzzle **99**
  Game Overview 100
  Blocks and Pieces 100
    Timing the Fall 101
    Keyboard Input 101
    Special Effects 101
  Making the Game 102
  Putting It All Together 111
  Game Variations 111
    Changing the Shapes 111
    Adding Color 112
    Keeping Score 112
    Speeding It Up 112
    Adding a Background 112

III.   Arcade Games **113**
  8.   Falling Objects **115**
    Game Overview 116
      Many Behaviors or One? 117
      Timing Drops 117
      Defining a Catch 117
      Game Over Options 118
      Penalty for Bad Catches 118
      Increasing Difficulty 118
      Distinguishing Good Objects from Bad 118
      Special Effects 119
    Making the Game 119
    Putting It All Together 128

Game Variations 129
  Educational Variants 129
  Changing Perspective 130
  Adding Animation 130
  Increasing Difficulty 130
  Catching a Bomb 130

9. Shooting Gallery **131**
Game Overview 132
  Types of Animation 133
  Random Appearances 133
  Limited Ammunition 134
  Screen Elements 134
  Point Values 134
  Special Effects 134
Making the Game 135
  Target Behavior 135
  Frame Behavior 141
  Blast Sprite Behavior 145
  Blocking Sprite Behavior 145
Putting It All Together 146
Game Variations 147
  A Richer Environment 147
  A Friendlier Environment 148
  More Animation 148

10. Sprite Invaders **149**
Game Overview 150
  Ship Movement 150
  Invader Movement 151
  A Lot of Bullets 151
  Levels 152
  Lives .152
  Special Effects 152
Making the Game 152
  Ship Behavior 152
  Invader Behavior 155
  Frame Behavior 158
  Bullet Behavior 162
  Invader Bullet Behavior 164
Putting It All Together 165
Game Variations 166
  Different Orientation 166

Product Placement 166
More Game Features 166

11. Space Rocks **167**
Game Overview 168
Ship Movement 168
Rock Movement 168
Breaking Rocks 169
Screen Wrap 169
Limited Ammunition 169
Levels 170
Special Effects 170
Making the Game 170
Frame Behavior 170
Ship Sprite Behavior 177
Rock Sprite Behavior 180
Bullet Sprite Behavior 182
Putting It All Together 183
Game Variations 184
Shields 184
Flying Saucers 184
Thruster Graphics 184
More Rock Variations 184
Using Vector Shapes 184
12. Paddle Bricks **185**
Game Overview 186
Moving the Paddle 186
The Ball 186
Bricks 187
Levels 187
Special Effects 187
Making the Game 187
Frame Behavior 188
Ball Behavior 190
Brick Behavior 195
Paddle Behavior 196
Putting It All Together 196
Game Variations 197
Decreasing Paddle Size 197
Colorful Arrangements 197
Turn It on Its Side 198
Multiple Balls 198

IV.   Word Games **199**

13. Trivia Game **201**

Game Overview 202

   The Question Database 202

   Screen Layout 203

   Buzzing In 203

   Time Running Out 203

   Penalties 203

   Disappearing Answers 204

   Special Effects 204

Making the Game 204

   Frame Behavior 204

   Button Behavior 208

Putting It All Together 210

Game Variations 211

   Number of Answers 212

   Levels of Play 212

   Randomizing the Questions 212

   The Clock Is Ticking 212

14. Cryptogram **213**

Game Overview 214

   Encoding the Phrase 214

   Displaying the Solution 215

   The Text Cursor 215

   Phrase Storage 215

   Capital Letters 216

   Special Effects 216

Making the Game 216

Putting It All Together 224

Game Variations 225

   Phrase Ideas 225

   Adding a Timer 226

   Levels of Difficulty 226

   Allowing Spaces 226

   Hints 226

   Give Up 226

15. Hangman **227**

Game Overview 228

   The Workspace 228

   Guessing Letters 228

   The Hangman 229

The Message Area 229

Next Phrase Button 229

Phrases 230

Special Effects 230

Making the Game 230

The Frame Behavior 230

The Letters Behavior 237

The New Phrase Button Behavior . . .237

Putting It All Together 238

Game Variations 239

Accepting Keyboard Input 239

Phrase Themes 239

Hangman Without the Hangman . . .240

16. Word Search **241**

Game Overview 242

The Matrix 243

The Word List 243

Selecting a Word 243

Marking Words 243

Populating the Matrix 243

Making the Game 244

Putting It All Together 255

Game Variations 256

Word Themes 256

Matrix Size 257

Word Direction 257

Selection Methods 257

17. Crossword Puzzle **259**

Game Overview 260

The Grid 260

The Clue List 261

Building the Puzzle 261

Character Entry 261

Special Effects 261

Making the Game 262

Frame Behavior 262

Grid Square Behavior 274

Clue List behavior 275

Putting It All Together 275

Game Variations 276

Crossword Themes 276

Stretching the Definition of a Word . .276
Storing Multiple Puzzles in One Game 277
Skipping the Puzzle-Building Step . . .277

V.   Card Games **279**
18. Video Poker **281**
Game Overview 282
The Deck of Cards 283
Three Screens 283
Poker Hand Values 284
Giving Values to Hands 286
The Draw 286
Special Effects 287
Making the Game 287
Frame Behavior 287
Hold Button Behavior 294
Other Button Behaviors 296
Putting It All Together 296
Game Variations 298
Colorful Background 298
Better Cards 298
No Card Backs 298
Win Sounds 299
Progressive Scoring 299
19. Blackjack **301**
Game Overview 302
The Shoe 302
The Cards As Sprites 303
Displaying Hands 304
Hand Values 304
Insurance 304
Double 305
Splits 305
Multiple Screens 305
Special Effects 306
Making the Game 306
Putting It All Together 321
Game Variations 324
Dealer Hits on Soft 17 324
Limiting Splits and Doubles 324
Cards and Background 324

Bets and the Wallet 324
Chips 325
20. Solitaire **327**
Game Overview 328
Deck of Cards 329
Naming Conventions 330
Sprite Arrangement 330
Card Movement 330
Special Effects 331
Making the Game 331
Frame Behavior 331
Card Drag Behavior 342
Other Behaviors 345
Putting It All Together 345
Game Variations 346
Las Vegas Rules 347
Animated Cards 347
Other Solitaire Games 347

**VI. Adventure and Strategy
Games** **349**
21. Adventure Game **351**
Game Overview 352
Rooms 352
Movement 353
Walls 353
Objects 353
Doors 354
Monsters 354
Signs 355
Containers 355
Points 355
The Puzzle 355
Special Effects 356
Making the Game 356
Character Behavior 356
Wall Behavior 362
Object Behavior 363
Door Behavior 364
Monster Behavior 365
Sign Behavior 368

Container Behavior 368
Points Behavior 369
Message Behavior 370
Putting It All Together 371
The Game Diagram 371
Creating the Rooms 372
Attaching the Behaviors 374
Game Variations 375
Scenarios 375
Multiple Monsters 375
Keys That Open Containers
That Have Keys 375
Secret Doors 376
More Behaviors 376
The Aftermath 376
Game Over 376

22. Maze Game **377**
Game Overview 378
Generating a Random Maze 378
Moving Around in the Maze 379
Graphics 379
A Goal 380
Special Effects 380
Making the Game 380
Maze Movie Script 380
Maze Frame Behavior 384
Putting It All Together 386
Game Variations 387
Better Walls 387
Different Size Maze 388
Different Maze Shape 388
Objects in the Maze 388
An Enemy in the Maze 388

23. Strategy Game **389**
Game Overview 390
Countries and Connections 390
Start of Play 391
Start of a Turn 391
Attacking 391
Victory 391
Artificial Intelligence 392

The Map 392
Special Effects 392
Making the Game 393
The Movie Script 393
Initialization Behavior 397
Country Behaviors 397
Initial Place Behavior 398
Player Place Behavior 400
Player Attack Behavior 401
Computer Place Behavior 404
Computer Attack Behavior 408
Putting It All Together 411
Game Variations 413
Better AI 413
Different Maps 414
Victory Determinants 414
Fortifications 414
Extra Armies 414
More Players 414

VII. Multiplayer Games 415

24. High Score Boards 417
Basic Method 418
HTML Forms 418
CGI Scripts 419
Implementations 419
HTML High Score Board 419
Built-In High Score Board 420
Score Rotation 420
Making the High Score Board 420
Submitting a High Score 421
Recording a High Score 422
Getting the High Score Board 425
Displaying the High Score Board . . .427
Using the High Score Board 428
Setup 428
Other Uses for High Score Boards 429
Contests 429
Surveys 429
Replacing HTML Forms 429
High Scores from a Projector 429

25. Multiplayer Game **431**
    Game Overview 432
        What You Will Need 432
        Running the Multiuser Server 433
        Making a Game Lobby 433
        Game Play 434
    Making the Game 434
        Movie Script 434
        User List Behavior 444
        Tic-Tac-Toe Behavior 444
        Game Sprite Behavior 447
    Putting It All Together 448
    Game Variations 449
        Input Validation 449
        Cancellation 449
        Multiple Challenges 449
        Better User Identification 449

VIII. Appendixes **451**
  A.   **Useful Lingo Index** **453**
  B.   **Useful Internet Resources** **457**
    Director and Lingo 458
    Shockwave Game Sites 459
    Game Design 459
    Game Programming 461
    Artificial Intelligence 462
    Classic Video Games 463
    General Game Information 464
  Index **467**

About the Author

Gary Rosenzweig is a game designer, programmer, entrepreneur, and the author of five books on Macromedia Director. He owns and operates CleverMedia, a Shockwave game-development company that runs four game sites on the Internet: `http://clevermedia.com`, `http://gamescene.com`, `http://gamespark.com`, and `http://flasharcade.com`.

Since founding CleverMedia in 1996, the company has produced more than 150 games. The games on the four sites that make up the "CleverMedia Network" are all free for Web surfers to play. Many of the games have also been licensed to other Web sites.

Rosenzweig started in the multimedia business by obtaining a bachelor's degree in computer science from Drexel University in Philadelphia. His interest in newspapers took him to the University of North Carolina in Chapel Hill where he earned a master's degree in journalism and mass communication.

From 1994 to 1996, Rosenzweig worked for Reuters and TCI as the Lingo expert for Ingenius, an educational software company. He wrote his first Lingo book in 1995 and distributed it for free on the Internet. In 1996, *The Comprehensive Guide to Lingo* was published by Ventana, followed the next year by *The Director 6 Book*. In 1999, *Special Edition Using Director 7* was published by Macmillan. Gary has also spoken at many Macromedia user conferences and the Game Developers Conference.

Gary reads a lot of classic science fiction books, likes to go to the movies, and enjoys travel. He lives in Denver, Colorado, with his wife, Debby, cat, Lucy, and dog, Natasha.

To email Gary, go to this Web page:

`http://clevermedia.com/resources/gamesbook/`

Dedication

This book is dedicated to my Mom and Dad, who have always had an unlimited supply of encouragement and support. They are the secret to my success.

Acknowledgments

Thanks to my wife, Debby, who enjoys challenging me to board games on our front porch and likes to test out the latest games at CleverMedia.

Thanks to my mom and dad, Jacqueline and Jerry, who always had a closet full of games while I was growing up and never complained that I was playing the Atari too much.

Thanks to my brother, Larry, who played games with me while we were growing up, even though he was several years younger than I, and I always won.

Thanks to my grandmom, Rebecca Jacob, who bought me my first computer. A week later, I had written my first game.

Thanks to my aunt and uncle, Barbara and Richard Shifrin, who collected chess sets and taught me how to win at Risk™.

Thanks to William Follett and Jay Shaffer, my friends and co-workers at CleverMedia. When you work with these guys, you realize that the only thing more fun than playing games is making them.

Thanks to all the people at Macmillan USA who helped put this book together: Karen Whitehouse, Beth Millett, John Nyquist, Julie McNamee, Brandon Penticuff, Anne Jones, Lori Lyons, Maribeth Echard, Eric S. Miller, Chris Barrick, and many others.

Tell Us What You Think!

As the reader of this book, *you* are our most important critic and commentator. We value your opinion and want to know what we're doing right, what we could do better, what areas you'd like to see us publish in, and any other words of wisdom you're willing to pass our way.

As an Associate Publisher for Que, I welcome your comments. You can fax, email, or write me directly to let me know what you did or didn't like about this book—as well as what we can do to make our books stronger.

Please note that I cannot help you with technical problems related to the topic of this book, and that due to the high volume of mail I receive, I might not be able to reply to every message.

When you write, please be sure to include this book's title and author as well as your name and phone or fax number. I will carefully review your comments and share them with the author and editors who worked on the book.

Fax: 317-581-4666

Email: hayden@mcp.com

Mail: Greg Wiegand
           Que
           201 West 103rd Street
           Indianapolis, IN 46290 USA

Introduction

For years, I have been contemplating writing a Lingo games book. What, exactly, would I put into such a book?

On one hand, I thought about what it would take to write a chapter for *every* basic computer game that I could possibly think of—literally hundreds. Another idea was not to teach even a single specific game, but rather to write about concepts and techniques used in games.

Both of these ideas had major flaws. The first would make a useful CD-ROM product, but wouldn't make a good book. I wouldn't be able to go into enough detail.

The second idea would be great for people who want to read about Lingo and ponder it, but not very useful for those who want to put it into practice.

So, I found a middle road. I would take 21 basic computer games and use those to illustrate many concepts and techniques used in making games. You can decide whether you want to focus on the games themselves, or on the techniques behind them.

In addition, because the games use advanced Lingo, I took the opportunity to ensure the book would be useful for those who want to use it to advance their Lingo skills, regardless of the game content.

What Is in This Book?

This book is full of games. Not just descriptions and theory, but the actual games themselves. This book contains all the source code for each game. You can read the code, learn from it, and even copy the code to make your own games.

The first two chapters introduce you to the world of games and making games in Director. They provide a background that will help those who prefer to read this book cover-to-cover.

The middle 21 chapters each take a specific game and show you how to create it. Every piece of Lingo code is in the book, as well as on the sample movies on the CD-ROM.

The last two chapters deal with two special topics. The first is how to make an Internet high score board. The last chapter shows you how to make a multiplayer game using the Macromedia Multiuser Server.

One of the things you will notice about this book if you quickly flip through the pages is the large amount of Lingo on its pages. This is a Lingo book, and you will find more Lingo here than probably in any other book.

The \SOURCE_FILES directory on the CD-ROM contains full, open-source examples of each movie in the book. There are 23 complete games representing Chapters 3 through 25.

Purposefully, the artwork in the examples is very simple. This way, you can focus on the Lingo, rather than the appearance of the games. Then, the games can also be turned into your own creations by replacing these placeholder graphics with some more color, finished artwork.

Whom Is This Book For?

This book has several different audiences. It is written mostly for intermediate- to advanced-level Lingo programmers, but can also be used in a different way by beginners, nonprogrammers, and non-Lingo programmers.

Intermediate to Advanced Lingo Programmers

After you reach a certain level as a Lingo programmer, you stop growing vertically and start growing horizontally. What I mean is that your skill level stays basically the same, but you begin to experiment with new techniques and concepts.

For instance, someone who has created business presentations for years with Lingo might have never tried to use Lingo to make a game. They have the basic skills required, but just need to learn how to redirect those skills to create something new.

This book is primarily written for those who understand the basics of Lingo and use it frequently. However, they want to expand their efforts beyond what they are doing now and create games.

Lingo Game Programmers

Another type of person that will find this book useful is someone who already uses Lingo to make games. In this case, this book is a timesaver. Instead of starting from scratch and creating a game, you can use the games in this book as a template for your own games.

This will not only save time, but will expose you to another person's way of thinking about Lingo programming and games.

Highly Motivated Beginners

So, can this book be used at all by beginners? Sure, it can. But you will have to be a highly motivated beginner. You need to be the sort of person who reads and rereads, digests and investigates, inquires and experiments.

If someone who did not know Lingo asked me if they could learn Lingo from this book, I would answer no. But, if someone decided to take this book and do it anyway, and they were motivated, I'm sure they would succeed.

This is especially true if you already have a background in other programming languages. In that case, this book could be a way for you to skip all the handholding beginner books and get right to programming.

Nonprogrammers

The byproduct of this book is 23 complete games. A Director user who is not a programmer could take these game files from the CD-ROM, change only the graphics, some text, and some Score arrangements, and make games.

One warning for those who want to do this: Do not expect to be able to alter or add to the Lingo code here. As the title states, it is "advanced" Lingo, and not easy for beginners to decipher or manipulate.

Despite this warning, I am sure that I will get many email messages from Lingo beginners and nonprogrammers asking me how they can modify a game to perform some task or another. My answer will have to be that if they want to modify the game, they will have to learn more about Lingo first.

Why Did I Write This Book?

I wrote this book because you asked for it. Well, maybe not you in particular, but a lot of Director users have. Even before my first mass-market book was published in 1996, friends and colleagues suggested that I write a book about Lingo games.

In 2000, the time is right for this book. Even Macromedia has acknowledged Director's use as a game platform by creating its own spin-off company to create Shockwave entertainment.

Although I am not aware of any actual statistics, I predict that most Director users create games of one sort or another. The rest of the Director users probably wish they did as well.

What Should You Already Know?

So, what exactly do I mean by *advanced* Lingo? What *advanced* means to one user can be totally different from what it means to another user.

I have seen people call themselves Lingo programmers even though they could write only *on mouseUp* handlers with a *go to frame 2* in it. That is not an advanced Lingo programmer. That is not even a beginner.

To give you an idea of what you should already know, I have constructed the following chart. You don't need to fit the chart exactly, but you should feel comfortable that what you don't know, you can learn. Of course, you should already be familiar with Director's interface elements, such as the Score, Cast, and Stage. Table I.1 lists Lingo skills that you should also have.

Table I.1   What You Should Know Before Using This Book

Skill	Know About	Used Before	Understand Thoroughly
Handlers	●	●	●
Variables	●	●	●
Loops	●	●	●
Lists	●	●	
Behaviors	●	●	
Behavior Properties	●	●	
Behavior Parameters	●		
Sprite Control	●	●	
Text Handling	●		

The preceding table lists specific elements of Lingo. However, there is also the matter of problem-solving skills. A programmer must be a problem-solver. You cannot expect to create anything with computers by just following instructions.

An advanced Lingo programmer must be a problem-solver. One who knows every Lingo command, but doesn't know how to put them together to perform a task is as bad off as someone who doesn't understand Lingo at all.

You should also be able to debug your own programs. A Lingo programmer who runs into a bug should start investigating it, determine the problem, and implement a solution. This goes beyond simply using the Lingo debugger. You must be able to understand the problem and understand your solution. Anything less and you will find yourself unable to create freely.

How to Use This Book

There are three ways that I foresee this book being used. The first is to make games. The second is to learn advanced Lingo. The third way is to learn nothing, steal the games, and use them in your Director projects.

Learning to Make Games with Lingo

This is the most straightforward use for the book. By reading the chapters and playing around with the sample movies on the CD-ROM, you will gain insight into how to create all sorts of games.

You should be able to take this insight and modify the games to make your own. You should also be able to create games by taking the techniques taught here and combining them in different ways.

Learning Advanced Lingo

The Lingo techniques in this book are far more advanced than what you find in your standard Director presentation. Therefore, by studying these chapters, you will improve your Lingo skills.

This is not a reference book, however. Do not expect to be able to look up a specific problem and find a solution here. Instead, expect to be able to learn techniques that will enable you to come up with your own solutions.

Steal the Games

Technically, because you paid for the book, it isn't really stealing. So, go ahead and take the source code files here and make your own games with them.

However, as I warned earlier in this introduction, don't expect to be able to modify the games very much if you are not willing to give yourself the chance to learn Lingo first.

The CD-ROM

Most computer books that you buy today come with a CD-ROM. However, many of these CD-ROMs contain very little information that you can actually use. With this book, on the other hand, the CD-ROM is very important. Check out the inside back cover for more details on software demos and useful collections. Each and every game in this book has a corresponding file on the CD, in the \SOURCE_FILES directory. This means that you don't have to type the lines of code yourself. In addition, you can open the files and play with the games and the code immediately.

I recommend that readers check out each game file on the CD before they read each chapter. This will give you a good sense of what information is in the chapter.

All the files here are Director 7-formatted files, so they will open in both Director 7 and Director 8. All the code works in both of those versions of Director.

Conventions

This book uses many conventions to make it easier for you to understand the code. If you see some code in a paragraph in italic, this means that the keyword or keywords are actual Lingo syntax that you can look up in the Director online help or other Director books. However, if the code is in quotation marks, then it means that the syntax is user-defined, such as variable or handler names.

So, for instance, *on exitFrame* is in italic because it is official Lingo syntax. You can look this up in other sources and find it. However, something such as "on showScore" is a custom-made handler. You will not find this in other materials because I made it up for the particular example. If you do find it in other materials, it will be a different handler made up for a different purpose.

In the sections of the book that show code, note that the double-dash (a "--") represents a comment line. You can have this either at the beginning of a line, if you want the entire line to be a comment, or in the middle of a line, if you want everything after the double-dash to be a comment.

Comments are nothing more than notes for the reader and do not affect the operation of the program at all. In fact, you could remove every single comment from the code examples, and they would work exactly the same.

In addition to the double-dash, you will often see the code continuation character, a "¬". This is rarely used in Director 7 or 8 because a single line can be as long as you want. However, it can still be used to indicate that the current line, and the one below it, are meant to be interpreted as one line of code, not two.

Because the pages in this book have a finite width, I use this continuation character to wrap my code lines at convenient places so that you can read them. You don't need to use them at all in your own code. Instead, you can just take the line of code in the book that follows a ¬ and add it to the end of the line above it.

Note that although this book uses Director 7-style continuation characters, the character has changed in Director 8. It is now a backslash: "\".

To help you read through some of the longer pieces of code in this book, I have included numbers that refer from the text to the lines in the code. When you see these numbers appear in the text, you will be able to glance forward at the code listing and see which line or lines I am referring to.

Updates and Communication

While writing and reviewing this book, I take great care to ensure that there are no errors or omissions. However, there are a lot of words here, and a lot of code. If I were to test each and every example until I was 100 percent satisfied that it was bug-free, then the book would probably never find its way to market.

So, it is inevitable that readers will discover minor issues with a movie or two. It is also probable that future versions of Director will introduce new syntax that will require changes in some of the code here. When this happens, I will post updates and corrections on a special section of my Web site. Here is the address:

`http://clevermedia.com/resources/gamesbook/`

This address contains updates, links to other resources, and a way for you to send feedback about the book.

In addition, if you find that you need to ask a question, or would like to seek help with something in this book, please use the forum I have set up at this address:

`http://clevermedia.com/resources/dcr/`

Why use a forum rather than emailing me directly? As the author of five books on Director, you can imagine that I would get a lot of email. However, my time is limited. In addition, when I help someone out directly through email, it helps only that one person.

With a forum, however, people can exchange ideas and help one another out. Chances are good that if you post a question there, some other user might be able to help you before I even see the message. Then, if I'm able to respond personally, the answer will help out others, as well as the person who originally asked the question.

When asking a question, however, please give a lot of thought to what you are asking. Many people ask questions that are too vague for anyone to be able to help. For instance, someone might ask, "How do I make a Centipede game?" The only answer, other than a 25-page book chapter, would be, "Learn Lingo, and then write the game."

Have Fun

I hope you enjoy this book. Many people will use this book at work or in school. They are buying it for professional reasons. However, this book is about games. The only reason to play games is to have fun. If you are like me, you will find that making games is even more fun than playing them.

Part I:
Writing Games with Lingo

● ● ● ●

1 Creating Games with Director and Lingo **11**

2 An Introduction to Games **27**

Creating Games with Director and Lingo

Macromedia Director is a great environment for creating games. The key to creating them is Director's built-in programming language, Lingo.

The advanced Lingo programmer can create a wide variety of games, from simple to complex. This is not only a lot of fun, but can also be very profitable.

Games and Macromedia Director

At its root, Director is an animation and presentation tool. However, it has evolved over the years into a complete programming environment.

Like any such environment, developers want to use it to make games. And Director is very accommodating to that purpose.

However, Director gets no respect in the game development industry. I think this actually comes out of the early success of Director. A lot of people bought and used Director versions prior to version 4. Many of the people in the game development industry still think of Director as the same, simpler tool that it was in version 3, and not the complex development environment that Director 8 is today.

Director is capable of quite a lot, but it has the reputation of being a slow, limited, presentation tool. It is still categorized with PowerPoint and HyperCard, rather than with C++ and Java where it should be.

However, thousands of games have been created with Director. Some are as simple as matching games, and others are complex role-playing or strategy games.

Director's Strengths

Let's look at Director's strengths and weaknesses as they apply to game creation. Let's start with Director's strengths:

- **Rapid Development**—Nothing I have seen beats Director here. I am amazed when I hear about 2-, 3-, or 4-year development times for games. Then, they still don't work until the company releases the second patch. Director enables you to create simple games in days rather than weeks, and complex games in months rather than years.

- **Multimedia**—Adding images, sounds, and even video in Director is an easy task. Most of the work has already been done for you by the Director engineers. You just need to drag and drop. The quality is also as high as you want: CD-quality sound and 32-bit color.

- **Lingo**—Lingo is a powerful programming environment. You can play sounds and move graphics with single lines of code. At the same time, you can construct complex data structures and perform tricky math. No complex libraries "includes" as with C++ and Java.

- **Delivery**—Director gives you a lot of options when the game is finished. Imagine what other companies need to do to take a Windows game and port it to the Macintosh. You just need to open the file and create a new Projector.

Director's Weaknesses

Now, let's look at Director's weaknesses as a game development tool:

- **3D Graphics**—You can create 3D graphics and place them in Director movies and you can simulate simple 3D graphics with mathematical algorithms applied to sprites. But, if you are looking for *Quake III* quality, you are out of luck. The only 3D Xtras available are slow and/or expensive.

- **Closed Programming Environment**—Suppose you create a game that uses something that no one has tried before in Director. Then, you find out that there is a limitation in Director that causes your game to not work because of this unique feature. If this were a custom environment such as the big game companies use, you could simply fix it. However, with Director, the best you can do is submit a bug report to Macromedia and wait for the next version of Director to come out. This is a disadvantage of any closed environment.

- **Limited Feature Set**—Director has a huge feature set, enormous compared to its multimedia tool competitors. However, if you use your own engine, you can add features by doing system-level programming. You can do this in Director to some extent by adding Xtras, but it cannot be done using Lingo. Xtras are compiled plug-ins that add functionality to Director. Because you need to create them in a C++ or similar environment, they are difficult to add, but they can be very powerful in some cases.

- **Speed**—Director 7 and 8 are very fast compared to previous versions. However, speed will always be a problem because Lingo is an interpreted language and there is no way to match the C++ or even assembly code that big game-development companies use.

Even these limitations have their advantages. The speed issue is counterbalanced by the fact that Lingo is much easier to program in than C++ or Java. The closed environment and limited feature set are offset by the fact that Macromedia does all the work on the engine, and you get it all for less than $1,000 instead of the cost of your own engineering team.

All said, Director is a great environment for creating games. If you don't already believe it, this book should prove it to you.

Game Lingo

The purpose of this book is twofold: to show you how to make games with Director and Lingo, and to teach advanced Lingo along the way.

As mentioned in the introduction, this book is not meant for absolute beginners. You should have a good understanding of how the Stage, Score, and Cast work together. You should also know how to write basic and intermediate Lingo scripts.

That said, I don't want to bog the first few chapters of the book down by going over Lingo basics. There are plenty of other good books on the market that do this. This book assumes that you already know the basics found in the first half of any general Director and Lingo book.

NOTE

If you feel you need some more Lingo training, try Que's *Special Edition Using Director 7* or *Special Edition Using Director 8* books by the same author. They both start at the beginner level and advance the reader up to the level of this book.

One of the purposes of this chapter is to look at some intermediate and advanced Lingo techniques so that you can begin creating games.

Programming Step by Step

When someone asks me for Lingo programming help, I find that there is one answer that covers most of the questions. This is that the person is trying to tackle too big of a problem all at once. They need to break the problem down into smaller ones. If they can't solve those problems, then they need to break them down into still smaller ones.

This is a basic principle of programming. Every large problem is really several smaller ones.

Take, for instance, the case in which a beginner programmer wants to have a button that changes when the user moves the mouse over it. However, the programmer is not sure how to do this with Lingo.

So, he breaks it down into smaller pieces. The first piece is, can he detect when the mouse moves over the sprite? The *on mouseUp* command turns up when searching the Lingo dictionary. So, he tries it:

```
on mouseUp
  put "Here!"
end
```

This is as simple as a handler can get. The programmer then runs the movie and sees that when the cursor enters the sprite area, the word "Here!" appears in the Message window.

Next, the programmer wants the sprite to change. So, he creates the second member that represents the changed button. A little more research turns up that he can set the *member* property of a sprite. So, he adds this to the script:

```
on mouseUp
  sprite(1).member = member("rollover button")
end
```

Step, by step, the programmer discovers the *on mouseLeave* handler to turn off the rollover state, the *me* parameter which is used by the handlers so that they can use *me.spriteNum* instead of hard-coding the sprite number, and he can keep on going until the script meets his needs.

Although this is a simple example that might already seem easy to you, it demonstrates the power of breaking down programming problems to their basic parts. It is important to understand this technique and use it while creating games.

One-Frame Movies

The Score is an animator's tool. It is used by nonprogrammer Director developers to create presentations involving many screens.

However, for a game developer, the Score is not nearly as important. It is mostly used for the arrangement of sprites vertically, rather than the arrangement of frames horizontally.

This is because most games take place in one frame. If there are any other frames at all, they are for things such as introductions, instructions, and "game over" screens. Most of the work goes into the main game frame.

NOTE

When you create a sprite by dragging a member to the Stage or Score, Director creates a long sprite span, usually 28 frames long. This is a useful starting point for animators, but not for game developers. You will probably want to change this preference to create new sprites with a single-frame sprite span. You can modify this preference by choosing File, Preferences, Sprite.

This main frame is a looping frame. At the least, its frame script channel contains the simple looping behavior that all Lingo programmers should be familiar with.

```
on exitFrame me
  go to the frame
end
```

The purpose of such a behavior is to catch the movie just as it is about to leave the current frame and advance to the next. Then, to send it back to replay the frame again. This way, the frame loops over and over.

The *on exitFrame* handler is also used to set off certain timed events and to check to see whether any keys are pressed.

Object-Oriented Thinking

Since Director 6, you can't help programming in an object-oriented manner. As a matter of fact, you would have to go out of your way to program any other way.

Each sprite is an object. Each frame is an object. You use behavior scripts to control these objects.

Even though most programming in Director is already object oriented, it helps to think in an object-oriented way when planning your game.

For instance, if the game has various moving pieces, is each an object? Or, are these elements controlled by the frame, which is an object? Are the elements similar enough to be controlled by the same behavior, but with different parameter settings? Or, should you write unique behaviors for each?

Using Behaviors

Many old-school Lingo programmers have still not adjusted to the modern behavior-style programming. But behaviors are great for game programming. They are a much better way to organize your code than the old style of using a large movie script and a lot of global variables. Even if the result is the same as the old school programming, your code will be easier to create, understand, and reuse.

If you are not familiar with behaviors, here is a quick primer. Behaviors are script members that can be attached to an individual sprite, many sprites, a frame, or a span of frames.

Behaviors control the object that they are attached to. So, a sprite behavior controls the sprite, whereas a frame behavior controls a frame. Director makes no distinction between these two types of behaviors. That is up to you and how you code the behavior.

One of the key elements of a behavior is the capability to have parameters that can be set when the behavior is added to the Score. You can set the parameters differently for different sprites.

So, for instance, you could have a behavior that controls an alien spaceship in a game. The behavior could have a parameter that determines the speed of the spaceship. When you assign it to one sprite, you could set the speed to one value. Then, when you assign it to another sprite, you could use another value. It is the same behavior, but the sprites exhibit different traits because the parameters are set differently.

The key to using parameters is to understand the *on getPropertyDescriptionList* handler. This handler enables you to specify parameters that will be defined when a behavior is first attached to a sprite. For instance, you could have the *pSpeed* property start off with different values. Here is an example:

```
on getPropertyDescriptionList me
  list = [:]
  addProp list, #pSpeed, [#comment: "Speed", #format: #integer, #default: 25]
  return list
end
```

The property "pSpeed" would have been declared at the top of the behavior script. The handler works by populating and returning a list with each property to be set, and a smaller list as the values. Each of these small lists has at least the standard properties of *#comment*, *#integer*, and *#default*. They are all used to compile a dialog box that appears when the behavior is attached to a sprite. Figure 1.1 shows the dialog box created by this example.

Figure 1.1
A behavior property settings dialog box changes depending on what the on get PropertyDescription List *handler contains.*

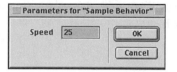

After a behavior is created, it can be used on many different sprites or frames in the movie. It can even be used in other movies. In fact, the behavior library that comes with Director is simply a collection of premade behaviors that Macromedia has included for novices. You'll see many examples of handlers in the chapters of this book.

Lists

Most beginner Lingo programmers can do a lot of work before they have to figure out lists. However, to make games, you really need to be able to use and understand them.

Lists are groups of values held together in a single variable. They are called *arrays* in other programming languages. Here are some examples:

```
[1,2,3,4,5]
[4.5,23.2,12.2]
["Gary", "Debby", "Lucy", "Natasha"]
```

Each of these is an example of a simple *linear* list. A *linear* list is just a list of values. You can even store lists inside of lists, or lists that have all sorts of different types of values.

```
[[1,4],[5,6],[3,7],[5,2]]
[6,7.2,"games"]
```

Another type of list is called a *property* list. A *property* list contains pairs of information. The first part of any item is the property and the second part is the value. Here is an example:

```
[#speed: 7, #power: 4, #defense: 9]
```

This example uses *symbols* as the properties, and integers as the values. You can actually use any type of data for either.

NOTE

Symbols, which always start with a "#", are used frequently in property lists. Some of Director's functions, such as the *on getPropertyDescriptionList* handler seen earlier in this chapter, require them. In addition, symbols are useful for creating object-oriented lists and variables values.

To handle lists, you refer to item numbers with brackets and properties with dot syntax. There also are a variety of functions and commands. Here is an example from the Message window:

```
myList = [101,103,104]
put myList[2]
-- 103
myList = [#this: 101, #that: 106, #other: 108]
put myList.that
-- 106
put getProp(myList,#that)
-- 106
put getPropAt(myList,2)
-- #that
deleteProp(myList,#this)
```

The preceding code starts by creating a linear list, and then getting an item from it. Then, it creates a property list and gets a property from it in two different ways. Finally, it gets a property name at a specific location and then shows you how to remove a property.

Lists are useful structures for storing such things as game boards, game pieces, moves, and so on.

Making Games

Each time I create a game, I use a slightly different process. However, I often get asked how it is done. So, I will suggest a method of creating games, but this is by no means that only way to go about it.

I use a variety of factors to determine how I will create a game. I take into account the type of game, its complexity, and the amount of time I have to create it. Sometimes, I choose one method over another simply because I feel like a change of pace, or I want to experiment with different styles of programming.

Game Screens

It is sometimes useful to have a checklist of things that need to be done to make a product. Games vary greatly in what they include, but there are some elements of games that keep reappearing. Think of these elements before planning your game. All of them are optional, however.

- **The Introduction Screen**—This is usually simply the screen that has the a button that reads something like "click to begin." However, you can color this screen up with graphics and text to get the user in the mood to play. Figure 1.2 shows one of my favorite game introduction screens.

Figure 1.2
The introduction screen to The Peanut Butter and Jelly Wars game. This game is just a simple Reversi game. However, the introduction screen proposes a metaphor to the player.

- **The Instruction Screen**—Some game developers, myself among them, argue that you should try to make your game so easy to play that instructions are not necessary. However, even when you are successful at that, you should provide an instruction page simply because some people will appreciate it. Figure 1.3 shows a sample instruction screen.

Figure 1.3
Here is an example of an instruction screen. This one uses a little humor, based on the fact that objects in arcade games don't always have real names, to lighten up the game a bit.

- **The Backstory Screen**—Although an introduction screen might suggest a metaphor for the game, a backstory screen is more direct. It tells the player, with text or narration, what has happened to bring them to this point. It could be as simple as "you have entered a race" or "prepare to play in the U.S. Open." It can also be as complex as a story involving an alien invasion against which you are the last line of defense.

● **The Game Background**—The screen where the action takes place can also have a lot of other elements. Will there be a "score" field? How about "level" or rank"? Sometimes, there is a summary of which keys do what. You will also want to add graphics that continue to suggest a theme introduced in the previous screens. For instance, in my game *Meltdown*, the background image, seen in Figure 1.4, suggests an industrial machine of some sort. The music soundtrack carries that even further.

Figure 1.4

Here is an example of a game background screen. The industrial theme of Meltdown *turns a simple puzzle game into a deeper experience.*

● **Between Levels Screen**—If your game has levels, you might want to add a screen that appears between each level. This gives users a break, and lets them ready themselves for the next level. For instance, in a space invaders game, it could simply say "Ready for level 4." In a golf game, it could recap the score and show a preview of the next hole. Figure 1.5 shows an example.

Figure 1.5

This example of a "between levels screen" is from my game Rapid Fire.

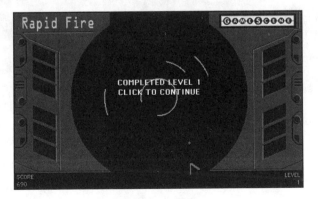

● **End Game Screen**—When the game is over, you can recap the score and ask whether the user wants to play again. You can also place a button that takes them to a high-score screen. Figure 1.6 shows an example.

Figure 1.6
The "end game" screen for my game Bomb Squad. This also enables the player to submit a high score to the Internet.

- **High Score Screen**—This screen enables the user to enter her name and then saves the score to a high-score board. It could be a local high score board, recording scores played only on that computer, or an Internet high score board where players compete from around the world. You could combine this screen and the end-game screen into one, as shown previously in Figure 1.6.

- **High Score Display Screen**—This can be at the start or end of a game. It displays the high scores in a list, just as the classic game machines did. This could give the players incentive at the start of the game, or simply let them compare their score at the end of the game. Figure 1.7 shows an example.

Figure 1.7
The "high-score display" screen for my game Aztec Underworld.

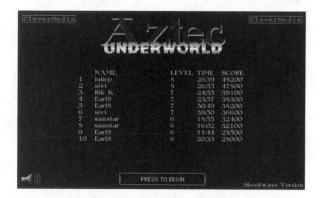

- **Payoff Screen**—Another version of the end-game screen is the payoff screen. This screen rewards the player for completing the game. You usually do this for games where there is no score other than winning. Or, you could use a payoff screen as a reward for reaching a certain score by the end of the game. Deciding what to include on a payoff screen is sometimes tougher than making the game itself. Most developers who use the payoff screen usually end up creating an animation of some sort. Or, you can make the payoff real by linking to a prize on the Internet, such as a coupon or a sweepstakes entry.

Planning and Preparation

The first step in developing any game is to come up with an idea. Sometimes, this is a totally new idea. But, more often, the idea has some roots in a previously made game. Maybe you are out to remake an arcade classic. Or, maybe you want to translate a non-computer game.

Either way, you want to define the game as well as you can. What elements are involved? What are the rules by which the elements move or change? What is the goal of the game?

For instance, in a game such as *Asteroids*, you would determine that the game elements are a spaceship, some asteroids, and a flying saucer. The rules are that the ship can rotate, thrust, and fire shots. The asteroids move around and break apart when they are hit. The flying saucer moves around, fires shots, and explodes when hit. The goal is simply to get a good score.

These are the basic rules of an *Asteroids* game. Of course, there are more details to be worked out, which you work out if you were actually planning to make the game.

The next step is to determine how the user will interact with the game. A key choice is whether to use the mouse, keyboard, or both. Then, you need to determine what the mouse button, mouse movement, or certain keys will do.

After this, you can begin to plan out your Cast and Lingo code. What sort of behaviors will you use? How many cast members are needed? How will all the elements interact?

There are usually many answers to these questions. You can't necessarily determine that one way is right and another wrong. Ten Lingo programmers will probably create a certain game ten different ways.

It's important that you think about your method, however. Try to make a plan. Make a list of which cast members you will need and which scripts you will need to create.

All this planning, however, can't predict the problems that might arise while creating the game. Be prepared to make changes as you go.

Where to Start

Now that all your planning is done, it's time to get down to programming. Just as with planning, there is no one right way to go about doing it. Here are some suggestions, however.

You could start by gathering all your media together. You make, or get someone else to make, the bitmaps, sounds, and other elements. Then, you gather all this together in the Cast before doing any programming.

You could also jump right into the programming, and fill the media elements in as you go along. This works especially well if the programmer and artist or sound designer is a different person. Then, you are all working in parallel.

if any bugs turn up that night and the next day, we can fix them quickly, or even postpone the launch of the game. CD-ROM game developers do something similar by giving preview versions of their games out to fan sites and magazines.

Distribution

After the game is complete, you need to get it to the people who want to play it. Rejoice in the fact that Director gives you more distribution options than the game engines used by the largest development companies.

Director movies are already cross-platform, which, in this case, means that they can be played on both Macintosh and Windows computers. If you are making a standalone application, called a *Projector*, you need to make a Macintosh Projector and a Windows Projector.

Projectors enable you to deliver games on CD-ROM or other hard media. You could also deliver a Projector over the Internet as a download.

If you are creating a game for Web delivery, your compressed Shockwave file will work on players with either type of computer.

Shockwave delivery is an extremely powerful feature of Director. You can't exactly make *Quake III* with Director, but you can reach millions of people over the Internet with almost no distribution cost.

Shockwave works with both Netscape Navigator and Microsoft Internet Explorer. It even works with other browsers that support the Netscape plug-in architecture.

In addition to the Projector and Shockwave delivery, there are also some variations. Director 7 and 8 enable you to make Shockwave projectors. These are small Projectors that use the Shockwave engine installed on the user's computer. If they do not have Shockwave installed, it enables the user to install it.

The best part about distributing your Director-based game is that you don't have to decide the format at all. You can create the game even if your distribution method has not yet been decided.

Before putting these techniques into practice, take a look at Chapter 2, "An Introduction to Games," to review the history of gaming and computer games, and to see where Director fits in.

An Introduction to Games

2

Imagine a world without computer games. It's not that hard considering the first computer game, *Space War*, was created in 1962. Then, it wasn't until the 1970s that the general public could play the first video games.

Imagine being the person to create the first computer game. There was little inspiration to draw on. Today, we can look back on countless video games and home computer games. Almost everything we create is derivative of something out of the past.

That first computer game was totally original. Since then, computers have revolutionized the world of games. Plus, we have a lot of inspiration.

From *Senet* to *Space War*

Games predate written history. It seems that we have always been interested in building little virtual realities where we can compete.

The Evolution of Board Games

The first board games were racing games, much like today's backgammon. One of the oldest game boards in existence is a game called *Senet*, which was popular in Egypt more than 2,000 years ago (see Figure 2.1).

Figure 2.1
Senet was played by the ancient Egyptians.

The game involved two players, each of whom had several pieces. The players threw sticks, because dice had not yet been invented, and moved their pieces along the board. The goal was to get your pieces to the end, which represented heaven.

This same game was adopted by other cultures for more than a thousand years. Each culture changed the playing pieces, and what the game's goal represented, but for the most part the game was the same.

NOTE

Senet's goal was actually to get your pieces to the last few spaces, which represented heaven. Many games used this as their goal. Today's game of hopscotch actually has the same goal, even though most people who play it don't know that the last space represents heaven.

In addition to racing games, another early type of game was a variety of *Nine Men's Morris*. This game involved a board with connected points. Each player had nine pieces and could move one piece per move along one connection to another point. If a player had three pieces in a row, they were allowed to remove one of their opponent's pieces.

This type of game evolved into games such as checkers and chess. The goal was to remove your opponent's pieces, while at the same time protecting yours.

Games such as this simulated an all-too-common theme in human history: war. Other cultures developed games like it, such as *Go* in Japan.

The ultimate war game, chess, evolved out of these early simple games. It started in 6th century India, but did not adapt modern features, such as the powerful queen, until the 15th century.

Chess spread throughout the world quickly, and is seen today by many as the ultimate game: easy to learn, but hard to master. The best chess players in the world are seen as celebrities, and chess tournaments make headlines.

The world of board games changed to what it is today in the late 19th century and early 20th. Companies such as Milton Bradley and Parker Brothers started inventing, mass-producing, and marketing games. New standards such as *Scrabble* and *Monopoly* were born out of old ideas. In addition, older games were codified by people such as Sir Edmund Hoyle, setting their rules in stone.

In America during the 20th century, a closet shelf full of board games became a standard. Games rose and fell in popularity as efforts by game companies to market them succeeded and failed.

War and Role-Playing Games

Board games are a casual experience for the most part. A typical game is easy to learn and can be played in an hour or two. However, some gamers desired a more engaging experience.

War games have existed in some form or another throughout history. However, the first modern war games were played in the 19th century. Military experts used large tables covered with sand and elaborate figures to plan out and test strategies.

The main purpose of the first war games was to plan out real battles. However, they soon came to be used as training tools as well. Military students would re-enact battles and make up scenarios. It was, and still is, a valuable tool.

Simplified versions of war games began to be used for recreation. The author H.G. Wells is often cited as the inventor of the first recreational war game. Boards with grids replaced the large tables. Instead of doing complex calculations, simple dice rolls and rules were used to decide the outcome of moves.

In the 1960s and '70s, war games were mass-produced in boxes with booklets that described the rules and large paper grids to play on. Several new games were produced annually, and magazines were even published on the subject.

From the world of war games came the world of role-playing games. The inventors of *Dungeons & Dragons* were simply out to make an interesting war game scenario that involved soldiers from the middle ages going in to an old castle and dungeon. Before they completed the scenario, they ended up with a whole new game complete with a telephone-book–sized set of rules. When they published a simplified version of these rules, they created a gaming phenomenon.

Dungeons & Dragons spawned many competitors and also many other types of role-playing games. Just about every type of adventure could be found in a box at your local hobby store: science fiction, espionage, old West, and even game systems to handle any type of world.

The role-playing games broke down the idea of what a game was and how long of an experience it was. It created a cottage industry of game companies, and players that were willing to try new things. This set the stage for the computer age of games.

From *Space War* to *Pong*

The first computer game was created by Steve Russell and other graduate students in 1962 on a PDP-1 mainframe computer at the Massachusetts Institute of Technology. It involved two space ships that floated around in the gravity-free environment of space and shot pixels at each other. The graphics were actually much better than what was to follow. The game even included a mathematically generated star field behind the ships.

This first game was addicting and fun. It was made freely available by the creators, so it soon found itself on just about every PDP-1 computer at every college that had one. However, commercial success was out of the question, as PDP-1 computers were too expensive to make into arcade machines, and no one owned a personal computer yet.

Meanwhile, the computer game evolved. A game called *Lunar Lander* consisted of absolutely no graphics, but could be played on computers that had no screen—only a spool of paper as an output device. A line of text would appear to tell you your position, velocity, and fuel remaining. You made a move, and the new position, velocity, and fuel update were printed. The object was to land before running out of fuel.

Not far behind these games was the classic *Adventure*. This was a precursor to all computer adventure and role-playing games. The game was purely text-based. It simply described your location and you gave it commands such as "go north" or "pick up sword."

The computer game first came into the public eye with early arcade games such as *Pong*. These games were first placed in shopping malls, right next to pinball machines and other coin-operated devices. But they soon took over the arcades.

From *Pong* to *Pac-Man*

The first coin-operated video game was Nolan Bushnell's *Computer Space*. It was like *Space War*, with the user controlling a ship out to destroy an enemy flying saucer. The machine accepted quarters.

Computer Space was not very successful. It turned out that the concept and controls were too advanced for people who had never seen a computer before.

Bushnell took his modest profits, only $500, and created his own company: Atari.

NOTE
Atari is the warning call that players give each other in the Japanese game of *Go*.

Atari's first creation was *Pong*, a game much simpler than *Computer Space*. The game was a success. Atari distributed the game through the same channels as pinball machines.

The next step for Atari was to sell *Pong* into homes. Atari teamed up with Sears to sell a home version of the game in 1975. Then, in 1976, Atari introduced *Breakout*, the first of the more complex video game classics. Not only was *Breakout* notable because it brought video games to a new level, but also because it was designed by Steven Jobs, who later revolutionized the personal computer industry.

In 1979, a Japanese company, Taito, developed *Space Invaders*, the first genuine video game hit. It began to take over the arcades (see Figure 2.2). Atari fought back with its own hit, *Asteroids*.

Figure 2.2
The heyday of video arcade games was in the early '80s, but the machines still remain popular today.

Also during 1979 and 1980, dozens of other games were invented in which players fought robots and aliens. However, the next big hit came from a simple maze game in which the hero was a yellow dot.

Pac-Man was not expected to be a hit. It was seen as too "cute" to be taken seriously. But kids in the arcades loved it. It was also the first arcade game that appealed to girls as well as boys and the first video game to bring in money from merchandising.

In 1982, there were 1.5 million arcade game machines in America in about 24,000 arcades and many miscellaneous locations. At the same time, 20 million home video games were sold, which cut heavily into the amount of television watched at home. In 1982, the video game industry was bringing in twice as much revenue as the American film industry.

The early '80s saw a constant stream of new video games by competing companies. The video arcade industry peaked around that time, and then fell back to the more stable level that we have today. This decline was caused by several factors, including the modernization of the mall and the advent of home game systems.

The Video Game Comes Home

In the late 1960s, an electrical engineer named Ralph Baer began creating the first home video game system (see Figure 2.3). His first models didn't even use microchips. However, they did connect directly to a standard television set. This eventually became the Odyssey game system.

The Odyssey included 12 different games printed on circuit cards. In addition, players had to place a transparent screen over their televisions to provide the background. Players also had to keep track of their own scoring by marking little sheets of paper.

The next advancement was provided by the General Instruments Corporation, which developed a microchip that manufacturers could buy for $5 or $6 that allowed more complex home video games to be developed. Coleco used it to develop the Telstar system.

Soon, companies such as Fairchild, RCA, Atari, and Mattel introduced new game systems that could be programmed. This allowed other companies to develop cartridges for them. The Atari Video Computer System eventually dominated the field. It sold more than 12 million units and more than 200 game cartridges were created for it.

Figure 2.3
The home video game system became a household item in the 1980s.

The home video game system is still just as popular today, but the players are different. Sony's PlayStation and Nintendo's N64 system are the two most popular. Although the Sega Saturn was not as popular, Sega may be regaining ground in the video game wars with the recent release of *Dreamcast*.

These modern home systems rival both the personal computer and the coin-operated arcade machine. The processors are fast, and the CD media or cartridges contain quite a bit of data.

Games Invade Computers

At the same time, the introduction of the personal computer meant that more complex games could be played as well. A huge library of games existed for computers such as the Apple II. It was easy for any programmer, with almost no money, to develop games for computers, as opposed to the expensive manufacturing process of the video game console.

In the 1980s, just about every successful video arcade game was translated to a game for the personal computer. Some of these games were legitimate versions made by their original creators, and others were imitations.

In addition, new games sprang up for the personal computer. Because no hardware had to be built to make the games available, it cost less to develop a game for a computer. The only things you needed to actually manufacture were the floppy disks and any printed materials.

This meant that games with a smaller potential audience could be produced. When modems and bulletin board systems became popular in the late 1980s, you could even make a game and distribute it for free.

Eventually, the CD-ROM drive gave game developers the chance to create games with a multimedia flair. The game *Myst* set the standard for CD-ROM adventure games that is still followed today. This game has hundreds of detailed still images.

Today's CD-ROM adventure games feature even more detailed images, along with soundtracks and complex interfaces. In the mid-1990s, *Phantasmagoria* used seven CD-ROMs to create an intense environment.

In addition to volume, computers also enabled developers to experiment with new techniques. Games such as *Doom* started the "first-person 3D shooter" genre. By the mid-1990s, just about every action game on the market fit into this category.

Games and Macromedia Director

Director does not get the respect it deserves in the development world. It is still seen as the simpler animation and presentation tool that it was before Director 4.

However, there are thousands of games made with Director. Some are small puzzle games and others are complex strategy simulations. Thanks to Shockwave, Director-based games are easy to distribute, which makes it hard for the industry to ignore them.

In the past, educational games were the primary type of game made with Director. Teachers and institutions were able to use simple games to teach children or college students. The use of games to provide instructional learning has been around for more than two decades, and Director is a tool that has been used to create many of these.

Recently, however, Director has also been used to create games meant purely for entertainment. This is largely because of Shockwave, which has enabled developers such as myself to distribute games at a low cost on the Web.

Recently, Macromedia itself has embraced this game concept and has started promoting Director as a game development tool. It even started to use it to make its own games.

Macromedia created the ShockRave site first, and then evolved that into the Shockwave.com site and ShockMachine, a standalone game browser for Shockwave content.

These moves by Macromedia had an important side effect. Macromedia added new features and speed to Director 7 and 8 specifically for game development, which helped not only its own content, but also external game developers.

Either way, Director 7 and 8 are now great platforms to develop games with, and future versions will likely continue this trend. Now, let's start making some games.

Further Reading

If you are interested in the history of games and computer games, here are some books that you might want to check out:

Screen Play: The Story of Video Games
George Sullivan
Copyright 1983
Publisher: Frederick Warne & Co., Inc., New York, NY

Content: History of computer and video games.

Joystick Nation
J.C. Herz
1997
Published by Little, Brown & Company Limited

Content: History of computer and video games.

The World of Games
Jack Botermans, Tony Burrett, Pieter van Delft, Carla van Splunteren
1987
Published by Facts on File, Inc., New York and Oxford

Content: History of games. Many illustrations.

The Greatest Games of All Time
Matthew J. Costello
1991
John Wiley & Sons, Inc.

Content: Interesting stories about old and new games, the game industry, and video games. Highly recommended.

Game Over: Press Start to Continue
David Sheff
1993
Random House

Content: The history of Nintendo. Highly recommended.

According to Hoyle
Richard L. Frey
1956, 1965, 1970
Fawcett Columbine

Content: Game rules.

The Oxford History of Board Games
David Parlett
1999
Oxford University Press

Content: The history of games.

Family Fun & Games
1992
Sterling Publishing Company

Content: Game rules.

A Brief History of Home Video Games
(An Online Book)
Sam Hart
1996-1999
http://newton.physics.arizona.edu/~hart/vgh

Content: Essays about different video game machines.

Part II:
Puzzle Games

3 Matching Game **39**

4 Memory Game **55**

5 Jigsaw Puzzle **71**

6 Sliding Puzzle **87**

7 Falling Blocks Puzzle **99**

Mars

Jupiter

Venus

Saturn

argest
Planet

Largest
Volcano

Rings

Close
o Ear

Matching Game

3

CD-ROM File: 03matching.dir

Useful Lingo in This Chapter

- ♠ Behaviors: Using parameters
- ♠ Graphics: Changing sprite members with Lingo
- ♠ Graphics: Moving sprites
- ♠ Graphics: Using a set of bitmaps
- ♠ Graphics: Using registration points
- ♠ Interface: Dragging and dropping
- ♠ Members: Using a naming convention
- ♠ Programming: Collision detection
- ♠ Programming: Using a case statement

Clicking and dragging is a standard computer user interface action. You see it done in the operating system as users click and drag file icons around.

This can be made into a game by placing draggable objects on one side of the screen, and destination objects on the other side. The goal is to drag the items to their correct counterpart.

This type of game is usually used for education or computer-based training. However, it can also be a useful trivia game with the right content.

Game Overview

A typical scenario is to have objects on the left and right side of the screen. The player's objective is to drag items on the right to items on the left. However, the items are not in order and there is only one correct pairing for each item.

Figure 3.1 shows a sample screen for the completed game. The items on the right, in this case some text members, can be moved to the graphics on the left. If a player moves the item to the wrong place, the item is rejected and it snaps back to its original position. However, if a match is correct, then the item should lock into place and remain there for the rest of the game.

Figure 3.1
A possible screen layout for a click-and-drag matching game.

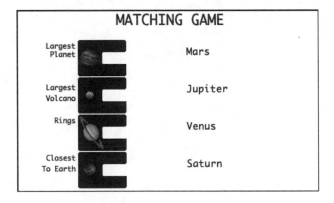

Try out the game before reading any further. It can be found on the book's CD-ROM, named 03matching.dir.

Close Enough for a Match

This game sounds simple, but there are a lot of details to be worked out. For instance, how close does the player have to get to make a match? If we require the player to place the item in the exact right location, with pixel precision, then it will be a very hard game to play. Instead, we should make it so that if the player is relatively close, the sprite should snap into location automatically. This should be good enough to convince the player that, if a match is rejected, it is rejected because the match was incorrect, not because the player did not place the item close enough.

Each sprite has two properties that can come in handy when deciding whether one sprite has been dropped onto the other. The first property is its location, or *loc*. This is the point on the Stage where the registration point of a bitmap, or the upper-left corner of a text member, is located. The other property is the rectangle, or *rect*, of the sprite. This is the bounding box of the entire sprite. Figure 3.2 shows both the registration point and the bounding box of a sprite.

Figure 3.2
This diagram shows the bounding box, or rect *of the sprite, as well as the registration point, which corresponds to the sprite's exact location on the Stage.*

Registration Point

Bounding
Box

NOTE
The registration point is the location in a bitmap sprite that is used to decide its placement on the Stage. If a sprite is placed at location 75, 125 on the Stage, it's actually its registration point that is located at 75, 125. By default, the registration point for bitmaps is at the center of the bitmap, but this can be changed in the Paint window. For text sprites, the registration point is always set to the upper-left corner of the text.

The simplest way to determine whether two sprites are being brought together is by examining their *loc* properties. However, the *loc* properties will match up only if the two sprites are in the exact same location. So, this is not a good method to use unless you want to drive the player crazy.

Another method is to compare the *rects* of the two sprites. You can use the *intersects* comparison in Lingo to determine whether two sprites overlap. However, this method is too vague. Large sprites can appear to be quite far away, and yet still have their bounding boxes touching at one point. More importantly, it's easy to have one sprite's bounding box overlap the bounding boxes of several other sprites. Determining which sprite the user meant as the destination can be a problem.

A good compromise is to compare the location of one sprite to the rectangle of another. You can do this with the Lingo *inside* function. This tells you whether the *loc* of the dragged sprite is inside the *rect* of the destination sprite.

Correct Matches

Another factor to take into consideration is how the items on the right know which item on the left they are supposed to match. The Lingo code cannot magically know which items are meant for each other. The person creating the game must establish this some-time, preferably without having to change any Lingo code.

Both the draggable item and the destination item are really just sprites on the Stage. One way to go about matching up items is by developing a system in which an item in one sprite channel is matched with an item in either the sprite channel before it or after it. For instance, the item on the right can be in sprite channel 7. The item that it matches on the left can then be in sprite channel 6. The Lingo code knows that these two sprites match up, because the movable sprite should always match the sprite one channel away. Figure 3.3 shows what the Score might look like with such a system.

Figure 3.3

This Score window shows a group of sprites. Sprites 6, 10, 14, and 18 are the movable sprites, and sprites 5, 9, 13, and 17 are the sprites they are meant to match.

NOTE

Remember that just because the sprites are arranged in a certain way in the Score, it does not mean that they have to be arranged in a similar way on the Stage. Two sprites can be in adjacent channels in the Score, but on totally different parts of the Stage.

It's also a good idea to offer a few options that can be changed when the behavior is used. We can make our code adjust to one of three situations. The first is when the sprite is meant to match the sprite in the previous channel. The second is when the sprite matches the sprite in the next channel. The third option should enable the author to specify any sprite by number. Building versatility into your code like this can make your behaviors much more useful. They can also cut down on the number of times that a non-Lingo Director user utilizing your code needs to request changes to the behavior.

Locking Sprites into Place

After a user drags a movable sprite on to another one, and it has been determined that a match has been made, the next step is to lock the movable sprite to its final position.

A simple way to do this is to set the movable sprite to the same location as the destination sprite. If the two sprites are identical in size and shape, then the movable sprite locks into a position on top of the destination sprite. However, by playing around with the registration points of both of these sprites, you can have them lock into position in many different ways.

For instance, the destination sprites can look as if they are missing a piece. The movable sprites can look just like that missing piece. When a correct match is made, the two sprites are positioned so that they appear to be a complete graphic.

One problem that this presents is what happens if both the destination and the movable sprites are text? In that case, you can't easily adjust either of the sprites' registration points. The code must make a decision about what to do in this case. In the game we will develop here, we will assume that when two text members are matched, the movable one gets placed just to the right of the destination one.

Game Over

A game such as this usually ends when the user correctly matches all the items. We need to recognize this event in our code.

The perfect time to test for this game-over condition is just after a match has been made. After all, this is the only point in the game where the end can possibly be reached. It cannot be reached when the user is doing nothing, or when the user makes an incorrect match.

At this point, we need to check through all the possible matches and verify that they are all complete. If even one is not complete, then the game is not yet over and no action needs to be taken.

If the game is found to be complete, then we can specify a frame that the movie will go to. This can be a "game-over" frame, or possibly the next level of the game.

Special Effects

In addition to the standard functionality like dragging, dropping, matching and locking, our game can have a little more pizzazz. Quite simply, we can add sound.

There should be at least two sounds associated with the actions in the game. They should be the sounds that play when the user is finished dragging a sprite. One sound signifies a completed match, and the other signifies an incorrect match.

More sounds could be added as well. You can have a "pick-up" sound when the user first clicks on an item to drag it. You could also have a sound that plays when the game is complete.

Making the Game

The game consists mostly of one large behavior. This is the script that controls the items on the right side of the screen. When the player clicks on one of these sprites, the behavior allows him or her to drag it anywhere on the screen. When the player releases the mouse button, the behavior tests to see whether a match has been made.

This section of this chapter looks at this behavior, piece by piece. You can see this same behavior in the sample movie for this chapter on the CD-ROM. The behavior is called "Drag, Drop and Match Game Behavior."

Now, let's look at each handler individually to examine how the behavior works. The goal is to have a behavior that can be used by the programmer, or possibly a nonprogrammer multimedia author. This author could take this behavior, without knowing any Lingo at all, and make a game from it.

The first part of this behavior, as in any, is the declaration of properties. In this case, we have several properties that the author will set when placing each sprite on the Stage. The rest are of no concern to the author. They are used by the behavior to keep track of the sprite's progress in the game.

```
-- Settable properties
property pMatchWith, pMatchSprite, pNoMatchAction
property pMatchSound, pNoMatchSound, pAllMatchedFrame

property pDrag -- if sprite is being dragged
property pDragOffset -- offset of click from registration point of sprite
property pOrigLoc -- remember the original location to "snap back" to
property pMatch -- if the sprite has been locked to another
```

Because the first six properties need to be defined in the *on getPropertyDescriptionList* anyway, we leave the comments for those properties for that handler. Meanwhile, the comments after the other properties show their purpose.

The first handler in any behavior should be the *on getBehaviorDescription* handler. The only purpose for this is to provide a description for the behavior in the behavior inspector.

Many programmers like to make this description very long, and include details about the settable properties as well. You can do that if you think it will be useful in your production process. For the purposes of this book, we will keep these short, or not use them at all.

```
on getBehaviorDescription me
   text = "Allows the sprite to be dragged."
   put "Will lock the sprite to another specific sprite if it is dragged to it." after¬
   text
   put "Goes to a new frame when all sprites are locked." after text
   return text
end
```

The *on getPropertyDescriptionList* provides all the options that the author can change to make the behavior fit his or her needs. Here is the handler. Look at each item that is added to the list and see whether you can determine what the behavior's settings dialog box, shown in Figure 3.4, will look like. The explanation of this handler follows the code.

NOTE

The ¬ character is Lingo's continuation character. Instead of pressing Return or Enter to advance to the next line of code, type an Option+L on Macintosh or an Alt+L in Windows. It is used to wrap long lines of code without really breaking them apart. When programming in Lingo, you don't need to use them at all as your lines can be as long as they want. However, because a book's pages have a finite width, I use them in the book.

```
on getPropertyDescriptionList me
  list = [:]

  -- Allow the author to have the sprite match with the previous,
  -- next, or a specific sprite
① addProp list, #pMatchWith,¬
    [#comment: "Match With",¬
    #format: #string,¬
    #range: ["Previous Sprite","Next Sprite","Specific Sprite"],¬
    #default: "Previous Sprite"]

  -- if a specific sprite is to be used, what is its number?
  addProp list, #pMatchSprite,¬
    [#comment: "  Specific Sprite",¬
    #format: #string,¬
    #default: 0]

  -- when a sprite is dropped to the wrong spot, what is done?
② addProp list, #pNoMatchAction,¬
    [#comment: "When No Match",¬
    #format: #string,¬
    #range: ["Nothing", "Snap Back"],¬
    #default: "Snap Back"]

  -- when a sprite is matched, what sound is played?
  addProp list, #pMatchSound,¬
    [#comment: "Match Sound",¬
    #format: #string,¬
    #default: ""]
```

continues

continued

```
    -- when a sprite is not matched, what sound is played?
    addProp list, #pNoMatchSound,¬
      [#comment: "No Match Sound",¬
       #format: #string,¬
       #default: ""]

    -- when all sprites are matched, which frame should the movie go to?
    addProp list, #pAllMatchedFrame,¬
      [#comment: "All Matched Frame",¬
       #format: #marker,¬
       #default: #next]
    return list
  end
```

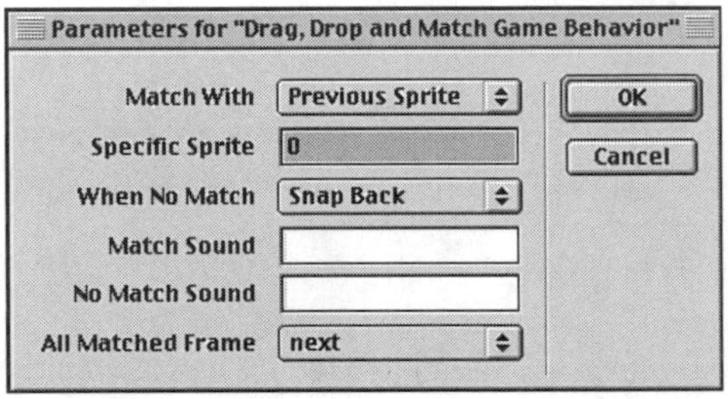

Figure 3.4

The Parameters dialog box for our game behavior.

The first property, "pMatchWith", gives the author three options ①. The first two, "Previous Sprite" and "Next Sprite", use the sprite's current location in the Score to determine the location of the sprite that it is supposed to match. The third option, "Specific Sprite", enables the author to specify the exact destination sprite, regardless of where the movable sprite is located in the Score. It uses the "pMatchSprite" property, which would otherwise go unused.

The next property, "pNoMatchAction", determines what happens when the user places an item in the wrong spot ②. The default is to have the sprite snap back to its original location. Also offered is the option of just leaving the sprite where the user dropped it.

The next two properties are the sounds that will be played when the sprite is dropped onto a location. One sound is for a correctly placed drop, and the other is for an incorrectly placed drop. If these properties are left blank, no sound is played at all.

The last property is the name of the frame that the movie jumps to when all the items have been matched.

Now, let's look at the other handlers in the behavior. The *on beginSprite* handler initializes the "pMatch", "pDrag", and "pOrigLoc" properties. It also sets the "pMatchSprite" property.

```
on beginSprite me
  -- initialize values
  pMatch = FALSE
  pDrag = FALSE
  pOrigLoc = sprite(me.spriteNum).loc

  -- set pMatchSprite if a specific sprite is not chosen
  case pMatchWith of
    "Previous Sprite":
      pMatchSprite = me.spriteNum - 1
    "Next Sprite" :
      pMatchSprite = me.spriteNum + 1
  end case
end
```

When the user clicks down on the mouse, the dragging begins. Thereafter, until the mouse is released, the sprite should follow the cursor. However, this is more complex than it seems.

Setting a sprite to a specific location is easy—just set the *loc* property of the sprite. Because the sprite is to follow the cursor, it makes sense to set the location of the sprite to the location of the cursor. However, this means that the registration point of the sprite will be positioned under the cursor. But what if the user did not click the registration point? In that case, the first thing that would happen when the user clicks is that the sprite would seem to jump so that its registration point is aligned with the cursor.

NOTE

The Lingo property *the clickLoc* is used to get the Stage location of a click. It is valid only in handlers such as *on mouseUp*, *on mouseDown*, or the handlers that they call. It returns a *point* structure.

A better way to do this is to record the offset between the location of the sprite and the click. Then, use this offset while dragging the sprite. This method keeps the cursor and the spot clicked on aligned, creating a much more natural feel to the drag.

The *on mouseDown* handler records this offset in the "pDragOffset" variable. It also sets the "pDrag" variable to *TRUE*. Before it does anything, however, the *on mouseDown* handler checks the "pMatch" variable to see whether this sprite has already been matched to its destination sprite. In that case, no dragging should be done.

```
-- the user begins the drag
on mouseDown me
  if pMatch then exit -- already locked in place
  pDrag = TRUE
  pDragOffset = the clickLoc - sprite(me.spriteNum).loc
end
```

NOTE

The constants *TRUE* and *FALSE* in Lingo are actually just substitutes for the numbers 1 and 0. When used in comparisons, a value of 0 is taken as false and any other numerical value is taken as true. However, the constants *TRUE* and *FALSE* make your code much easier to read.

When the user lifts up the mouse button, the drag is over. The *on mouseUp* handler sets the "pDrag" variable to *FALSE* and then calls our own custom "on checkForMatch" handler.

```
-- the user ends the drag
on mouseUp me
  if pMatch then exit -- already locked in place
  pDrag = FALSE
  checkForMatch(me)
end
```

If the player is dragging the sprite fast enough, it is possible that they could release the mouse button at a time when the sprite has not yet been redrawn to be under the cursor. In that case, an *on mouseUpOutside* handler is called instead of *on mouseUp*. Because, in this case, we don't care that the sprite was not actually under the cursor, we just redirect this call to the behavior back to the *on mouseUp* handler.

```
-- user moved the mouse quickly, record as mouseUp anyway
on mouseUpOutside me
  mouseUp(me)
end
```

The *on exitFrame* handler is called on a regular basis as the movie loops on the frame. It is here that we need to reposition the sprite if a drag is in progress. We set the *loc* of the sprite to the cursor's position, remembering to subtract the drag offset we recorded in the *on mouseDown* handler.

```
-- if a drag is in progress, reposition the sprite
on exitFrame me
  if pDrag then
    sprite(me.spriteNum).loc = the mouseLoc - pDragOffset
  end if
end
```

The *on mouseUp* handler calls "on checkForMatch" when a drag is complete. This handler needs to determine whether the sprite is not over its mate. To do this, it uses the *inside* function to compare the location of the sprite to the rectangle of the sprite it should match.

If a match is found, the "pMatch" variable is set to *TRUE*. Then, a sound is played if the game's creator supplied a "pMatchSound" property. The "on lockInPlace" handler is called to give the sprite its permanent, correct, position ③ . Finally, the "on checkForAllMatch" handler is called to see whether the game is over.

In the case in which the sprite is not over its mate, the "pNoMatchSound" property is examined and a sound is played if needed. Also, if the "pNoMatchAction" is set to the default "Snap Back", then the sprite's location is reset to its original value ④ .

```
-- check to see if the sprite is over its match
on checkForMatch me
  -- see if the location of the sprite is inside the rect of the matching sprite
  if inside(sprite(me.spriteNum).loc, sprite(pMatchSprite).rect) then
    -- record the match
    pMatch = TRUE
    -- play a sound if one is needed
    if pMatchSound <> "" then puppetSound pMatchSound
    -- lock the sprite into position
③→ lockInPlace(me,pMatchSprite)
    -- see if all the sprites are matched
    checkForAllMatch(me)
  else
    -- play a sound if one is needed
    if pNoMatchSound <> "" then puppetSound pNoMatchSound
    case pNoMatchAction of
      "Snap Back":
        -- put the sprite back in its original location
④→     sprite(me.spriteNum).loc = pOrigLoc
    end case
  end if
end
```

The "on lockInPlace" handler sets the location of the dragged sprite to the location of the destination sprite. However, in the case that both sprites are text members, it sets the dragged sprite to match the upper-right corner of the destination sprite, thus placing the two sprites side-by-side.

```
on lockInPlace me , otherSprite
  if (sprite(otherSprite).member.type = #text) and (sprite(me.spriteNum).member.type =¬
  #text) then
    -- if both are text, then loc the sprite to the upper right corner
    loc = point(sprite(otherSprite).rect.right, sprite(otherSprite).rect.top)
  else
    -- if not text, then lock both sprites exactly together
    -- and leave spacing up to the registration points
    sprite(me.spriteNum).loc = sprite(otherSprite).loc
  end if
end
```

Every time a match is successfully made, the "on checkForAllMatch" handler is called. This handler loops through all the sprites in the current frame. It calls a handler in these sprites named "on getMatch". This handler returns the value of "pMatch" for the sprite.

NOTE
The Lingo *sendSprite* command sends a message to a sprite, in effect calling a handler there. This is one way for behaviors to contact one another and send or request information.

The beauty of the *sendSprite* command here is that it returns a value of *VOID* if the sprite does not have a behavior attached that responds to the "getMatch" message. We can test for this with the *voidP* function, and then disregard these sprites; we only want the results from sprites with this behavior attached.

After the handler finds a sprite that has a "pMatch" of *FALSE*, the handler knows that the game is not over and uses the *exit* command to terminate the handler ⑤. However, if it makes it through the loop without finding an unmatched sprite, the handler knows that the game is over and goes to the frame in the "pAllMatchedFrame" property.

```
-- check all sprites to see if any are not matched
on checkForAllMatch me
  -- loop through all sprite channels
  repeat with i = 1 to the lastChannel
    -- get the value of pMatch for the sprite
    match = sendSprite(sprite(i),#getMatch)
    -- if it is a VOID value, then it is not the right type of sprite anyway
    if voidP(match) then next repeat
    -- if the sprite is not yet matched, then the game is not yet done
⑤→ if match = FALSE then exit
  end repeat
  -- if here, then all sprites found must be matched
  go to frame pAllMatchedFrame
end
```

The last handler we need is the one that responds to the "getMatch" message. This is a simple handler that just returns the value of "pMatch".

```
-- when requested, return the value of pMatch
-- for use by the checkForAllMatch handler
on getMatch me
  return pMatch
end
```

To better understand this behavior, it's best to look at it together in the script member in the example on the CD-ROM. If you don't understand something in it, play the game and examine how it works.

Putting It All Together

The only other piece of code needed to make the game work is the simple frame script that causes the movie to loop on a single frame.

```
on exitFrame
   go to the frame
end
```

Besides the code, you need to worry about the appearance of the bitmap members and the text in the text members. Remember that you can use either type of member for the movable sprites and the destination sprites. However, for bitmap sprites, you need to pay careful attention to the registration point because it will be used to determine how the sprites lock to each other.

The positioning of the sprites in both the Score and on the Stage is important as well. You don't want the items to be directly across from their correct destination sprites. Instead, you want to mix them up a little to make the game more interesting.

Game Variations

A game like this can be adapted for many purposes. It can be used for entertainment or education. It's a good exercise for computer-based training applications, too. This is because, as a teaching tool, the game reinforces what it is teaching by requiring the user to perform an action that associates two items.

To this end, you can make a variety of improvements to this basic game.

Making a Longer Game

If you want to make a longer game out of this, you need to make a set of several frames, each one a small matching game in itself. The game can then evolve over the series of frames.

For instance, for a trivia game, you could have each frame represent a different topic. Or, for an educational game, each frame can pose more difficult challenges.

Keeping Score

You don't need to keep score in a game like this. However, if you want, you can keep track of the number of correct matches and the number of incorrect matches. Of course, the number of correct matches will always be the same each time the game is played, because all matches need to be correct for the game to end.

To keep track of this, add 1 to a global variable each time a match is made, and each time an incorrect match is attempted. Here is an example:

```
gNumberCorrect = gNumberCorrect + 1
```

You could do the same with a "gNumberIncorrect" global. Both of these globals need to be set to 0 at the start of the movie.

The lines of code that increment the score counters can be placed at the same spot as the *puppetSound* commands in the "on checkForMatch" handler. In addition, you can set a text member to show the update to the score. You can do this with a new handler that is called *every* time the score is changed.

```
on showScore me
   member("score").text = "Score:"&&gNumberCorrect&&"correct."&& ¬
gNumberIncorrect&&"incorrect."
End
```

These changes can be seen in the script "Drag, Drop and Match Game Behavior w/Score" in the sample movie for this chapter. If you turn off script auto coloring by choosing File, Preferences, Script, and then deselecting the Auto Color option, you can see the new lines added in red. You must do this before opening the movie, because Auto Coloring will remove the red color that I have placed on this text.

Timing the Player

Another way to keep score is to keep track of how long the player takes to complete the match. You can do this by recording the time at the start of the frame, and then checking it against the time when the matching is complete.

To record the time, add a property called "pStartTime" and set it to *the ticks* during the *on beginFrame* handler.

```
pStartTime = the ticks
```

NOTE

There are three system properties in Lingo that keep track of the time since Director, the Projector, or the Shockwave applet started. They are *the ticks*, *the milliseconds*, and *the timer*. *The ticks* and the timer measure 1/60ths of a second, and *the milliseconds* measures 1/1000ths of a second. The timer can be reset to 0 with the *startTimer* command.

When the matching is all done, you can determine the final time by subtracting the "pStartTime" property from the current value of *the ticks*. The result is divided by 60 to convert it to seconds.

```
finalTime = (the ticks - pStartTime)/60
```

You can place this value in a text member to display to the user at the end of the game. Or, you can constantly display the current time. Do this by calling a handler like this in the *on exitFrame* handler.

```
on showTimer me
  finalTime = (the ticks - pStartTime)/60
  text = "Time:"&&finalTime
  if member("score").text <> text then
    member("score").text = "Time:"&&finalTime
  end if
end
```

This handler not only calculates the time in seconds and creates a string based on that, but also checks the "score" member to ensure that an update is necessary. Because every sprite that uses this behavior will attempt to update the score, and the movie is probably moving at many frames per second, the timer member is not usually in need of an update. Because changing a text member takes time, be sure that the time, in seconds, is different before setting the member to a new value.

The code for the timer can also be found in the sample movie in the script member named "Drag, Drop and Match Game Behavior w/Timer". Be sure to turn off script auto coloring before opening the movie so that you can see the changes in red.

Creative Screen Layout

A simple way to make something different out of this game, without doing any additional coding, is to change the scenario from two columns of items to more of a collage of images. For instance, the background can be a forest with all sorts of animals: a monkey hanging from a tree, a tiger on the ground, a bird on a branch, and fish in a pond. Then, the movable sprites are the words "monkey," "tiger," "bird," and "fish." The player, probably a young child for this game, would have to match the words to the animals.

Randomness

One final idea for this game is to add a bit of randomness to the screen layout. You could have the items shuffle on the screen before the game begins. This would place the items in different spots every time the user plays.

There are many ways to achieve this. One way is to have an additional behavior placed on the item sprites. This behavior seeks out another sprite with the same behavior and swaps screen positions with it. However, it would maintain the same Score position, so the game knows which items match up with which.

Here is a quick randomizing behavior:

```
on beginSprite me
  -- loop and determine all of the other sprites that
  -- share this behavior
  spriteList = []
repeat with i = 1 to the lastChannel
```

continues

continued

```
        s = sendSprite(i,#getSpriteNumber)
        if voidP(s) then next repeat
        add spriteList, s
    end repeat

    -- pick a random sprite from the list
    randomItem = random(spriteList.count)
    s = spriteList[randomItem]

    -- swap positions with that sprite
    newpos = sprite(s).loc
    sprite(s).loc = sprite(me.spriteNum).loc
    sprite(me.spriteNum).loc = newpos
  end

-- return my sprite number to anyone that asks
on getSpriteNumber me
  return me.spriteNum
end
```

This behavior is not perfect. Some of the shuffling techniques we will use in card games later on get more into proper randomization like this. This behavior, for one, has the flaw that it cannot contact sprites further down in the Score from itself because the *sendSprite* command won't work on sprites that have not yet run their *on beginSprite* handler. However, for the purposes of this game, it works quite well.

Memory Game

4

CD-ROM File:04memory.dir

Useful Lingo in This Chapter

♠ Animation: Creating a delay with Lingo

♠ Behaviors: Calling handlers in other behaviors

♠ Behaviors: Using parameters

♠ Behaviors: Using a ranged parameter

♠ Graphics: Changing sprite members with Lingo

♠ Graphics: Making sprites disappear

♠ Graphics: Using a grid of bitmaps

♠ Graphics: Using a set of bitmaps

♠ Input: Selecting with mouse clicks

♠ Math: Using random numbers

♠ Members: Using a naming convention

♠ Programming: Creating a timer

One game stands out as probably the most common game created with Director. This memory/matching game, best known under the brand name *Concentration*, is simple, yet challenging.

The game has an educational feel, even though it does not teach anything. However, it can be argued that the game helps to improve the player's memory. Usually, however, this game is classified as an entertaining distraction rather than a game of skill.

Game Overview

The basic idea is that the screen is filled with a number of face-down cards. Each card is part of a matched pair. The player can turn any two cards over at a time to look at them. If the player turns two matching cards over, those cards are removed from the table. Otherwise, both cards are turned back to face-down.

The goal, of course, is to remove all the cards from the table. As the player turns over cards, he or she should remember which cards are where to make it easier to find matches in the future.

Figure 4.1 shows a game in progress. This game consists of 100 cards, which is a high number. A game with 25 or 36 is more common. In the figure, some cards are missing. These have already been matched. In addition, two cards are turned over, indicating that the player has just selected the second card in an attempt to make a match.

Figure 4.1
A matching game in progress.

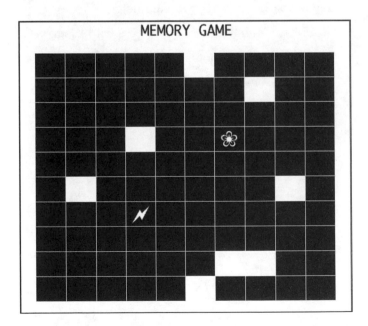

Try the game out before reading any further. It can be found on the book's CD-ROM, in the folder for this chapter.

Shuffling the Deck

As opposed to the matching game in Chapter 3, "Matching Game," this game is one that can be played over and over by the same person. For it to be challenging, however, the cards should not be in the same position each time.

To make a random board, you need to have the cards shuffled each time the game is played. This is done in a similar way that a real-life deck of cards is shuffled.

First, the deck of cards is created as a Lingo list. This deck of cards is in order. Then, a random one is picked from this deck and placed in a second pile. Then, another card is picked. This goes on until the deck is empty and the pile is full. The result is that the pile is a randomly sorted deck of cards. They are then dealt out onto the table for the game.

We'll look at the Lingo code for this later in the chapter. This shuffling technique comes in handy for a lot of the games in this book.

Time for Pause

When the game starts, all the cards are face-down on the table. The player then clicks on a card. This card is turned over and its value revealed.

Then, the user clicks on a second card. If this card is a match, both cards should be taken off the table. If it isn't a match, both cards are turned back down.

However, there is one thing that needs to be taken into account: a pause. If the player turns over the second card, and both are immediately turned back or taken off, then the player never gets to see the value of the second card. This is unimportant if the cards match, but it's important if the cards don't. Seeing the second card is a crucial part of the game, because the player will want to note its value for future reference.

You need to create a pause of a certain length when the second card is turned over. After this pause, both cards are turned back down or removed from the table. In addition you should allow the player to end the pause by clicking the next card. This allows fast players to continue playing without waiting.

The Hidden Picture

A typical motivation for this type of game is to have a picture hidden under the cards. As the cards are removed from the screen, the picture is revealed.

This allows the game to take on a theme. For instance, a site promoting a movie, for instance, can have a still image from the movie underneath.

To add this hidden picture element to the game actually requires no additional programming at all. The game takes place in a series of sprites in a frame. The picture needs to merely reside in a lower-numbered frame channel than the cards. The image is under the game at all times and is revealed as the sprites are removed from the Stage.

The Cards

The cards can be any size and shape, as long as they are all the *same* size and shape. The way the code is written in this chapter, the cards need to be placed in their own cast library. This cast library should have absolutely nothing else in it besides the cards. This makes it easy for the behavior to figure out how many cards there are and where in the cast they are.

In addition, there needs to be a single graphic of a card turned face-down. This bitmap should be in the default, internal cast library, not the "Cards" cast library.

This face-down card bitmap needs to be placed on the Stage in as many sprites as there are to be cards on the screen. For instance, in Figure 4.1, shown previously, there are 100 of these cards needed.

The position of each card on the Stage is irrelevant to the game, but is usually a grid as shown earlier in Figure 4.1. Note that there needs to be exactly twice as many sprites on the Stage as there are cards in the "Cards" cast library. This is because each card graphic represents a pair of cards.

The game behavior expects the cards to be placed in consecutive sprites in the Score. For instance, in the game on the CD-ROM, they are in sprite channels 11 through 110.

The cards themselves can have any sort of image on them. You can use photographs, drawings, colors, symbols, letters, or even words. The game on the CD-ROM uses simple symbols taken from various specialty fonts. Figure 4.2 shows the "Cards" cast library.

Figure 4.2
The "Cards" cast library contains all the cards used in the game.

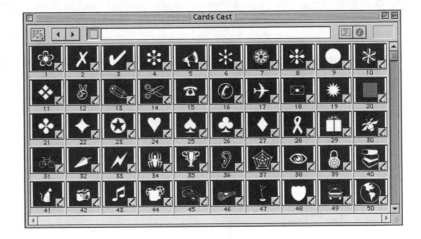

Game Over

As in the previous chapter, a game-over condition is reached when all the cards have been matched. Because we are removing sprites from the Stage when each match is made, the program just needs to check out all the sprites. If any are still on the Stage, then the game is still in progress.

Because the only way a game can end is by the user making a final match, it's necessary to check for the end of the game only when a match is made.

Special Effects

As in all games, sounds can be added to spice things up a bit. A sound would make sense when a match is made. This would signify the two cards being removed from the board.

However, it's not always a good idea to have a sound when the second card does not match. This is because this situation occurs a lot, especially during the beginning of the game. A sound for a nonmatch can get annoying. Still, it's a good idea to include an option for a sound and decide when setting up the Score.

In addition, a sound can be played when a card is clicked. This little bit of feedback makes it a more pleasant experience for the player.

Making the Game

In the last chapter, we had one behavior that was used on each sprite in the game. In addition, we had a simple frame behavior that simply looped on the frame.

In this chapter, we'll do the opposite. The frame behavior will actually be the main piece of code, controlling the game play. The sprites, in turn, will have a simple behavior on them that just passes mouse clicks to the frame behavior.

This all-powerful frame behavior starts off as any other behavior, with a list of properties. The first six are properties that are set when the behavior is assigned to a frame in the Score. The rest are listed here with descriptions.

```
-- Settable Properties
property pSpriteOffset, pDisplayDelay, pGameOverFrame
property pClickSound, pMatchSound, pNoMatchSound

property pNumberOfCards -- number of cards in the game
property pBoard -- holds a list of what cards are where
property pCard1 -- the first card in a pair clicked on
property pCard2 -- the second card in a pair clicked on
property pCardTimer -- the time that the second card was clicked
```

The *on getPropertyDescription* handler returns the information you want displayed in the behavior inspector.

```
on getPropertyDescription me
   text = "Used on a frame script to make a matching game."&RETURN
   put "Will shuffle a list of cards from the 'Cards' cast library"&RETURN after text
```

```
     put "and will assign them to certain sprites based on the sprite offset."&RETURN
  after text
     put "Will allow the user to click on a pair of sprites and"&RETURN after text
     put "then remove them if they refer to the same card."&RETURN after text
     return text
  end
```

The *on getPropertyDescriptionList* behavior is much like the one from the previous chapter. One difference is the way we set a range for the "pDisplayDelay" property. Instead of just allowing the author to type in a number for this property, we are going to have a small slider in the behavior Settings dialog box. You do this by including a *#range* property, with a list that has a *#min* and a *#max* value. The result is the slider seen in Figure 4.3.

Figure 4.3

The Parameters dialog box for the Matching Game Frame Behavior, which includes a slider for one of the values.

```
  on getPropertyDescriptionList me
     list = [:]

     -- pSpriteOffset is used to determine how far from
     -- the top of the Score the first card is
     -- so, if the first card starts in channel 11,
     -- the offset would be 10 (10 away from channel 1).
     addProp list, #pSpriteOffset,¬
        [#comment: "Card Sprite Offset",¬
         #format: #integer,¬
         #default: 0]

     -- pDisplayDelay is how many ticks the pair of
     -- cards will be kept on the screen for the player
     -- to see before they are removed or turned back over
     addProp list, #pDisplayDelay, ¬
        [#comment: "Display Delay",¬
         #format: #integer,¬
         #default: 60,¬
         #range: [#min: 0, #max: 240]]
```

```
-- when a sprite is clicked, what sound is played?
addProp list, #pClickSound,¬
  [#comment: "Click Sound",¬
   #format: #string,¬
   #default: ""]

-- when a sprite is matched, what sound is played?
addProp list, #pMatchSound,¬
  [#comment: "Match Sound",¬
   #format: #string,¬
   #default: ""]

-- when a sprite is not matched, what sound is played?
addProp list, #pNoMatchSound,¬
  [#comment: "No Match Sound",¬
   #format: #string,¬
   #default: ""]

-- when all sprites are matched, which frame should the movie go to?
addProp list, #pGameOverFrame,¬
  [#comment: "Game Over Frame",¬
   #format: #marker,¬
   #default: #next]
  return list
end
```

TIP

Instead of using the *#string* format for the sound parameters, you could use the *#sound* format. This presents a pop-up menu of all the sound members in the movie. However, this would also force you to use assign a sound always. Using the *#string* format is not as convenient, but it does allow you to leave the entry blank, indicating that you do not want to use a sound.

The *on beginSprite* handler is the one that needs to shuffle the cards to provide a random layout each time the game is played. It starts by getting the number of members in the "Cards" cast library ①. It then adds each card twice to a list ②. Then, a random item from this first list is taken and put into a new list ③, the "pBoard" property. When all the items from the first list have been randomly shuffled into the second, the game is ready to begin.

```
-- shuffles the cards to build the pBoard list
-- initializes the game properties
on beginSprite me
```

continues

continued

```
                -- refers to the "Cards" cast library to see how many cards there are
①→  pNumberOfCards = the number of members of castLib "Cards"

        -- build a list with each card in the list twice
        list = []
②→  repeat with i = 1 to pNumberOfCards
          add list, i
          add list, i
        end repeat

        -- fill the pBoard list up randomly with items from
        -- the previously created list
        pBoard = []
        repeat while list.count > 0
          r = random(list.count)
③→      add pBoard, list[r]
          deleteAt list, r
        end repeat

        -- initialize the game properties
        pCard1 = 0
        pCard2 = 0
    end
```

Each time a sprite is clicked, it sends a "turnCard" message to the frame behavior. This is then handled by the "on turnCard" handler below. The sprite number is also passed to this handler.

With the sprite number, and the "pSpriteOffset" property, the code determines the card number. It records this in either "pCard1" or "pCard2".

In addition, the card is turned over ④. This simply means that the sprite on the Stage is replaced with the appropriate bitmap from the "Cards" cast.

No decision is made in this handler as to whether a match has been made. Instead, the "pCardTimer" property is set when the second card is turned over ⑤. This is monitored by the *on exitFrame* handler, and the comparison occurs after a specified amount of time passes.

In the meantime, if the player tries to turn another card over, then the time delay ends and the comparison is made immediately. You can see this bit of code in the final *else* portion of the handler: ⑥

```
    -- called by the sprites when the user clicks
    -- the spriteNumber parameter is the sprite number clicked
  on turnCard me, spriteNumber
      -- play sound, if there is one
      if pClickSound <> "" then puppetSound 1, pClickSound
```

```
    -- determine the card number
    cardNumber = spriteNumber - pSpriteOffset

    if pCard1 = 0 then -- first card clicked
      -- record this card
      pCard1 = cardNumber
      -- turn it over
④→    sprite(spriteNumber).member = member(pBoard[cardNumber],"Cards")

    else if pCard2 = 0 then -- second card clicked
      -- ignore if it is the same card
      if cardNumber = pCard1 then exit
      -- record this card
      pCard2 = cardNumber
      -- turn it over
      sprite(spriteNumber).member = member(pBoard[cardNumber],"Cards")
      -- set the timer
⑤→    pCardTimer = the ticks

⑥→else -- two cards are already turned over
      -- this happens if the user clicks very quickly
      -- force a look at the two cards
      returnCards(me)
      -- make sure the card was not clicked on twice
      if sprite(spriteNumber).memberNum = 0 then exit
      -- record new card as the first card
      pCard1 = cardNumber
      -- turn it over
      sprite(spriteNumber).member = member(pBoard[cardNumber],"Cards")
    end if
end
```

The "on returnCards" handler does the comparison. This handler is also responsible for dealing with the results—either turning the cards back over ⑦, or removing them ⑧. If a successful match is made, it calls the "on checkAllMatched" handler to see whether the game is over.

```
    -- looks at the two cards turned over and compares them
    on returnCards me
      if pBoard[pCard1] = pBoard[pCard2] then -- they are a match
        -- play sound, if there is one
        if pMatchSound <> "" then puppetSound 2, pMatchSound
⑧→      -- remove both sprites
        sprite(pCard1+pSpriteOffset).memberNum = 0
        sprite(pCard2+pSpriteOffset).memberNum = 0
```

continues

continued

```
            -- check for game over
            if checkAllMatched(me) then
              go to frame pGameOverFrame
            end if
          else -- no match
            -- play sound, if there is one
            if pNoMatchSound <> "" then puppetSound 2, pNoMatchSound
(7)-->     -- turn both cards back
            sprite(pCard1+pSpriteOffset).member = member("Card Back")
            sprite(pCard2+pSpriteOffset).member = member("Card Back")
          end if

          -- reset the game properties
          pCard1 = 0
          pCard2 = 0
        end
```

The *on exitFrame* handler plays an important part in this game. It checks for the situation in which two cards are turned over. If that is true, then it checks to see whether it's a certain amount of time past the time set in "pCardTimer". If this is also true, then it calls "on returnCards" to compare them.

This behavior is also responsible for the critical *go to the frame* command. This keeps the game looping on the current frame.

```
on exitFrame me
  if pCard1 <> 0 and pCard2 <> 0 then -- two cards are turned
    if the ticks > pCardTimer + pDisplayDelay then -- time has expired
      -- check the cards to see if there is a match
      returnCards(me)
    end if
  end if

  -- loop on the frame
  go to the frame
end
```

The last handler checks to see whether the game is over. It simply looks at all the sprites where a card should be and sees whether there is one there. If it finds any cards (9), then the game is not over, and a *FALSE* is returned. Otherwise, a *TRUE* is returned.

```
-- check to see if the game is over
on checkAllMatched me
  -- loop through all cards
  repeat with i = 1 to pNumberOfCards
    -- determine the card's sprite
```

```
         spriteNumber = i + pSpriteOffset
         -- if it is still a card, then the game is not over
⑨→      if sprite(i).memberNum <> 0 then return FALSE
      end repeat

      -- all cards missing, so game over
      return TRUE
   end
```

In addition to this one long behavior for the frame script channel, there needs to be a behavior on each of the individual card sprites. This behavior is just one line of code inside an *on mouseUp* handler.

```
on mouseUp me
   -- simply tell the frame script that this sprite was clicked
   sendSprite(0,#turnCard,me.spriteNum)
end
```

NOTE

When you want to send a message to the frame script, use *sendSprite* with a sprite number of 0. In Director 7, you can actually use any sprite number to send a message to the frame script, so long as the sprite does not already have a behavior that handles the same message. Strangely enough, if you were to ask the frame behavior for the value of *me.spriteNum*, however, it would return -5.

The *sendSprite* command here sends its message to the frame script channel. To do this, a sprite number of 0 is used as the first parameter. The command also sends an extra parameter, the sprite number.

Putting It All Together

Using the behaviors described previously to create this game is fairly simple. First, you need to create the "Cards" cast. Figure out how many cards you want, remembering that each card will be used twice to make a matching pair. Then, create your bitmaps.

The "Cards" cast should look like Figure 4.2, shown previously. There should be nothing but face-up cards in the cast. The face-down card needs to be placed in another cast library, probably just the default internal cast. Be sure that the cards, and the face-down bitmap, are all exactly the same size.

Next, you need to place the face-down bitmap in the Score twice for every card you have. So, if the "Cards" cast has 18 cards, then you need to make 36 sprites. These sprites should be in a continuous sprite block. It's best not to start the sprite block at sprite 1, because you might want to place a background image there. I usually put something like this starting at sprite 11, which gives me 10 sprites that will be underneath them if I need them.

Select all the card sprites and add the simple "Matching Game Sprite Behavior" to them. This allows them to pass the mouse clicks back to the main behavior, which will be in the frame script channel. Drop the "Matching Game Frame Behavior" there.

When you drop the "Matching Game Frame Behavior", you are asked to fill out the Parameters dialog box for this behavior. This dialog box was shown in Figure 4.3. Start by indicating the sprite offset for the block of card sprites. If the block starts at sprite 11, for instance, then the offset is 10.

You can also modify the delay time for cards to be shown, and the sounds that are played at various points of the game. If you don't have a sound for a particular event, just leave it empty.

Finally, tell the behavior which frame it should go to when the game is over. In many cases, just using the default "next" setting works fine.

That's all you need to do to get a game going. However, there are many ways in which this game can be improved beyond the basics.

Game Variations

Although the basic game is good as a memory exercise, scoring features can make it even more exciting. There are two ways to keep score: You can record the number of guesses and the number of correct matches, and you can time the player. In addition, a two-player version of the game can turn it into a competition.

Keeping Score

The sample movie on the CD-ROM includes frames and behaviors that represent all four versions of the game discussed in this chapter. If you look at the "Matching Game Frame Behavior w/Score" behavior, you will see a script similar to the basic game's script, except that script also keeps track of the score.

Furthermore, if you turn off script auto coloring by choosing File, Preferences, Script, Auto Coloring, you can see that I have marked the changes in red. This will help you find the changes that are mentioned in the following paragraphs. You need to turn auto coloring off before opening the movie, however.

The first such change is to add two properties that keep track of the score. You need to add a property that counts the number of guesses that the user makes, and a property that counts the number of correct matches.

```
property pScoreGuess, pScoreMatch -- remember the score
```

Next, in the *on beginSprite* handler, set these properties to 0.

```
-- initialize the score
  pScoreGuess = 0
  pScoreMatch = 0
  showScore(me)
```

The last line shown previously calls a new handler. This will simply display the current score in a text member. Call this in the *on beginSprite* handler to be sure that this text member displays the initialized score when the game begins.

```
on showScore me
  -- show the score
  member("score").text = "Score:"&&pScoreMatch&"/"&pScoreGuess
end
```

In the "on returnCards" handler, you need to add 1 to the "pScoreGuess" property each time a pair of cards is compared.

```
-- record the guess
  pScoreGuess = pScoreGuess + 1
```

Further down in the same handler, add 1 to the "pScoreMatch" if a correct match has been made.

```
-- record the match
    pScoreMatch = pScoreMatch + 1
```

Finally, the "on returnCards" handler should call the "on showScore" handler to display the change in the score.

This completes the changes to the code. The only change to the movie beyond that is to create the "score" text member and place it on the Stage. You should also place this "score" text member on the end game frame, so that the final score is present on the screen when the game is over.

Adding a Timer

An alternative way to score this sort of game is to keep track of the amount of time it takes the player to complete the puzzle. This is done by simply recording the time the game started, and then checking to see how much time has elapsed since then.

The example on the CD-ROM also includes a "Matching Game Frame Behavior w/Timer" behavior. If you turn off the script auto coloring, you will see that the new pieces of code are in red.

The first such line just added the "pGameTimer" property to the top of the behavior.

```
property pGameTime -- the start time of the game
```

After that, this property needs to be initialized in the *on beginSprite* handler.

```
-- set the start time
```

```
pGameTime = the ticks
showTimer(me)
```

The "on showTimer" handler is called right away to show the starting time, 0, on the screen. This same handler will be used to update the time throughout the game.

```
on showTimer me
  -- the current time, as a string
  currentTime = string((the ticks - pGameTime)/60)
  -- if this is different than the time displayed, update
  if member("score").text <> currentTime then
    member("score").text = currentTime
  end if
end
```

Notice that there is a lot more to this "on showTimer" handler than just placing the time in a text member. First, the time is calculated by subtracting the start time from the current time. Then, this result is divided by 60 to get seconds. This number is converted to a string.

This string is then compared to the text in the "score" text member. If the time is different from the number shown there, the text member is changed to show the new time.

The reason this is done is simply for speed. Every time you set a text member, Director takes the time to rerender the text on the screen. Because the movie is running faster than one frame per second, you will be asking for an update to the timer several times a second. For instance, if the "score" text member shows 3, to indicate that three seconds have passed since the beginning of the game, then you will probably be asking for a timer update many more times before the time changes to 4. Because the time shown is the same as the actual time, setting the text member won't do any good. All that will happen is that the member will rerender the text, taking a small amount of time to do so, probably milliseconds. However, these are still wasted milliseconds, so it's better not to force the text member to update unless it really needs to.

The last change you need to make to the script is to add a call to the "on showTimer" handler in the *on exitFrame* handler. The system property *the ticks* is constantly changing, so there is never a need to actually increment a timer of any sort. Just by calling this handler once per frame, you can update the timer.

```
-- update the time
showTimer(me)
```

That's all it takes to add a timer to the game. You can see that it actually takes less code than adding the scoring functionality of the last section.

Be sure that the "score" text member is in the Cast and on the Stage. You will also want this to be in the end game frame so that the user can examine his final time. Because the end game frame does not have your game behavior script on it, the "score" member is no longer updated. So, the time remains frozen on the screen on the end game frame, which is *exactly* what you want.

Two-Player Game

Making this game a two-player game is a little more difficult. However, it can be done using the same behavior framework developed here. As before, the changes described in the following paragraphs can be found in the "Matching Game Frame Behavior for Two Players" behavior marked in red.

First, you need to add two new properties—one to keep track of which player is up, and the other to keep track of the scores for both players.

```
property pPlayerTurn -- indicates whose turn it is
property pScores -- a list with the players' scores
```

These two properties need to be set at the end of the *on beginSprite* handler; the text members on the screen need to be set as well.

```
-- initialize player information
pPlayerTurn = 1
  pScores = [0,0]
  showTurn(me)
  showScore(me)
```

Two text members are needed for this version of the game. As before, you need the "score" text member, but this time two lines are needed to show the two scores. So, be sure that the text member is large enough on the Stage to allow two lines of text.

The second text member indicates which player's turn it is. We'll name this text member "turn". Here are the handlers that update these text members:

```
on showTurn me
  member("turn").text = "Player"&&pPlayerTurn
end

on showScore me
  text = ""
  repeat with i = 1 to pScores.count
    put "Player"&&i&":"&&pScores[i]&RETURN after text
  end repeat
  member("score").text = text
end
```

Notice that the "on showScore" behavior is not hard-coded for exactly two players. Instead, it looks to the "pScores" list to determine how many players to list. This will come in handy if you ever want to make this game for even more players to play at once.

The other handler you need increments the "pPlayerTurn" property when a turn is over.

```
on endTurn me
  pPlayerTurn = pPlayerTurn + 1
  if pPlayerTurn > pScores.count then
    pPlayerTurn = 1
  end if
  showTurn(me)
end
```

The "on endTurn" handler also does not assume two players, but instead looks at the number of items in "pScores" to determine when the turn should go back to player 1. This handler works with any number of players.

Now the "on returnCard" handler needs to be modified to record the score and call "on endTurn". This game differs from the earlier score-keeping version in that we are interested only in matches, not the number of guesses. So, we need to increment the score only in the case of a match. Here are the lists to be added:

```
-- record the score
    pScores[pPlayerTurn] = pScores[pPlayerTurn] + 1
    showScore(me)
```

Finally, we need to call "on endTurn" at the end of the "on returnCard" handler to indicate that the next player is up.

```
    endTurn(me)
```

This completes the changes to the behavior. Be sure that both the "turn" and the "score" members are present on the Stage, although only the "score" member needs to be present at the end game frame.

To make this game work with more than three players, you need only to add more 0's to the "pScores" list in the *on beginSprite* handler. This has the potential to be a challenging party game with four, five, or even six players. Each player will want to pay attention to the other players' guesses to try to find matches. Remember to expand the "turn" text member to accommodate all the extra lines of the score needed.

Jigsaw Puzzle

5

CD-ROM File: 05jigsaw.dir

Useful Lingo in This Chapter

- ♠ Behaviors: Calling handlers in other behaviors
- ♠ Behaviors: Using parameters
- ♠ Graphics: Adjusting sprite layers
- ♠ Graphics: Moving sprites
- ♠ Graphics: Using a set of bitmaps
- ♠ Graphics: Using registration points
- ♠ Graphics: Using points
- ♠ Input: Dragging with the mouse
- ♠ Interface: Dragging and dropping
- ♠ Lists: Using linear lists
- ♠ Lists: Using property lists
- ♠ Lists: Lists that contain lists
- ♠ Math: Using random numbers

The idea of computer jigsaw puzzles seemed ridiculous at first. I had made my first jigsaw puzzle program as more of a programming exercise, than a realistic game. I thought, who would want to play a jigsaw puzzle on a computer, when the real thing worked so well?

Well, it was a good thing that I took a chance on that first jigsaw puzzle game. The Jigsaw puzzle is now one of the most popular of games at my site. People like the fact that they don't take up an entire table and they can't lose the pieces. They play them as they would play a solitaire game. Jigsaws are a simple distraction that some players even use as meditation and for stress-relief.

Game Overview

Jigsaw puzzles involve a number of playing pieces that fit together to form a complete picture. The actions by the user are simple click-and-drag actions. They do, however, expect that the pieces will join to one another to form larger pieces.

Figure 5.1 shows the example jigsaw puzzle game from the CD-ROM. This example includes a puzzle where all the pieces are simple squares, and another where they are odd shapes.

Figure 5.1
This jigsaw puzzle is partially completed. The pieces that are linked together will move together.

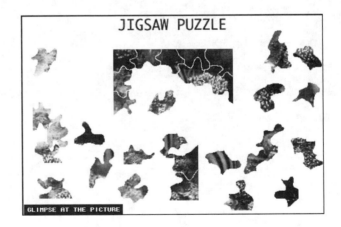

Dragging

Clicking and dragging is something that was used in the game in Chapter 3, "Matching Game." However, there are several important differences here.

First, when pieces are dragged, they should move to the front of the screen, on top of other pieces. We don't want the user losing the piece under another when we are trying to create the illusion that they have lifted it up off the table.

Second, when one piece has been successfully linked to another, both pieces should be dragged together from then on. This gets even more complex when several pieces have been joined.

Creating Puzzle Pieces

A big issue that should not be overlooked is how to create the puzzle pieces. There are many ways to do this, but not a single one that is simple.

You can start with a full picture and start cutting pieces out from it to form other bitmap members. However, while doing this, you must keep the registration points matched. All the pieces created should have a registration point at the center of the whole puzzle, not the center of each piece. By doing it this way, the program knows when pieces are correctly positioned relative to one another because their *loc* properties are the same.

Figure 5.2 shows two paint windows side-by-side. You can see two different puzzle pieces, with the registration points for each. Notice how the registration points are at the center of the puzzle, not the center of the pieces. Check out the puzzle pieces in the example movie on the CD-ROM as well. It's important to understand this fundamental element of the jigsaw puzzle programs.

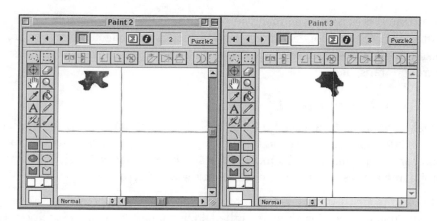

Figure 5.2   *The registration points for the puzzle pieces need to be lined up so that the registration point is always at the center of the completed picture.*

One way to make jigsaw pieces is to draw a box around the image. Place this box many pixels out from the sides of the image. The bitmap now looks like a picture inside a box. The box helps keep the registration point stable while you cut out pieces. Then, duplicate the bitmap member, but cut out the image itself, leaving only the box. Make many copies of this box bitmap in the cast. Return to the original image and cut out a piece of it with the lasso tool. Cut it—don't copy it. Then, go to one of your box bitmaps and paste it in there. It should appear in the same space as it originally occupied, but now all by itself. Repeat this until there is no original image left. Now, return to each piece and remove the box around it by using the fill tool to fill the box pixels with white.

Of course, there are many other ways to create puzzle pieces. I'm surprised that someone hasn't created a program that does it. Either way, you end up with a set of puzzle pieces. Place them in a separate cast library for organizational purposes. An example is shown in Figure 5.3. To keep things simple, these pieces are just plain squares.

Figure 5.3
A Cast library filled with square puzzle pieces.

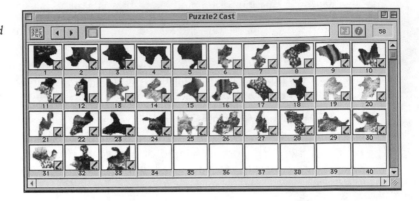

If your puzzle pieces have been made correctly, then you should be able to drag all the pieces to the Stage or Score and they should fit together perfectly. Don't worry if they look like a mess at first, you will probably need to change the ink of all those sprites to "background transparent."

Random Placement

Now that all your pieces are on the Stage, you'll notice that the puzzle is all done! To make it a little more of a challenge for the player, you might want to mix them up a little. You can do this manually, by moving the sprites around. However, this would mean that the game always starts with the pieces in the same location.

A better way to do this is to use Lingo to place each piece randomly on the Stage at the start of the game. This Lingo code has the additional task of making sure no pieces hang off the edge of the Stage, or touch other pieces.

Payoff

The reward for playing a jigsaw puzzle game should be just seeing the finished puzzle. But, alas, some players (and producers) demand more. As in past chapters, this game detects when the puzzle is complete and automatically goes to another frame. Here, you can place the final image, or perhaps a congratulatory animation.

Special Effects

Although you can place sounds in the game for both clicking and dropping, all this game really requires is a sound for the case in which two pieces become linked together.

Another special effect that can be used for this game is the cursor change. We can have the cursor change into a hand when it is above a piece, and change into a closed hand when the player grabs a piece.

Making the Game

Most of this game will actually be one large behavior that is attached to each and every jigsaw piece sprite. However, we will start by looking at the frame behavior script.

The Frame Behavior

This script serves three purposes. The first is to register the first and last sprite in the block of sprites that make up the jigsaw pieces. The Frame behavior takes these as parameter properties, and then passes those values on to global variables to use them there.

Here is the beginning section of the "Jigsaw Puzzle Frame Behavior." All lines but the last line in the *on beginSprite* handler deal with setting up the sprite range.

```
-- these two globals allow the sprite range
-- to be passed to all the sprites for use
global gFirstSprite, gLastSprite

-- these properties are just used to get
-- the sprite range
property pFirstSprite, pLastSprite

-- the only two parameters are to set the sprite range
on getPropertyDescriptionList me
  list = [:]

  addProp list, #pFirstSprite,¬
    [#comment: "First Puzzle Piece Sprite",¬
     #format: #integer,¬
     #default: 1]

  addProp list, #pLastSprite,¬
    [#comment: "Last Puzzle Piece Sprite",¬
     #format: #integer,¬
     #default: 1]

  return list
end
```

Figure 5.4 shows the Parameters dialog box for this behavior. It reflects the list built in the *on getPropertyDescriptionList* handler.

Figure 5.4
*The Parameters
dialog box for the
sprite behavior.*

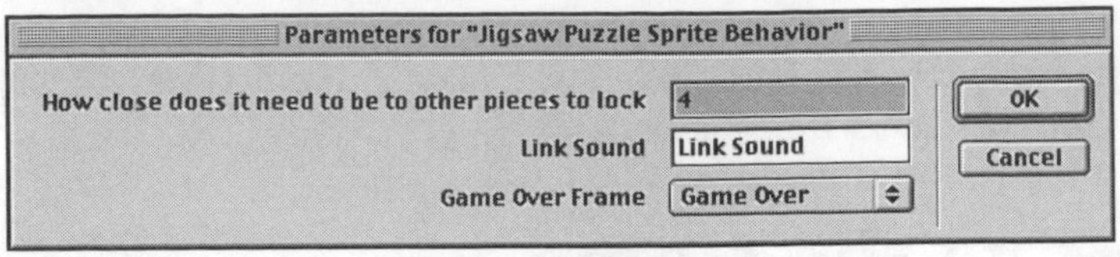

```
-- when the frame begins, set up the sprite range globals
-- and randomize the pieces
on beginSprite me
  gFirstSprite = pFirstSprite
  gLastSprite = pLastSprite
  randomizePieces(me)
end
```

The sprite range could have been established many different ways. These two globals could have been properties in the main sprite behavior instead, which would require them to be set exactly the same for every sprite. Having them set in the one and only frame behavior guarantees that they will not be set to different values by accident.

The last line of the *on beginSprite* handler calls the custom "on randomizePieces" handler. This handler loops through all the sprites and sets them to random positions on the Stage ① . This is the second purpose for this behavior. The behavior makes sure the edges of the rectangles for the sprites are not off of the Stage ② , and that no piece touches any other on the Stage ③ .

```
-- move the pieces around the Stage until all are
-- completely on the Stage and none are overlapping
on randomizePieces me
  numTries = 0
  repeat with i = gFirstSprite to gLastSprite
    repeat while TRUE
      -- see if it may be locked up because of lack of sprite
      numTries = numTries + 1
      if numTries > 1000 then
        i = gFirstSprite
        numTries = 0
      end if
①→    -- pick a random location
      x = random((the stage).rect.width)
      y = random((the stage).rect.height)
      sprite(i).loc = point(x,y)
②→    -- see if the sprite is hanging over the edge
      if sprite(i).rect.left < 0 then next repeat
      if sprite(i).rect.right > (the stage).rect.width then next repeat
      if sprite(i).rect.top < 0 then next repeat
      if sprite(i).rect.bottom > (the stage).rect.height then next repeat
```

```
③ ➤ -- see if the sprite is overlapping another
      touchingOtherPiece = FALSE
      repeat with j = gFirstSprite to i-1
        if j = i then next repeat
        if sprite j intersects i then
          touchingOtherPiece = TRUE
          exit repeat
        end if
      end repeat
      if touchingOtherPiece then next repeat
      -- this piece is set, go on to next
      exit repeat
    end repeat
  end repeat
end
```

A peculiar thing can happen with this handler every once in a while. If the pieces are placed just right, the handler can run out of space on the Stage to place additional pieces. No matter how hard it tries, it cannot find a spot on the Stage where the last remaining piece or pieces can fit. In that case, the "numTries" counter in the handler reaches a high number, such as 1,000, and the handler restarts the process by setting the "i" variable back to 0. This is an important part of the handler, because it ensures that the handler won't loop infinitely. In addition, you must test your puzzle to ensure enough space is available on the Stage for the pieces to coexist without their rectangles overlapping.

The third and final purpose for this behavior is to do the traditional frame looping.

```
on exitFrame me
  go to the frame
end
```

The Sprite Behavior

The main code for this game is in the sprite behavior. This behavior needs to be attached to *every* puzzle piece sprite in the Score.

The properties and globals used by the behavior are explained in the comments at the beginning of the script.

```
-- these two globals are set by the frame script
-- and contain the sprite range
global gFirstSprite, gLastSprite

property pOffset -- click and drag offset
property pDrag -- is the sprite being dragged
property pLinks -- which other sprites are linked to this one?
property pCloseness, pLinkSound, pGameOverFrame
```

continues

continued

```
on getPropertyDescriptionList me
  list = [:]

  -- how near this piece needs to be to another to link it
  addProp list, #pCloseness,¬
    [#comment: "How close does it need to be to other pieces to lock",¬
     #format: #integer,¬
     #default: 4]

  -- sound to play when a link is made
  addProp list, #pLinkSound,¬
    [#comment: "Link Sound",¬
     #format: #string,¬
     #default: ""]

  -- frame to jump to when game is over
  addProp list, #pGameOverFrame,¬
    [#comment: "Game Over Frame",¬
     #format: #marker,¬
     #default: #next]

  return list
end
```

Figure 5.5 shows the Parameters dialog box for this behavior. It reflects the list built in the *on getPropertyDescriptionList* handler.

Figure 5.5

The Parameters dialog box for the frame behavior.

Each sprite keeps track of the others that are linked to it by the use of the "pLinks" property. This property is a list of these sprite numbers. This list also includes the sprite's own number. This list is set up in the *on beginSprite* handler.

```
-- start by including self in links
on beginSprite me
  pLinks = [me.spriteNum]
end
```

One of the special effects of this game is the cursor change. We want the cursor to change into an open hand when the user passes the cursor over a piece. We also want the cursor to change back when it isn't over any pieces. The *on mouseEnter* and *on mouseLeave* handlers take care of this. The cursor number for an open hand is 260.

NOTE

There are many ways to change the cursor in Director. For games like this, it's often useful to set the *cursor* property of a sprite for rollovers. This way, if the game ends or the user selects an option that takes him or her suddenly to another frame, the cursor is sure to switch back to normal as soon as the sprite is gone.

```
on mouseEnter me
  -- open hand cursor
  sprite(me.spriteNum).cursor = 260
end

on mouseLeave me
  -- reset cursor
  sprite(me.spriteNum).cursor = -1
end
```

When the user starts a drag, the cursor needs to change into the closed hand cursor, which is number 290. In addition to setting the "pDrag" property and the "pOffset" property (as you saw in the two previous chapters), we will also call the "on moveToFrontZ" handler, which allows the piece to be drawn on top of all the others on the Stage as the user drags it.

```
-- start a drag
on mouseDown me
  pDrag = TRUE
  -- closed hand cursor
  sprite(me.spriteNum).cursor = 290
  -- get click offset
  pOffset = the clickLoc - sprite(me.spriteNum).loc
  -- use locZ property to move this piece and all links to front
  moveToFrontZ(me)
end
```

When the user drops the piece being dragged, the cursor changes back into an open hand. In addition, the sprite, and all the sprites it is already linked to, are checked to see whether they are in a position that would link them to more sprites.

A *repeat with…in* loop is used to cycle through all the values in the "pLinks" property. The sprites are all set to the new location at the end of the drag. Then a message is sent to each sprite, which includes the current one, to execute the "on checkForNewLinks" handler.

Notice that the "on restrictLoc" handler is called as a function with the mouse location. This "on restrictLoc" handler ensures the location value is within the limits of the Stage, thus preventing someone from dragging a piece off the Stage, where they could never pick it up again.

The *on mouseUp* handler also calls "on moveToNormalZ" to ensure that the sprites do not stay on top of others during future drags.

```
on mouseUp me
  -- if not being dragged, then ignore
  if not pDrag then exit

  -- open hand cursor
  sprite(me.spriteNum).cursor = 260

  pDrag = FALSE
  -- set all linked pieces to current position
  -- check each piece to see if any can be linked to them
  repeat with s in pLinks
    newLoc = restrictLoc(me,the mouseLoc) - pOffset
    sprite(s).loc = newLoc
    sendSprite(s,#checkForNewLinks)
  end repeat

  -- move all sprites back to normal locZ
  moveToNormalZ(me)
end

-- send mouseUpOutsides to mouseUp
on mouseUpOutside me
  mouseUp(me)
end
```

The *on exitFrame* handler takes care of all the dragging. It uses the same "on restrictLoc" handler to restrict the mouse location. This handler also loops through all the values in "pLinks" to ensure they follow the sprite being dragged.

```
-- drag piece and all links
on exitFrame me
  if pDrag then
    -- drag piece
    newLoc = restrictLoc(me,the mouseLoc) - pOffset
    sprite(me.spriteNum).loc = newLoc
    -- drag links as well
    repeat with s in pLinks
      sprite(s).loc = newLoc
    end repeat
  end if
end
```

Here is the "on restrictLoc" handler. It looks at the horizontal and vertical values of the location point and ensure they are within the limits of the Stage. For extra assurance, we will ensure it isn't within 10 pixels of the edge of the Stage.

```
-- make sure a point is within the Stage
on restrictLoc me, loc
  if loc.locH < 10 then loc.locH = 10
  if loc.locH > (the stage).rect.width-10 then¬
     loc.locH = (the stage).rect.width-10
  if loc.locV < 10 then loc.locV = 10
  if loc.locV > (the stage).rect-10.height then¬
     loc.locV = (the stage).rect.height-10
  return loc
end
```

After a drag has been completed, the "on checkForNewLinks" handler is called for *every* sprite involved in the drag. It loops through all the sprites, being sure to ignore ones that are already linked to the current sprite.

The "on checkForNewLinks" handler calls the "on closeEnough" handler to see whether a piece is in the proper position to be linked to the current sprite. It then plays a sound and calls "on addLink" to add this new sprite to the "pLinks" property. The handler then sets the position of all the sprites linked together to the current sprite's position ④ , thus locking all the sprites together. Lastly, the "on checkForNewLinks" handler calls the "on checkGameDone" handler to see whether the game is over.

```
-- see if this sprite touches any others
on checkForNewLinks me
  repeat with s = gFirstSprite to gLastSprite
    -- make sure the piece isn't already linked
    if getOne(pLinks,s) then next repeat
    -- see if the piece is close enough to be linked
    if closeEnough(me,s) then
      -- play sound
      if pLinkSound <> "" then puppetSound pLinkSound
      -- add to list of links
      addLink(me,sprite(s).pLinks)
      -- set all old and new linked pieces to the right location
      repeat with ss in pLinks
④ ➤    sprite(ss).loc = sprite(me.spriteNum).loc
      end repeat
      -- check to see if puzzle is done
      checkDoneGame(me)
      -- need look no further
      exit
    end if
  end repeat
end
```

The "on closeEnough" handler checks three conditions to determine whether two sprites are correctly positioned to be linked. First, it checks the horizontal difference, then, the vertical difference, and finally, it compares the two sprites' rectangles to see whether they overlap. In fact, we add one pixel on every side to expand the bounding rectangle of the current sprite to be sure sprites that are just barely touching will be considered close enough.

In every comparison, the "pCloseness" property is used to determine the amount of leeway the sprites have to be considered close enough to link up.

NOTE
The *intersects* function is a good way to determine whether two rectangles overlap. However, the result is the actual rectangle that represents the intersection. So, to make a test out of *intersects*, we need to see whether it's *not* equal to "rect(0,0,0,0)", which is the value returned if there is no intersection at all.

```
-- see if a sprite is close enough to this one to link
on closeEnough me, s
  -- close enough horizontally
  if abs(sprite(me.spriteNum).locH - sprite(s).locH) < pCloseness then
    -- close enough vertically
    if abs(sprite(me.spriteNum).locV - sprite(s).locV) < pCloseness then
      -- see if the sprite rectangles are close enough
      if intersect(sprite(s).rect,sprite(me.spriteNum).rect+¬
        rect(-pCloseness-1,-pCloseness-1,pCloseness+1,pCloseness+1))¬
        <> rect(0,0,0,0) then
        -- close enough
        return TRUE
      end if
    end if
  end if
  -- not close enough
  return FALSE
end
```

The "on addLink" handler takes the "pLinks" property from both the current sprite, and the new sprite, and combines them into one new variable. The handler then assigns this value to the "pLinks" property of both sprites, as well as all the sprites involved. This ensures that all the sprites linked together by this drag action now have the same value for the "pLinks" property.

```
-- merge the links of this sprite with the links of the
-- new sprite and set the pLinks property for all
-- of these sprites to be the new list
-- this effectively links this sprite to the others
-- and the others to this one
on addLink me, list
  newlist = []
```

```
   -- add all the links for this sprite
   repeat with s in pLinks
     add newlist, s
   end repeat
   -- add all the links for another sprite
   repeat with s in list
     add newlist, s
   end repeat
   -- set all sprites involved to have the same list
   repeat with s in newlist
     sprite(s).pLinks = newlist
   end repeat
 end
```

Checking to see whether the game is over is a simple task. The "pLinks" property holds the list of all the sprites that are linked to the current one. When the puzzle is complete, all the sprites are linked, so all the "pLinks" properties will be a list of all the sprites in the puzzle. So, all that is needed to determine the end of the game is to check the current sprite and see whether the number of items in "pLinks" is equal to the total number of sprites.

```
 -- if this is linked to all other pieces
 -- then game must be over
 on checkDoneGame me
   -- how many pieces are there?
   totalLinks = gLastSprite - gFirstSprite + 1
   -- are all linked?
   if pLinks.count = totalLinks then
     go to frame pGameOverFrame
   end if
 end
```

The final two handlers take care of moving the sprites to the front of the screen for dragging, and then back to their normal layer when the drag is over. This is done by altering the *locZ* property of these sprites.

The *locZ* property overrides the natural sprite layering determined by the sprite's channel in the Score. Because the Score in Director 7 can go up to only channel 1,000, we will use a *locZ* value of 1,001 for each sprite to ensure they are above all the sprites on the Stage.

```
 -- move all sprites in pLinks to be on top
 on moveToFrontZ me
   repeat with s in pLinks
     sprite(s).locZ = 1001
   end repeat
 end
```

To reset the *locZ* properties of the sprites, just set the *locZ* to the sprite's channel number.

```
-- move all sprites in pLinks to normal locZ
on moveToNormalZ me
  repeat with s in pLinks
    sprite(s).locZ = s
  end repeat
end
```

Putting It All Together

For organizational purposes, place the puzzle pieces in a separate cast library. You can even make this an external cast library, which would make it easy to swap out with a new puzzle later on.

Then, drag and drop all the puzzle piece members from the Cast to the Score at once. They will probably all be set to "copy" ink, so select them all again and change them to "background transparent" ink. Now, if your registration points are set correctly, you should be able to see the completed puzzle on the Stage.

Move the sprites in the Score so that they are positioned where you want them. You might want to start them at sprite channel 11 or thereabouts, so you have a few sprite channels left for items that will appear under the pieces as they move about.

Then, drag and drop the "Jigsaw Puzzle Frame Behavior" to the frame script channel. You are prompted for the first and last sprite channel numbers, so enter those.

Now, select all the puzzle pieces again, and use the script pop-up menu at the top of the Score window to add the "Jigsaw Puzzle Sprite Behavior" to all of them at once. Enter a link sound, if any, and a game over frame. You can also change the closeness property. If you need to change these values later on, the best way is to select all the sprites, remove the behavior, and then add it again. This way, all the parameters can be set at once.

Now the game is ready to go. Remember to create your game over frame and your link sound.

Game Variations

You can add the most variety to your jigsaw puzzles through the images themselves. You can make difficult puzzles that use images with repeating patterns, like a field of grass, or simple puzzles that have distinct objects in the image.

However, there are a few other features you can add to this game. You can allow the player to examine the complete image from time to time, just as jigsaw puzzle players sometimes look at the box to see where pieces go. You can also create nonrectangular puzzles.

Looking at the Box

It's a good idea to allow the player to glimpse the entire puzzle from time to time to get a hint as to where pieces go. One simple way to do this is to place a small button on the Stage that the user can click to see the image. The image will appear only until the user lifts up the mouse button.

A behavior to do this is very simple. It just swaps out the button sprite's member for the member in the next Cast slot. As soon as the mouse button is lifted, the sprite reverts to the button member.

```
property pOrigMemberNumber

on beginSprite me
  -- remember the original member
  pOrigMemberNumber = sprite(me.spriteNum).memberNum
end

on mouseDown me
  --show the next member
  sprite(me.spriteNum).memberNum = pOrigMemberNumber+1
end

on mouseUp me
  -- revert back to original member
  sprite(me.spriteNum).memberNum = pOrigMemberNumber
end

on mouseUpOutside me
  mouseUp(me)
end
```

Check out how this is done in the example movie on the CD-ROM. The button and the complete image are in Cast members right next to each other. Also, their registration points are set so that if the button is in the lower-left corner of the Stage, the image also appears there. You can play with the button's Stage position and the two members' registration points to have them appear anywhere on the Stage.

For the image to appear on top of any pieces on the Stage, the button should be in a higher-numbered sprite channel than the pieces.

You may also want to place the completed image on the "game over" screen for the player to look at. This is much nicer than simply jumping to mostly blank frame as the example movie does.

Different Puzzle Shapes

The code in this chapter will work regardless of the shape of the puzzle. It just uses the registration points of the pieces and their rectangles to determine which pieces link to which. So, you could create a circular image, for instance, and then cut pieces out of that.

Sliding Puzzle

6

CD-ROM File: 06slidingpuzzle.dir

Useful Lingo in This Chapter

- ♠ Behaviors: Using parameters
- ♠ Graphics: Moving sprites
- ♠ Graphics: Using points
- ♠ Lists: Using linear lists
- ♠ Math: Using random numbers

The sliding puzzle game, like the jigsaw puzzle, is a real-world physical game that has been adapted to the computer screen. Also, like jigsaw puzzles, they can be used for many purposes. Because an image is at the center of the game, it can be used to promote things, or it can simply be given a theme. For instance, a sliding puzzle with an illustration for a children's book can be used in an educational CD-ROM, whereas a movie still image can be used to promote a film on the Web.

Game Overview

A sliding puzzle has puzzle pieces that are usually square, and are fixed to the board. One piece is missing. Figure 6.1 shows a typical setup.

Figure 6.1
The sliding puzzle game is played by moving one piece at a time into the empty slot.

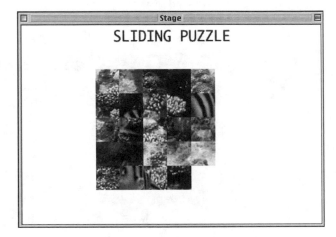

The user arranges the pieces by sliding one into the empty slot from either the left, right, top, or bottom. By continuously moving pieces around, any arrangement can be obtained, although the combination of movements needed to get a certain arrangement is not always obvious.

Puzzle Pieces

A sliding puzzle game is similar to a jigsaw puzzle in that you start with a cast library filled with puzzle pieces. Because the pieces must slide by one another, they should be square, or at least rectangular. They should all be exactly the same size.

In addition, we do not have to use the same registration point alignment that we used for the jigsaw puzzles. The registration point for each piece should be in the center of the bitmap. This makes it much easier to build the pieces, as anyone who has played with Director 7's Paint Window knows.

One peculiar thing about the sliding puzzle is that one piece is always missing. It is almost always the bottom-right corner piece. This is fundamental, because the player needs an empty slot to slide the first piece into.

Figure 6.2 shows a cast library with 24 puzzle pieces. The puzzle is meant to be a 5×5 square puzzle, with the bottom-right corner piece missing at the start of the game.

Figure 6.2
A cast library with the pieces for a sliding puzzle game.

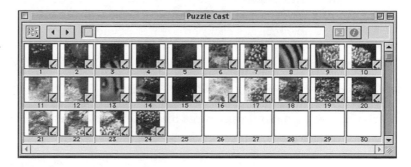

The Sliding Motion

In many Director-based versions of this game, when the user clicks on a piece, it jumps into an adjacent vacant slot. Although this gets the job done, let's go for something a little nicer here by actually having the sprites animate into the new spot, giving a smooth feel to the game.

To do this, we will attach a sprite behavior to every piece that will get the signal to animate and where to animate to. The sprite behavior will then take care of that animation independent to the main game behavior. By making things like this independent of the game code, we avoid complicating the code with special effects that have little to do with the game logic.

Detecting Game Over

Because all the puzzle pieces have their registration points marked in the center, there is no easy way, as there was with the jigsaw puzzles, to determine whether the puzzle is complete. Instead, we will use a technique that relies on two facts. First, the sprites will be arranged in the Score in the same order in which they appear on the Stage. So, the sprite in the upper-left corner will be in the first sprite channel, the next piece to the right will be in the next channel, and so on. Second, the empty spot in the puzzle will be at the bottom right.

These facts then enable us to look through the sprites and determine whether each sprite is in its proper position throughout the puzzle. Thus, we can determine whether the game is over.

Special Effects

In addition to the sliding animation, we will be adding sound and cursor changes to this game. The sound will be a simple one to go along with the sliding animation. The cursor change just consists of a finger cursor to be applied to each puzzle piece, indicating that it is clickable.

Making the Game

This game consists of two behaviors, one for the frame and one for the sprite. The frame behavior is the main one, keeping track of the game state, whereas the sprite behavior simply registers clicks and performs the animation.

Frame Behavior

The frame behavior uses five parameters and four properties. The parameters are used to determine the sprite range, the empty spot at the start of the game, and the frame that the movie jumps to when the game is over.

```
-- parameters
property pFirstSprite, pLastSprite
property pOpenSpot, pGameOverFrame
property pSlideSound
```

The properties hold the calculated value of the width and height of the pieces. A property will also hold the location of the upper-left puzzle piece as a landmark for the location of the other pieces.

The fourth property is one that will become quite common throughout the rest of this book. We name it "pMode" because it determines what mode the game is in. In this case, we will have two modes. One mode will be #normal for when the game is waiting for user input. The other will be #animate for when the puzzle pieces are moving. During the #animate mode, we will not allow the user to click on a puzzle piece.

```
-- properties
property pPieceWidth, pPieceHeight
property pUpperLeftLoc, pMode
```

The *on getPropertyDescriptionList* handler has its defaults set for a 5×5, or 24-piece, puzzle. The 25th slot is the open one. Figure 6.3 shows the Parameters dialog box for this behavior.

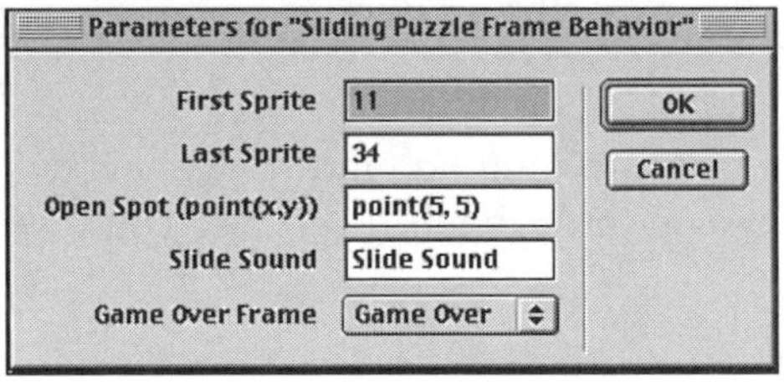

Figure 6.3

The Parameters dialog box for the "Sliding Puzzle Frame Behavior."

Parameters for "Sliding Puzzle Frame Behavior"		
First Sprite	11	OK
Last Sprite	34	Cancel
Open Spot (point(x,y))	point(5, 5)	
Slide Sound	Slide Sound	
Game Over Frame	Game Over	

```
on getPropertyDescriptionList me
  list = [:]

  -- the first puzzle piece channel
  addProp list, #pFirstSprite,¬
    [#comment: "First Sprite",¬
     #format: #integer,¬
     #default: 11]

  -- the last puzzle piece channel
  addProp list, #pLastSprite,¬
    [#comment: "Last Sprite",¬
     #format: #integer,¬
     #default: 34]

  -- the open spot, usually the bottom right corner
  addProp list, #pOpenSpot,¬
    [#comment: "Open Spot (point(x,y))",¬
     #format: #point,¬
     #default: point(5,5)]

  -- the sound to be played during a slide
  addProp list, #pSlideSound,¬
    [#comment: "Slide Sound",¬
     #format: #string,¬
     #default: ""]

  -- frame to jump to when the puzzle is solved
  addProp list, #pGameOverFrame,¬
    [#comment: "Game Over Frame",¬
     #format: #marker,¬
     #default: #next]

  return list
end
```

When the frame is entered, the *on beginSprite* handler calculates the values of "pPieceWidth" and "pPieceHeight" based on the first puzzle piece sprite. All pieces should be the same dimensions. The "pUpperLeftLoc" is also set this way. The "pMode" is set to #normal, and then the "on randomizePieces" handler is called.

```
-- set properties and randomize puzzle
on beginSprite me
  -- get the piece width and height from the first piece
  pPieceWidth = sprite(pFirstSprite).width
  pPieceHeight = sprite(pFirstSprite).height
```

continues

continued

```
-- get the location of the upper left piece to use as a landmark
pUpperLeftLoc = sprite(pFirstSprite).loc
-- start in normal mode, which allows clicks
pMode = #normal
-- mix it up
randomizePieces(me)
end
```

To randomize the pieces on the Stage, we shuffle their positions. First, a "posList" variable is created. Then, it is filled with the positions of all the sprites. Next, all the sprites are assigned one position from the list.

```
-- this handler shuffles the piece positions
on randomizePieces me
  -- create a list with all positions
  posList = []
  repeat with s = pFirstSprite to pLastSprite
    add posList, sprite(s).loc
  end repeat
  -- randomly assign positions to sprites
  repeat with s = pFirstSprite to pLastSprite
    r = random(posList.count)
    sprite(s).loc = posList[r]
    deleteAt posList, r
  end repeat
end
```

When a puzzle piece is clicked, the sprite behavior sends a #clickPuzzle message to the frame behavior. This message includes the sprite's number as a second parameter.

The first thing that the "on clickPuzzle" handler does is ensure that the "pMode" is #normal. Otherwise, it will ignore the click. This happens when there is animation in progress. You'll see where we set the "pMode" to #animate later in this behavior.

The handler then determines the location of the sprite in the puzzle by using its location, the location of the upper-left corner of the puzzle, and the width and height of each piece ① . This position is stored in the two variables: "x" and "y."

Then, the empty space in the puzzle, represented by the "pOpenSpot" property, is compared to the position of the piece to see whether the two are next to each other. If so, then the "on move" handler is called with the horizontal and vertical difference between the two positions ② . This "on move" handler takes care of swapping the piece for the empty slot.

```
-- the sprite behaviors call this handler with their sprite number
-- it determines if the piece is next to the empty space
-- and moves it there if it is
on clickPuzzle me, spriteNumber
  -- make sure we are in normal mode
  if pMode <> #normal then exit
  -- determine the x and y position of the piece
① x = (sprite(spriteNumber).locH-pUpperLeftLoc.locH)/pPieceWidth+1
  y = (sprite(spriteNumber).locV-pUpperLeftLoc.locV)/pPieceHeight+1
  -- see if the open spot is to the left, right, above or below
  if pOpenSpot.locV = y then -- move horizontally
    if pOpenSpot.locH = x-1 then -- move left
      move(me,spriteNumber,-1,0)
    else if pOpenSpot.locH = x+1 then -- move right
      move(me,spriteNumber,1,0)
    end if
  else  if pOpenSpot.locH = x then -- move vertically
    if pOpenSpot.locV = y-1 then -- move pup
②    move(me,spriteNumber,0,-1)
    else if pOpenSpot.locV = y+1 then -- move down
②    move(me,spriteNumber,0,1)
    end if
  end if
end
```

The "on move" handler takes the difference between the puzzle piece position and the empty slot as two variables: "dx" and "dy." Variables with these names are often used to indicate the "difference" between two locations.

The new location of the piece is calculated. Then, the new "pOpenSpot" property is calculated. Finally, the sprite is sent the #changeLoc message, which kicks off the animation to slide the piece into the empty slot. The "pMode" for the frame behavior is also changed, so clicks are ignored until the animation is done.

```
-- move a sprite into the empty spot
on move me, spriteNumber, dx, dy
  -- determine new location from dx, dy
  newloc = sprite(spriteNumber).loc + point(dx*pPieceWidth,dy*pPieceHeight)
  -- change the open spot to be where the piece was
  pOpenSpot = pOpenSpot - point(dx,dy)
  -- tell the sprite to animate to the new location
  sendSprite(spriteNumber,#changeLoc,newloc)
  -- set the mode, so that no clicks are allowed until animation is done
  -- play the sound
  if pSlideSound <> "" then puppetSound pSlideSound
  -- change the mode to no allow clicks until slide is complete
  pMode = #animate
end
```

When the sprite is done animating, it sends a #resetMode message back to the frame behavior. This does two things. First, it resets the "pMode" to #normal, thus allowing clicks to be recognized again. Second, it calls the "on checkForGameOver" handler to see whether the puzzle is complete.

```
-- when animation is done, sprite will call this to allow more clicks
on resetMode me
  pMode = #normal
  -- also see if all pieces are now in the correct spots
  if checkForGameOver(me) then
    go to frame pGameOverFrame
  end if
end
```

To determine whether the game is over, the "on checkForGameOver" handler loops through all the sprites. The sprites are arranged in the order of the solved puzzle, with the upper-left corner piece first, the one to the right of it second, and so on. First, it checks to see whether the sprite is just to the right of the sprite before it ③ . If this is so, then these two sprites are in order. Otherwise, it checks to see whether the next sprite is the start of a new row ④ . If so, then the sprites are still in order. However, if there is any deviation from this, then it means that the sprites are out of order on the screen, and a *FALSE* is returned.

```
-- loop through all pieces starting with the second one
-- if each piece come either to the right, or starts a new row,
-- then the puzzle is done
on checkForGameOver me
   -- get loc of first sprite
  prevLoc = sprite(pFirstSprite).loc
  repeat with i = pFirstSprite+1 to pLastSprite
    -- get loc of this sprite
    nextLoc = sprite(i).loc
    -- see if they are next to each other
③► if nextLoc.locH <> prevLoc.locH + pPieceWidth then
      -- or, see if it is the first of the next row
      if (nextLoc.LocV <> prevLoc.locV + pPieceHeight) or¬
      ④►  (nextLoc.locH <> pUpperleftLoc.locH) then
        -- neither, so must be out of order
        return FALSE
      end if
    end if
    -- ready to look at next piece
    prevLoc = nextLoc
  end repeat
  -- made it here, so all pieces must be in order
  return TRUE
end
```

The last function of the frame behavior is the standard looping frame code.

```
-- loop on the frame
on exitFrame
  go to the frame
end
```

The Sprite Behavior

The sprite behavior starts off by simply setting the *cursor* property of the sprite to 280, which is the finger cursor. This is a good way to indicate, without instructions, that the player is to click on the puzzle pieces.

In addition, the sprite behavior also has a "pMode" property. We use the same two values for this "pMode" property as we did in the frame behavior: #normal and #animate.

```
property pNewLoc, pMode

on beginSprite me
  -- use the finger cursor for this sprite
  sprite(me.spriteNum).cursor = 280
  -- normal mode (do nothing)
  pMode = #normal
end
```

When the sprite is clicked, the #clickPuzzle message is sent along to the frame behavior to be dealt with.

```
-- pass mouse clicks along to the frame behavior
on mouseUp me
  sendSprite(0,#clickPuzzle,me.spriteNum)
end
```

When the frame behavior determines that the sprite needs to change location, it calls the "on changeLoc" handler shown here. A parameter tells the sprite where the destination is. The "pMode" of the sprite behavior is changed to #animate.

```
-- frame behavior calls this to initiate an animation
on changeLoc me, newloc
  -- record the destination location
  pNewloc = newloc
  -- allow the animation
  pMode = #animate
end
```

The "on exitFrame" behavior uses the "pMode" property to determine whether it's supposed to be doing anything. If it is, the "on exitFrame" behavior then examines its current position with the "pNewLoc" position, and brings it one pixel closer to the destination. ⑤

If the destination is reached ⑥ , a message, #resetMode, is sent back to the frame behavior, and the "pMode" of the sprite behavior changes back to #normal.

```
on exitFrame me
  -- if the destination does not equal the current position
  if pMode = #animate then
    -- move the location by one pixel in the right direction
    curloc = sprite(me.spriteNum).loc
    if curloc.locH < pNewLoc.locH then
⑤➤   curloc = curloc + point(1,0)
    else if curloc.locH > pNewLoc.locH then
⑤➤   curloc = curloc - point(1,0)
    else if curloc.locV < pNewLoc.locV then
⑤➤curloc = curloc + point(0,1)
    else if curloc.locV > pNewLoc.locV then
⑤➤   curloc = curloc - point(0,1)
    end if
    sprite(me.spriteNum).loc = curloc
    -- if this ends the animation, tell the frame script
    -- so its pMode can be changed to #normal
    -- and set the sprite's pMode to #normal too
⑥➤   if curloc = pNewLoc then
       sendSprite(0,#resetMode)
       pMode = #normal
    end if
  end if
end
```

Note that the position of the sprite is changed by one pixel at a time. The sample movie on the CD-ROM is set to 120 frames per second. So, a 40×40 piece should slide into a new position in one-third of a second. However, if you feel that you need to make the game work smoothly for slower computers—ones that cannot do 120 frames per second—you might want to move the pieces more than one pixel at a time. You can change to four *point* values in the previous handler to use any number of pixels you want. However, be sure that it uses a number divisible by the dimensions of the pieces.

For instance, if the pieces are 40 pixels wide and 40 pixels high, then 1, 2, 4, and 8 work well. However, if the pieces move 3 pixels at a time instead, they will overshoot the destination location because 40 is not divisible by 3.

Putting It All Together

To make the game work, first you need to drop all the pieces on the Stage. Then, arrange them so that the pieces appear as they should at the end of the game. This means that the pieces should line up perfectly and the bottom-right slot should be empty. This is harder to do than in the jigsaw puzzle game, because the pieces do not all share a common registration point.

Drop the sprite behavior on the sprites, and the frame behavior on the frame. The frame behavior will ask for some parameters. Provide it with the first and last sprite used by the puzzle pieces, the empty slot as a *point*, the sound name, and the end game frame.

Finally, just create the end game frame and the slide sound.

Game Variations

As with the jigsaw puzzle, the easiest variation you can do is to use different images. You can make the puzzle represent any topic you want that way. The following sections present some other ideas.

Rectangular Pieces

Computer screens are not square. Browser windows even less so. So, why make a square puzzle? You can make a rectangular puzzle using square pieces, or even a rectangular puzzle using rectangular pieces.

This variation requires only that you cut the pieces differently. The game itself doesn't care whether the piece width and height differ, just as long as all the pieces are the same dimensions.

You could even use round pieces if you want. The pieces still act as if they are square or rectangular, but you can just make them look round, like circles that the user can slide around. This works well with the next variation.

Sliding Number Puzzles

Another common type of puzzle is a sliding number puzzle. This is where each of the squares is simply a number, rather than a piece of an image. The object is to arrange the numbers in order. So, the 24-piece puzzle discussed previously would just be the numbers 1 through 24.

The sliding number puzzle is really exactly the same game. Only the puzzle piece bitmaps are different.

Falling Blocks Puzzle

7

CD-ROM File: 07fallingpuzzle.dir

Useful Lingo in This Chapter

♠ Behaviors: Calling handlers in other behaviors

♠ Graphics: Making sprites disappear

♠ Graphics: Moving sprites

♠ Graphics: Using a grid of bitmaps

♠ Input: Accepting arrow keys

♠ Lists: Using linear lists

♠ Lists: Using property lists

♠ Lists: Lists that contain lists

♠ Math: Using random numbers

♠ Programming: Collision detection

Up until this chapter, all the games have been turn-based. That means the player takes a turn and then has as long as he or she wants to make the next turn.

Puzzle games are often done this way, but they don't have to be. You can have action-based puzzles as well.

In this chapter, we will build a game called the "Falling Blocks Puzzle." This is probably the most popular form of computer action puzzle game. You might recognize it.

Game Overview

The way this game works is a little more complex than most puzzle games. Groups of blocks fall from the top of the screen. The player can move them left and right as they fall, as well as rotate them. When they land on the bottom of the screen, or on top of another piece, they stop. The screen quickly fills up with blocks. However, if any complete, solid row of blocks is completed by the user, that row disappears, making room for more.

The game ends when the user places a piece too high up on the screen. This usually happens when the screen is just about full.

Figure 7.1 shows a game in progress. The set of three blocks in the middle of the screen is a falling piece. The rest of the blocks in the middle are pieces that have previously fallen.

Figure 7.1
This Falling Blocks puzzle is shown in progress.

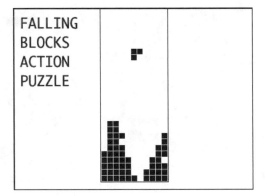

Blocks and Pieces

For the purposes of this chapter, a "block" is defined as a single square element on the screen. A "piece" is a collection of blocks that fall together from the top of the screen. Blocks never fall by themselves. They are always a part of a piece.

To make these pieces, we will use a list that contains the positions of each block in a piece. Here is an example:

```
[[0,0],[0,-1],[1,0]]
```

Each small list contains the position of a block. The position [0,0] means that the block will be located at exactly the center of the piece. The [0,-1] means that the block will be one space up from the center. The [1,0] means that the block will be one space to the right of the center.

In addition to this description, we also have to provide descriptions for each of the orientations of the piece. The user will be able to turn the pieces in 90-degree increments, which creates a potential of four descriptions that we need per piece. Some shapes will need only two positions, if their third and fourth orientation is the same as the first and second. Some pieces look the same no matter what the rotation, so we will need only one description.

Timing the Fall

Each piece should fall at a certain rate. We could have the piece drop one space every frame, which would enable us to set the drop rate by simply setting the movie's tempo.

However, if we lock the drop rate to the tempo, we are also restricting the number of moves that the user can make over time. They will be able to move the piece only one space to the left or right for every space it drops.

A better way to do this is to use a timer to determine the frequency of drops. Then, you can have the tempo set very high, and allow the user to move left and right as much as he or she wants in any given period of time.

The way a timer works is that every time a drop occurs, a property variable is set to the time when the next drop should occur. Then, once per frame, the timer is checked to see whether it's time for the next fall. On fast machines, hundreds of frame loops could go by before the timer triggers a drop. On slow machines, only a few frame loops might occur. No matter how fast the machine is, the drops should happen at a constant rate.

Keyboard Input

Instead of using the mouse for user interaction with this game, we will use the keyboard. There are several ways to take keyboard input in Director.

One is to use the *on keyDown* and *on keyUp* handlers. They work like *on mouseDown* and *on mouseUp*. The only difference is that the key's value is present in these handlers as both *the key* and *the keyCode*. The first is the actual character of the key pressed, and the second is a special set of values for things such as arrow keys.

At least four keys are needed for this game. The first two are the left- and right-arrow keys, which will be used to move the pieces left and right. Keys are also needed to enable the user to rotate the pieces left and right.

Special Effects

Because this game is more complex than most in this book, and because there is a lot of code, I've left out sounds. However, a Lingo programmer should have no problem finding the right spots to add the *puppetSound* command. Examples of using sound in games can be found in most other chapters.

Making the Game

The script for this game is long and complicated. It uses everything from property lists to multiline comparison statements. You will definitely want to check out the file on the CD-ROM before reading the rest of the chapter.

Even though there is a lot of code, it all still fits in just one frame behavior. This behavior controls everything in the game.

Instead of using an *on getPropertyDescriptionList* handler, we will do something different here. Because it's unlikely that a multimedia author will want to drag, drop, and customize this game, we are putting all the game constants in the *on beginSprite* handler. It's still easy to find one of these properties and change it if necessary.

The behavior starts by declaring these properties, as well as a bunch of others. These other properties will be used to keep track of the game state throughout play. Descriptions for each can be read in the following comments.

```
--properties set in on beginSprite
property pSpeed
property pEntryLocation
property pLeftWall
property pRightWall
property pFloor
property pRowMax
property pBlockSize
property pFirstSprite

property pPieceList -- list of piece types
property pPieceType -- current piece type
property pPieceOrientation -- current piece orientation
property pPieceSprites -- sprites used by the piece
property pPieceLoc -- location of the piece
property pNextMoveTime -- when next drop will happen
```

As promised, the *on beginSprite* handler starts by setting all the game constants. These constants determine the game speed, playing area, block size, and the sprites used in the Score.

```
on beginSprite me
  pSpeed = 20 -- 20 ticks need to pass before a drop
  pEntryLocation = point(200,0) -- starting spot of the drop
  pLeftWall = 150 -- leftmost block position
  pRightWall = 250 -- rightmost block position
  pFloor = 280 -- bottommost block position
```

```
   pRowMax = 11 -- how many rows there are
   pBlockSize = 10 -- space separating the blocks
   pFirstSprite = 11 -- first sprite that can be used by a block

   getPieceList(me) -- initialize piece list
   pNextMoveTime = the ticks -- set next move for now
   dropNewPiece(me) -- create a new piece
end
```

The *on beginSprite* handler ends by calling "on getPieceList", setting the "pNextMoveTime" property, and dropping the first piece. The "on getPieceList" handler creates the game constant "pPieceList". This is a list of all the pieces and their configurations for different orientations.

For instance, take the first piece type. It shows a [[-1,0],[0,0],[1,0]] as the first orientation. This means there is one block one space to the left of center, one block at the center, and one block one space to the right of center. Figure 7.2 shows this piece if we were using hollow squares for each block. When it is rotated to the right, the next orientation, [[0,-1],[0,0],[0,1]], is used. This has one block above the center, one block at the center, and one block to the right of the center. Figure 7.3 shows the piece with the rotation. Because another rotation to the right returns the piece to the same shape as the first orientation, no more is needed. For other shape types, up to four orientations are needed.

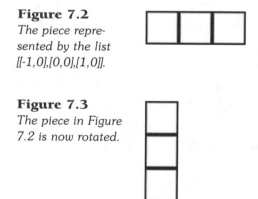

Figure 7.2
The piece represented by the list [[-1,0],[0,0],[1,0]].

Figure 7.3
The piece in Figure 7.2 is now rotated.

```
-- Initializes pPieceList with a list of all the pieces
-- Each piece includes all the different rotations
on getPieceList me
  pPieceList = []
```

continues

continued

```
          -- three blocks, straight
          list = []
          add list, [[-1,0],[0,0],[1,0]]
          add list, [[0,-1],[0,0],[0,1]]
          add pPieceList, list

          -- three blocks, bent
          list = []
          add list, [[0,0],[0,-1],[1,0]]
          add list, [[0,0],[1,0],[0,1]]
          add list, [[0,0],[0,1],[-1,0]]
          add list, [[0,0],[-1,0],[0,-1]]
          add pPieceList, list

          -- two blocks, straight
          list = []
          add list, [[0,0],[1,0]]
          add list, [[0,0],[0,1]]
          add list, [[0,0],[-1,0]]
          add list, [[0,0],[0,-1]]
          add pPieceList, list

          -- four blocks, square
          list = []
          add list, [[0,0],[1,0],[0,-1],[1,-1]]
          add pPieceList, list
        end
```

The "on dropNewPiece" handler starts a piece dropping at the beginning of the game. It is also used just after a piece lands to drop the next piece.

This handler is responsible for picking a random piece and a random orientation. It also looks through the sprites in the Score to find sprites not in use. It uses these sprites to display the blocks of the piece.

The property "pFirstSprite" is used to tell the code where a large span of sprites begins. These sprites are available to be used as blocks on the game. In this example, "pFirstSprite" is set to 11. The sprite channels from 11 to 318 contain block bitmap members. Because the game screen is a grid that is 11 blocks wide and 28 blocks high, we know that we will never need more than 308 sprites (11 times 28) no matter how well the player packs in the blocks. If you change the dimensions of the board, you might want to change the number or sprites as well.

These sprites are then taken by the "on dropNewPiece" handler and put into the "pPieceSprites" list ①. The "on drawPiece" handler uses these sprites to draw the current piece as it falls. When the piece lands, the sprites are still used by the same blocks as they lie at the bottom of the screen.

If a sprite is in use, it will have a positive locV value. If it is not in use, it will have a negative locV value and thus be out of sight above the top of the Stage. So, we start all 308 sprites above the top of the screen. They will all have negative *locV* values. As we use sprites, they are drawn on the screen and are given positive *locV* values. If a sprite is removed from the screen, which happens when a row clears, then the sprite is placed at a negative *locV*. This not only takes the sprite off the Stage visually, but also lets the "on dropNewPiece" handler find it when it's time to drop the next piece.

```
-- create a new piece and drop from the top
on dropNewPiece me
  -- choose a random piece
  pPieceType = random(pPieceList.count)
  -- find some empty sprites
  pPieceSprites = []
  numSpritesNeeded = pPieceList[pPieceType][1].count
  repeat with i = pFirstSprite to the lastChannel
    if sprite(i).locV < 0 then -- sprite not in use
      add pPieceSprites, i
      if pPieceSprites.count = numSpritesNeeded then exit repeat
    end if
  end repeat
  -- pick a random orientation
  pPieceOrientation = random(pPieceList[pPieceType].count)
  -- starting location
  pPieceLoc = duplicate(pEntryLocation)
  drawPiece(me)
end
```

The "on drawPiece" handler takes the sprites in "pPieceSprites" and uses them to display the blocks in the piece. It uses the "pPieceLoc" as well as the data from the "pPieceList" to draw each block.

```
-- display a piece in the proper orientation
on drawPiece me
  -- loop through all sprites
  repeat with i = 1 to pPieceSprites.count
    -- set the location of the sprite
    sprite(pPieceSprites[i]).loc = pPieceLoc +¬
      point(pPieceList[pPieceType][pPieceOrientation][i][1]*pBlockSize,¬
      pPieceList[pPieceType][pPieceOrientation][i][2]*pBlockSize)
  end repeat
end
```

When the time comes, each piece must drop one space down. This is simply done by changing the "pPieceLoc". However, two events must be looked for first. Both of these events result in the piece stopping, and a new piece being dropped from the top.

The first event is when the piece lands on top of another piece. The second event is when the piece hits the bottom. Both of these are handled by their own handler functions.

In addition, if one of these two conditions is met, then some other checks must be conducted. The rows of blocks in the game need to be examined to see whether any rows are complete. All the blocks need to be checked to see whether one has landed at the top of the screen, in which case the game is over.

```
-- move the piece down
on movePiece me
  -- see if it should stop
  if fallOnPiece(me) or hitBottom(me) then
    -- see if any rows are now complete
    checkRowsCompleted(me)
    -- see if the piece is stuck at the top
    checkGameEnd(me)
    -- get the next piece set
    dropNewPiece(me)
    -- return FALSE since no move was made
    return FALSE
  end if
  -- move down
  pPieceLoc.locV = pPieceLoc.locV + pBlockSize
  -- redraw sprites
  drawPiece(me)
  -- return TRUE since a move was made
  return TRUE
end
```

The "on hitBottom" handler checks all the sprites in the piece to see whether any are in the space just above the floor. If so, then the piece has hit the bottom and must stop.

```
-- check to see if the piece hit the floor
on hitBottom me
  -- loop through sprites
  repeat with s in pPieceSprites
    -- if a sprite touches the floor
    if (sprite(s).locV >= pFloor) then
      return TRUE
    end if
  end repeat
  return FALSE
end
```

The "on fallOnPiece" handler checks all the piece's sprites against all the other block sprites. If the piece appears to be just above another block, then it has landed on it and the block must stop.

```
-- check to see if the piece hit another piece
on fallOnPiece me
  -- loop through sprites
  repeat with i = pFirstSprite to the lastChannel
    -- see if the sprite is being used
    if sprite(i).locV < 0 then next repeat
    -- make sure it is not one of the sprites from the current piece
    if getOne(pPieceSprites,i) then next repeat
    -- loop through the piece's sprites
    repeat with s in pPieceSprites
      -- see if the sprite is run on top of another
      if (sprite(i).locH = sprite(s).locH) and¬
         (sprite(i).locV = sprite(s).locV+pBlockSize) then
        return TRUE
      end if
    end repeat
  end repeat
  return FALSE
end
```

The "on checkRows" handler looks at all the sprites and compiles a list of which sprites are in which row. If any row contains the maximum number of sprites, then that row must be removed ②.

```
-- check all sprites to see if any complete rows are formed
on checkRowsCompleted me
  -- start an empty property list
  list = [:]
  -- loop through all sprites
  repeat with i = pFirstSprite to the lastChannel
    -- if the sprite is in use
    if sprite(i).locV > 0 then
      -- if this row is not yet in the list
      if voidP(getAProp(list,sprite(i).locV)) then
        addProp list, sprite(i).locV, 1
      else -- add one to the number of sprites in the row
        setProp list, sprite(i).locV, getProp(list,sprite(i).locV)+1
      end if
    end if
  end repeat
  -- loop through all the rows
  repeat with i = 1 to list.count
```

continues

continued

```
        -- if the row has the maximum number of sprite
②→  if list[i] = pRowMax then
        -- clear the row
        removeRow(me,getPropAt(list,i))
      end if
    end repeat
  end
```

To remove a row, the code simply looks at *every* sprite in use. It takes away and recycles any sprites in the row to be removed. It also moves any sprite in rows above it down by one ③ .

```
  -- clear a row and move everything above it down
  on removeRow me, v
    -- loop through sprites
    repeat with i = pFirstSprite to the lastChannel
      if sprite(i).locV < 0 then -- sprite not used
        next repeat -- do nothing
      else if sprite(i).locV < v then -- sprite above row
③→  sprite(i).locV = sprite(i).locV + pBlockSize -- move down
      else if sprite(i).locV = v then -- sprite in row
        sprite(i).locV = -100 -- remove
      end if
    end repeat
  end
```

Checking for the end game is simple. Each sprite is checked to see whether it's at the top. If just one block is stopped at the top, the game is over.

```
  -- see if the current piece is stuck near the top
  -- and end the game if so
  on checkGameEnd me
    if pPieceLoc.locV <= 10 then
      go to frame "End"
      abort -- don't continue
    end if
  end
```

The *on exitFrame* handler calls the "on movePiece" handler to keep the piece dropping. It does this only when the value of *the ticks* reaches the value in "pNextMoveTime". It also resets "pNextMoveTime" to 20 ticks in the future.

```
  -- every frame, check to see if it is time for next drop
  on exitFrame me
    if the ticks > pNextMoveTime then
      movePiece(me)
```

```
            pNextMoveTime = the ticks + pSpeed
        end if
        go to the frame
    end
```

The user interacts with the game through five keys. The left- and right-arrow key move the piece left and right. The "." and "," keys, which also have the symbols ">" and "<" on them, are used to rotate the piece left and right. In addition, the spacebar is used for a special function. It tells the game to drop the current piece as fast as possible, so that the player does not have to wait for it to get to the bottom.

```
-- takes keyboard input
on keyUp me
    case the keyCode of
        124: -- right arrow
            if not hitOtherPiece(me,pBlockSize) then
                pPieceLoc.locH = pPieceLoc.locH + pBlockSize
            end if
        123: -- left arrow
            if not hitOtherPiece(me,-pBlockSize) then
                pPieceLoc.locH = pPieceLoc.locH - pBlockSize
            end if
    end case
    case the key of
        ".": -- rotate right
            pPieceOrientation = pPieceOrientation + 1
            if pPieceOrientation > pPieceList[pPieceType].count then pPieceOrientation = 1
        ",": -- rotate left
            pPieceOrientation = pPieceOrientation - 1
            if pPieceOrientation < 1 then pPieceOrientation = pPieceList[pPieceType].count
        SPACE: -- quickly drop
            drop(me)
    end case
    pushAwayFromEdges(me) -- make sure the piece doesn't go past edge
    drawPiece(me)
end
```

The *on keyUp* handler ends with a call to "on pushAwayFromEdges". This handler takes care of an odd situation in the game in which the user tries to move the piece past the left or right side of the playing area. However, it isn't as simple as just stopping the user from pushing past a limit. When pieces are rotated, they can also go past the limit. A piece that occupies column 1 and 2 in the playing area can attempt to rotate into column 0, for instance.

This handler takes care of any situation in which the piece is over the edge. It simply recognizes that this is happening ④ , and nudges the piece back toward the center by one column ⑤ .

```
-- special handler that looks to make sure the
-- piece is not past the edges, and moves it in
-- if it is
-- needs to be called when the user moves the piece
-- or rotates it
on pushAwayFromEdges me
  -- assume no problem
  pastLeftEdge = FALSE
  pastRightEdge = FALSE
  -- loop through piece's sprites
  repeat with i = 1 to pPieceSprites.count
    -- get sprite location
    x = pPieceLoc.locH + pPieceList[pPieceType][pPieceOrientation][i][1]*10
    -- see if it is too far right
    if x > pRightWall then pastRightEdge = TRUE
    -- see if it is too far left
    if x < pLeftWall then pastLeftEdge = TRUE
  end repeat
  -- move piece in if necessary
  if pastRightEdge then adjustment = -pBlockSize
  else if pastLeftEdge then adjustment = pBlockSize
  else exit
  pPieceLoc.locH = pPieceLoc.locH + adjustment
end
```

The "on hitOtherPiece" handler checks for a very unusual occurrence. If the user is moving the piece across the screen, and there are other blocks in the way, the game needs to prevent the user from moving the piece through the existing blocks. To do this, the handler checks the proposed new position of the piece ⑥ , and looks to see whether any blocks are in the way ⑦ . If so, a *FALSE* is returned. This tells the handler calling it—in this case, the *on keyUp* handler—not to allow the move.

```
-- check to see if the user tried to move the piece
-- into another piece
on hitOtherPiece me, changeLoc
  -- loop through the piece's sprites
  repeat with i = 1 to pPieceSprites.count
    -- determine the sprite's location
    thisloc = point(changeLoc,0) + pPieceLoc +¬
      point(pPieceList[pPieceType][pPieceOrientation][i][1]*pBlockSize,¬
      pPieceList[pPieceType][pPieceOrientation][i][2]*pBlockSize)
    -- loop through all the sprites
    repeat with j = pFirstSprite to the lastChannel
      -- make sure sprite is in use
      if sprite(j).locV < 0 then next repeat
      -- make sure sprite is not part of piece
      if getOne(pPieceSprites,j) then next repeat
```

```
               -- see if the locations are the same
  (7)-→ if sprite(j).loc = thisloc then return TRUE
       end repeat
    end repeat
    return FALSE
end
```

Finally, end with the simple "on drop" handler. This loops quickly with a *repeat* loop while calling "on movePiece". When "on movePiece" returns a *FALSE*, it means that the piece has reached a stopping point and the game continues as normal. The *updateStage* command is used here to force a screen redraw.

```
-- when user hits space, quickly drop the piece
on drop me
  repeat while TRUE
    -- move down until hits something
    if not movePiece(me) then exit
    -- force stage update
    updateStage
  end repeat
end
```

Putting It All Together

Creating the game from this script is the easiest part of this chapter. First, just create a little box bitmap. I made mine in the CD-ROM example movie 9 pixels square, which leaves a white line between boxes because they are spaced 10 pixels apart.

Then, drop this sprite in the Score in sprite channel 11. Use the arrow keys to move it up off the Stage. Then, copy and paste the sprite into channels 12 through 318.

Now, drop the behavior script onto the frame script channel. One additional touch would be to draw a rectangle shape around the playing area. You might have to run the game a few times and adjust this rectangle to get it to fit just right. Again, see the example movie if this is not clear.

Game Variations

There are many aspects of this game that can be varied. The whole metaphor for the game can be adjusted to suit a specific need. For instance, this game on my site is called "Meltdown" and is supposed to represent filling a nuclear reactor with fuel.

Changing the Shapes

The four shapes in the example movie are only suggestions. You could use the lists in the "on getPieceList" handler to make the shapes anything you want. Just remember to include all the rotation orientations.

Adding Color

You could make the blocks something a little different, such as stars or circles. Or, you could keep them as blocks and just change their color. You could assign a random color to each sprite as it is assigned in the "on dropNewPiece" handler. The code could look something like this:

```
sprite(i).color = getAt([rgb("FF0000"), rgb("00FF00"), rgb("0000FF")],random(3))
```

Keeping Score

The only event in the game worthy of earning points is when a row is cleared. But, you could also award points for *every* block that lands somewhere. You could keep track of this in a "pScore" property, and display it in a text member as shown in earlier chapters, as in the "Game Variations" section of Chapter 3, "Matching Game."

Speeding It Up

The "pSpeed" property is set to 20 in the *on beginSprite* handler. You could easily change this value as the score increases. So, after a certain number of points, it goes to 19, which is a little faster. Then, it could go to 18, and so on.

Adding a Background

This game requires a vertical playing field. Because computer screens are wider than they are tall, and browser windows even more so, there is usually a lot of space to the left and right of the playing area. You can color this up with images, and even photographs. You could have the image change at different score milestones.

Part III:
Arcade Games

8   Falling Objects   **115**

9   Shooting Gallery   **131**

10   Sprite Invaders   **149**

11   Space Rocks   **167**

12   Paddle Bricks   **185**

Falling Objects

8

CD-ROM File: 08fallingobjects.dir

Useful Lingo in This Chapter

- ♠ Behaviors: Using parameters
- ♠ Behaviors: Using a ranged parameter
- ♠ Graphics: Changing sprite members with Lingo
- ♠ Graphics: Moving sprites
- ♠ Graphics: Using a set of bitmaps
- ♠ Graphics: Using registration points
- ♠ Graphics: Using points
- ♠ Input: Dragging with the mouse
- ♠ Lists: Using linear lists
- ♠ Math: Using random numbers
- ♠ Members: Using Cast libraries
- ♠ Programming: Collision detection
- ♠ Variables: Keeping score

For our first arcade-style game, we'll look at a common Director game. The Falling Objects game has a simple premise: Objects fall from the sky and you have to catch them.

This game idea is probably used so much because the game can be adapted for so many different purposes. The objects can be promotional items that reflect the products a company sells, they can form an educational quiz, or they can simply be entertaining.

First, we'll look at the basics of the game, then we'll build it, and finally we'll discuss the ways in which the game can be used.

Game Overview

In this game, there are two different types of objects. The first is the one under the player's control. This object, which is represented as a baseball glove in the example movie, is used to catch the falling objects. The player can move this object from left to right across the bottom of the screen.

The other type of object is one that falls from the top of the screen. We must allow for one or more of these to be falling at one time. We also have to take into account the fact that some objects are desirable, whereas others are not.

For instance, in our sample game, the objects falling are going to be objects from the world of sports: baseballs, footballs, basketballs, and so on. The object of this particular version of the game is to catch the baseballs, but to avoid the other objects. Figure 8.1 shows this game in action.

Figure 8.1
The falling objects game uses objects from different sports.

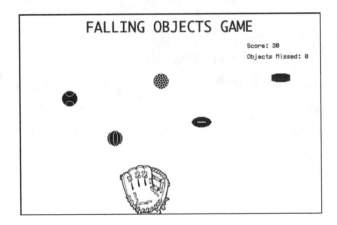

As always, there are a lot of different techniques that need to be considered before the programming begins, the most important of which is to determine what code is needed.

Many Behaviors or One?

When designing the code for this game, it is tempting to write a behavior for the glove and a behavior to be used for the falling objects. This makes sense at first, until you think about the fact that all items are closely related to one another and need to be in constant communication.

For instance, the game needs to know when to drop new objects. At the start of the game, approximately one object at a time should drop, but then the frequency should increase as the player scores more points. In addition, as each item is dropped, it needs to be assigned a sprite, and that sprite needs to use a member. This needs to be a sprite that is not already in use. The messaging between sprites gets to be increasingly complex with the addition of other features as well. The result is that it is actually better to create one game behavior that gets assigned to the frame, rather than a behavior that gets assigned to each and every sprite.

This frame behavior keeps track of all sprites and the general game properties. This also makes the game easy to set up after the behavior is complete.

Timing Drops

A game like this definitely needs to get harder as the player does better. We can do this one of two ways, or both. First, we can increase the speed at which items drop. Second, we can increase the frequency of drops.

At the start of the game, the frequency of drops should be at about the right speed so that there is one item falling at any given time. Then, as the user racks up points, the frequency increases. Soon, the screen is filled with many items at once.

Defining a Catch

In this game, it's important to define when a catch occurs. Is it when the rectangles of the object and the glove intersect? Is it when the location of the object enters the rectangle of the glove? We will offer both these options.

In addition, we will offer the option of defining a catch as when the rectangle of the object contains the registration point of the glove. This is useful if the objects are going to be much bigger than the glove. This option will be a parameter that you will set when you drop the behavior onto the Score.

We will also have two purely mathematical ways of determining whether there is a catch. The first uses the horizontal and vertical location of the object and the glove. If both these measurements are within a certain amount, a catch is made. The other method uses the distance calculated with the standard mathematical equation.

These last two distance methods enable us to determine that a catch has been made irrelevant to the size of the two sprites involved.

Game Over Options

There are three ways in which our example game can end. The first happens when the player misses a certain number of items that he or she is supposed to catch.

The second option is to count the number of times the player catches an item that he or she is not supposed to. When this count gets too high, the game is over.

A third option is not nearly as useful, but is still included. This game over option simply waits for the player to attain a certain score.

Although I have not added the capability to combine the options in the example game, the code can easily be adapted to that. In one scenario, you might want to have the game end and go to a "you lose" frame if the player misses a certain number of objects. The same game would go to a "you win" frame if the player attains a certain score.

Penalty for Bad Catches

If there are some objects that the player is supposed to catch, and others that the player is supposed to avoid, what happens in the latter case? If a player catches a bad object, they should obviously not be awarded points. But, should they be penalized?

If you have the game set to end when the user catches a certain number of bad items, then they are already penalized for this. However, if the game ends because of another condition, you might want to also subtract points from the user's score when they catch a bad item.

Increasing Difficulty

A game like this should start off easy, and get more and more difficult as time goes on. We can do this simply by increasing the frequency of falling objects.

This can be done over time, or a little each time the player adds to the score. We'll use the latter in this example.

Distinguishing Good Objects from Bad

The member from each object is chosen at random each time. Sometimes, the falling object will be a good one, meaning that the player should catch it. Sometimes, the object will be a bad one, meaning that the player should avoid it.

A simple method of determining which items are good and which are bad is to use the member names. We'll just name the bitmaps that represent good objects "good" and the bad objects "bad." When a catch is made, the member name is examined to determine which one it is.

Special Effects

We're going to include more sounds than usual in this game. We want a sound when a play catches an object. There should be one for catching a good object, and one for catching a bad object. There should also be a sound for when the object first falls from the sky.

A fourth sound would be used to represent when a good object has fallen to the ground, thus being missed by the player.

All these sounds are optional, as in earlier chapters.

Making the Game

As mentioned before, all the game code is contained in one long frame behavior. This makes it very easy to implement this game with just the one behavior and a collection of bitmaps.

The property declarations have useful descriptions after them, with the exception of the parameters that are defined in the *on getPropertyDescriptionList* handler.

```
-- Parameters
property pFirstSprite, pLastSprite
property pGloveSprite
property pSpeed
property pDropFrequency
property pCatchRequirement, pCatchDistance
property pScoreIncrement
property pEndGameCondition, pEndGameNumber
property pCatchBadPenalty
property pDropSound, pCatchSound
property pMissSound, pBadCatchSound
property pEndGameFrame


-- Other Properties
property  pScore -- Player Score
property pUsingSprites -- Sprites currently in the action
property pNumberMissed -- Number of good objects missed
property pNumberBadCaught -- Number of bad objects caught
property pNextDropTime -- next time an object is scheduled to fall
```

This behavior contains the longest *on getPropertyDescriptionList* handler that we have seen so far in this book. Thus, this game is highly customizable. I've scattered some additional comments inside the handler text that follows. Figure 8.2 shows the resulting Parameters dialog box.

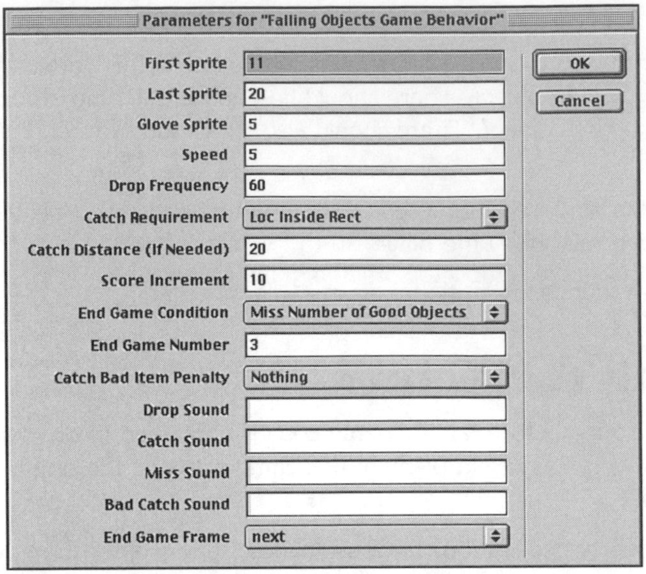

Figure 8.2

The Parameters dialog box for the falling objects game has quite a few customizable parameters.

Parameters for "Falling Objects Game Behavior"		
First Sprite	11	OK
Last Sprite	20	Cancel
Glove Sprite	5	
Speed	5	
Drop Frequency	60	
Catch Requirement	Loc Inside Rect	
Catch Distance (If Needed)	20	
Score Increment	10	
End Game Condition	Miss Number of Good Objects	
End Game Number	3	
Catch Bad Item Penalty	Nothing	
Drop Sound		
Catch Sound		
Miss Sound		
Bad Catch Sound		
End Game Frame	next	

```
on getPropertyDescriptionList me
  list = [:]

  -- First sprite with object
  addProp list, #pFirstSprite,¬
    [#comment: "First Sprite",¬
     #format: #integer,¬
     #default: 11]

  -- last sprite with object
  addProp list, #pLastSprite,¬
    [#comment: "Last Sprite",¬
     #format: #integer, #default: 20]
```

The last two parameters tell the behavior where the sprites in the score are located that will be used as the falling objects. You can put in as few or as many of these as you want. The game will not try to assign more falling objects at one time than there are sprites. So, if you want to limit the number of items that can be falling at once to eight, have only eight sprites available.

```
  -- sprite that catches objects
  addProp list, #pGloveSprite,¬
    [#comment: "Glove Sprite",¬
     #format: #integer,¬
     #default: 5]
```

```
-- starting speed of fall
addProp list, #pSpeed,¬
  [#comment: "Speed",¬
   #format: #integer,¬
   #default: 5]
```

The "pSpeed" property sets the number of pixels that each falling object moves for each frame. Another important factor in the speed of the game is the Score tempo. Be sure you set the Score tempo to something like 15 or 30 frames per second before playing around with the "pSpeed" parameter. Try to keep the tempo constant as you adjust "pSpeed".

NOTE

In most games, the speed of the game is determined by both the behavior parameters, such as "pSpeed" and the Score's tempo. On fast machines, you can use a low parameter value, and a high tempo to make a smooth game. However, slower machines might not be able to keep up with the high tempo of the movie. If you want your game to work fast on slower machines, use a high behavior parameter such as "pSpeed", and a low tempo. Experiment with different values on both a low-speed test machine and your high-speed development computer.

```
-- how often to drop objects
addProp list, #pDropFrequency,¬
  [#comment: "Drop Frequency",¬
   #format: #integer,¬
   #default: 60]
```

This property can be confusing because a lower number means that objects fall more often. More precisely, it is the number of ticks that must pass before another object falls.

```
-- test to be performed to determine catch
addProp list, #pCatchRequirement,¬
  [#comment: "Catch Requirement",¬
   #format: #string,¬
   #range: ["Rects Touch", "Loc Inside Rect",¬
            "Rect Touches Loc", "Square Distance",¬
            "Circular Distance"],¬
   #default: "Loc Inside Rect"]
```

The "pCatchRequirement" parameter sometimes needs an accompanying number value to define it. This number is used in case either of the distance methods is chosen. The "pCatchDistance" parameter is used for that. If neither of the distance methods is used, the "pCatchDistance" parameter is ignored.

```
-- distance measurement for catch test
addProp list, #pCatchDistance,¬
  [#comment: "Catch Distance (If Needed)",¬
   #format: #integer,¬
   #default: 20]
```

The next parameter determines how many points are awarded for each correct catch, as well as how many points should be subtracted for an incorrect catch.

```
-- how many points to be awarded for each catch
addProp list, #pScoreIncrement,¬
  [#comment: "Score Increment",¬
   #format: #integer,¬
   #default: 10]
```

Like the "pCatchRequirement", the "pEndGameCondition" needs a number value to fully define the end game condition. In the case of the first two choices, this number is used to determine how many objects must be missed, or caught, to end the game. In the case of the "Obtain Certain Score" choice, the number is used as the score that must be obtained.

```
-- how does the game end
addProp list, #pEndGameCondition,¬
  [#comment: "End Game Condition",¬
   #format: #string,¬
   #range: ["Miss Number of Good Objects",¬
            "Catch Number of Bad Objects",¬
            "Obtain Certain Score"],¬
   #default: "Miss Number of Good Objects"]

-- number associated with the end game condition
  addProp list, #pEndGameNumber,¬
    [#comment: "End Game Number",¬
     #format: #integer,¬
     #default: 3]
```

The next parameter enables you to specify whether you want points to be subtracted when the player catches the wrong object.

```
-- what happens when a bad item is caught
addProp list, #pCatchBadPenalty,¬
  [#comment: "Catch Bad Item Penalty",¬
   #format: #string,¬
   #range: ["Nothing",¬
            "Lose Points"],¬
   #default: "Nothing"]
```

The next four parameters are the sounds to be used in the game. If you leave them blank, no sound is played at all.

```
-- sound to play when item drops
addProp list, #pDropSound,¬
  [#comment: "Drop Sound",¬
   #format: #string,¬
   #default: ""]
-- sound to play when item is caught
addProp list, #pCatchSound,¬
  [#comment: "Catch Sound",¬
   #format: #string,¬
   #default: ""]
-- sound to play when item is missed
addProp list, #pMissSound,¬
  [#comment: "Miss Sound",¬
   #format: #string,¬
   #default: ""]
-- sound to play when bad item is caught
addProp list, #pBadCatchSound,¬
  [#comment: "Bad Catch Sound",¬
   #format: #string,¬
   #default: ""]
```

The last parameter is the frame to which the movie advances when the game is over.

```
-- Frame to go to when game is over
addProp list, #pEndGameFrame,¬
  [#comment: "End Game Frame",¬
   #format: #marker,¬
   #default: #next]

  return list
end
```

The *on beginSprite* handler resets all the score-like properties, clear the *pUsingSprites* list and set the value of the score text on the screen.

```
-- reset score and sprite list
on beginSprite me
  pScore = 0
  pNumberMissed = 0
  pNumberBadCaught = 0
  pNextDropTime = the ticks
  showScore(me)
  pUsingSprites = []
end
```

All action in the game takes place in the *on exitFrame* handler. First, the glove sprite is aligned to match the current cursor position. Then, each falling object is moved down a bit. Next, all the objects are checked to see whether any have been caught. Finally, the time is checked to see whether another object should drop.

```
-- regularly timed events
on exitFrame me
  -- match glove sprite to cursor
  sprite(pGloveSprite).locH = the mouseH
  -- move objects down
  letObjectsFall(me)
  -- see if an object has been caught
  checkCaught(me)
  -- see if another item can be dropped
  if the ticks > pNextDropTime then
    dropObject(me)
    pNextDropTime = the ticks + pDropFrequency
  end if
  -- loop on the frame
  go to the frame
end
```

The "on letObjectsFall" handler loops through the sprites in use and moves them down according to "pSpeed" ① . If the sprite has passed out of view on the bottom of the screen, then the sprite is recycled by removing it from the "pUsingSprites" list ② .

A check is also made to see whether the object is a "good" object. If so, then it was missed by the player and gets added to the "pNumberMissed" property ③ . If the game is set to end when the player misses a certain number of good objects, then the "on checkEndGame" handler is called to end the game.

```
-- move all existing objects down
on letObjectsFall me
  repeat with i = pUsingSprites.count down to 1
    -- get sprite number
    s = pUsingSprites[i]
    -- get vertical location
    y = sprite(s).locV
    -- increase vertical location
①→ y = y + pSpeed
    sprite(s).locV = y
    if y > (the stage).rect.height + sprite(s).rect.height/2 then
      -- sprite is beyond bottom of screen, remove object
      if sprite(s).member.name = "Good" then
        if pMissSound <> "" then puppetSound pMissSound
③→     pNumberMissed = pNumberMissed + 1
        showScore(me)
        checkEndGame(me)
      end if
②→   deleteAt pUsingSprites, i
    end if
  end repeat
end
```

When it is determined that it's time to drop a new object, the "on dropObject" handler is called. This handler first loops through the sprite range to find a sprite not being used ④ . Then, it assigns it a random member from the cast library of objects. It also picks a random horizontal location and a vertical location that puts the object just above the top of the screen.

```
-- create a new falling object
on dropObject me
  -- loop through sprites
  repeat with s = pFirstSprite to pLastSprite
    -- see if it is being used
    if not getOne(pUsingSprites,s) then
      -- pick a random member
      r = random(the number of members of castLib "Objects")
      mem = member(r,"Objects")
      -- random horizontal location that still
      -- has entire member on the screen
      screenWidth = (the stage).rect.width
      memberWidth = mem.rect.width
      x = random(screenWidth-memberWidth)+memberWidth/2
      -- set vertical loc to just above screen
      memberHeight = mem.rect.height
      sprite(s).loc = point(x,-memberHeight/2)
      -- set member
      sprite(s).member = mem
      -- add to list
      add pUsingSprites, s
      -- no need to look further
      if pDropSound <> "" then puppetSound pDropSound
      exit repeat
    end if
  end repeat
end
```

The "on checkCaught" handler checks each sprite that is in use and determines whether it has been caught by the glove. It uses one of the five methods to determine this, depending on the "pCatchRequirement" parameter.

If a catch has been made, the "on checkCaught" handler must deal with it being either a good object or a bad one. In the latter case, the "pNumberBadCaught" must be incremented ⑤ . If it's a good catch, "on addScore" is called ⑥ . Either way, the "on checkEndGame" handler must be called.

```
-- check to see if any objects were caught
on checkCaught me
  repeat with i = pUsingSprites.count down to 1
    s = pUsingSprites[i]
    if pCatchRequirement = "Rects Touch" then
      if sprite s intersects pGloveSprite then
        catch = TRUE
      end if
    else if pCatchRequirement = "Loc Inside Rect" then
      if inside(sprite(s).loc, sprite(pGloveSprite).rect) then
        catch = TRUE
      end if
    else if pCatchRequirement = "Rect Touches Loc" then
      if inside(sprite(pGloveSprite).loc, sprite(s).rect) then
        catch = TRUE
      end if
    else if pCatchRequirement = "Square Distance" then
      if (sprite(s).locH - sprite(pGloveSprite).locH) <= pCatchDistance and¬
         (sprite(s).locV - sprite(pGloveSprite).locV) <= pCatchDistance then
        catch = TRUE
      end if
    else if pCatchRequirement = "Circular Distance" then
      if sqrt(power(sprite(s).locH - sprite(pGloveSprite).locH,2)+¬
              power(sprite(s).locV - sprite(pGloveSprite).locV,2))¬
         <= pCatchDistance then
        catch = TRUE
      end if
    end if
    if catch then
      sprite(s).locV = -30
      deleteOne pUsingSprites, s
      if sprite(s).member.name = "Good" then
        if pCatchSound <> "" then puppetSound pCatchSound
```
⑥➤ `        addScore(me)`
```
      else
        if pBadCatchSound <> "" then puppetSound pBadCatchSound
        if pCatchBadPenalty = "Lose Points" then
          subtractScore(me)
        end if
```
⑤➤ `        pNumberBadCaught = pNumberBadCaught + 1`
```
        showScore(me)
      end if
      checkEndGame(me)
    end if
  end repeat
end
```

If a catch has been made, the score increases, and the drop frequency decreases.

```
-- add to the score and increase drop frequency
on addScore me
  pScore = pScore + pScoreIncrement
  pDropFrequency = pDropFrequency - 1
  showScore(me)
end
```

If a bad object has been caught, and the "pBadCatchPenalty" is set to "Lose Points", then the "on subtractScore" handler is used to decrease the score. Care is given not to allow the score to fall below zero. If you prefer not to take pity upon bad players, you can remove that line and let the score fall into negative values.

```
-- subtract points
on subtractScore me
  pScore = pScore - pScoreIncrement
  if pScore < 0 then
    -- don't allow score to go under 0
  pScore = 0
  end if
  showScore(me)
end
```

The "on showScore" handler works as it did for earlier games, but has an addition here. If the "pEndGameCondition" is set to "Miss Number of Good Objects", then the "pNumberMissed" is shown as well as the score. If the "pEndGameCondition" is set to "Catch Number of Bad Objects", then the "pNumberBadCaught" is shown. Either helps the user determine how close he or she is to the end of the game, thus adding a little tension to the gameplay.

```
-- update the onscreen text member
on showScore me
  text = "Score:"&&pScore&RETURN
  -- add second line depending on the type of game
  if pEndGameCondition = "Miss Number of Good Objects" then
    put "Objects Missed:"&&pNumberMissed after text
  else if pEndGameCondition = "Catch Number of Bad Objects" then
    put "Bad Objects:"&&pNumberBadCaught after text
  end if
  member("score").text = text
end
```

The "on checkEndGame" handler looks at each of the three possible ways the game can end, and goes to a new frame if any are true. You might want to make it so the game can end on a combination of the end game conditions, rather than just one. A little modification of the code could have this handler ignore the "pEndGameCondition" property and instead just check for all the conditions.

```
-- see if the necessary game over condition is met
on checkEndGame me
   if pEndGameCondition = "Miss Number of Good Objects" then
      if pNumberMissed >= pEndGameNumber then
        go to frame pEndGameFrame
      end if
   else if pEndGameCondition = "Catch Number of Bad Objects" then
      if pNumberBadCaught >= pEndGameNumber then
        go to frame pEndGameFrame
      end if
   else if pEndGameCondition = "Obtain Certain Score" then
      if pScore >= pEndGameNumber then
        go to frame pEndGameFrame
      end if
   end if
end
```

Putting It All Together

The way the example code is set up, the game requires two cast libraries. The first is the standard internal cast, which needs to have the behavior itself, and also the "glove" bitmap, or whatever you are using to catch the falling objects.

The second cast should have only bitmaps that represent the falling objects. They should all be called "good" or "bad," depending on the type of object.

NOTE

You could also change the code to see whether the name of the members *contain* "good" or "bad." This way, you could name the bitmaps with little descriptions, such as "baseball good" and "football bad."

To build the game from these members, just drag a few objects to the Stage in a range of sprite channels. For instance, you could use channels 11 through 20. Be sure that the sprites are positioned above the top of the screen, so they are not seen until they are used by the behavior. You can use any member you want for these, because the member is set randomly before each falls.

Also, you must place the glove bitmap in a sprite channel. Then, when you assign the game behavior to the script channel, you need to specify the object sprite range and the glove's sprite.

The rest of the behavior's properties also need to be set. Don't forget to set the movie tempo, or perhaps the tempo channel of that particular frame as well.

Taking a look at the example movie on the CD-ROM will show you how the Score and Stage are set up. Figure 8.3 shows the Score. In this example, I use various types of sports objects. However, only the baseball is a "good" object, as specified by its name in the Cast.

Figure 8.3
The Score window shows the three frames used in the Falling Objects game. Game play takes place on the middle frame where there is a bank of sprites available to become falling objects.

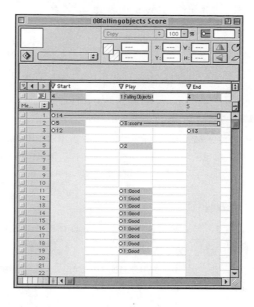

Game Variations

As mentioned at the beginning of this chapter, this game can be easily customized, perhaps more so than any game in this book. You can not only change the objects in the game to represent different things, but you can also change the metaphor of the game without altering the code.

Educational Variants

Because the object of the game is to catch "good" objects and avoid "bad" ones, you can easily adapt this to education. The "good" objects need to fit a certain criterion, for instance, "countries in Africa." The falling objects would be country names. The player is then faced with the task of identifying the continent that the country is located on before deciding whether to catch it. As the game play continues, the correct answers are reinforced with the sounds and score changes that occur as the player catches country names.

The same idea can be applied to words in any set. You could have the player pick out primary colors, or prime numbers. A language game could have the player select adjectives out of falling words. Just about any subject can be incorporated into a "falling objects" game.

Changing Perspective

Why does the top of the screen have to represent "up"? You could paint a background of a river, with a boat rather than a glove. As the boat moves up the river, the player can move it from left to right to pick up floating objects.

The same idea can be done with a street and a car, an airplane, or a spaceship. With some modification to the code, you can make the objects go from left to right or right to left instead of top to bottom.

Adding Animation

A sprite does not have to contain a static bitmap member. It can contain a Director film loop member. This would mean that the objects would animate as they fall. The only difference this would make is that the game will look nicer.

Increasing Difficulty

To make the game a little more challenging, you can make the pieces fall diagonally or randomly move left and right while falling.

This would require some changes to the code, of course. A diagonally falling object would have to change its horizontal location while falling.

This would make items harder to catch, and might even take some items off the sides of the screen while falling. This can just be a hazard of the game, or you can include code to ensure that the items reverse direction when they get too far to the left or right.

Catching a Bomb

One variation of the game that might not be readily apparent is that you could set the "pEndGameCondition" to "Catch Number of Bad Objects" and set the "pEndGameNumber" to 1. Then, include a lot of good objects, and just one bad one that looks like a bomb.

When the player accidentally catches the bomb, the game ends. Perhaps in the end game frame, a huge explosion occurs to drive the point home. This makes for an exciting and tension-filled game.

Shooting Gallery

9

CD-ROM File: 09shootinggallery.dir

Useful Lingo in This Chapter

♠ Behaviors: Using parameters

♠ Behaviors: Using a ranged parameter

♠ Graphics: Making sprites disappear

♠ Graphics: Moving sprites

♠ Graphics: Using points

♠ Input: Selecting with mouse clicks

♠ Interface: Using custom cursors

♠ Variables: Keeping score

Clicking a button on the screen is typical computer user interface behavior. However, if the objects start moving around and ducking behind other objects, then it becomes a game.

This type of game can be used to represent a carnival shooting gallery, or a hunting experience. It can also be used for colorful holiday games such as a "Turkey Shoot" for Thanksgiving.

Game Overview

The Lingo code at the heart of this game takes mouse clicks and records them as hits or misses. The cursor becomes a gun sight, and the mouse button becomes the trigger.

The rest of the code concerns itself mostly with the movement of the targets. A good shooting gallery should have targets that move in all sorts of different ways, at different speeds, and pop out at different times.

Figure 9.1 shows one way that a shooting gallery game can be set up. It resembles a carnival shooting gallery. Ducks move across the bottom of the screen and up and down the sides. Three ducks near the bottom pop up occasionally, and three ducks behind the block in the center rotate around, popping their heads up like clockwork.

Figure 9.1

This shooting gallery game is set up like a carnival booth.

Another way to set up the game that is more challenging is to have all the ducks hide behind objects, occasionally peeking out with great irregularity. Figure 9.2 shows what this could look like. The three ducks on each side and the two ducks at the bottom appear every once and a while, at random. The player has to keep guessing where the next one will appear.

Figure 9.2

A shooting gallery game where all the targets hide and appear at random.

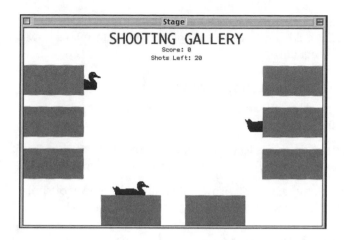

Types of Animation

The games shown in the two previous figures actually contain six different types of movement. Instead of creating six different behaviors, we'll create one behavior that handles them all.

The first two types of animation are a simple vertical and a simple horizontal movement. In the first case, the target moves up a certain number of pixels and then moves back down. The second has the target moving first left and then back to the right.

The next animation makes the target move in a circle of a certain radius. It should be able to move both clockwise and counterclockwise.

The fourth animation shrinks the target vertically, holding the bottom at the same position on the screen. This causes the target to appear as if it were falling backward, as though it were hinged at the bottom.

The last two animation types allow the target to move continuously across the screen or up or down it. The difference between these and the first two animations is that the targets move until they cross the screen, and then appear again on the other side.

For all these types of animations, we should be able to vary the speed. For some, we should be able to change the distance traveled. For the circular movement, we need to be able to change the radius of the circle.

We should also be able to change the starting point for each animation. So, for instance, we can tell the target where in the circle to start in the case of a circular animation.

Random Appearances

If targets appear at regular intervals during the game, the player has only to wait, cursor positioned at the right spot, and click at the right time.

To avoid this, there should be an element of randomness in the game. So, between animations, the targets should pause for a random length of time.

The pause should occur, of course, at a time when then target is out of harm's way. The behavior should enable us to set a value that determines how often the target begins an animated sequence.

Limited Ammunition

For a game like this we should keep score. For the score to mean something, we need to limit the playing time.

One way to do this is to have a timer so that the user has to hit as many targets as quickly as they can. Another way is to limit the number of shots that the player has.

For this example, we will allow only a limited number of shots. The score is then determined by the number of shots that actually hit targets.

Screen Elements

Only a few simple screen elements are required for this example game. However, you will want to have much more elaborate artwork for the game you create.

The first thing you need is a target—or, if you prefer, many different types of targets. In the example game, I used a simple duck silhouette.

In addition, you need background art, as well as foreground art. The latter is important because it will be used as objects that the targets can hide behind. In the example game, I just used simple blocks.

Point Values

Not every target should offer the same level of difficulty. Some will move faster and appear less frequently.

Our target behavior should enable us to set point values for each individual target. These will be the points awarded to the player when he or she hits the target.

Special Effects

The most important special effect here is the cursor. Because this is a shooting game, the cursor should reflect what you would see when looking through a gun sight.

We also need a little "blast" graphic to appear on the screen when the user takes a shot. This graphic appears only when a shot misses. Both the shot graphic and the cursor appear in Figure 9.3.

However, there should also be a screen reaction when the user hits. In that case, we will simply swap out the sprite's member with a new graphic. This will also signal to the player that he or she has already hit the target and should not attempt to do so again.

Figure 9.3
The Cast window shows the bull's-eye cursor and a small graphic to briefly mark where a shot has been fired.

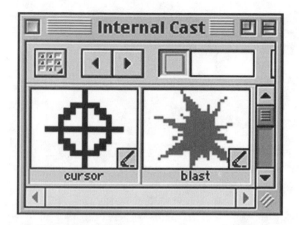

Of course, sound effects are a good addition to this game. A gunshot sound is an easy one, but you can also use sounds to reflect the targets. You can use different shot sounds for a hit or a miss.

Making the Game

This game requires four behaviors. The first is for the target sprites themselves, and contains the code to animate them. The second is the frame behavior that keeps track of the overall game state and handles events sent to the Stage. The third is a small behavior to enable some sprites to block shots to targets that are behind them. The last behavior is for a small blast graphic that appears when the user takes a shot and misses.

Target Behavior

The behavior that gets placed on any target on the screen is called the "Shooting Gallery Sprite Behavior" in the example on the CD-ROM. It's primarily in charge of the movement of the target. It also accepts mouse clicks on the sprite as hits.

Figure 9.4 shows the Parameters dialog box for this behavior. Following the figure, you'll see the property declarations and the *on getPropertyDescriptionList* handler, which is rather long. It includes a lot of parameters to provide a great deal of versatility in how the sprite can move. I have added comments to the individual parameters to better explain them.

Figure 9.4
The Parameters dialog box for the sprite behavior is shown here.

Parameters for "Shooting Gallery Sprite Behavior"		
Type of Movement	moveVert	OK
Speed	-10	Cancel
Amount	25	
Starting Step	0	
Points	10	
Frequency	1	

```
-- parameters
property pMovement
property pSpeed
property pAmount
property pStep
property pPoints
property pFrequency

-- other properties
property pOrigLoc -- remember the sprite's original location
property pOrigRect -- remember the sprite's original rect
property pOrigStep -- remember the starting step
property pHit -- has the sprite been hit recently

on getPropertyDescriptionList me
  list = [:]
```

The type of movement that a target sprite exhibits will fit one of the six types explained earlier in this chapter. Each will be seen later in the *on exitFrame* handler, where the actual code for executing the movement is located.

```
-- type of movement
addProp list, #pMovement,¬
  [#comment: "Type of Movement",¬
   #format: #symbol,¬
   #range: [#upDown, #leftRight, #circle,¬
            #layDown, #moveHoriz, #moveVert, #none],¬
   #default: #none]
```

The "pSpeed" parameter is used by all the movement types to determine how many pixels the sprite moves in one frame. In the case of circular movement, the "pSpeed" relates to the number of degrees around the circle that the sprite moves in one frame. With the "#layDown" movement type, the "pSpeed" and the "pAmount" are used to determine a fractional amount of movement.

```
-- how many pixels to move at one time
addProp list, #pSpeed,¬
  [#comment: "Speed",¬
   #format: #integer,¬
   #default: 1]
```

The "pSpeed" can also be set to a negative value to make the sprite move backward. This works for the "#circle", "#moveHoriz", and "#moveVert" types. The other types of movement are back-and-forth movements, and don't need to use a negative "pSpeed".

The "pAmount" parameter is used to determine how far a sprite should go in the case of "#upDown" and "#leftRight". In the case of "#circle", the "pAmount" is used as the radius of the circle. In the case of "#layDown", the "pSpeed" and "pAmount" are used as a fraction to determine how much to stretch the sprite in each frame.

```
-- total distance to move
-- for #circle, it is the radius
addProp list, #pAmount,¬
  [#comment: "Amount",¬
   #format: #integer,¬
   #default: 25]
```

The "pStep" parameter is necessary if you want the sprites to start at different positions. This property is actually used to increment the movement throughout the life of the sprite. By using it as a parameter as well, it enables you to have the sprite start a part of the way through the animation. So, if the movement type is "#upDown" and the "#pAmount" is 100, then you know that the sprite is supposed to move 100 pixels up, and then 100 back down, for a total of 200 steps. If you set "pStep" to start at 100, then the sprite will start at the top, and appear to move down and then up instead.

```
-- where the sprite begins
addProp list, #pStep,¬
  [#comment: "Starting Step",¬
   #format: #integer,¬
   #default: 0]
```

The "pPoints" parameter is simply the number of points that the user gets when they hit the target. You should determine how difficult a target is to hit and assign an appropriate number. A fast-moving target that appears rarely should be worth more than a slow moving target that is always on the screen.

```
-- number of points the sprite is worth when hit
addProp list, #pPoints,¬
  [#comment: "Points",¬
   #format: #integer,¬
   #default: 10]
```

The "pFrequency" parameter enables you to make the game more random. When the sprite hits the "pStep" that corresponds to where it started, it stops moving. Then, the "pFrequency" parameter is used to determine when it starts again. A low number, such as 1, means that it starts immediately. A high number, such as 100, means that it has a 1 in 100 chance of starting again on each frame.

When you are using a "pFrequency" of more than 1, be sure that the starting "pStep" for the target has it hiding behind a blocking sprite or off the screen. Otherwise, the target will be very easy to hit because it will be standing still.

```
-- how often the sprite should do its movement
addProp list, #pFrequency,¬
  [#comment: "Frequency",¬
```

```
        #format: #integer,¬
        #default: 1]

   return list
end
```

The *on beginSprite* handler is responsible for remembering the original location, rectangle, and "pStep" of the sprite. All of these are useful in one type of animation or the other.

```
-- get the starting location, rect, and step
on beginSprite me
  pOrigLoc = sprite(me.spriteNum).loc
  pOrigRect = sprite(me.spriteNum).rect
  pOrigStep = pStep
  pHit = FALSE
end
```

The *on exitFrame* handler is the workhorse of this behavior. It looks at "pMovement" and determines what type of movement to apply to the sprite.

Most types of movement first call "on checkForReset" and then "on allowAnimation". This first handler checks to see whether the sprite has completed an animation and should be reset if it was hit. The second handler advances the "pStep" property as long as the sprite is not currently in a stopped mode, waiting for its next chance to appear.

```
-- perform the animation
on exitFrame me
  case pMovement of
```

The "#upDown" and "#leftRight" movements are basically the same. If "pStep" is less than "pAmount", then the sprite is on its way up or to the left. If it is greater than "pAmount", then it's on its way back. The sprite's location is set according to the original location and the value of "pStep".

```
        #upDown: -- move vertically
          checkForReset(me) -- see if animation has completed one sequence
          allowAnimation(me) -- next step of animation
          if pStep > pAmount*2 then pStep = 0 -- sequence complete
          if pStep <= pAmount then -- first half of sequence
            y = pOrigLoc.locV - pStep -- up
          else -- second half of sequence
            y = pOrigLoc.locV - pAmount*2 + pStep -- down
          end if
          sprite(me.spriteNum).locV = y -- set sprite location

      • #leftRight: -- move horizontally
          checkForReset(me) -- see if animation has completed one sequence
```

```
allowAnimation(me) -- next step of animation
if pStep > pAmount*2 then pStep = 0 -- sequence complete
if pStep <= pAmount then -- first half of sequence
  x = pOrigLoc.locH - pStep -- left
else -- second half of sequence
  x = pOrigLoc.locH - pAmount*2 + pStep -- right
end if
sprite(me.spriteNum).locH = x -- set sprite location
```

The circular animation works very differently. It uses "pAmount" as the radius, and "pStep" as a number of degrees. It then uses *sin* and *cos* to create a location.

```
#circle: -- move in circle
    checkForReset(me) -- see if animation has completed one sequence
    allowAnimation(me) -- next step of animation
 -- sequence complete, clockwise or counterclockwise
    if pStep >= 360 then pStep = pStep - 360
    else if pStep < 0 then pStep = pStep + 360
angle = 2.0*pi()*pStep/360.0 -- convert to radians
    x = cos(angle)*pAmount -- calculate x from angle and radius
    y = sin(angle)*pAmount -- calculate x from angle and radius
    sprite(me.spriteNum).loc = point(x,y) + pOrigLoc -- set sprite location
```

The "#layDown" movement type uses "pStep" over "pAmount" as a fraction and then sets the height of the sprite to that fraction. When "pStep" is at 0, the height is 0, and the sprite appears to be flat. When "pStep" is the same as "pAmount", the height is equal to the original height of the sprite, and it appears normal. In between, the sprite looks like it is getting lifted up, and then falling back down again.

```
#layDown: -- compress rectangle
    checkForReset(me) -- see if animation has completed one sequence
    allowAnimation(me) -- next step of animation
    if pStep > pAmount*2 then pStep = 0 -- sequence complete
percent = float(pStep)/float(pAmount) -- percent of shrink
if percent > 1 then percent = 2.0-percent -- second half of sequence
height = percent*(pOrigRect.height) -- calculate actual height of rect
newRect = duplicate(pOrigRect)
newRect.top = newRect.bottom - height -- calculate new rect
    sprite(me.spriteNum).rect = newRect -- set the rect of the sprite
```

The "#moveHoriz" and "#moveVert" types don't need to use the "pAmount" parameter. This is because they move all the way across the screen. When the sprite reaches the opposite side of the screen, it is simply reset to the other side.

```
#moveHoriz: -- move across screen continuously
    x = sprite(me.spriteNum).locH -- current location
    x = x + pSpeed -- add to current location
    spriteWidth = pOrigRect.width
```

```
    stageWidth = (the stage).rect.width
    if pSpeed > 0 and x-spriteWidth/2 > stageWidth then -- off screen?
      reset(me)
      x = x - stageWidth - spriteWidth -- move to other side
    else if pSpeed < 0 and x+spriteWidth/2 < 0 then -- off screen?
      reset(me)
      x = x + stageWidth + spriteWidth -- move to other side
    end if
    sprite(me.spriteNum).locH = x -- set the loc of the sprite

  #moveVert:
    y = sprite(me.spriteNum).locV -- current location
    y = y + pSpeed -- add to current location
    spriteHeight = pOrigRect.height
    stageHeight = (the stage).rect.height
    if pSpeed > 0 and y-spriteHeight/2 > stageHeight then -- off screen?
      reset(me)
      y = y - stageHeight - spriteHeight -- move to other side
    else if pSpeed < 0 and y+spriteHeight/2 < 0 then -- off screen?
      y = y + stageHeight + spriteHeight -- move to other side
      reset(me)
    end if
    sprite(me.spriteNum).locV = y -- set the loc of the sprite

  end case
end
```

Several utility handlers are called from the "on exitFrame" handler. The first is one that checks to see whether the "pStep" is back to its original value. If it is, then it's reset to the "Target" member and "pHit" is set to *FALSE*. This is needed in case the sprite was hit by the player, thus changing the member to the "Target Hit" member.

```
-- see if sprite is back at the start of a sequence
on checkForReset me
  if pStep = pOrigStep then
    reset(me)
  end if
end

-- reset the sprite if it was hit
on reset me
  if pHit then
    sprite(me.spriteNum).member = member("Target")
    pHit = FALSE
  end if
end
```

The "on allowAnimation" handler checks to see whether "pStep" is set to its original value. If it is, then the handler only advances the movement of the sprite providing that a random number from 1 to "pFrequency" is equal to 1. If "pFrequency" is 1, then this happens 100 percent of the time. If "pFrequency" is more than 1, then the sprite might have to wait for a number of frames before moving past the original "pStep" value again.

```
-- only advance the animation if it is in the middle
-- of a sequence, or if it is time to start a new sequence
on allowAnimation me
  if pStep = pOrigStep then -- start of sequence
    -- pFrequency used to randomly determine if it is time to start again
    if random(pFrequency) = 1 then
      pStep = pStep + pSpeed
    end if
  else
    pStep = pStep + pSpeed
  end if
end
```

Almost separate from the animation handlers in this behavior is the *on mouseDown* handler. This is a simple way to detect whether the player has hit the sprite with a shot.

If this happens, the frame behavior is notified via the "on addScore" handler. The sprite's member is changed to reflect the hit, and the "pHit" property is set to *TRUE*.

This "pHit" property is then used to prevent the player from hitting the sprite again. The "pHit" property is reset when the sprite reaches its home state. So, when a target moves onto the screen, the player can hit it once, and it changes into a new member. Then the player can't hit that target again until it moves off the screen and then back on again.

```
-- if the user clicks, then it represents a gunshot
on mouseDown me
  if not pHit then -- not already hit
    sendSprite(0,#addScore,pPoints) -- add to score
    sprite(me.spriteNum).member = member("Target Hit") -- new member
    pHit = TRUE
  else
    pass -- pass to frame behavior so it can be recorded as a miss
  end if
end
```

Frame Behavior

The frame behavior has the responsibility of keeping track of the score, the number of shots fired, and adding effects such as the cursor and sounds.

The *on getPropertyDescriptionList* handler needs to get only four parameters: the number of shots the player has, two sound names, and the frame to jump to when the game is over. These are similar parameters to the ones we have used in most of the previous games. The resulting dialog box is shown in Figure 9.5.

Figure 9.5

The frame behavior Parameters dialog box.

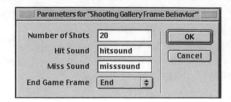

```
-- parameters
property pNumberOfShots
property pEndGameFrame
property pHitSound
property pMissSound

property pScore -- the player's score

on getPropertyDescriptionList me
  list = [:]

  -- starting number of shots the player gets
  addProp list, #pNumberOfShots,¬
    [#comment: "Number of Shots",¬
     #format: #integer,¬
     #default: 20]

  -- hit something sound
  addProp list, #pHitSound,¬
    [#comment: "Hit Sound",¬
     #format: #string,¬
     #default: ""]

  -- miss sound
  addProp list, #pMissSound,¬
    [#comment: "Miss Sound",¬
     #format: #string,¬
     #default: ""]

  -- frame to jump to when it is over
  addProp list, #pEndGameFrame,¬
    [#comment: "End Game Frame",¬
     #format: #marker,¬
     #default: #next]
```

```
    return list
end
```

The *on beginSprite* marks the start of the game. Because we want to use a custom cursor for the entire game, we can set it here. Instead of using a cursor from the standard set of cursors that are embedded inside Director, Projectors, and Shockwave, we will make our own custom cursor. We activate this cursor with the *cursor* command.

```
-- set cursor to crosshairs, score to 0
on beginSprite me
    cursor([member("cursor")]) -- set cursor to crosshairs
    pScore = 0
    showScore(me)
end
```

NOTE

The *cursor* command can actually be used in three different ways. You can use it with a number to use a standard cursor such as a hand or a magnifying glass. You can use it with a list or one or two members to make a simple custom cursor, or you can use it with a special animated cursor member to make a color cursor or an animated cursor. The last option requires the animated cursor Xtra that comes with Director.

The custom cursor, in this case, is an old-fashioned custom cursor that has been around in Director for many versions. Figure 9.6 shows the member for this cursor. It must be a 1-bit bitmap member.

Figure 9.6
A 1-bit bitmap is used as the cursor in this game.

You could also use an animated cursor instead. This would enable you to use color and make the cursor size bigger. However, for this example game, all we need is a simple cursor.

The next handler updates the "score" text member.

```
-- put score in text member
on showScore me
    member("score").text = "Score:"&&pScore&RETURN&¬
                           "Shots Left:"&&pNumberOfShots
end
```

The "on addScore" handler does more than just increase the score. It also reduces the number of shots remaining, and checks for the end of the game.

```
-- add points to score
on addScore me, p
  if pHitSound <> "" then puppetSound pHitSound
  pNumberOfShots = pNumberOfShots - 1 -- reduce shots
  pScore = pScore + p -- add score
  showScore(me)
  checkEndGame(me)
end
```

The "on mouseDown" handler gets called when the user clicks on an empty part of the screen, or when the user clicks on a sprite that has no *on mouseDown* handler of its own. We also use the *pass* command in the sprite behavior to pass along "mouseDown" messages to the frame behavior when the player tries to shoot a target that has already been hit.

This "on mouseDown" handler is called only when the player shoots and misses. So, we must subtract one from the number of shots left and check for the end of the game. In addition, a message is sent to the blast graphic sprite to position itself where the shot was fired.

```
-- click missed an object and went to frame
on mouseDown me
  if pMissSound <> "" then puppetSound pMissSound
  pNumberOfShots = pNumberOfShots - 1 -- reduce shots
  sendSprite(40,#display,the clickLoc) -- place blast graphic
  showScore(me)
  checkEndGame(me)
end
```

The "on checkEndGame" handler needs to see whether all shots have been fired to determine whether the game is over.

```
-- see if all shots are gone
on checkEndGame me
  if pNumberOfShots = 0 then
    go to frame pEndGameFrame
  end if
end
```

In addition to all the previous code, the frame behavior is responsible for creating the one-frame loop. This is all that is needed in the *on exitFrame* handler.

```
-- loop on the frame
on exitFrame me
  go to the frame
end
```

Blast Sprite Behavior

The blast sprite is a little graphic that is used to mark the screen each time the player misses. It acts as visual feedback to the user that the shot has been fired, even though a target was not hit.

This behavior just needs to move into position when the frame behavior tells it to. Then, it should wait at that location for a specific amount of time before disappearing.

The blast sprite behavior does its disappearing by going back to its original location, which should be off the Stage. The time is determined by counting down from 10 every time the frame loops. When 0 is reached, the sprite should disappear.

```
property pOrigLoc, pTimer


on beginSprite me
  pOrigLoc = sprite(me.spriteNum).loc -- remember original location
  pTimer = 0 -- start property at 0
end


-- called by frame behavior to tell blast graphic to move
on display me, loc
  sprite(me.spriteNum).loc = loc -- new location
  pTimer = 10 -- begin counting down
end


on exitFrame me
  if pTimer > 0 then -- counting down
    pTimer = pTimer - 1
    if pTimer = 0 then sprite(me.spriteNum).loc = pOrigLoc -- done counting, reset
location
  end if
end
```

Blocking Sprite Behavior

Targets should not always be vulnerable to the player's shots. This would make the game pretty easy. One way to protect them is to have them move and rest off the screen. Another way is to hide them behind other sprites.

Figures 9.1 and 9.2 showed some of these objects as simple blocks. These blocks need to have a behavior attached to them to eat the "mouseDown" messages so that they do not get to the target sprites.

You can do this by simply having an empty *on mouseDown* handler. However, we want to be sure that these shots get recorded as misses, just as a shot on the background would be. So, the "mouseDown" message should be passed directly to the frame behavior. Here is the handler that does this:

```
on mouseDown
  sendSprite(0,#mouseDown)
end
```

Putting It All Together

To build this game, you need at least five different graphics. First, you need the graphics for the targets themselves. In the example on the CD-ROM, a duck silhouette is used. You can see this duck, along with an image of it after it has been hit, in Figure 9.7.

Figure 9.7
The Cast window shows the target both before and after it has been hit.

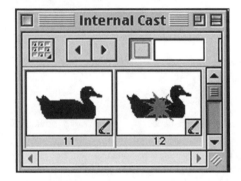

Then, you need an image that represents the target after it has been hit. The example movie just uses the same duck graphic, but with a blast image placed over it.

The third item you need is the blast graphic. This graphic represents a shot that has hit the back of the screen or a nontarget object.

The fourth graphic is an object that provides some cover for the targets. The example movie uses a simple rectangle, but you might want to use something better, such as boxes or trees.

The last graphic needed is the one-bit bitmap for the cursor.

After all the pieces are ready, and you have the four behaviors ready to go, you just need to do some assembly in the Score.

Start by dropping the frame behavior on the frame. Then, add the blast member to a sprite channel high in the Score, such as channel 50.

To add targets, do it one at a time. Drop a target member in the Score. Position it on the Stage approximately where you want it to go. Then, attach the sprite behavior to it. You'll have to fill in all the parameters to make the target move the way you want it to.

Before adding any more targets, first test this one. Run the movie and see how it moves. Stop the movie and make adjustments to the parameters and the sprite's position. Keep doing this until the sprite is moving exactly as you want it to.

Continue to add targets one by one. Test each one before moving on to the next.

After all your targets have been added, just add the nontarget objects on higher-numbered sprite channels so that they cover the targets.

In some cases, the blocking objects will be in front of some targets, but behind others. This enables you to have some targets that appear in front of some objects. For instance, one duck can peek out from behind a tree, while another duck runs across the screen and in front of that same tree.

You need to remember to drop the blocking object behavior on the objects you add.

Game Variations

The nature of the sprite behavior in this game lends itself to countless variations. The example movie on the CD-ROM includes two variations. The first is a carnival-like game, shown previously in Figure 9.1, and the second is closer to something like *Whack-A-Mole*, shown in Figure 9.2

The carnival-style game is not that challenging. Because there are many targets always on the screen, it is only a matter of figuring out which ones are worth more points and hitting only those.

The second game has an element of twitch-style arcade games. You have to react fast to catch a target, and it's easy to miss because you are too slow.

To vary the game even more, you can just play with the sprite behavior parameters or work with the graphics themselves.

A Richer Environment

Instead of the plain-looking screens shown in the example movie, you should create a rich environment that reflects a theme. You can also use many different types of targets instead of just one. Here are some ideas:

- A barnyard setting with bales of hay, farm machines, and farm animals
- A forest scene with trees and jungle animals
- A field with little groundhog or prairie dog holes
- A wilderness scene with bushes, trees, and deer
- An alien landscape with little alien creatures that pop out of craters

If you want to have different types of targets, such as chickens, ducks, and turkeys, you could use different "Target" members for each. This also means using different "Target Hit" members for each. You can do this by adding another parameter to the sprite behavior to specify the first word of the members to be used. For instance, a value of "Chicken" means that the target member is "Chicken" and the hit member is "Chicken Hit."

A Friendlier Environment

If you are like me, and the idea of blowing away little creatures is not appealing, then consider the other ways in which things can be "shot." Here are some examples to use in place of a gun and bullets:

- A camera and taking pictures
- A dart gun
- A pair of lips that kiss (great for young children)
- Guns and bullets, but shooting inanimate objects such as bottles and cans

More Animation

When a target is hit, it immediately changes the member of the target sprite to the "Target Hit" member. You could make this a Director film loop or an animated GIF. This way, the act of getting hit also results in animation.

The final frame of this animation could be blank, so the target appears to disappear at the end, until it is later reset. You could have the target explode, for instance.

If you are going to use an alternative to bullets, you can have the animation reflect that. For instance, if you have a camera as the user's weapon, the hit animation could show the targets smiling or posing for the camera.

Sprite Invaders

CD-ROM File: 10spriteinvaders.dir

Useful Lingo in This Chapter

♠ Animation: Creating a delay with Lingo

♠ Behaviors: Calling handlers in other behaviors

♠ Behaviors: Using parameters

♠ Graphics: Changing sprite members with Lingo

♠ Graphics: Making sprites disappear

♠ Graphics: Moving sprites

♠ Graphics: Using points

♠ Input: Accepting arrow keys

♠ Math: Using random numbers

♠ Programming: Collision detection

♠ Variables: Keeping score

When most people old enough to remember the 1970s are asked about arcade games, they inevitably think of the hit game "Space Invaders." Millions of these games were sold, and hundreds of other games like it were developed.

It is common for a Director game developer to get asked to create an "invaders"-style game. Let's look at the basic parts of such a game and develop our own "Sprite Invaders."

Game Overview

The basic idea of the game is to have a formation of invaders march down the screen. They go right and then left, dropping lower each time they change direction.

The player, on the other hand, remains vertically stationary at the bottom of the screen. He or she can move the "ship," "gun," "turret," or whatever you want to call it, back and forth, and fire bullets at the oncoming invaders.

The game ends when either the invaders reach the bottom of the screen, or fire back at the player's ship, hitting it. Figure 10.1 shows the game at its start.

Figure 10.1

The screen at the start of a Sprite Invaders game.

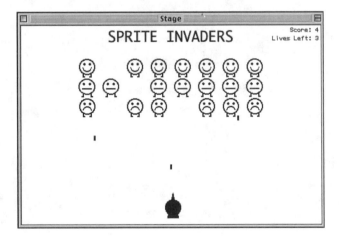

Our example movie uses three different invader graphics, and the screen is arranged with a row of each.

Ship Movement

The ship in this game is controlled by the keyboard rather than by the mouse. When the mouse is used to control such an item, as in Chapter 8, "Falling Objects," the player has the ability to move the item across the screen very quickly. In fact, if the user pulls the mouse to one side or the other fast enough, it is really jumping from one location to the other without passing through any intermediate points. In addition, it is easy for the player to have the cursor positioned off the game, where a mouse click will simply react with the computer's desktop rather than the game.

Keyboard control means that the ship must move one step at a time. This is important in this game because a major factor is to avoid the falling bullets of the invaders.

We will use the left- and right-arrow keys for movement. We will also restrict the ship to staying at least 20 pixels away from the left and right sides of the screen.

Invader Movement

The invaders primarily move horizontally. When one or more invaders comes up against a side of the screen, all the invaders reverse direction. At the same time, they drop down the screen a little. Thus, they approach their goal by staggering.

An important factor is that all the sprites must move in unison. So, when a single sprite determines that it is too close to a wall, it must send a message to all the sprites to drop and start moving in the other direction.

A Lot of Bullets

The player should be able to fire bullets at a certain rate. Certainly, this rate needs to be limited, or the invaders would never stand a chance. However, the player should be able to fire fast enough to have several bullets travelling on the screen at once.

This means that we cannot simply have one bullet sprite. Instead, we need to have a bank of bullet sprites.

By using a clever behavior, we can make these sprites work together to determine which sprites should be used when a new bullet is fired. The first sprite in the bank is always asked first: "Can you fire?" If the sprite is not being used, it fires and begins its movement. However, if it is already moving, it passes the message on to the next sprite. This sprite then either fires or passes the message on.

After a sprite reaches the top of the screen, or it hits an invader, it becomes inactive and is ready for the next time it is asked to fire.

Using this method, all we need to do each time a bullet is fired is ask the first sprite in the sprite bank to fire. From then on, the behavior assigned to this sprite and the others after it will pass the message along until a sprite takes on the responsibility of being the bullet.

We use this same strategy for the bullets fired by the invaders. All you need to do is to be sure that there are enough sprites available. For instance, if the player holds down the spacebar, how many sprites will be needed to display the maximum number of bullets that can appear at once? Figure this out, either by math or by trial-and-error and you have your answer.

Levels

This game requires more than one level. A novice user might not be able to destroy all the invaders before getting killed or before they land. However, most people will be able to clear the board. What then?

The second level can have faster invaders. Maybe there will be more of them, too. You can even have them in different patterns.

We can set this game up to support as many levels as you want to build. If a player clears the board, the movie goes to another frame for the next level. The sprite behaviors there are set to make that level more difficult.

Lives

In video games, you almost always get more than one life. That would certainly be expected in a game like this one.

When the player is hit with an enemy bullet, they lose a life. In addition, the game should pause for a second to allow the player to catch their breath. Then, the level should start over.

However, if the invaders land, the game should be considered over, even if the player has never died. You might decide otherwise, but the example on the CD-ROM works this way.

Special Effects

At least three sounds are needed. The first is for when the player fires a shot. The second is for when a bullet hits an invader. The third is for when an enemy bullet hits the player's ship.

In addition to the sounds, a little animation is traditional in a game like this. The invaders can switch between members as they march across the screen. To do this, you will need two members for each invader.

Making the Game

This game uses five behaviors. The game state is controlled by the frame behavior. There is a behavior for the invaders and a behavior for the ship. In addition, there is a behavior for the player's bullets and a behavior for the invader bullets.

Ship Behavior

The ship behavior is responsible for controlling the position of the ship. Because it monitors the keyboard to do this, we will also look for a key press that signifies the firing of a bullet.

The *on getPropertyDescriptionList* handler enables you to set a speed for the player's ship when attaching the behavior to a sprite. It also sets the fire sound. The "pFireDelay" parameter is the number of ticks that the player must wait before another shot is allowed. The smaller this number, the more quickly the shots will appear if the player holds down the spacebar. Figure 10.2 shows the Parameters dialog box for this behavior.

Figure 10.2

Set the speed for the ship behavior in the Parameters dialog box.

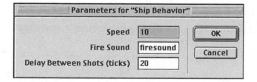

```
property pSpeed
property pFireSound
property pFireDelay
property pLastFireTime

on getPropertyDescriptionList me
  list = [:]

  -- how many pixels the ship moves at a time
  addProp list, #pSpeed,¬
    [#comment: "Speed",¬
     #format: #integer,¬
     #default: 5]

  -- sound to use when firing a bullet
  addProp list, #pFireSound,¬
    [#comment: "Fire Sound",¬
     #format: #string,¬
     #default: ""]

  -- how many ticks to wait before allowing another bullet
  addProp list, #pFireDelay,¬
    [#comment: "Delay Between Shots (ticks)",¬
     #format: #integer,¬
     #default: 30]

  return list
end
```

The "pLastFireTime" property is set in the *on beginSprite* handler. This property is used to determine whether it's too soon to fire another shot. When the user fires a shot, the "pLastFireTime" property is set to the current time, but for now, it is set to 0.

```
on beginSprite me
  pLastFireTime = 0
end
```

The *on exitFrame* handler mainly looks for keys that are pressed. If the left- or right-arrow keys are down, it moves the ship in the appropriate direction.

If the spacebar is down, the *on exitFrame* handler checks to be sure that it has been long enough since the last shot ① , and then sends a message for another shot to be fired.

NOTE

The *keyPressed* function is an alternative to using *on keyDown* to detect key presses. Instead of responding to an event such as *on keyDown*, the *keyPressed* function looks at the current state of the keyboard and determines whether a specific key is being held down. It is ideal for arcade games because you can detect multiple keys and determine whether they are being held down rather than just detecting the initial key press.

```
on exitFrame me
  -- left arrow
  if keyPressed(123) then
    x = sprite(me.spriteNum).locH
    x = x - pSpeed
    if x < 20 then x = 20
    sprite(me.spriteNum).locH = x
  end if

  -- right arrow
  if keyPressed(124) then
    x = sprite(me.spriteNum).locH
    x = x + pSpeed
    if x > (the stage).rect.width-20 then x = (the stage).rect.width-20
    sprite(me.spriteNum).locH = x
  end if

  -- check spacebar, plus check to make sure did not fire last frame
  if keyPressed(SPACE) then
    -- space, fire
①→ if the ticks < pLastFireTime + pFireDelay then exit
    if pFireSound <> "" then puppetSound 1, pFireSound
    sendSprite(6, #fire, sprite(me.spriteNum).loc)
    pLastFireTime = the ticks
  end if
end
```

Invader Behavior

The main purpose of the invader behavior is to keep the invaders moving. The movement is from left to right, then right to left, then left to right again, and so on. Each time the invaders change direction, there must be a small vertical drop as well.

The behavior keeps track of the current horizontal direction with the property "pDirection". It starts off as 1, and changes to -1 when the direction is reversed. The change in position for the sprite is "pSpeed" multiplied by "pDirection".

The property "pSpeed" is set through the *on getPropertyDescriptionList* handler. You can make it faster on harder levels. You should set the speed of every invader on the screen to the same amount, or you will have chaos on the screen. Figure 10.3 shows the Parameters dialog box for the invader behavior.

Figure 10.3
Set the speed
for the invader
behavior in the
Parameters
dialog box.

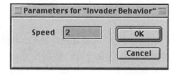

```
property pSpeed
property pDirection
property pMemNum
property pHit
property pOrigLoc

on getPropertyDescriptionList me
  list = [:]

  addProp list, #pSpeed,¬
    [#comment: "Speed",¬
     #format: #integer,¬
     #default: 2]

  return list
end
```

When the sprite begins, it remembers the original location in the "pOrigLoc" property. This will be used to reset the sprite should the level need to start over again.

The "pMemNum" property is set to the original member number as well, and it is used to create the two-member animation. The "pHit" property records whether the sprite is still alive.

```
on beginSprite me
  pOrigLoc = sprite(me.spriteNum).loc
  pMemNum = sprite(me.spriteNum).memberNum
  pDirection = 1 -- start moving to right
  pHit = FALSE
end
```

When the user dies, the level should start over again. The "on reset" handler is called for all sprites. This handler resets the sprite's location, the "pHit" property, and the "pDirection" property.

```
on reset me
  pDirection = 1 -- start moving to right
  pHit = FALSE
  sprite(me.spriteNum).loc = pOrigLoc
end
```

All the action takes place in the *on exitFrame* handler. It first checks to see whether the sprite is already out of action, and does nothing if it is ② .

Otherwise, it moves the sprite one step horizontally. It checks to see whether the sprite is now up against a side of the screen ③ . If so, it sends a message to the frame behavior.

This handler also swaps the member to create the simple animation ④ . The member is either the original member used by the sprite, or it is the very next member in the Cast.

Finally, based on a 1 in 300 chance, the invader fires a bullet ⑤ . This is passed on to the first invader bullet sprite's behavior. In this case, the sprite is number 55. If you change the location of this sprite, be sure you change this number as well.

```
    on exitFrame me
      if pHit then
②►     exit
      else
        -- move
        x = sprite(me.spriteNum).locH
        x = x + pDirection*pSpeed
        sprite(me.spriteNum).locH  = x
        -- hit a wall?
③►     if pDirection > 0 and x > (the stage).rect.width-20 then
          sendSprite(0,#hitWall)
③►     else if pDirection < 0 and x < 20 then
          sendSprite(0,#hitWall)
        end if
        -- toggle to other member to create animation
④►     if sprite(me.spriteNum).memberNum = pMemNum then
          sprite(me.spriteNum).memberNum = pMemNum + 1
```

```
        else
          sprite(me.spriteNum).memberNum = pMemNum
        end if
        -- fire 1 out of 300 times
(5)→    if random(300) = 1 then
          sendSprite(55, #fire, sprite(me.spriteNum).loc)
        end if
      end if
    end
```

If any sprite has signaled the frame behavior that it has hit the side of the screen, then the frame behavior notes it and signals back to all invaders later on in the code to change direction. The following handler takes care of that message, dropping the sprite down a bit as well.

```
on changeDirection me
  -- move down
  y = sprite(me.spriteNum).locV
  y = y + pSpeed
  sprite(me.spriteNum).locV = y
  -- hit bottom?
  if y > sprite(5).rect.top then sendSprite(0,#hitBottom)
  -- reverse direction
  pDirection = -pDirection
end
```

If a player's bullet intersects an invader, the invader sprite is notified through a call to the "on hit" handler. This handler displays the "Invader Hit" member for a moment, and then removes the invader member altogether. The "on hit" handler also sets "pHit" to *TRUE*, so this sprite will do nothing for the rest of the level.

```
-- called by bullet behavior to notify of a hit
on hit me
  sprite(me.spriteNum).member = member("Invader Hit") -- change to hit graphic
  updateStage  -- show now, since sprite will disappear next frame
  sprite(me.spriteNum).memberNum = 0
  pHit = TRUE
end
```

The last handler in this behavior is the "on invaderAlive" handler. This is called by the frame behavior every time an invader dies. The frame behavior is searching for an invader that is still alive and kicking. If it finds one, then it knows that the level is not yet over.

```
-- called by frame behavior to see if any invaders remain
on invaderAlive me
  return not pHit
end
```

Frame Behavior

The frame behavior keeps track of things that go beyond a single object. For instance, because all the invaders should change direction in unison, this event gets channeled through the frame behavior. The frame behavior also checks for and handles the case where the player dies, or the invaders land. The frame behavior is responsible for keeping track of the score as well. Figure 10.4 shows the Parameters dialog box that results from the *on getPropertyDescriptionList* handler.

Figure 10.4
The Parameters dialog box for the frame behavior.

```
property pHitSound
property pDieSound
property pEndLevelFrame
property pEndGameFrame

property pScore
property pLives
property pInvadersHitWall
property pInvadersHitBottom

on getPropertyDescriptionList me
  list = [:]

  addProp list, #pHitSound,¬
    [#comment: "Hit Sound",¬
     #format: #string,¬
     #default: ""]

  addProp list, #pDieSound,¬
    [#comment: "Die Sound",¬
     #format: #string,¬
     #default: ""]

  addProp list, #pEndLevelFrame,¬
    [#comment: "End Level Frame",¬
     #format: #marker,¬
     #default: #next]
```

```
addProp list, #pEndGameFrame,¬
  [#comment: "End Game Frame",¬
   #format: #marker,¬
   #default: #next]

return list
end
```

The *on beginSprite* handler initializes the number of lives remaining and the score.

```
on beginSprite me
  pLives = 3
  pScore = 0
  showScore(me)
end
```

When any invader gets close to the side of the screen, it sends the "hitWall" message to the frame behavior. This is noted by setting the "pInvadersHitWall" property to *TRUE*. This property is then used in the *on enterFrame* handler.

```
on hitWall me
  pInvadersHitWall = TRUE
end
```

The same idea is used when the invaders hit the bottom of the screen. In this case, the "pInvadersHitBottom" property is set.

```
on hitBottom me
  pInvadersHitBottom = TRUE
end
```

The *on enterFrame* handler is called just after the screen is drawn for the next frame. This handler is used to check for the case in which the invaders need to change direction, or have hit the bottom of the screen. In the first case, all the invaders are sent the message to change direction. In the second case, the game ends.

NOTE

The *on enterFrame* handler is called in every behavior just after the frame is drawn. It will thus be called for *every* behavior before the first *on exitFrame* handler is called of any behavior. This means that we can use it to execute code that needs to happen before all *on exitFrame* handlers are executed. In this case, we use it to change direction of all invaders before any of them has the chance to move.

```
on enterFrame me
  -- see if an invader hit a wall
  if pInvadersHitWall then
    sendAllSprites(#changeDirection)
  end if

  -- an invader hit the bottom
  if pInvadersHitBottom then
    go to frame pEndGameFrame
  end if

  -- reset wall hit flag for this frame
  pInvadersHitWall = FALSE
end
```

When an invader is hit, the "on addScore" handler is called to add to the score, update the text on the screen, and check to see whether the level is over.

```
-- message sent when an invader is hit
on addScore me
  if pHitSound <> "" then puppetSound 2, pHitSound
  pScore = pScore + 1
  showScore(me)
  checkEndLevel(me)
end
```

The level is over if all the invaders are dead. This next handler loops through all the sprites and sends the "invaderAlive" message to each. If it ever gets back a *TRUE* as an answer, it knows that an invader is alive.

Note that this is a very time-consuming process that works only in this case because we are not doing it very often. The only time the handler is called is when an invader dies; it's not called every single frame.

```
on checkEndLevel me
  -- loop through all sprites
  repeat with i = 1 to the lastChannel
    -- if one is still alive, look no further
    if sendSprite(i,#invaderAlive) then exit
  end repeat
  -- not invaders left, level is over
  go to frame pEndLevelFrame
end
```

The "on showScore" handler places the score and the number of lives left in the text member on the screen. The "on showScore" handler is called only when either the score or the number of lives left changes.

```
on showScore me
  text = ""
  put "Score:"&&pScore&RETURN after text
  put "Lives Left:"&&pLives after text
  member("Score").text = text
end
```

When the player's ship is hit, the "on shipHit" handler performs a series of actions. First, it displays a new graphic in place of the ship. In this example movie, we just use the same graphic that is shown for the exploding invaders.

Next, the number of lives remaining is changed. If the number of lives remaining is now less than 0, then the game ends. Otherwise, all the sprites are sent the "reset" message.

When the player dies, there is also a call to the "on freeze" handler. This handler performs a loop for two seconds, thus freezing the screen and the computer for that time.

This is not a good method for creating a pause. However, it is a simple method, and is used here to try to keep from complicating the game code further.

If I were making this game for my site, I would probably not use "on freeze", but instead have the movie go to another frame that displays a "Press Any Key to Try Again" button.

```
-- message sent when the player is hit
on shipHit me
  sprite(5).member = member("Invader Hit") -- ship explodes
  updateStage
  sprite(5).member = member("Ship")
  pLives = pLives - 1
  if pDieSound <> "" then puppetSound 2, pDieSound
  if pLives < 0 then
    go to frame pEndGameFrame
  else
    sendAllSprites(#reset)
    showScore(me)
    freeze(me)
  end if
end

-- pause all operation for 2 seconds
on freeze me
  freezeTime = the ticks + 120
  repeat while the ticks < freezeTime
  end repeat
end
```

Finally, the frame behavior has the responsibility of keeping the frame looping.

```
on exitFrame
  go to the frame
end
```

Bullet Behavior

As previously mentioned in this chapter, the bullet sprites exist as a bank of sprites. The first sprite in this bank is always the one that is asked to play the role of the latest bullet being fired. If it's busy already, it passes the message down the line until a sprite that isn't doing anything can act as the new bullet.

The following behavior is placed on all the sprites in this bank. The behavior starts with an *on getPropertyDescriptionList* handler that lets the author define the speed of the bullet. Figure 10.5 shows the Parameters dialog box that results. There is also an *on reset* handler that resets the bullet in the case where a player dies.

Figure 10.5

The Parameters dialog box is shown here for the bullet behavior.

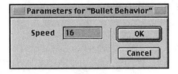

```
property pSpeed
property pMoving

on getPropertyDescriptionList me
  list = [:]

  addProp list, #pSpeed,¬
    [#comment: "Speed",¬
     #format: #integer,¬
     #default: 16]

  return list
end

on beginSprite me
  reset(me)
end

on reset me
  sprite(me.spriteNum).locV = -100
  pMoving = FALSE
end
```

The "on fire" handler is called when the player presses the fire key. It first checks the "pMoving" property to see whether the sprite is already firing. If it is, the "on fire" handler passes the message to the next sprite. If not, the sprite positions itself to where it is told, and the "pMoving" property is set to *TRUE*.

```
on fire me, loc
  -- got signaled to fire
  if pMoving then -- busy, send to next sprite
    sendSprite(sprite(me.spriteNum+1),#fire,loc)
  else
    sprite(me.spriteNum).loc = loc
    pMoving = TRUE
  end if
end
```

The *on exitFrame* handler checks to see whether the "pMoving" property indicates that the sprite is in use. If it is, then it moves vertically up, according to "pSpeed" ⑥ . A call to "on didIHit" checks to see whether the bullet hit anything.

```
on exitFrame me
  if pMoving then
    -- move bullet up
    y = sprite(me.spriteNum).locV
⑥→ y = y - pSpeed
    sprite(me.spriteNum).locV = y
    if y < 0 then -- reached top of screen
      pMoving = FALSE
    else
      didIHit(me) -- check for hit
    end if
  end if
end
```

The "on didIHit" handler loops through the invader sprites to see whether any intersect the bullet. The first and last invader sprites are hard-coded here as 30 and 53 ⑦ , respectively, so be sure to adjust these if you change your Score.

```
on didIHit me
⑦→ repeat with i = 30 to 53 -- loop through invader sprites
    if sprite i intersects me.spriteNum then -- see if it hit
      sendSprite(sprite i, #hit)
      -- get rid of bullet
      sprite(me.spriteNum).locV = -100
      pMoving = FALSE
      sendSprite(0,#addScore)
    end if
  end repeat
end
```

Invader Bullet Behavior

The invader bullets behave in an opposite way from the player's bullets. They move down, instead of up. They also look for an intersection with the player's ship, rather than with an invader sprite. Otherwise, you will recognize most of the code from the previous behavior.

```
property pSpeed
property pMoving

on getPropertyDescriptionList me
  list = [:]

  addProp list, #pSpeed,¬
    [#comment: "Speed",¬
     #format: #integer,¬
     #default: 16]

  return list
end

on beginSprite me
  reset(me)
end

on reset me
  sprite(me.spriteNum).locV = -100
  pMoving = FALSE
end

on fire me, loc
  if pMoving then -- busy, send to next sprite
    sendSprite(sprite(me.spriteNum+1),#fire,loc)
  else
    -- set loc, mode
    sprite(me.spriteNum).loc = loc
    pMoving = TRUE
  end if
end

on exitFrame me
  if pMoving then
    -- move down
    y = sprite(me.spriteNum).locV
    y = y + pSpeed
    sprite(me.spriteNum).locV = y
    if y > (the stage).rect.height then -- hit bottom
```

```
      pMoving = FALSE
    else
      didIHit(me) -- hit gun?
    end if
  end if
end

on didIHit me
  if sprite 5 intersects me.spriteNum then -- hit gun?
    sendSprite(0,#shipHit)
  end if
end
```

Putting It All Together

Each level of this game needs its own frame. Inside this frame, there should be three banks of sprites. The first bank is for the invaders; the second bank is for the player's bullets; and the third bank is for the invaders' bullets. In addition, the player's ship needs to be placed in the score as well.

The location of all these sprites is referred to by hard-coded numbers in the behaviors. Here is a list, then, of where the sprites should be located:

- Sprite 5: The Player's Ship
- Sprites 6–26: The Player's Bullets
- Sprites 30–53: The Invaders
- Sprites 55–75: The Invader Bullets

Any of these numbers can be changed, but the code would have to be changed in the appropriate place to reflect the difference.

After all the sprites are in place, the behaviors need to be dropped on them. Most of the behaviors require at least the speed of the element to be set. The frame behavior also needs to be dropped into the Score.

Note that the bullet sprites all need to be positioned off the Stage so that they are not visible. The invader sprites need to be positioned relative to one another so that they are in formation.

Remember to also add the second member for each invader. Don't forget to add the sounds that you want as well.

After a single frame has been built, you can then make the frames to represent other levels. If you want the last level to be repeated until the player dies, then you can just duplicate it and have those last two levels refer back and forth to each other. For instance, the frame for the seventh level can have the frame for the eighth level as the next level, and the frame for the eight level can have the frame for the seventh level as the next level. Thus, the user plays the seventh and eighth levels over and over until the game ends.

Game Variations

The rules of an invaders game are pretty tight. You can't really go too far with a variation before it becomes a completely different game. However, there are a few things you can do.

Different Orientation

Who says that up has to be up? The game could be showing a top-down view of the action. Instead of space, the screen could be a field and the invaders could be approaching insects.

Also, consider the possibility that the invaders are not moving down, but the player is moving up. The game is the same, but the background image moves down along with the invaders themselves. The illusion is that the player is slowly advancing while the invaders move back and forth.

Product Placement

What if the invaders were soda cans, soap, or groceries? The game would make little sense, but who says a video game has to make sense?

More Game Features

A good Lingo programmer can add a lot of features to make this game more complex. Extra lives can be awarded when the player passes certain scores. Other invaders can come flying across the screen to allow the player to score bonus points. Little boxes can act as shields that the player's ship can hide under. The example game presented here is actually fairly basic compared to some of the more complex invader-style games out there.

Space Rocks

CD-ROM File: 11spacerocks.dir

Useful Lingo in This Chapter

- ♠ Behaviors: Calling handlers in other behaviors
- ♠ Behaviors: Using parameters
- ♠ Graphics: Changing sprite members with Lingo
- ♠ Graphics: Making sprites disappear
- ♠ Graphics: Moving sprites
- ♠ Graphics: Using points
- ♠ Graphics: Rotating sprites
- ♠ Input: Accepting arrow keys
- ♠ Math: Using random numbers
- ♠ Members: Using a naming convention
- ♠ Programming: Collision detection
- ♠ Strings: Building member names
- ♠ Variables: Keeping score

This type of game has been around for a while, but is still seen as challenging. Since the early days of video arcade games, players have been piloting ships through star fields trying to blast asteroids and meteors before they get blasted themselves.

Although hardly educational, this game does require quick reaction times and lots of practice to master. It's also an easy game to learn, thus making it a favorite of sites that want Shockwave game content.

Game Overview

In "Space Rocks," you pilot a small ship in a field of large objects. If one of the objects hits your ship, you die. However, you can avoid the objects in two ways: You can blast them with your gun, or you can fly away.

Figure 11.1 shows a game in progress. The game started with four big rocks, but one was blasted into two medium-sized rocks by the player. The ship still remains in the middle of the screen because the player has not yet applied any thrust.

Figure 11.1
Space Rocks game in progress.

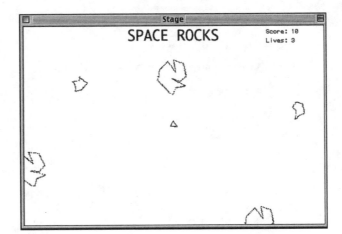

Ship Movement

The player's ship starts out in the middle of the screen. The player can rotate it in any direction. This determines both the ship's aim and its direction of movement.

The player moves by firing the ship's thrusters. When this happens, the ship gains momentum in the direction in which the ship is pointed.

The player can also fire a bullet in the direction that the ship is pointing. There is only a limited number of bullets that can appear at any given time, usually five.

Rock Movement

Rocks, like the player's ship, have both a direction and a speed. Unlike the player's ship, the rocks start off moving at the beginning of the level, and they don't stop unless they are hit by a player's bullet. They do not change direction or speed unless they are hit, in which case the big rock ceases to exist and two new rocks, with new directions and speeds, are created to replace it.

We use the term *momentum* to describe the case where an object on the screen is constantly moving. To easily handle momentum, we will break it into two components: horizontal momentum and vertical momentum. Combined, they can make the object move in any direction in the computer screen's two dimensions.

Breaking Rocks

Instead of just disappearing, as our sprite invaders did in the previous chapter, the rocks break into two smaller pieces when they are hit. The rocks start off as "big" size rocks, and then break into two "medium" rocks. When a "medium" rock is hit, it breaks into two "small" rocks. Finally, when a "small" rock is hit, it disintegrates.

We will do this by getting rid of the large rock, and placing two smaller rocks at the same location. These new rocks will have a random direction.

Screen Wrap

The screen is a finite space. However, the rocks need to keep moving in the same direction. So, what happens when a rock moves off the screen?

Although it breaks the "outer space" metaphor a bit, we take the rock and place it on the other side of the screen. It retains the same speed and direction. It just appears to have "wrapped" around to the other side.

This "wrap" happens for both the horizontal and vertical edges of the screen. The same idea is applied to the player's ship, but not the bullets the player fires.

Wrapping is achieved by simply adding or subtracting vertical and horizontal values. For instance, if the screen is 500 pixels wide, and a rock moves to a horizontal position of 505, we simply subtract 500 and place the rock at a horizontal position of 5.

Limited Ammunition

The player cannot be allowed to let loose an endless stream of bullets because it would make the game too easy. Instead, there should be a limit to the number of bullets allowed on the screen at one time. In addition, the bullets should be spaced apart in time a bit.

Because we are using a bank of bullet sprites, we just need to limit this bank to five sprites. In the Score position that would contain the sixth sprite, we place no sprite at all. This way, when the fifth bullet sprite asks the sixth bullet sprite to fire, the message just gets ignored.

In the sample movie on the CD-ROM, we allow only five bullets on the screen at one time. Not only does this enable us to predict how many sprites are necessary, but it makes the game more difficult for the player.

Levels

Like the game in Chapter 10, "Sprite Invaders," this game has levels of increasing diffi-culty. Each level is a separate frame. The frame behavior sets the number of rocks and the speed of the rocks higher for each level.

Special Effects

We have established that we will need at least three rock graphics: large, medium, and small. However, we will actually have two variations of each type. This makes the game screen look a little less uniform. After all, rocks are not supposed to be all the same.

In addition, we will put a spin on the rocks. It is unlikely that rocks in space will maintain the same orientation as they fly by, so a little spin makes them look more realistic. The spin is created by changing the *rotation* property of the sprites.

Sounds for this game include rock explosions and the ship firing. We can also have one for the ship explosion.

Making the Game

The code for the game is spread over four behaviors. The main behavior is the frame behavior. However, there are smaller behaviors for the rocks, the ship, and the bullets.

Frame Behavior

This frame behavior contains all the options for the game. The *on getPropertyDescriptionList* is the largest we have seen yet. It contains properties for the speed of the rocks ①, the num-ber of rocks to start with ②, the sprites that will be used by the rocks, the ship and bullets ③, the frames to go to when a level ends ④ or the user dies ⑤, and various sounds that can be used. Figure 11.2 shows the resulting Parameters dialog box.

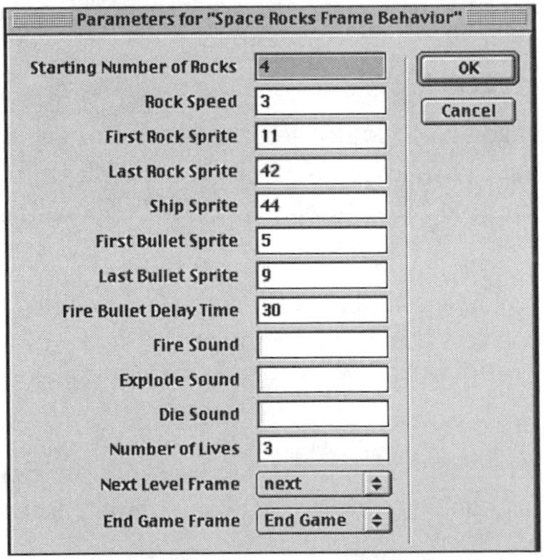

Figure 11.2
The Parameters dialog box for the Space Rocks frame behavior.

Parameters for "Space Rocks Frame Behavior"

Starting Number of Rocks	4
Rock Speed	3
First Rock Sprite	11
Last Rock Sprite	42
Ship Sprite	44
First Bullet Sprite	5
Last Bullet Sprite	9
Fire Bullet Delay Time	30
Fire Sound	
Explode Sound	
Die Sound	
Number of Lives	3
Next Level Frame	next
End Game Frame	End Game

OK   Cancel

```
property pStartNumRocks
property pRockSpeed
property pFirstRockSprite, pLastRockSprite
property pShipSprite
property pFirstBulletSprite, pLastBulletSprite
property pFireDelay
property pFireSound
property pExplodeSound
property pDieSound
property pStartingLives
property pNextLevelFrame
property pEndGameFrame

property pLastFireTime
property pSetUpFlag

global gLives, gScore

on getPropertyDescriptionList me
  list = [:]
```

(2)➤ `-- how many large rocks appear on the screen at the start`
```
    addProp list, #pStartNumRocks,¬
      [#comment: "Starting Number of Rocks",¬
       #format: #integer,¬
       #default: 4]
```

(1)➤ `-- how fast the rocks move`
```
    addProp list, #pRockSpeed,¬
      [#comment: "Rock Speed",¬
       #format: #integer,¬
       #default: 3]
```

(3)➤ `-- bank of rock sprites`
```
    addProp list, #pFirstRockSprite,¬
      [#comment: "First Rock Sprite",¬
       #format: #integer,¬
       #default: 11]
    addProp list, #pLastRockSprite,¬
      [#comment: "Last Rock Sprite",¬
       #format: #integer,¬
       #default: 42]

    -- player's ship sprite
    addProp list, #pShipSprite,¬
      [#comment: "Ship Sprite",¬
```

continues

continued

```
            #format: #integer,¬
            #default: 44]

    -- bank of bullet sprites
    addProp list, #pFirstBulletSprite,¬
      [#comment: "First Bullet Sprite",¬
       #format: #integer,¬
       #default: 5]
    addProp list, #pLastBulletSprite,¬
      [#comment: "Last Bullet Sprite",¬
       #format: #integer,¬
       #default: 9]

    -- how many ticks to wait until next shot allowed
    addProp list, #pFireDelay,¬
      [#comment: "Fire Bullet Delay Time",¬
       #format: #integer,¬
       #default: 30]

    -- sounds
    addProp list, #pFireSound,¬
      [#comment: "Fire Sound",¬
       #format: #string,¬
       #default: ""]
    addProp list, #pExplodeSound,¬
      [#comment: "Explode Sound",¬
       #format: #string,¬
       #default: ""]
    addProp list, #pDieSound,¬
      [#comment: "Die Sound",¬
       #format: #string,¬
       #default: ""]

    -- number of lives, only for use in first level
    addProp list, #pStartingLives,¬
      [#comment: "Number of Lives",¬
       #format: #integer,¬
       #default: 0]

④→ -- frame to go to when all rocks are gone
    addProp list, #pNextLevelFrame,¬
      [#comment: "Next Level Frame",¬
       #format: #marker,¬
       #default: #next]
```

⑤ ━━► ‑‑ frame to go to when lives run out
```
    addProp list, #pEndGameFrame,¬
      [#comment: "End Game Frame",¬
      #format: #marker,¬
      #default: #next]


    return list
  end
```

In this game, each frame represents a level. Therefore, the properties shown previously can be set differently for each frame, making each level harder.

The frame for the first level should have its "pStartLives" set to a nonzero value, such as 3. This starts the global variable "gLives" off at that value. All other frames should have the "pStartLives" property set to 0, which causes the *on beginSprite* handler to not reset "gLives" ⑥ .

The *on beginSprite* handler would normally set up everything in the frame. However, because this would require sending messages to other sprites, it's an impossible task. This is because the *on beginSprite* handler for the frame behavior executes before the sprites have been initialized. So, any messages sent to a sprite would be ignored.

Instead, we will send these messages in the *on exitFrame* handler. However, because this handler executes every single time the frame loops, we will use a property called "pSetupFlag" to be sure it sets up the sprites in the frame only the first time the frame loops. We set "pSetupFlag" to *TRUE* in the *on beginSprite* handler ⑦ . Then, when the "on setup" handler is called by the *on exitFrame* handler, it sets "pSetupFlag" to *FALSE*. After it is set to *FALSE*, the "on setup" handler knows not to execute its code again. Thus, the setup is performed only once.

```
  -- set score, lives, and prime for setup
  on beginSprite me
```
⑥ ━━►`  if pStartingLives <> 0 then`
```
      gLives = pStartingLives
    gScore = 0
    end if
    showScore(me)
    pLastFireTime = 0
```
⑦ ━━►`  pSetupFlag = TRUE -- set up rocks on next exitFrame`
```
  end
```

The "on setup" handler sends messages to the appropriate number of rock sprites. These sprites then become visible rocks that have a random location and direction.

```
  -- create initial set of rocks
  on setup me
    repeat with i = 1 to pStartNumRocks
      sendSprite(pFirstRockSprite,#randomRock,pRockSpeed)
```

```
   end repeat
   pSetupFlag = FALSE -- setup complete
end
```

The frame behavior is responsible for detecting the user's input on the keyboard. The left- and right-arrow keys are used to rotate the ship ⑧ . The up arrow is used to fire the thrusters ⑨ . The down arrow is used to stop the ship ⑩ . The spacebar is used to fire a bullet ⑪ . All these events, except the last, result in a message being sent to the ship sprite.

```
-- accept keyboard input
on keyboardInput me
```

⑧► ```
   -- rotate
   if keyPressed(124) then
     sendSprite(pShipSprite,#rotate,5)
   else if keyPressed(123) then
     sendSprite(pShipSprite,#rotate,-5)
   end if
```

⑨► ```
   -- move forward
   if keyPressed(126) then
     sendSprite(pShipSprite,#shipThrust)
   end if
```

⑩► ```
   -- stop movement
   if keyPressed(125) then
     sendSprite(pShipSprite,#stopShip)
   end if
```

⑪► ```
   -- fire bullet
   if keyPressed(SPACE) then
     fireBullet(me)
   end if
end
```

When the user fires a bullet, the "on fireBullet" handler is called. This checks to be sure that enough time has elapsed since the last firing to allow another. It then sends location and orientation information to a bullet sprite so that a bullet can be created ⑫ .

```
on fireBullet me
   -- only allow a fire if enough time has passed since last
   if the ticks > (pLastFireTime + pFireDelay) then
     if pFireSound <> "" then puppetSound 1, pFireSound
     -- use ship's angle and location for bullet
     rot = sprite(pShipSprite).pAngle
     loc = sprite(pShipSprite).pLoc
```

```
      angle = 2.0*PI*rot/360.0
      -- send message to bank of bullets
(12)-> sendSprite(pFirstBulletSprite,#fire,loc,angle)
      -- remember the time
      pLastFireTime = the ticks
   end if
 end
```

This next handler compares the locations of all the rocks against the locations of all the bullets to see whether any make contact. It uses the distance formula to compute whether a bullet is close enough to a rock ⑬ .

If a bullet makes contact, then the rock is destroyed, but two smaller rocks are created to take its place. However, if the rock is already the smallest type, then the two new rocks are not created ⑭ .

Although this handler is examining the rock sprites, it makes a note if it can find at least one rock. This is stored in the "rockExists" variable. If no rocks are found, then the level is over ⑮ .

```
  -- check all bullets and rocks to see if any collide
  on checkHit me
    rockExists = FALSE -- assume all rocks gone
    -- loop through rocks
    repeat with rock = pFirstRockSprite to pLastRockSprite
      if sprite(rock).pMoving = FALSE then next repeat -- this rock not being used
      rockExists = TRUE -- at least one rock still here
      -- loop through bullets
      repeat with bullet = pFirstBulletSprite to pLastBulletSprite
        if sprite(bullet).pMoving = FALSE then next repeat -- bullet not being used
(13)->  -- calculate distance
        dist = sqrt(power(sprite(bullet).locH-sprite(rock).locH,2)+¬
                    power(sprite(bullet).locV-sprite(rock).locV,2))
        -- estimate rock radius
        radius = sprite(rock).rect.width/2
        -- see if the two are close enough
        if dist < radius then
          if pExplodeSound <> "" then puppetSound 2, pExplodeSound
          -- what size should smaller rocks be?
          if sprite(rock).pSize = "big" then
            newSize = "medium"
          else if sprite(rock).pSize = "medium" then
            newSize = "small"
          else
            newSize = "none"
          end if
```

continues

continued

```
        loc = sprite(rock).loc -- get this rock's location
        sendSprite(rock,#die) -- remove rock
        sendSprite(bullet,#die) -- remove bullet
    ⑭→ if newSize <> "none" then
          -- add two smaller rocks
        sendSprite(pFirstRockSprite,#newRock,loc, ¬
pRockSpeed,newSize)
          sendSprite(pFirstRockSprite,#newRock,loc, ¬
            pRockSpeed,newSize)
        end if
        -- add to score
        gScore = gScore + 10
        showScore(me)
      end if
    end repeat
  end repeat
⑮→ -- if no rocks exist at all, then the level is over
  if not rockExists then
    go to frame pNextLevelFrame
    abort -- don't continue with Lingo commands
  end if
end
```

This next handler is similar to the last. Instead of checking the positions of rocks and bullets, it checks the positions of rocks as compared to the ship. If one is too close ⑯ , then the ship has been hit.

```
-- see if a rock is close to the ship
on checkShipHit me
  -- allow a grace period for new ships
  if the ticks < sprite(pShipSprite).pGracePeriod then exit

  -- loop through rocks
  repeat with rock = pFirstRockSprite to pLastRockSprite
    if sprite(rock).pMoving = FALSE then next repeat -- this rock not being used
    -- see if the two are close enough
    dist = sqrt(power(sprite(pShipSprite).locH-sprite(rock).locH,2)+¬
                power(sprite(pShipSprite).locV-sprite(rock).locV,2))
    -- estimate rock radius
    radius = sprite(rock).rect.width/2
    -- see if they hit
⑯→ if dist < radius then
      if pDieSound <> "" then puppetSound 2, pDieSound
      -- remove life
      gLives = gLives - 1
```

```
         if gLives < 0 then -- no lives left, game over
            go to frame pEndGameFrame
            abort -- don't continue with Lingo commands
         else -- still some lives left
            sprite(pShipSprite).member = member("ship explode")
            updateStage -- briefly show explosion
            sprite(pShipSprite).member = member("ship")
            showScore(me) -- update score
            sendSprite(pShipSprite,#reset) -- reset ship
         end if
      end if
   end repeat
end
```

The "on showScore" handler is a utility for updating the onscreen text with the current score and the number of lives left.

```
-- update text on screen
on showScore me
   text = ""
   put "Score:"&&gScore&RETURN after text
   put "Lives:"&&gLives&RETURN after text
   member("score").text = text
end
```

Finally, the frame behavior ends with the *on exitFrame* handler. This calls the handlers previous that need to do something each and every frame.

```
on exitFrame me
   if pSetupFlag then setup(me) -- initial setup of rocks (done once)
   keyboardInput(me) -- check keyboard
   checkHit(me) -- see if bullets hit rocks
   checkShipHit(me) -- see if rocks hit ship
   go to the frame -- loop on the frame
end
```

Ship Sprite Behavior

The behavior for the ship's sprite needs to handle all the messages from the frame behavior. These are all reactions to player key presses. In addition, the ship sprite behavior needs to keep the ship moving if the ship has momentum.

```
property pLoc -- sprite location
property pOrigLoc -- reset location
property pAngle -- sprite angle
property pOrigAngle -- reset angle
property pShipDX, pShipDY -- momentum
property pGracePeriod -- period where ship is invulnerable
```

The last property listed, "pGracePeriod", refers to a short span of time just after a new life for the player begins. During this short span of time, the ship cannot be hit by a rock. This grace period is used *every* time the ship is destroyed and a new one is created. It ensures that the player does not die immediately after being reborn just because a rock happened to be there at that time.

The *on beginSprite* handler saves the original location and direction of the ship for use when the ship is reset after being destroyed. It initializes the "pLoc" and "pAngle" properties as well, and starts the momentum, represented by both the "pShipDX" and pShipDY" properties.

```
-- get starting properties
on beginSprite me
  pOrigLoc = sprite(me.spriteNum).loc
  pLoc = pOrigLoc
  pOrigAngle = sprite(me.spriteNum).rotation
  pAngle = pOrigAngle
  pShipDX = 0
  pShipDY = 0
  pGracePeriod = 0
end
```

When the player dies, the "reset" message is sent to all the sprites. Some of our behaviors will handle this message and others will not. In the case of the ship's behavior, the ship is reset to its starting location and direction, all momentum is taken away, and a grace period of three seconds is started.

```
-- reset after a life lost
on reset me
  pLoc = pOrigLoc
  sprite(me.spriteNum).loc = pLoc
  pAngle = pOrigAngle
  sprite(me.spriteNum).rotation = pAngle
  pShipDX = 0
  pShipDY = 0
  pGracePeriod = the ticks + 3*60 -- invulnerable for 3 seconds
end
```

When the user presses the left- or right-arrow keys, the "rotate" message is sent to the ship. The "pAngle" property is changed and the sprite's *rotation* property is then changed to draw the ship sprite at the proper rotation.

```
-- rotate ship
on rotate me, angle
  pAngle = pAngle + angle
  sprite(me.spriteNum).rotation = pAngle
end
```

When the user presses the up-arrow key, it means that he wants the thrusters to push the ship forward. The "on shipThrust" handler determines the horizontal and vertical components of this thrust as variables "dx" and "dy." It then adds this to the "pShipDX" and "pShipDY" properties. No actual movement is performed here, only a change in momentum. It is the *on exitFrame* handler's responsibility to move the ship according to this momentum.

```
-- apply thrust
on shipThrust me
  angle = 2.0*PI*pAngle/360.0
  dx = cos(angle)
  dy = sin(angle)
  pShipDX = pShipDX + dx
  pShipDY = pShipDY + dy
end
```

NOTE

The *cos* and *sin* functions enable you to translate a point on a circle to a horizontal and vertical point on a grid. The *cos* function takes an angle and converts it to the horizontal position of the point on a circle, and the *sin* function gives you the vertical position of the point. Using these, we can get *x* and *y* values given just an angle.

A little thrust here and there can soon send the ship speeding off almost uncontrollably. To help the player out, we allow them to hit the down-arrow key to stop the ship. This simply means taking away all momentum.

```
-- stop ship dead
on stopShip me
  pShipDX = 0
  pShipDY = 0
end
```

The only responsibility of the *on exitFrame* handler is to move the ship. To this end, it takes the ship's current location and adds the momentum values ⑰ . It then checks to see if the ship's position is off the screen and wraps it around if so ⑱ .

```
-- move ship according to momentum
on exitFrame me
  -- get ship location
  x = pLoc.locH
  y = pLoc.locV
⑰ -- move
  x = x + pShipDX
  y = y + pShipDY
⑱ -- check to see if the ship is off the screen
  if x < 0 then x = x + (the stage).rect.width
```

continues

continued

```
        if x > (the stage).rect.width then x = x - (the stage).rect.width
        if y < 0 then y = y + (the stage).rect.height
        if y > (the stage).rect.height then y = y - (the stage).rect.height
        -- set ship location
        pLoc = point(x,y)
        sprite(me.spriteNum).loc = pLoc
      end
```

Rock Sprite Behavior

The rock sprite's behavior is mostly concerned with the same thing as the ship sprite's behavior: momentum. However, it begins with two handlers that deal with initializing the rock sprites. The first creates a big rock at a random position, with a random momentum ⑲. This is for the beginning of a level, when several new rocks are created at once.

```
      property pMoving -- is rock moving?
      property pLoc -- rock location
      property pAngle -- movement angle
      property pSpeed -- rock speed
      property pSize -- rock member size
      property pType -- rock member type
      property pRotate -- speed of tumble

      -- create a random big rock at the start of a level
      on randomRock me, speed
        if pMoving then -- pass to next rock
          sendSprite(me.spriteNum+1,#randomRock,speed)
        else
          pMoving = TRUE
          x = 0 -- between left and right sides
⑲ ➤     y = random((the stage).rect.height) -- any vertical location
          pLoc = point(x,y)
          pAngle = random(2.0*PI*100)/100.0 -- any angle
          pSpeed = speed
          pSize = "big"
          pType = random(2) -- one of two types
          pRotate = random(2) -- tumble 1 or 2 degrees at a time
          if random(2) = 1 then pRotate = -pRotate -- 50% of negative tumble
        end if
      end
```

The second handler that deals with rock creation is called when a large rock is broken into two smaller pieces. This "on newRock" handler creates a rock of a specific size at a specific location ⑳. The size is one less than the rock destroyed and the position is the same as the position of the rock that was destroyed.

```
  -- create a new rock at a specific location with specific size
on newRock me, loc, speed, size
  if pMoving then -- pass to next rock
    sendSprite(me.spriteNum+1,#newRock,loc,speed,size)
  else
    pMoving = TRUE
20▶ pLoc = loc
    pAngle = random(2.0*PI*100)/100.0 -- any angle
    pSpeed = speed
    pSize = size
    pType = random(2) -- one of two types
    pRotate = random(2) -- tumble 1 or 2 degrees at a time
    if random(2) = 1 then pRotate = -pRotate -- 50% of negative tumble
  end if
end
```

When a rock is hit, the sprite needs to note that the rock is no longer moving and move the image off the screen so that it isn't visible.

```
  -- take rock out of the action
on die me
  pMoving = FALSE
  sprite(me.spriteNum).loc = point(-100,-100)
end
```

The *on exitFrame* handler is similar to the ship sprite's *on exitFrame* handler. It just deals with the change in the ship's position due to its momentum ㉑ . It also provides the screen wrapping so that the rock is never off the screen ㉒ .

```
  -- move rock according to momentum
on exitFrame me
  if pMoving then
    -- get location
    x = pLoc.locH
    y = pLoc.locV
21▶ -- calculate movement
    dx = cos(pAngle)*pSpeed
    dy = sin(pAngle)*pSpeed
    -- move
    x = x + dx
    y = y + dy
22▶ -- see if the rock is off the screen
    if x < 0 then x = x + (the stage).rect.width
    if x > (the stage).rect.width then x = x - (the stage).rect.width
    if y < 0 then y = y + (the stage).rect.height
    if y > (the stage).rect.height then y = y - (the stage).rect.height
```

continues

continued

```
      -- set the location
      pLoc = point(x,y)
      sprite(me.spriteNum).loc = pLoc
      sprite(me.spriteNum).member = member("Rock"&&pSize&&pType)
      -- set the rotation
      rot = sprite(me.spriteNum).rotation
      rot = rot + pRotate
      sprite(me.spriteNum).rotation = rot
    end if
  end
```

One other thing that the *on exitFrame* handler does is rotate the rock a bit. This does not affect the momentum at all, but simply makes the rock appear as if it is tumbling. This is purely a special effect and does not affect the game play.

Bullet Sprite Behavior

The bullet sprite behavior does not introduce anything new. It uses the same basic method of handling bullets as the Sprite Invaders game from the last chapter. However, it is using the same horizontal and vertical momentum as the ship and the rocks.

The "on fire" handler deals with creating a new bullet. It passes the message on if the current sprite is too busy ㉓ .

```
property pMoving -- is bullet being used?
property pLoc -- sprite location
property pAngle -- movement angle


-- fire a new bullet
on fire me, loc, angle
  if pMoving then -- pass on to next sprite
      sendSprite(me.spriteNum+1,#fire,loc,angle)
    else
      -- start moving
      pMoving = TRUE
      pLoc = loc
      pAngle = angle
    end if
  end
```

When the bullet hits something, or leaves the screen, it is reset.

```
-- remove bullet
on die me
  pMoving = FALSE
  sprite(me.spriteNum).loc = point(-100,-100)
end
```

The *on exitFrame* handler moves the bullet sprite according to momentum ㉔ and also checks to see whether the bullet has left the screen ㉕ .

```
-- move bullet according to momentum
on exitFrame me
  if pMoving then
    -- get location
    x = pLoc.locH
    y = pLoc.locV
    -- calculate movement
    dx = cos(pAngle)*10.0
    dy = sin(pAngle)*10.0
    -- move
    x = x + dx
    y = y + dy
    -- see if the bullet is off the screen
    if (x < 0 or x > (the stage).rect.width) or¬
      (y < 0 or y > (the stage).rect.height) then
      -- bullets do not loop around screen, they die instead
      die(me)
    else
      -- set location
      pLoc = point(x,y)
      sprite(me.spriteNum).loc = pLoc
    end if
  end if
end
```

Putting It All Together

As with Sprite Invaders, this game requires one frame for every level. Place the frame behavior on the frame, and then start adding the sprites.

In the sample movie on the CD-ROM, sprites 5 through 9 are used as the bullet sprites. Then, sprites 11 through 42 are used as the rock sprites. This allows for a maximum of 32 rocks on the screen at one time. Because each big rock can eventually give birth to four small rocks, 32 sprites can handle an initial value of 8 big rocks.

Sprite 44 is used as the ship sprite. It is placed in a higher-numbered channel so that it appears above any rocks or bullets on the screen.

The "score" text member is placed in sprite 3, which places it underneath passing rocks, bullets, and the ship.

After several levels have been laid out, the first level is set to have a "pStartingLives" value of 3. The rest of the frames have this set to 0, so that the number of lives and the score are not reset.

Each frame has "next" as the frame for the next level, but the "End Game" frame for the game over frame.

Instead of having the levels go immediately from one to the next, you might want to have an intermediate "get ready for the next level" frame in between. This also enables you to loop and repeat the last level over and over again instead of just ending the game after three levels.

Game Variations

This version of Space Rocks does not have all the bells and whistles of similar games. Adding these could considerably increase the amount of code. However, I would be remiss if I did not mention them.

Shields

The game already has a grace period built in for a short time after a new ship appears. You could also allow the user a limited number of shields that can be activated with a special key press. When the shield is up, the ship cannot be hit. You can use the same grace period code for this. For added effect, you might want to change the member that represents the ship to a bitmap that also shows the shield during this time.

Flying Saucers

You could have a flying saucer appear every once in a while that is worth extra points. A simple one could just behave like a rock, except that it flies across the screen only once. A more complex one can change direction, and even shoot bullets back at the player.

Thruster Graphics

You can have a second ship graphic member that represents the ship while the thrusters are being fired. This member is put in place of the ship while the user holds down the up-arrow key.

More Rock Variations

The sample game includes two variations of each size of rock. You can have just one variation, to keep the file size down. You can also have many more variations to enrich the game. Just be sure you name the new variations properly and change the code to reflect that it has more than two choices for each rock. You could even have the rocks change as the player moves up levels.

Using Vector Shapes

Instead of using bitmap shapes for the rocks, you can use vector shape members. There are two main advantages to this. The first is that they draw nicely no matter what angle the sprite is set to. The second is that you can accurately detect whether a bullet has hit one rather than using the distance formula estimate.

With a vector shape, you can use *hitTest* to determine whether any point on the Stage is inside the boundaries of the vector shape.

Paddle Bricks

12

CD-ROM File: 12paddlebricks.dir

Useful Lingo in This Chapter

- ♠ Behaviors: Calling handlers in other behaviors
- ♠ Behaviors: Using parameters
- ♠ Behaviors: Using a ranged parameter
- ♠ Graphics: Coloring sprites with Lingo
- ♠ Graphics: Making sprites disappear
- ♠ Graphics: Moving sprites
- ♠ Graphics: Using a rectangle shape member
- ♠ Input: Dragging with the mouse
- ♠ Programming: Collision detection
- ♠ Programming: Bouncing objects off walls
- ♠ Variables: Keeping score

The idea of a ball and a paddle goes back to the genesis of video games. Since the original "Pong," many variations have been used to keep the idea fresh. One of the most popular variations, almost more popular than Pong, is having elements on the screen, called "bricks," that the ball must strike and destroy.

Game Overview

This game consists of a paddle at the bottom of the screen that the user can move back and forth. The purpose of the paddle is to hit a ball that moves in two dimensions.

In addition, a group of bricks appear at the top of the screen that must be destroyed by the ball. The player uses the paddle to direct the bouncing ball and hit the bricks until all are destroyed. If the player misses the ball, it falls off the bottom of the screen and the player loses a life. Figure 12.1 shows the game in progress.

Figure 12.1
This Paddle Bricks game is in progress.

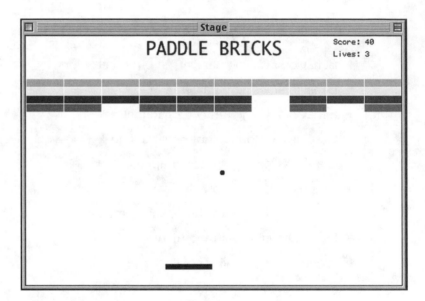

Moving the Paddle

The paddle's vertical position remains stationary, while the horizontal position matches that of the cursor. This is done simply by changing the *locH* property of the paddle's sprite.

The Ball

The ball must bounce off the sides and top of the screen. It should also bounce off the bricks.

It would be easy to have the ball also bounce off the paddle. However, a true bounce would mean that the ball bounces off in exactly the opposite angle from which it hit. If we used this standard law of physics, then the paddle would be little more than a device used to prevent the ball from falling off the screen.

Instead, we will change the angle of reflection according to where the ball hits the paddle. If the ball hits on the right side of the paddle, then the ball will fly up and to the right. If the ball hits the left side of the paddle, then the ball will fly off and to the left. The slope of the angle depends on how far from the center of the paddle the ball hits. So, if the ball hits in the center of the paddle, it will fly straight up. This enables the player to direct the movement of the ball.

Bricks

The only purpose of the bricks is to wait until the ball hits them. When it does, the brick disappears, the ball is reflected, and points are scored. When all bricks are gone, the level is over and the game should advance to a more difficult level.

The look of the bricks can vary from brick to brick. You can use different members. In the sample movie on the CD-ROM, a single one-bit member is used, but the brick sprites have different colors applied to them to make the game more interesting.

Levels

As with "Space Rocks" and "Sprite Invaders," one level is represented by one frame. The ball behavior has a setting for speed that can be increased for every level.

In addition, the bricks can take on a different layout for each level. You can place more bricks and make them worth different amounts of points. You can even place strange-looking bricks surrounded by normal bricks. The strange-looking ones can be worth a lot of points and play different sounds when hit.

Special Effects

In addition to being worth different amounts of points and using different members or colors, the bricks can also play different sounds when hit. You will probably not want to have a different sound for every brick, but rather assign points and sounds to groups of bricks.

This method enables you to have a musical-sounding game. Each row of bricks, for instance, can play a different note when hit. Unusual bricks can play tunes or explosion sounds.

Making the Game

Behaviors are necessary for the frame, paddle, ball, and bricks.

Frame Behavior

In this game, the frame behavior doesn't do as much as in the previous two chapters. It delegates collision detection to the ball sprite, because it is the only object that collides with anything.

The frame behavior is mostly concerned with working with the score and the number of lives, or balls, remaining.

```
property pNextLevelFrame
property pEndGameFrame
property pStartLives

global gScore, gLives
```

The *on getPropertyDescriptionList* handler enables you to set the number of lives that the player starts with. This should be set for only the first level. A value of 0 for the other levels should be used as a signal not to reset the lives and score. Figure 12.2 shows the Parameters dialog box that results.

Figure 12.2
The frame behavior Parameters dialog box.

```
on getPropertyDescriptionList me
  list = [:]

  -- number of lives to start with, or 0 if not first level
  addProp list, #pStartLives,¬
    [#comment: "Starting Lives",¬
     #format: #integer,¬
     #default: 0]

  -- next level
  addProp list, #pNextLevelFrame,¬
    [#comment: "Next Level Frame",¬
     #format: #marker,¬
     #default: #next]

  -- game over
  addProp list, #pEndGameFrame,¬
    [#comment: "End Game Frame",¬
     #format: #marker,¬
     #default: #next]
```

```
      return list
   end
```

When the frame starts, it determines whether the number of lives and the score should be reset.

```
on beginSprite me
   -- if pStartLives is not 0 then set gLives, reset score
   if pStartLives <> 0 then
     gLives = pStartLives
     gScore = 0
   end if
   showScore(me)
end
```

The frame behavior is in charge of incrementing the score and also displaying it.

```
on addPoints me, n
   gScore = gScore + n
   showScore(me)
end

on showScore me
   text = ""
   put "Score:"&&gScore&RETURN after text
   put "Lives:"&&gLives after text
   member("score").text = text
end
```

When a ball goes past the bottom of the Stage, the "on endLife" handler in the frame behavior is used to subract the life, send the reset message, and also determine whether the game is over.

```
-- missed ball, lose life
on endLife me
   gLives = gLives - 1
   if gLives < 0 then
     go to frame pEndGameFrame
   else
     showScore(me)
     sendAllSprites(#reset) -- send reset to ball
   end if
end
```

When all the bricks are gone, the "endLevel" message is sent to the frame behavior. The purpose for this is to keep the "pNextLevelFrame" property as a frame behavior property rather than separating it from "pEndGameFrame".

```
on endLevel me
  go to frame pNextLevelFrame
end
```

And, of course, the *on exitFrame* handler keeps the frame looping.

```
on exitFrame
  go to the frame
end
```

Ball Behavior

The ball sprite behavior is the main behavior in this game. It is in charge of the movement of the ball, and determining whether the ball hits anything. The ball sprite behavior checks to see whether the ball hits a brick, a wall, or the paddle, and whether it falls off the bottom of the screen. Each occurrence has its consequence.

```
property pMoveX,  pMoveY -- momentum
property pOrigMoveX, pOrigMoveY -- original momentum
property pOrigLoc -- original location
property pLoc -- current location
property pSpeed -- vertical speed
property pRadius -- radius of ball
property pPaddleSprite -- paddle sprite
property pMaxHitSlope -- slope to use when ball hits edge
property pPaddleSound, pWallSound
```

The ball behavior has a long list of parameters that can be set when the game is being created. Each of these can vary on different levels because the ball sprite exists individually on these frames.

The starting momentum is recorded in the "pOrigMoveX" and "pOrigMoveY" parameters. This is used to start the ball off at the beginning of the level, and is used to start a new ball after the player misses one. The channel number for the paddle sprite is also asked for.

The "pMaxHitSlope" determines how steep the angle at which the ball will fly off will be when it hits the paddle. This value is equivalent to the horizontal speed of the ball. The parameter "pSpeed" determines the vertical speed of the ball.

Two sounds are also asked for. You can use the same sound for the ball hitting the wall or the paddle, or you can come up with two different sounds. Figure 12.3 shows the resulting Parameters dialog box.

Figure 12.3
The ball behavior Parameters dialog box.

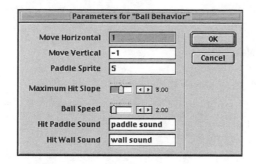

```
on getPropertyDescriptionList me
  list = [:]

  -- direction of initial movement
  addProp list, #pOrigMoveX,¬
    [#comment: "Move Horizontal",¬
     #format: #integer,¬
     #default: 1]
  addProp list, #pOrigMoveY,¬
    [#comment: "Move Vertical",¬
     #format: #integer,¬
     #default: -1]

  -- paddle sprite
  addProp list, #pPaddleSprite,¬
    [#comment: "Paddle Sprite",¬
     #format: #integer,¬
     #default: 5]

  -- how much of an angle will ball fly off at if the
  -- ball hits the edge of the paddle
  addProp list, #pMaxHitSlope,¬
    [#comment: "Maximum Hit Slope",¬
     #format: #float,¬
     #range: [#min: 1.0, #max: 5.0],¬
     #default: 3.0]

  -- vertical speed of ball
  addProp list, #pSpeed,¬
    [#comment: "Ball Speed",¬
     #format: #float,¬
     #range: [#min: 1.0, #max: 8.0],¬
     #default: 2.0]
```

continues

continued

```
-- hit paddle sound
addProp list, #pPaddleSound,¬
  [#comment: "Hit Paddle Sound",¬
   #format: #string,¬
   #default: ""]

-- hit wall sound
addProp list, #pWallSound,¬
  [#comment: "Hit Wall Sound",¬
   #format: #string,¬
   #default: ""]

return list
end
```

The ball sprite starts off by recording the original position of the ball and getting its radius for future reference in other handlers. It then calls "on reset" to set the location and momentum of the ball.

```
-- record original location, get radius
on beginSprite me
  pOrigLoc = sprite(me.spriteNum).loc
  pRadius = sprite(me.spriteNum).width / 2
  reset(me)
end

-- start momentum and current position
on reset me
  pMoveX = pOrigMoveX
  pMoveY = pOrigMoveY
  pLoc = pOrigLoc
end
```

The *on exitFrame* handler changes the position of the ball and then checks to see whether any collisions occur. Four handlers are called to determine collisions. Those handlers directly follow the *on exitFrame* handler in the script.

```
-- move ball and check for impact
on exitFrame me
  pLoc = pLoc + pSpeed*point(pMoveX,pMoveY)
  checkHitSides(me) -- hit sides of screen
  checkHitPaddle(me) -- hit paddle
  checkMissedBall(me) -- fell through bottom
  sprite(me.spriteNum).loc = pLoc -- set new location
  checkHitBricks(me) -- hit a brick
end
```

NOTE

Notice that you can multiply structures such as points and rects by regular numbers. The result is the same type of structure, but with each value inside it individually multiplied by the number. So, multiplying point(5,9) by 2 results in point(10,18).

The "on checkHitSides" handler determines whether the ball has hit the top, left, or right sides of the screen. It does a lot more that just detect it, actually. It also computes how much past the edge the ball went ① and resets its position to match where the ball should be in real life ② . It then reverses the momentum in that direction.

```
     -- see if the ball hit the left, right or top of screen
    on checkHitSides me
①►   amountPastTop = 0 - (pLoc.locV - pRadius)
       if amountPastTop >= 0 then
         if pWallSound <> "" then puppetSound pWallSound
②►     pLoc.locV = pLoc.locV + amountPastTop
         pMoveY = -pMoveY
       end if

①►   amountPastSide = 0 - (pLoc.locH - pRadius)
       if amountPastSide >= 0 then
         if pWallSound <> "" then puppetSound pWallSound
②►     pLoc.locH = pLoc.locH + amountPastSide
         pMoveX = -pMoveX
       end if

①►   amountPastSide = (pLoc.locH + pRadius) - (the stage).rect.width
       if amountPastSide >= 0 then
         if pWallSound <> "" then puppetSound pWallSound
②►     pLoc.locH = pLoc.locH - amountPastSide
         pMoveX = -pMoveX
       end if
    end
```

The next handler checks to see whether the ball has hit the paddle. It uses the Lingo *inside* function to determine whether contact has been made.

If there is a hit, the vertical momentum of the ball is reversed. The horizontal momentum, however, is thrown away and totally replaced by a new value depending on where on the paddle the ball hit ③ .

```
     -- see if the ball hit the paddle
    on checkHitPaddle me
       if inside(pLoc,sprite(pPaddleSprite).rect) then
         amountPastPaddle = (pLoc.locV + pRadius) - sprite(pPaddleSprite).rect.top
```

continues

continued

```
        if pPaddleSound <> "" then puppetSound pWallSound

        pLoc.locV = pLoc.locV - amountPastPaddle
        pMoveY = -pMoveY

        paddleWidth = sprite(pPaddleSprite).rect.width
        ballHitSpot = pLoc.locH - sprite(pPaddleSprite).locH

        -- send off in a slope relative to how close to the center
        -- of the paddle the ball hit
        pMoveX = 3.0*ballHitSpot/paddleWidth
      end if
    end
```

If the ball falls below the bottom of the screen, it means that the player missed it with the paddle. The ball is lost and the "on endLife" handler in the frame behavior is called.

```
  -- see if ball is below the bottom of the screen
  on checkMissedBall me
    if pLoc.locV > (the stage).rect.height then
      sendSprite(0,#endLife)
    end if
  end
```

The goal of the game is to hit bricks. This next handler checks for that. It sends a "checkHit" message to each brick sprite. If any of these messages returns a *TRUE*, then it means that the brick was hit. The brick takes care of removing itself, but the ball behavior must handle reversing the momentum of the ball.

This handler also keeps track of the case where no sprites at all return a value. If a brick is hit by the ball, it returns a *TRUE*. If it has not been hit, but is still on the screen, it returns a *FALSE*. However, if the sprite is no longer on the screen, or the sprite is not even a brick, it returns *VOID*. If all inquiries return *VOID*, then the "someBricksRemain" variable is still *FALSE* when the loop is done, and the level is over.

```
  -- see if the ball hit a brick
  on checkHitBricks me
    someBricksRemain = FALSE -- assume all bricks are gone

    repeat with s = 1 to the lastChannel
      check = sendSprite(s,#checkHit,me.spriteNum)
      if check then
        pMoveY = -pMoveY -- bounce
      else if not voidP(check) then
        someBricksRemain = TRUE -- note that at least one brick remains
      end if
    end repeat
```

```
  -- if no bricks remain, then level is over
  if not someBricksRemain then
    sendSprite(0,#endLevel)
  end if
end
```

Brick Behavior

Bricks have their own behavior even though they do not move during the game. Using the parameters of this behavior we can make each brick play a different sound, and have each brick worth a different amount of points.

The behavior is also in charge of checking to see whether the brick is currently in contact with the ball. If so, the brick should disappear.

The *on getPropertyDescriptionList* handler just needs to find out how many points the brick is worth, and what sound to play when it is hit. Figure 12.4 shows the Parameters dialog box.

Figure 12.4
The Parameters dialog box for the brick behavior.

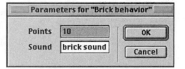

```
property pHit -- has brick been hit?
property pSound -- sound to play when hit
property pPoints

on getPropertyDescriptionList me
  list = [:]

  -- how many points is brick worth
  addProp list, #pPoints,¬
    [#comment: "Points",¬
      #format: #integer,¬
      #default: 10]

  -- how many points is brick worth
  addProp list, #pSound,¬
    [#comment: "Sound",¬
      #format: #string,¬
      #default: ""]

  return list
end
```

continues

continued

```
-- start off not hit
on beginSprite me
  pHit = FALSE
end
```

The "on checkHit" handler is called by the ball sprite behavior. If this brick determines that it has been hit, then it returns a *TRUE* after making itself disappear. If the brick is already gone, it returns a *VOID* instead of a *TRUE* or *FALSE* to notify the ball sprite behavior that it is no longer in play ④.

```
  -- see if the ball is hitting this brick right now
  on checkHit me, ballSprite
④►if pHit then return VOID -- already hit, don't check

  if sprite me.spriteNum intersects ballSprite then -- a hit
    sprite(me.spriteNum).loc = point(-100,-100) -- remove brick
    pHit = TRUE -- remember I'm hit
    if pSound <> "" then puppetSound pSound
    sendSprite(0,#addPoints,pPoints) -- increase score
    return TRUE -- I was hit
  else
    return FALSE -- I was not hit
  end if
end
```

The brick behavior is also in charge of sending the "addPoints" message to the frame behavior so that the score can be increased.

Paddle Behavior

The frame, ball, and brick behaviors take care of everything in the game except for one aspect: the movement of the paddle. This is simply accomplished by setting the horizontal location of the paddle to the horizontal location of the cursor.

```
-- paddle follows cursor
on exitFrame me
  sprite(me.spriteNum).locH = the mouseH
end
```

Putting It All Together

The sample movie on the CD-ROM has been set up with two levels. Each level has the ball in sprite channel 3 and the paddle in sprite channel 5.

The bricks are contained in a whole set of channels from 11 on up. The second level has more bricks than the first.

The bricks are also colored by changing the color of the sprites themselves. This is done manually in the Score. However, you could also use different members for the bricks rather than doing what I have by using the same member with a different color assigned to the sprite.

The frame behavior goes in the script channel for each frame. For the first level, set the number of lives to 3, but set it to 0 for all the rest. Also set the next level frame name for each, as well as the end game frame.

The paddle sprite behavior goes on the paddle sprite without needing any parameters filled in. However, the ball sprite takes a lot of parameters. You should have the ball speed increase with each level. You can also make the maximum slope value larger to match it.

Finally, you need to just add the brick behavior to all the bricks. If you have a set of bricks that share the exact same point value and sound, then you can add the behavior to all of these at once, and set the parameters for all of them at once. Otherwise, you have to set them all individually if they differ.

NOTE

If you need to change the parameters for a whole set of sprites, it is usually easier to use the Score window to remove the behavior from all the sprites at once, and then reassign the behavior to all the sprites at once. That way, you need to fill out the Parameters dialog box only once, and all the sprites will have the same values. However, if you select several sprites, bring up the behavior Parameters dialog box, and change something, this changes only the first sprite in the group.

Game Variations

You can do a lot of little things to make this game different from your standard paddle bricks game. Some of these don't even involve any programming, whereas others require some rewriting.

Decreasing Paddle Size

There is no reason why each level needs to use the same paddle graphic. In fact, you could make the paddle a little smaller for each level, thus increasing the difficulty of the game. You could even make the ball smaller as well.

Just create paddle members that are different sizes and use the appropriate one on each level. The behavior will recognize the sprite's paddle width and use it.

Colorful Arrangements

Don't underestimate the idea of being able to use any image as a brick. You could have bricks that resemble objects. Or, you could just have bricks arranged in interesting patterns. You can have sounds to match the image or color as well. Another idea would be to have an image behind the bricks that is revealed as the bricks are removed.

Turn It on Its Side

By changing all the horizontal Lingo properties to vertical properties, and vice versa, you could make this a game that plays from left to right instead of up and down. This is one way to make your version stand out. You could even place a paddle on both sides of the screen with a little programming work.

Multiple Balls

Instead of just having one ball on the screen at a time, some higher levels can have two. You can do this with the code as it is by just placing two ball sprites on the screen at once. However, the ball behavior will reset both balls when only one is missed. With a little extra work, the behaviors can be altered to accommodate this.

Part IV:
Word Games

13 Trivia Game **201**

14 Cryptogram **213**

15 Hangman **227**

16 Word Search **241**

17 Crossword Puzzle **259**

13

Trivia Game

CD-ROM File: 13triviagame.dir

Useful Lingo in This Chapter

♠ Behaviors: Using parameters

♠ Graphics: Making sprites disappear

♠ Interface: Using button down states

♠ Math: Using random numbers

♠ Strings: Storing data in text members

♠ Strings: Using items

♠ Strings: Comparing strings

♠ Variables: Keeping score

Trivia games for computers have become amazingly popular because they are simple to play and addictive. They are also undoubtedly educational, even if all you learn are a few trivial facts.

Trivia games can be easily made with Director. Because trivia games are essentially text-based, we will be using a lot of Lingo's string handling functions to create this trivia game.

Game Overview

The main aspects of a trivia game are the display of the question and the interface to let the user answer. There are many ways to do this, of course, but for our example, we will use questions with a choice of four answers. So, a sample screen will look something like Figure 13.1.

Figure 13.1
Each turn in the trivia game consists of a question and four possible answers.

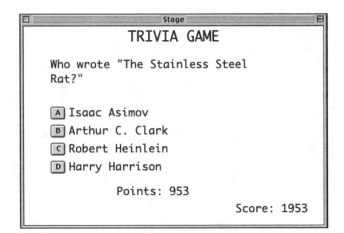

The Question Database

The hardest part of making a trivia game is actually not the code—it's coming up with the trivia questions themselves. It sounds easy enough to come up with a dozen or so, but you need at least a few hundred to make a decent trivia game. However, if you are making a short, educational questions-and-answers-game, you might be fine with only a dozen questions.

The questions should be plain text and in a format that makes it easy for a nonprogrammer to create them. This way, you can do all the work of making the trivia game, and someone else, or a whole group of people, can make the questions. In the sample game on the CD-ROM, the questions are stored in a text member, with one question per line. Here is an example:

```
What is the fastest animal on Earth?;Spotted Leopard,Cheetah,Giant Turtle,Llama;2
```

The format of each line starts with the question, followed by a semicolon. Then, there are the four answers, each separated by a comma. Finally, there is another semicolon and then a number that represents the position of the correct answer.

Screen Layout

Looking at Figure 13.1, shown previously, you can see the basic screen layout. There is the question above the four answers. Next to each answer is a button. When the question appears, the player must decide which answer is correct and click its button.

The question is a text member and so are each of the four answers. The button next to each answer is a bitmap member.

Buzzing In

In addition to the four buttons on the screen, the player will also be able to use the keyboard to answer the questions. Each button is mapped to a different key on the keyboard. Because the buttons shown earlier in Figure 13.1 are labeled "A" through "D," those same keys are used.

It's the responsibility of the frame behavior to handle keyboard messages. However, we'll use the button behaviors to map the keys to the buttons. To do this, we make the frame behavior pass on the key presses to the sprite behaviors, which will then determine whether one matches a button.

Time Running Out

To make the game more exciting, a timing element is involved. When the player is first asked the question, they can earn 1,000 points by immediately answering correctly. However, with each frame loop that goes by, the amount of potential points they can earn decreases by one. So, if they take one second to answer, and the movie is playing at 15 frames per second, they will get only 985 points. This adds a sense of urgency to the game.

Penalties

So, what if the player gets the wrong answer? Instead of just scoring zero points and moving on, they are penalized. If they answer incorrectly, they will have 100 fewer potential points. So, a player that takes one second to answer, but gets it wrong, and then takes another second to try another answer, and gets it right, will score 870 points. This is because they lost 15 points waiting the first second, then they lost 100 points with a wrong answer, and then they lost another 15 points waiting another second. 1,000–15–100–15 = 870.

Disappearing Answers

In addition to losing points when the player guesses wrong, they will also see that answer's button removed from the screen. This prevents them from choosing the same wrong answer twice. It also helps them think more clearly about the remaining answers.

Special Effects

We'll need sounds for both right and wrong answers. We'll also want to put a little thought into the answer buttons on the screen. Because they are the primary interface through which the user interacts with the game, they should behave somewhat nicely, with a down state and proper button behavior.

Making the Game

Only two behaviors are needed for this game. The main one—the frame behavior—controls the game flow, the questions and answers, the player's score, and the timer. The second behavior is the button behavior, which sends messages to the frame behavior and handles key presses.

Frame Behavior

The frame behavior only needs to know which member holds the question-and-answer data, and which frame to go to when the last question is over. In addition, you can supply two sounds to be used when the user attempts an answer. Figure 13.2 shows the resulting Parameters dialog box.

Figure 13.2
The frame behavior Parameters dialog box.

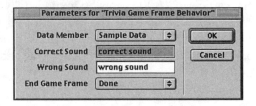

```
property pDataMember -- question text
property pQuestionNum -- current question
property pPossiblePoints -- points to add to score
property pScore -- current score
property pCorrectAnswer -- which is current correct answer
property pCorrectSound, pWrongSound -- sounds
property pEndGameFrame -- frame to go to when game is over

on getPropertyDescriptionList me
  list = [:]
```

```
addProp list, #pDataMember,¬
  [#comment: "Data Member",¬
   #format: #text,¬
   #default: VOID]

addProp list, #pCorrectSound,¬
  [#comment: "Correct Sound",¬
   #format: #string,¬
   #default: ""]
addProp list, #pWrongSound,¬
  [#comment: "Wrong Sound",¬
   #format: #string,¬
   #default: ""]

addProp list, #pEndGameFrame,¬
  [#comment: "End Game Frame",¬
   #format: #marker,¬
   #default: #next]
return list
end
```

NOTE

Notice how you can specify *#text* as the format for the "pDataMember" parameter. This results in a pop-up menu of text members. You can use other member types as well, such as *#bitmap* or *#sound*. If you use *#member*, a pop-up menu appears that contains all member types.

When the frame starts, the question number is set to 1, the score set to 0, and the first question is asked.

```
on beginSprite me
  pQuestionNum = 1
  pScore = 0
  showScore(me)
  askQuestion(me)
end
```

The "on askQuestion" handler takes the text from the member specified and extracts the question, answers, and number of the correct answer from it. It populates the question text member ① as well as the four answer text members ②.

```
on askQuestion me
  -- get the data
  text = pDataMember.text.line[pQuestionNum]
```

continues

continued

```
          -- reset all the button sprites
          sendAllSprites(#makeVisible)

          -- get the question, answers and correct answer number
          the itemDelimiter = ";"
          question = text.item[1]
          answers = text.item[2]
          pCorrectAnswer = value(text.item[3])

          -- display the question
          member("Question").text = question

          -- display the answers
          the itemDelimiter = ","
          repeat with i = 1 to 4
             member("Answer"&&i).text = answers.item[i]
          end repeat

          -- start the potential points at 1000
          pPossiblePoints = 1000
          showPossiblePoints(me)
      end
```

NOTE

The Lingo property *the itemDelimiter* specifies the character to be used to separate items in a text string. You can set it to any character, such as a semicolon or comma, and then use the *item* descriptor to extract segments of a string.

The next two handlers are in charge of updating the potential points text member and the score text member.

```
-- update the possible points display
on showPossiblePoints me
  if pPossiblePoints < 0 then pPossiblePoints = 0
  member("Possible Points").text = "Points:"&&pPossiblePoints
end

-- update the score display
on showScore me
  member("Score").text = "Score:"&&pScore
end
```

When the user clicks a button, the message is sent back to the frame behavior. The frame behavior determines whether the answer is correct.

```
-- see if an answer is correct
on clickAnswer me, n
  if n = pCorrectAnswer then
    if pCorrectSound <> "" then puppetSound pCorrectSound
    -- add to score
pScore = pScore + pPossiblePoints
    showScore(me)
    -- move on to next question
    nextQuestion(me)
    return TRUE
  else
    if pWrongSound <> "" then puppetSound pWrongSound
    -- subtract from potential score
    pPossiblePoints = pPossiblePoints - 100
    showPossiblePoints(me)
    return FALSE
  end if
end
```

When the player gets the right answer, this next handler moves the game on to the next question. If there are no more questions, it moves the game on to the "pEndGameFrame".

NOTE

To determine the number of elements in a string, use the *count* property. For instance, "myText.word.count" returns the number of words in "myText". You can also use "myText.line.count", "myText.item.count", and "myText.char.count". The latter example is the same as "myText.length".

```
-- move on to next question
on nextQuestion me
  pQuestionNum = pQuestionNum + 1
  if pQuestionNum > pDataMember.text.line.count then
    -- no more questions
    go to frame pEndGameFrame
  else
    askQuestion(me)
  end if
end
```

The *on exitFrame* handler needs to decrease points from "pPossiblePoints" in addition to looping on the frame.

```
on exitFrame me
  -- subtract from potential score
  pPossiblePoints = pPossiblePoints - 1
```

```
  showPossiblePoints(me)
  go to the frame
end
```

Because key press messages come to the frame behavior, we need to handle them here. However, the button behaviors will know which button responds to which key. So, we will send the "keyHit" message to all the sprites and let the button behaviors take it from there.

```
-- take any key presses and send to the button sprites
on keyDown me
  sendAllSprites(#keyHit,the key)
end
```

Button Behavior

The button behavior needs only to react to the player's input. This can come from either a mouse click or a key press.

This behavior resembles a typical button behavior more than anything else. It records the original member number as the normal state of the button. It assumes that the very next member is the down state of the button. When the user clicks down on the button, the down state is shown. When the user releases the mouse button, the action is taken. If the user moves off the button before releasing the mouse button, then the action is not taken, but instead the button is returned to the normal state.

The behavior starts off by gathering two important pieces of information in the *on getPropertyDescriptionList* handler. The first bit of information is which answer number the button corresponds to. The second is which key on the keyboard the button maps to. Figure 13.3 shows the Parameters dialog box.

Figure 13.3

The button behavior Parameters dialog box.

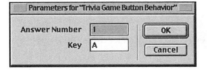

```
property pOrigMemNum -- normal member number
property pPressed -- whether the button is being pressed
property pAnswerNum -- which answer the button corresponds to
property pKey -- which key the button is mapped to

on getPropertyDescriptionList me
  list = [:]

  -- which answer number the button represents
  addProp list, #pAnswerNum,¬
    [#comment: "Answer Number",¬
```

```
        #format: #integer,¬
        #default: 1]

  -- which key the button is mapped to
  addProp list, #pKey,¬
    [#comment: "Key",¬
     #format: #string,¬
     #default: ""]

  return list
end
```

The behavior starts by getting the current member number of the sprite to be used as the normal state of the button. The "pPressed" property is used throughout the behavior to tell whether the button is currently being held down by the player.

```
-- remember original, normal, member
on beginSprite me
  pOrigMemNum = sprite(me.spriteNum).memberNum
  pPressed = FALSE
end
```

At the start of a question, the frame behavior asks all the sprites to reset by sending the "makeVisible" message. This resets the buttons to their normal states. This is needed because some buttons might have been removed due to wrong answers by the player.

```
-- respond to frame behavior's message to reset
on makeVisible me
  sprite(me.spriteNum).memberNum = pOrigMemNum
end
```

The clicking process starts when the player presses down on the button. The "pPressed" property is set to *TRUE* and the sprite's member is changed to the down state.

```
-- user clicks down on button
on mouseDown me
  pPressed = TRUE
  -- change to down state
  sprite(me.spriteNum).memberNum = pOrigMemNum + 1
end
```

The click process ends if the player lifts up the mouse button while the cursor is over the sprite. If so, the button is returned to the up state ③, and the answer is sent to the frame behavior to be checked ④. If the answer is wrong, we remove the button by setting its *memberNum* to 0.

```
-- user finished click
on mouseUp me
```

continues

continued

```
    if pPressed <> TRUE then exit
    pPressed = FALSE
    -- reset to up state
③→sprite(me.spriteNum).memberNum = pOrigMemNum
    -- check to see if the answer was right
④→if not sendSprite(0,#clickAnswer,pAnswerNum) then
      -- remove the button
      sprite(me.spriteNum).memberNum = 0
    end if
  end
```

Another way to end a click is to move the mouse off the button before releasing. In this case, we want to give the player the benefit of the doubt and assume that they did not want to click the button in the first place.

```
  -- user did not complete click
  on mouseUpOutside me
    pPressed = FALSE
    -- reset button
    sprite(me.spriteNum).memberNum = pOrigMemNum
  end
```

When a key on the keyboard is hit, the message is sent to the frame behavior. In turn, our frame behavior sends a "keyHit" message to all the sprites. When one of these button behaviors gets this message, it compares the key that was pressed to the key that the button is supposed to be mapped to ⑤. If they match, the button acts just like it has been clicked.

```
  -- respond to the frame behavior's "on keyHit" message
  -- if this button is mapped to that key
  on keyHit me, key
⑤→ if key = pKey then
      -- check to see if the answer was right
      if not sendSprite(0,#clickAnswer,pAnswerNum) then
        -- remove the button
        sprite(me.spriteNum).memberNum = 0
      end if
    end if
  end
```

Putting It All Together

Before even touching the Score, you need to set several members. You need a text member that contains all the questions and answers in the format mentioned previously. In the sample movie, this is called "Sample Data."

Then, you need a "question" member and four "answer" members. The latter should be named "answer 1", "answer 2", and so on.

You also need a text member called "possible points" and one called "score". Finally, you need four buttons, each with a bitmap for the up state and a bitmap for the down state.

After you have all these members, you can place them in the Score and arrange them on the Stage. Figure 13.4 shows the Score with these present. Sprite channel numbers are not important in this game because they are never referred to in the code.

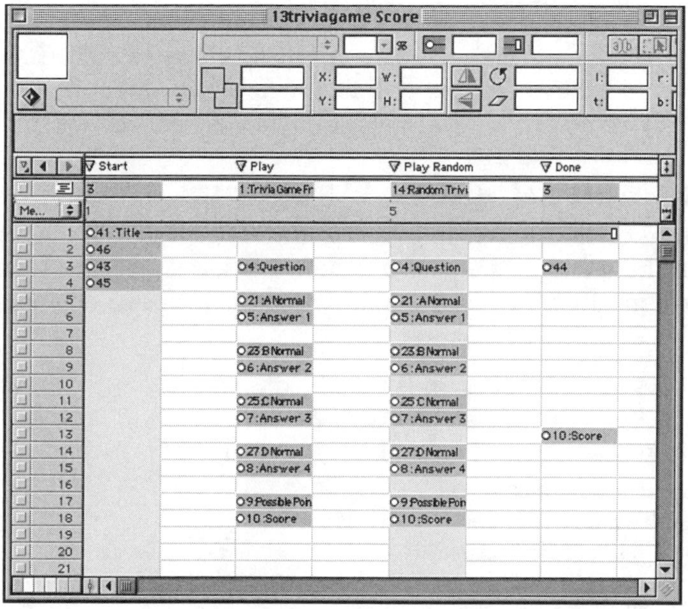

Figure 13.4

The Score shows all the sprites needed for the Trivia game.

All that remains is for you to drop the frame behavior on the frame and fill in the appropriate parameters. Then, drop the button behavior on the four buttons and set their answer numbers and key mappings. If you leave the key mapping parameter blank, it will not use that feature at all.

In the sample movie, the game also has a start frame and an end frame.

Game Variations

The biggest way that you can vary a trivia game is through the questions. They can represent one topic or many. They can be easy or difficult. They can even use humor to lighten up the game.

Besides the questions, you can vary the mechanics of the game in several ways.

Number of Answers

This sample movie uses four possible answers for each question. However, there is nothing in the code that specifies "four." You could just as easily use three. All you need to do is remove the fourth button and text member, and be sure that there were only three answers listed for each question in the database.

Levels of Play

When a set of questions is finished, the "pEndGameFrame" doesn't necessarily have to take the user to a "Game Over" frame. It can instead take them to another set of questions. You can then create multiple levels, with each level getting harder and harder.

With a little more coding, you could make the score cumulative instead of resetting after every frame. You can also count the number of correct answers on each level and let the user move on to the next level only if they get enough correct.

Randomizing the Questions

Instead of having a group of questions that get asked in the same order each time, you could have a large group of questions and have a random sampling of them asked. This would involve using the *random* function to choose a random question instead of using the "pQuestionNum" property.

To be sure that a question is not asked twice, you could store the number of each question asked in a list, and then use *getOne* to check to see whether the question has already been asked. It would look something like this:

```
repeat while TRUE
  r = random(pDataMember.text.line.count)
  if not getOne(pAlreadyUsedList,r) then exit repeat
end repeat
add pAlreadyUsedList, r
text = pDataMember.text.line[r]
```

You must remember to initialize "pAlreadyUsedList" by setting it to [] in the *on beginSprite* handler. You also have to add it to the property declarations at the start of the behavior.

If you look at the example on the CD-ROM, you will see that there is also a frame with this type of game on it. The behavior is called "Random Trivia Game Frame Behavior" and you can look at it to see the exact changes that were made to randomize the questions. If you turn off script coloring before loading the movie, the new lines show up in red.

You can also use a similar technique to randomize the order of the answers.

The Clock Is Ticking

One simple improvement would be a looping "tick" sound on the game frame. This should make it sound like a clock is ticking and increase the feeling of urgency.

BK CNAK SXQCRSV QX TKNG

ULQ TKNG RQZKMT.

Cryptogram

CD-ROM File: 14cryptogram.dir

Useful Lingo in This Chapter

- ♠ Behaviors: Using parameters
- ♠ Behaviors: Using a ranged parameter
- ♠ Graphics: Using a "reverse" ink sprite as a text cursor
- ♠ Input: Accepting arrow keys
- ♠ Input: Accepting typed input
- ♠ Lists: Using linear lists
- ♠ Lists: Using property lists
- ♠ Strings: Using ASCII codes
- ♠ Strings: Converting strings to uppercase
- ♠ Strings: Parsing strings
- ♠ Strings: Replacing characters in strings
- ♠ Text Members: Using monospaced fonts to align text
- ♠ Text Members: Using text members to store data

One of the most popular types of word games, cryptograms, are essentially puzzle games where the player needs to decipher the secret code to reveal the hidden message. It is easy to learn how to solve cryptograms, but they make such intriguing mind exercises that players can continue to play the daily cryptogram that appears in their local newspaper for their entire lives.

In addition, cryptograms lend themselves to many different themes because they can use any short phrase as the hidden message. This phrase can then be tailored to meet the needs of your CD-ROM or Web site. Cryptograms can also be used as part of a larger game, where it is just one puzzle to solve in a larger adventure scenario.

Game Overview

The cryptogram screen should consist of two overlapping text members. The first member displays the encoded message and never changes throughout the game. The second text member changes as the player guesses which letter matches which. Figure 14.1 shows the game screen with a game in progress.

Figure 14.1
The cryptogram game is shown here in progress. On a color screen, the higher letters are in red, and the lower letters are in black.

A third element on the Stage is the cursor. This is seen in Figure 14.1 over the first lower letter. It's a simple bitmap box member that uses the "reverse" ink to highlight the letter underneath it. The user can move this cursor and then use the keyboard to guess which letter matches which.

Encoding the Phrase

The message is a line of text that consists of letters, spaces, and some punctuation. We need to encode the letters and leave the rest alone.

To encode the letters, you randomly assign another letter to represent every letter. For instance, "G" can represent "A." This means that every place "A" is present in the message, the letter "G" is used in the encoded message instead.

The one catch is that we do not want to have a letter represent itself. So, if it happens that "A" is randomly picked to represent "A," you should encode the message again rather than leave it like that.

The encoding is done by starting with a list of the 26 letters of the alphabet. Then, each letter is assigned another letter as its encoded translation. The result is a property list that matches real letters to encoded ones.

After this translation list has been built, the phrase is translated into its encoded form and stored in a property variable. It is also displayed on the screen.

Displaying the Solution

Overlaid on top of the encoded message on the screen is another text member. This text member starts off containing underscore characters in place of letters. As the player guesses which letters go where, the underscores are replaced with letters.

As the player gets closer to solving the puzzle, this text member begins to resemble the solution.

NOTE

Why not use spaces to represent blank letters rather than underscores? A space is used by the text member as a possible location of a line wrap. This could mean that the solution text member could wrap in different places than the encoded text member, and the two text members will no longer line up. If you really want to use blank spaces rather than underscores, you might want to think about using the *color* property of text to color the underscores white, rather than black, thus making them invisible onscreen.

The Text Cursor

The interface needs to make it clear which letter the player is concentrating on. To do this, a small rectangular bitmap is used as a text cursor. It is placed on top of the text members on the Stage, and is set to use "reverse" ink. This has the effect of inverting the letter underneath it as shown previously in Figure 14.1.

This cursor needs to move during the game to point to which letter the player is concentrating on. We will provide two ways to do this. The first will be to allow the user to click on a letter and have the cursor move there. The second way will be to allow the player to use the arrow keys to move the cursor forward or backward in the phrase.

Phrase Storage

The phrase itself has to be stored somewhere in the movie to be used by the game. We could have it hard-coded in the behavior, or use *on getPropertyDescriptionList* to allow an author to set the phrase for each frame. However, both of these methods assume that we want to use only one phrase per game.

For this game, we'll store the phrase in a text member. As a matter of fact, we'll store many phrases in the text member. Instead of the game using only one phrase, it will present a series of phrases in either sequential or random order. These phrases will be stored, one per line, in a single text member.

At the start of the game, all these phrases are read into a list. If the game is to use them in order, it chooses the first phrase first, and removes it from the list. Then, when the player solves this phrase, the game asks for the next phrase.

In the case where the phrases are to be used in random order, a random phrase is chosen from the list, and then used and removed from the list. This happens until there are no more phrases left.

Capital Letters

In cryptograms, the distinction between uppercase and lowercase letters becomes problematic for both the puzzle maker and the puzzle solver. As a result, the phrase is usually presented in all uppercase, and no lowercase letters are used.

However, to help the person making the phrase list—whether that is you are someone else—we will allow the phrases to be in mixed case. Before the program uses the list of phrases, however, it will convert all the text to uppercase. So, by the time the phrases are used in the game, they are guaranteed to be all capital letters.

Likewise, we won't need to ask the player to use only capital letters. As a player presses keys on the keyboard to enter letters, these letters are converted to uppercase before being used in the game.

Special Effects

In this game, sounds are strictly optional. I have included no sounds, nor hooks for them, in the sample movie. However, you could certainly add *puppetSound* commands if you want.

Making the Game

All the code for this game is kept in the frame behavior script. Thus, the game lives completely in one frame.

The behavior starts off with the *on getPropertyDescriptionList* where it gathers information about the cursor and text sprite locations, the source of the phrases, the order in which the phrases should be used, and the frame to jump to when all the phrases have been used up. Figure 14.2 shows the Parameters dialog box this creates.

Figure 14.2
The Parameters dialog box for the cryptogram frame behavior.

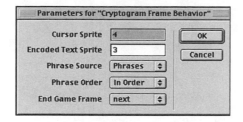

```
property pPhraseList -- list of phrases taken from text member
property pRealPhrase -- the actual phrase
property pEncodedPhrase -- the encoded phrase shown to the player
property pSolvedPhrase -- the phrase as the player solves it
property pCursorPos -- the position of the player's typing cursor

property pCursorSprite
property pEncodedTextSprite
property pPhraseSource
property pPhraseOrder
property pEndFrame

on getPropertyDescriptionList me
  list = [:]

  -- which sprite to use as the typing cursor
  addProp list, #pCursorSprite,¬
    [#comment: "Cursor Sprite",¬
     #format: #integer,¬
     #default: 4]

  -- which sprite to use as the typing cursor
  addProp list, #pEncodedTextSprite,¬
    [#comment: "Encoded Text Sprite",¬
     #format: #integer,¬
     #default: 3]

  -- the text member with the phrases in it
  addProp list, #pPhraseSource,¬
    [#comment: "Phrase Source",¬
     #format: #text,¬
     #default: VOID]

  -- what order to present the phrases
  addProp list, #pPhraseOrder,¬
    [#comment: "Phrase Order",¬
```

continues

continued

```
              #format: #string,¬
              #range: ["In Order", "Random"],¬
              #default: 3]

    -- the frame to go to when the last phrase is solved
    addProp list, #pEndFrame,¬
      [#comment: "End Game Frame",¬
       #format: #marker,¬
       #default: #next]


    return list
  end
```

The *on beginSprite* handler gets the phrases, sets up the first phrase, and initializes the cursor.

```
-- get phrases, set up the first phrase
on beginSprite me
  getPhrases(me)
  setUpPhrase(me)
  pCursorPos = 1
  showCursor(me)
end
```

The "on getPhrases" handler gets the phrase text member and stores all the text in a variable called "text." It then converts each of the characters in the variable to upper-case. Finally, it places each of the lines into an item in "pPhraseList".

```
-- read phrases from text and put into list
on getPhrases me
  pPhraseList = []
  text = member(pPhraseSource).text

  -- make phrases all capital letters
  repeat with i = 1 to text.length
    put convertToCaps(me,text.char[i]) into char i of text
  end repeat

  -- add each to list
  repeat with i = 1 to text.line.count
    if text.line[i].length = 0 then next repeat -- skip empty lines
    add pPhraseList, text.line[i]
  end repeat
end
```

The "on setUpPhrase" handler either takes the first item in the phrase list ①, or picks a random item ②. It then removes this item from the list so that it isn't used again.

Next, it creates a translation list ③. This is a property list in which each property is a letter of the alphabet and its value is the letter that it maps to. This translation is then applied to our phrase to encode it ④.

One thing that this translation list cannot include is a letter that maps to itself. If one is found ⑤, that is noted and a new translation list is generated ⑥. This keeps happening until a translation list in which each letter is mapped to a letter other than itself is created.

Finally, the handler builds the "pEncodedPhrase" property and the "pSolvedPhrase" property ⑦. The first is a text string in which all the letters have been encoded according to the translation list. The second is a text string in which all the letters are shown as an underscore. Both properties are placed in a different text member so that they appear on the screen.

```
-- set up a phrase
on setUpPhrase me
  -- get next phrase in list
  if pPhraseOrder = "In Order" then
①► pRealPhrase = pPhraseList[1]
    deleteAt pPhraseList, 1 -- remove phrase

    -- pick a random phrase from list
  else if pPhraseOrder = "Random" then
    r = random(pPhraseList.count)
②► pRealPhrase = pPhraseList[r]
    deleteAt pPhraseList, r -- remove phrase
  end if

  -- clear encoded and solved text
  pEncodedPhrase = ""
  pSolvedPhrase = ""

③► -- create random translation list
  repeat while TRUE
    translationList = [:]
    listGood = TRUE -- assume translation list is good

    --- make ordered list of letters
    list = []
    repeat with i = 1 to 26
      add list, numtochar(64+i)
    end repeat
```

continues

continued

```
        -- loop through letters and assign a random translation
      repeat with i = 1 to 26
        r = random(list.count) -- pick random
        addProp translationList, numtochar(64+i), list[r] -- add to list
⑤→    if i = r then listGood = FALSE -- if translation is a match, list is bad
        deleteAt list, r -- remove character from ordered list
      end repeat

        -- keep generating translation lists until one is good
⑥→  if listGood then exit repeat
    end repeat

④→  -- create encoded and solved phrases
    repeat with i = 1 to pRealPhrase.length
      realChar = pRealPhrase.char[i] -- correct character

        -- if it is in translation list, then translate
      if not voidP(getAProp(translationList,realChar)) then
        code = getProp(translationList,pRealPhrase.char[i])
        put code after pEncodedPhrase -- build encoded phrase
        put "_" after pSolvedPhrase -- build solved phrase

          -- if not in translation list, assume it is a space or punctuation
      else
⑦→    put realChar after pEncodedPhrase -- build encoded phrase
        put realChar after pSolvedPhrase -- build solved phrase
      end if
    end repeat

      -- assign encoded and solved phrases to text members
    member("encoded").text = pEncodedPhrase
    member("solved").text = pSolvedPhrase
  end
```

This next handler is a utility handler used by both "on getPhrases" and *on keyUp*. It converts a single character to uppercase. If the character is already uppercase, or is not a letter at all, it simply returns the original character. However, if it's a lowercase letter, it returns the converted character.

NOTE

The *charToNum* and *numToChar* functions convert single character strings to code numbers and vice versa. These code numbers are values from 0 to 255. These are called ASCII codes (American Standard Code for Information Interchange). Code 65 is a capital "A" and code 90 is a capital "Z." A lowercase "a" is 97 and a lowercase "z" is 122. Therefore, you can convert a lowercase letter to a capital letter by subtracting 32 from its ASCII value.

```
-- utility handler that takes a character and converts it to uppercase
on convertToCaps me, c
  ascii = charToNum(c) -- get character code
  if ascii >= chartonum("a") and ascii <= charToNum("z") then -- is it lowercase?
    c = numToChar(ascii-32) -- convert to uppercase
  end if
  return c
end
```

The *on mouseUp* handler takes a mouse click from the user and tries to reposition the text cursor to the letter underneath the mouse cursor.

First, the *on mouseUp* handler checks to see whether the mouse cursor is even over the text sprite. If it is, the handler uses *pointToChar* to determine which character the cursor is over and then the handler sets the text cursor position to that character.

If this character is not a letter of the alphabet, then the cursor position is set to 0, which tells the "on showCursor" handler not to display the cursor at all. The same is true if the mouse cursor is not even over the text member at all.

```
-- when the player clicks on the text, select that character
on mouseUp me
  if rollover(pEncodedTextSprite) then -- clicked on text
    -- get character clicked
pCursorPos = pointToChar(sprite pEncodedTextSprite, the mouseLoc)
    -- make sure it is not a space or punctuation
    if (" ,.-" contains pRealPhrase.char[pCursorPos]) then
      pCursorPos = 0
    end if
  else -- clicked outside of text
    pCursorPos = 0
  end if
  showCursor(me)
end
```

The "on showCursor" handler is responsible for setting the position of the text cursor sprite according to "pCursorPos". It uses *charpostoloc* to determine the pixel position of the character in the text member, and then adds the location of the sprite to that to determine the position on the Stage.

If "pCursorPos" is 0, then the text cursor is simply moved off the Stage completely, making it invisible to the player.

```
on showCursor me
  if pCursorPos <> 0 then
    -- select character
    sprite(pCursorSprite).loc =¬
      charPosToLoc(sprite(pEncodedTextSprite).member, pCursorPos) +¬
      sprite(3).loc
  else
    -- remove cursor from screen
    sprite(pCursorSprite).loc = point(-100,-100)
  end if
end
```

The *on keyUp* handler performs two tasks in this game. First, it determines whether the player has pressed an arrow key and moves the text cursor appropriately. Second, it accepts letter characters and applies those to the solution that the player is trying to piece together.

In the case of the arrow keys, the left- and right-arrow keys are distinguished by their *keyCode* ⑧ . Then, the "d" variable is set to the amount that the cursor should move. The cursor is moved this amount, and then a check is performed to see whether the cursor is over a valid letter ⑨ . If it isn't, the cursor continues to move in that direction. This prevents the player from selecting a space or punctuation. The handler also prevents the text cursor from pointing to a character beyond the end or before the beginning of the text.

```
  -- accept keystrokes to make letter guess and to move the cursor
  on keyUp me
    -- arrow keys
    if the keyCode = 123 or the keyCode = 124 then
      -- assign the character movement amount to d
⑧→  if the keyCode = 123 then d = -1
      else if the keyCode = 124 then d = 1

      -- keep moving the cursor until a valid character is selected
      repeat while TRUE
        pCursorPos = pCursorPos + d -- move cursor
        -- wrap from end to beginning or beginning to end
        if pCursorPos > pRealPhrase.length then pCursorPos = 1
        else if pCursorPos < 1 then pCursorPos = pRealPhrase.length
        -- if not punctuation, then cursor is done moving
⑨→    if not (" ,.-" contains pRealPhrase.char[pCursorPos]) then exit repeat
      end repeat
      showCursor(me)
```

The next part of the *on keyUp* handler takes a letter and places it into the solution. First, it converts the letter to uppercase. Then, it checks to see whether the letter is really a letter, not some other key. Next, it searches through the entire phrase to find every place where the same letter should be used and replaced by the letter in the "pSolvedPhrase" property ⑩ .

This means that if the player wants to replace the letter "G" with an "A," this game automatically does that throughout the phrase. A pencil-and-paper game requires that the user do this manually.

At this point, there is no check to see whether the player entered the correct letter. That would make cryptograms very easy.

```
-- make a letter guess
  else
    -- get capitalized key
    k = convertToCaps(me,the key)


    -- see if it is a letter
    ascii = chartonum(k)
    if ascii >= chartonum("A") and ascii <= chartonum("Z") then
      -- see if the cursor is over a valid letter
if pCursorPos > 0 then
        -- repeat through solved text and replace letter
        letterReplaced = pRealPhrase.char[pCursorPos]
⑩   repeat with i = 1 to pRealPhrase.length
          if pRealPhrase.char[i] = letterReplaced then
            put k into pSolvedPhrase.char[i]
          end if
        end repeat
        -- set text member
        member("solved").text = pSolvedPhrase
      end if

      -- check to see if the cryptogram is solved
      if pRealPhrase = pSolvedPhrase then
        phraseSolved(me)
      end if
    end if
  end if
end
```

When the *on keyUp* handler is used to replace a letter in the solution, a check is made to see whether the solution phrase is the same as the real phrase. If so, that means that the user has solved the cryptogram.

The "on phraseSolved" handler is then called to determine what to do next. If all the phases have been used, then the movie moves on. Otherwise, a new phase is presented and the cursor is reset.

```
-- if solved, then go to next phrase, or end game
on phraseSolved me
  if pPhraseList.count < 1 then
    go to frame pEndFrame
  else
    setUpPhrase(me)
    pCursorPos = 1
    showCursor(me)
  end if
end
```

Last, but not least, the *on exitFrame* handler needs to cause the frame to loop.

```
-- frame loop
on exitFrame
  go to the frame
end
```

Putting It All Together

First, you need to create a text member to hold the encoded text. Place some sample text in it—a phrase or just some randomly typed letters—so that you can position the member on the Stage.

You should use a monospaced, or fixed width, font for this member, because if you use a variable width font, the phrase will shift around on the screen as the user tries different letters in different places. In the sample game, I used an embedded version of Monaco. Another good font to use is Courier or Courier New. Also, set the text member to the default "Adjust To Fit" rather than "Fixed" size. This enables the member to grow larger for a larger phrase.

After you have this member on the Stage and ready to go, duplicate it in the Cast, and then drag this duplicate member to the Stage. You need to position this member so that it appears just over the other one. Set the ink for both members to "Background Transparent" so one can be seen through the other.

You should select the text in this member and change its color to red or something other than black to distinguish it from the text in the other member. Figure 14.3 shows the screen as it should look now.

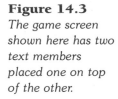

Figure 14.3

The game screen shown here has two text members placed one on top of the other.

The final element is the text cursor. It should be a rectangle about the size of a single letter in your text members. You might have to experiment with sizes until you get it just right. Place that in the Score as well, but in a higher-numbered sprite channel than the other two members.

The text cursor is set to be "reverse" ink in the sample movie. If you want to use a different type of cursor, such as an outlining box or an arrow pointing to a character, then you might want to use another ink instead.

To complete the Score setup, just drop the frame behavior onto the frame script channel. Fill in the Parameters dialog box with the sprite locations of the encoded text member and the text cursor. Also, specify the text member that holds the phrases. If you haven't made that yet, you can come back to the Parameters dialog box and set this later.

The text member with the phrases is the only other element needed. If you want to make this a one-phrase cryptogram, just include one line in the text member. Otherwise, include as many as you like.

Game Variations

As in many word games, the theme of this game can be changed by simply changing the content, rather than the code. In the case of cryptograms, you can have the nature of the phrases used suggest a theme. In addition, there are a few things that can be done to the code to make the game different.

Phrase Ideas

The types of phrases that can be used are limited only by your imagination. Here are some suggestions:

Humorous Quotations

Profound Quotations

Useful Sayings

Quotations in the News

Movie Titles

Book Titles

Song Titles or Lyrics

Trivia Facts

Adding a Timer

A clever programmer might want to attempt to add a timer to this game. The timer can either limit the amount of time the player has to figure out a phrase, or can subtract from the total amount of points that a player earns by solving a phrase.

This second idea is much like the timer used in the trivia game in Chapter 13, "Trivia Game." This turns the game from a quiet pastime to a hectic race.

Levels of Difficulty

Instead of having the entire game in one frame, you can have the game in several frames, each one calling on a different pool of phrases. Each of these phrase sets can be more difficult, adding more or fewer letters depending on which you consider more difficult.

You can also just keep the game in a single frame and order the phases from easiest to hardest.

Allowing Spaces

You might not want to limit the player to typing just the 26 letters of the alphabet. Instead, you might also want to allow them to use the spacebar to clear out a letter. This way, if they think that an "R" equals an "E," and then they realize that "E" is actually some other letter, they can position the text cursor over the "R," and press the spacebar to clear out all of the "R" letters, using an underscore for those once again.

Hints

With some additional programming, you could add a hint feature. Perhaps you could make it so that when the player hits a certain key, such as a question mark, the program will look to see which character is correct for that cursor slot and insert it.

Give Up

In addition to hints, you might want to allow the player to be able to give up. In this case, you should reveal the entire phrase. You can do this by writing a new handler that simply sets the encoded phrase to the real one and displays it.

```
I_ I HAVE _EE_ _A__HE_
_HA_ __HE__, I_ I_
_E_A__E I HAVE ____D __
_HE _H__LDE__ __ _IA___.

  BC  FG   K MNOPQRSTU
```

Hangman

15

CD-ROM File: 15hangman.dir

Useful Lingo in This Chapter

- ♠ Behaviors: Using parameters
- ♠ Behaviors: Using a ranged parameter
- ♠ Graphics: Changing sprite members with Lingo
- ♠ Input: Clicking on text as input
- ♠ Strings: Using ASCII codes
- ♠ Strings: Converting strings to uppercase
- ♠ Strings: Parsing strings
- ♠ Strings: Comparing strings
- ♠ Strings: Replacing characters in strings
- ♠ Text Members: Using text members to store data

A classic game for kids of all ages, Hangman combines grammar skills, probability skills, and sheer luck. Hangman is traditionally played by two players with pencil and paper. However, only one of the players is really playing the game[md]the other provides the word or phrase to be guessed and lets the player know whether letters he or she has selected are correct.

With a computer program, the game can be played with one player. The phrases are presented by the computer, which has the advantage of never tiring of playing.

Like cryptograms, the Hangman game can be used for a variety of different purposes ranging from education to pure entertainment. In addition, you can disguise a Hangman game to make it look and play like something completely different.

Game Overview

The idea of a Hangman game seems simple, but that's not the case when you start to think of all the elements required. You can see each of these elements in the screen shown in Figure 15.1.

Figure 15.1
The Hangman game screen is shown here, just after a player has lost.

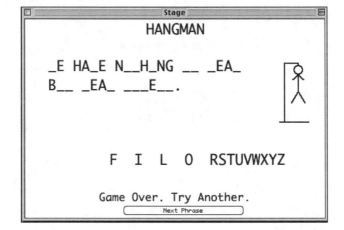

The Workspace

We will have a property in the game behavior that represents the workspace. In addition, we will place this text into a text member on the Stage for display.

Guessing Letters

Second, you need a way for the player to guess letters. You can use the keyboard for this, but because we cannot remove letters from the keyboard as the player guesses, it's better to have a visual element instead. This will be a list of the 26 letters of the alphabet.

The player will be able to click on any letter. As they make guesses, the letters disappear from the list. So, the list acts both as a set of buttons for the player to click, and as a reminder of what letters the player has yet to choose.

The Hangman

Next, you need the hangman graphic. The graphic starts as a simple line, representing the platform, but builds up to a full picture of a person swinging from the gallows. Figure 15.2 shows a sample set of bitmaps.

Figure 15.2

This set of bitmap members shows the Hangman at each stage.

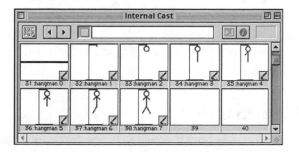

The Hangman is actually a series of eight bitmap images. The first is image zero, which represents just the platform as is shown at the beginning of the game. The other images add a bit of the picture until image number seven, which shows the full, gruesome, picture. We will name these in a standard fashion to allow the behavior to be able to figure out which image is needed at any given time.

The Message Area

In this game, you need to have a message area to pass along some information to the player. For instance, we want the game to be able to present more than one phrase. This means that the player's chance to solve one phrase will end at some point, but the game will not yet be over.

There is the situation where the Hangman is fully drawn, and the player has not yet guessed the phrase. In this case, the message "Game Over. Try Another." appears. At this point, the player cannot choose another letter.

The same situation arises when the player guesses all letters in the phrase. The player is not allowed to choose another letter at this point.

The message area relays to the user that they need to take an action other than guessing more letters.

Next Phrase Button

When the game is frozen because the player has figured out the phrase or the Hangman is complete, the player needs to be able to move on to the next phrase. For this purpose, there will be a "Next Phrase" button on the Stage.

This button can also be used by the player to abort any single phrase and move on early.

Phrases

Just as the cryptogram game (see Chapter 14, "Cryptogram") took its phrases from a pool of phrases in a text member, so will this game. Another similarity is that the phrases will be converted to all uppercase letters.

Special Effects

Sounds will really help this game to move along. We will use sounds for each of the two possible outcomes of a game sequence. We will also use a positive sound for when a player guesses a useful letter, and a negative sound for when a letter is guessed that draws more of the hangman.

Making the Game

Although there is a small behavior attached to the text sprite that contains the letters of the alphabet, the main script for this game is the frame behavior. This frame behavior is in charge of handling all aspects of the game except the keyboard interaction.

The Frame Behavior

There are many similarities between this frame behavior and the one for the cryptogram game. Our property declarations and *on getPropertyDescriptionList* reflect this, as we see many of the same properties show up.

We will have a "pPhraseSource" property that is a name of a text member. This member contains the list of phrases to be used in the game. The "pPhraseOrder" property works in the same way as in the previous chapter, too. The game can use the phrases sequentially, or in a random order.

In addition to these properties, there needs to be one that identifies the sprite channel location of the hangman graphic. There are also four sound properties to be used in various parts of the game. Figure 15.3 shows the Parameters dialog box for this behavior.

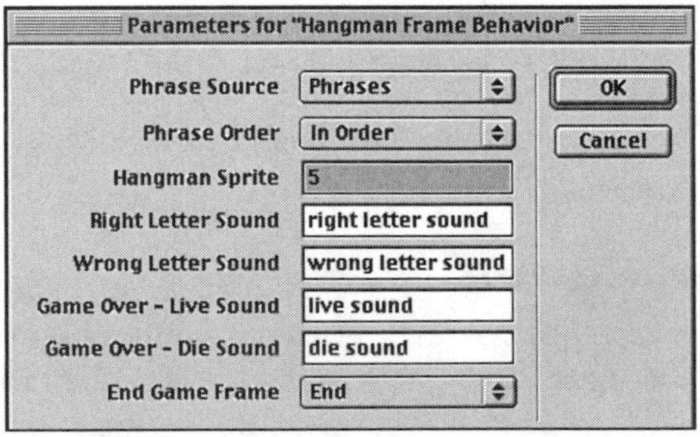

Figure 15.3
The Parameters dialog box for the frame behavior is shown here.

Parameters for "Hangman Frame Behavior"	
Phrase Source	Phrases
Phrase Order	In Order
Hangman Sprite	5
Right Letter Sound	right letter sound
Wrong Letter Sound	wrong letter sound
Game Over - Live Sound	live sound
Game Over - Die Sound	die sound
End Game Frame	End

```
property pPhraseList -- list of phrases taken from text member
property pPhrase -- the phase to be guessed
property pWorkspace -- the solution as it is being built
property pLetters -- the letters the player has used
property pHangmanNum -- progress of the hangman drawing
property pGameInProgress -- whether the player can make a guess

property pPhraseSource
property pPhraseOrder
property pHangmanSprite
property pRightLetterSound, pWrongLetterSound
property pLiveSound, pDieSound
property pEndFrame

on getPropertyDescriptionList me
  list = [:]

  -- the text member with the phrases in it
  addProp list, #pPhraseSource,¬
    [#comment: "Phrase Source",¬
     #format: #text,¬
     #default: VOID]

  -- what order to present the phrases
  addProp list, #pPhraseOrder,¬
    [#comment: "Phrase Order",¬
     #format: #string,¬
     #range: ["In Order", "Random"],¬
     #default: 3]

  -- where the hangman graphic is
  addProp list, #pHangmanSprite,¬
    [#comment: "Hangman Sprite",¬
     #format: #integer,¬
     #default: 5]

  -- sounds
  addProp list, #pRightLetterSound,¬
    [#comment: "Right Letter Sound",¬
     #format: #string,¬
     #default: ""]
  addProp list, #pWrongLetterSound,¬
    [#comment: "Wrong Letter Sound",¬
     #format: #string,¬
     #default: ""]
```

continues

continued

```
    addProp list, #pLiveSound,¬
      [#comment: "Game Over - Live Sound",¬
       #format: #string,¬
       #default: ""]
    addProp list, #pDieSound,¬
      [#comment: "Game Over - Die Sound",¬
       #format: #string,¬
       #default: ""]

    -- the frame to go to when the last phrase is solved
    addProp list, #pEndFrame,¬
      [#comment: "End Game Frame",¬
       #format: #marker,¬
       #default: #next]

    return list
  end
```

The behavior begins by getting the phrases out of the text member, and then setting up
the first phrase in the list. It converts the entire phrase to uppercase, even if it isn't in
uppercase while stored in the text member.

```
  -- get phrases, set up the first phrase
  on beginSprite me
    getPhrases(me)
    setUpPhrase(me)
  end

  -- read phrases from text and put into list
  on getPhrases me
    pPhraseList = []
    text = member(pPhraseSource).text

    -- make phrases all capital letters
    repeat with i = 1 to text.length
      put convertToCaps(me,text.char[i]) into char i of text
    end repeat

    -- add each to list
    repeat with i = 1 to text.line.count
      if text.line[i].length = 0 then next repeat -- skip empty lines
      add pPhraseList, text.line[i]
    end repeat
  end
```

To set up a phrase, the following handler first picks one from the list. If "pPhraseOrder" is "In Order," then it picks the next one in the list ①. Otherwise, it picks a random phrase ②. Either way, the phrase is removed from the list so that it isn't picked again.

Next, the "pWorkspace" property is built by calling our "on showWorkspace" handler. At the beginning of the game, this string contains the phrase, but with all underscore characters in the place of the letters. This string is presented in a text sprite, as well as a string of all the letters of the alphabet. The latter is built by calling "on showLetters".

In addition to these two text sprites, the message text is also cleared, and the hangman is drawn. Because this segment of the game is just beginning, the "pHangmanNum" is set to 0, and when the hangman is drawn, it's the first hangman graphic that is used, called "Hangman 0".

One thing that the "on setUpPhrase" handler does before anything else is check to be sure that there is a phrase left in the list. Because we will be calling this handler every time the user is done with one phrase and wants to move on to the next, this is the best place to check for this end-of-game condition.

```
-- set up a phrase
on setUpPhrase me
  -- make sure there are phrases left
  if pPhraseList.count < 1 then
    -- if not, advance the movie
    go to frame pEndFrame
    exit
  end if

  -- get next phrase in list
  if pPhraseOrder = "In Order" then
    pPhrase = pPhraseList[1]
    deleteAt pPhraseList, 1 -- remove phrase

    -- pick a random phrase from list
  else if pPhraseOrder = "Random" then
    r = random(pPhraseList.count)
    pPhrase = pPhraseList[r]
    deleteAt pPhraseList, r -- remove phrase
  end if

  -- clear workspace, letters and hangman
  pWorkspace = ""
  pLetters = []
  pHangmanNum = 0

  -- allow user to guess
  pGameInProgress = TRUE
```

continues

continued

```
            -- clear all screen displays
            member("message").text = ""
            showLetters(me)
            showWorkspace(me)
            showHangman(me)
        end
```

The "on showWorkspace" handler creates a string from scratch. The handler loops through each letter of the phrase and determines whether the letter is contained in "pLetters" ③. If so, the letter is added to the string ④. If not, an underscore character is added ⑤. The result is placed in the "workspace" text member.

```
      -- show the phrase in its current state of being solved
      on showWorkspace me
         -- recreate workspace each time
         pWorkspace = ""

         -- build workspace one character at a time
         repeat with i = 1 to pPhrase.length
           realChar = pPhrase.char[i] -- get correct character

           -- see if it is a letter
           ascii = chartonum(realChar)
           if ascii < 65 or ascii > 90 then
             put realChar after pWorkspace -- place non-letter

③→     else if getOne(pLetters,realChar) then
④→       put realChar after pWorkspace -- place letter

           else -- it is a letter, but not one guessed yet
⑤→       put "_" after pWorkspace -- put placeholder
           end if
         end repeat

         -- display the workspace
         member("workspace").text = pWorkspace
      end
```

The "on showLetters" handler works in a similar way. It loops through all the letters of the alphabet using ASCII values. If the letter is in "pLetters", then it has been chosen, and a space is placed in the string. Otherwise, the letter is placed in the string. The result is a string that contains only letters that have not yet been chosen. This is placed in the "letters" text member.

```
      -- show the letters that the user has not yet chosen
      on showLetters me
```

```
  -- start with empty string and build list
  letterText = ""

  -- loop through letters according to ASCII values
  repeat with i = 65 to 90
    letter = numtochar(i)

    -- place space if letter has been used
if getOne(pLetters,letter) then
      put SPACE after letterText

    else -- place actual letter if it has not yet been used
      put letter after letterText
    end if
  end repeat

  -- display letters
  member("letters").text = letterText
end
```

The "on showHangman" handler draws the hangman graphic on the screen. It takes the property "pHangmanNum" and determines which graphic to place in the sprite channel. If the handler figures out that the graphic is the last one in the sequence, it ends this portion of the game.

```
-- draw hangman graphic according to state of game
on showHangman me
  -- show a numbered bitmap
  sprite(pHangmanSprite).member = member("Hangman"&&pHangmanNum)

  -- if this is the last bitmap in the series, the game has been lost
  if the number of member ("Hangman"&&(pHangmanNum+1)) < 1 then
    if pDieSound <> "" then puppetSound pDieSound
    member("message").text = "Game Over. Try Another."
    pGameInProgress = FALSE -- do not allow more guessing
  end if
end
```

This next handler is identical to the "on convertToCaps" handler used in the previous chapter.

```
-- utility handler that takes a character and converts it to uppercase
on convertToCaps me, c
  ascii = chartonum(c) -- get character code
  if ascii >= chartonum("a") and ascii <= chartonum("z") then -- is it lowercase?
    c = numtochar(ascii-32) -- convert to uppercase
  end if
  return c
end
```

When the player clicks on a letter to try it out, the message is passed on to the frame behavior via the "on tryLetter" handler. This handler first ensures that a letter has been chosen ⑥ , and not a space or anything else. The handler then determines whether the letter is contained in the phrase anywhere ⑦ . If not, the "pHangmanNum" property is incremented. Either way, the letter is added to "pLetters".

This handler then calls both "on showWorkspace" and "on showLetters" to update all the text on the screen. The new "letters" text member will be missing the letter chosen, because it was added to "pLetters". For the same reason, the new "workspace" text member shows that letter in all the positions, if any, in which it appears in the phrase.

The "on tryLetter" handler is also responsible for seeing whether the "pWorkspace" property is identical to the "pPhrase" property. If they are, then the player has successfully guessed the phrase and this portion of the game is over.

You might also want to take note of the first code line of the "on tryLetter" handler. This checks to see whether the "pGameInProgress" property is *TRUE* before allowing the letter to be considered. The only reason that the "pGameInProgess" property would be *FALSE* would be if the current phrase on the screen had been solved, or if the hangman had been completed, but the player had not yet clicked the Next Phrase button.

```
-- message sent by text sprite click
-- allows the user to guess a letter
on tryLetter me, letter
  -- make sure this is still allowed
  if not pGameInProgress then exit

  -- make sure this is a letter and not a space or something
  ascii = chartonum(letter)
  if ascii < 65 or ascii > 90 then exit

  -- if the letter is not in the phrase, then advance hangman graphic
  if not (pPhrase contains letter) then
    if pWrongLetterSound <> "" then puppetSound pWrongLetterSound
    pHangmanNum = pHangmanNum + 1
    showHangman(me)
  else
    if pRightLetterSound <> "" then puppetSound pRightLetterSound
  end if

  -- add to list of letters guessed
  add pLetters, letter

  -- update screen
  showWorkspace(me)
  showLetters(me)
```

```
   --see if the phrase is complete
   if pWorkspace = pPhrase then
     if pLiveSound <> "" then puppetSound pLiveSound
     member("message").text = "Game Over. You Got It. Try Another."
     pGameInProgress = FALSE -- do not allow more guessing
   end if
end
```

The behavior also contains the usual frame loop code in the *on exitFrame* handler.

```
-- frame loop
on exitFrame
   go to the frame
end
```

The Letters Behavior

The sprite with the "letters" text member must have a short behavior attached to it to pass along letter choices. When the player clicks on the sprite, this behavior figures out which letter has been clicked and passes it along to the frame behavior.

```
on mouseUp me
   -- get the character position clicked on
   charPos = locToCharPos(sprite(me.spriteNum).member,¬
            (the clickLoc)-sprite(me.spriteNum).loc)

   -- see which letter that is
   letter = sprite(me.spriteNum).member.text.char[charPos]

   -- send it along to the frame behavior
   sendSprite(0,#tryLetter,letter)
end
```

The New Phrase Button Behavior

To allow the player to advance to the next phrase, there must be a button for the user to click. In the sample movie on the CD-ROM, this button is always available. The player can advance to the next phrase at any time, either when they are done with a phrase, or if they simply want to skip it.

The sample movie also places this script in a button cast member to make the Cast easier to view. However, you can place it on a screen element as a separate behavior.

```
on mouseUp
   sendSprite(0,#setUpPhrase)
end
```

Putting It All Together

The Stage needs to have three text members. The first is the "workspace" member. This member displays the phrase as a combination of underscores and letters, depending on how far along the game is. This member should use a monospaced, or fixed-width, font, so that the underscores and the letters that replace them are exactly the same width. Otherwise, the phrase might shift around as the user makes choices.

Figure 15.4 shows the hangman game screen as it might appear at the beginning of a game. The hangman graphic is just the platform of the gallows, whereas the phrase appears as all blanks and the letter list is full.

Figure 15.4

The hangman game is shown here at the beginning, before the user has tried a single letter.

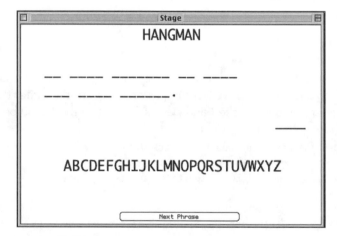

The next text member is the one that contains the letters. This member also needs to use a monospaced font so the letters and the spaces that replace them are the same size.

The last text member is the "message" member. This member contains the "game over" messages when the phrase has been solved, or the hangman is complete. This member doesn't necessarily have to use the same font as the previous two members, but I have done so for consistency.

The only other screen element is the sprite that holds the hangman graphics. This sprite starts out with the first, or zero-numbered graphic, so place that one in the Score. You need to construct all the other hangman graphics and name them properly. The first should be "hangman 0," the second "hangman 1," and so on.

The number of hangman graphics determines how many chances the player has to get the phrase right. With eight graphics, as in the sample movie, the player can afford to guess wrong six times. The seventh time the player guesses a wrong letter, they lose the game.

Finally, you need to populate a text member with phrases to be used. The next section gives some ideas as to what you can use.

Game Variations

Once again, the most striking variation between games is not in the graphics, but in the phrases used. However, the interesting thing about Hangman games is that they don't have to have a hangman in them at all (see the section "Hangman Without the Hangman" later in this chapter).

Accepting Keyboard Input

One minor modification to the game is that you might want to accept keyboard input in addition to allowing the player to click on letters on the screen. This can easily be done by taking the key pressed from an *on keyUp* handler in the frame behavior, and passing it right in to "on tryLetter".

Phrase Themes

Hangman games are unusual in that long phrases are usually easier to solve than shorter ones. This is because there is less likely a chance that the player would pick a wrong letter. As a matter of fact, it is easy for you to have phrases that are impossible *not* to solve. For instance, if the player can choose 7 wrong letters before losing, and the phrase uses 20 different letters, it is impossible to lose. This is because if 20 letters are used, only 6 are not used, so the maximum number of wrong guesses that the player can have is 6—but, it will take 7 wrong guesses to lose.

Although longer phrases make it harder to lose, they can also be more obscure to the player. So, sometimes a long phrase can be hard, even if it does include many letters.

In fact, many Hangman games are played with a single word rather than a phrase. Sometimes these words have a theme, and sometimes they do not. Here is a list of suggestions for themes for lists of words or short phrases.

> Movie Titles
>
> Book Titles
>
> Famous People
>
> Sports Terms
>
> Location Names
>
> Animals
>
> Landmarks
>
> Astronomical Objects
>
> Household Objects

Colors

Plants

Hangman Without the Hangman

Try replacing the hangman with something else. Take the eight bitmaps and draw a bomb counting down from seven to zero. Now, you have the same exact game, with the same exact code, but it appears totally different to the player.

You can suggest a theme to your game this way. If you like, you can get totally away from the morbid theme of traditional Hangman, and use something a little lighter. However, you want to stick with the idea that "something bad" will happen if the graphic sequence reached its end. Here are some suggestions.

A pirate walking the plank

A mouse stealing some cheese

A robber stealing some money from the bank safe

A house getting overgrown with weeds

A man chopping down a tree

A leaky bucket losing water

A candle burning down

You can also use a film loop instead of a static graphic for each stage of the hanging. This way, you can see the poor guy struggle.

Word Search

CD-ROM Example: 16wordsearch.dir

Useful Lingo in This Chapter

- ♠ Behaviors: Using parameters
- ♠ Graphics: Using line shape members
- ♠ Input: Dragging with the mouse
- ♠ Lists: Using linear lists
- ♠ Lists: Using lists that contain lists
- ♠ Strings: Using ASCII codes
- ♠ Strings: Converting strings to uppercase
- ♠ Strings: Parsing strings
- ♠ Strings: Replacing characters in strings
- ♠ Text Members: Using monospaced fonts to align text
- ♠ Text Members: Using text members to store data
- ♠ Text Members: Setting line spacing
- ♠ Text Members: Matching screen location and text
- ♠ Text Members: Coloring text

I've been told many times that word searches are the most popular puzzle game in the world. With its combination of simplicity and long play times, I believe it.

To play word search, you need both luck and logic. At the start of the game, you can quickly scan the matrix and notice a few words. But by the time you are down to the last few words, you are forced to examine the matrix letter by letter.

Although they hold no real educational value, other than teaching concentration and patience, word searches are still a good way to wrap a theme up into a game. The best word searches use words that are all related to one another, thus making the game more appealing, assuming you are interested in the theme that all the words share.

As a Lingo program, word searches present quite a few problems. This is probably why you see so few word-search games done with Director. Most notably, programmers have trouble generating a random arrangement of letters that contain the words and use graphics to highlight a player's selection. We'll look at those issues here and come up with solutions.

Game Overview

The sample movie on the CD-ROM does not offer many options. The puzzle matrix is locked in at 15×15, and specific methods are used to both select and mark words that are found. Even with these assumptions in the code, the game contains two fairly lengthy behaviors.

Lets take a look at what elements go into this game. Figure 16.1 shows the Stage with a game in progress. You can see several words that have already been found, as well as one in the process of being selected.

Figure 16.1

Letters that are grayed out are in words that have been found, and words are highlighted as the user is connecting the letters to find them.

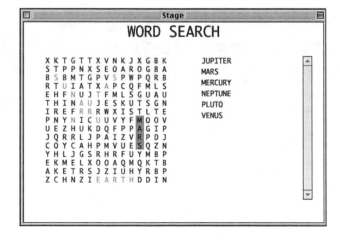

The Matrix

The main playing element here is a matrix of letters. This matrix is a text member with 15 rows of 15 characters each. Actually, each row contains 30 characters, with a space after each letter to widen the grid.

The characters use a monospaced, or fixed-width, font, so they all line up regardless of which characters are chosen. The height of the lines in the member is also altered so that the height of a line and the width of two characters are exactly the same. This makes for a nice, square matrix of letters.

The Word List

Next to the matrix is a list of words that can be found. This list is a noninteractive part of the game. It simply starts off containing all the hidden words, and shrinks as words are removed from it. The user doesn't click on it or anything.

Selecting a Word

In a pencil-and-paper version of word search, a player selects a word by circling it in the matrix. To translate that action into something that can be done with a mouse is tricky, but can be accomplished with a line sprite.

Line sprites are made by drawing a line on the Stage with the line tool. Lines are defined by their rectangle on the Stage, and whether the line is drawn from the upper left to the bottom right of the rectangle, or the upper right to the bottom left. We will use Lingo to set both of these properties of the line, as well as an extra-wide line width.

This line appears underneath the matrix sprite, which uses the "background transparent" ink. The line uses a shade of gray to stand out from the white background, while at the same time, allow the black letters to stand out from it.

Marking Words

Although the line serves as a way to highlight the word that the player is indicating, another method is used to mark words that have been previously found. The method is to change the color of letters in the matrix.

Populating the Matrix

A lot of the game code is involved with the initial populating of the matrix. Each word is randomly laid into the matrix. However, as it fills up, there are fewer and fewer spaces to fit each word. We have to watch for the case where the matrix fills up before the list of words is exhausted.

The manner in which the words are placed into the puzzle is also important. A simple word search game has words laid in horizontally and vertically. However, a more complex game has them diagonally as well. We are going to go one step further and have the words sometimes appear backward. This gives us a total of eight ways in which a word can appear in the matrix: horizontally, vertically, diagonally down, and diagonally up. Then, of course, the words could be backward in each of these placements, which gives us a total of eight ways.

Making the Game

This game's code is contained in one large script. This script is the sprite behavior that goes with the matrix text sprite. It creates the puzzle, maintains it during the game, monitors mouse actions, and deals with, well, everything else.

We'll start with the property declarations. Like the previous two chapters, we get a word list from a text member. We also have a "pEndGameFrame" property. There will be a large list of lists, stored in "pMatrix" that contains the whole letter matrix. The width and height of this square matrix will be stored in "pMatrixSize".

The rest of the properties have to do with the player's current selection in the matrix. We have one property, "pFirstChar", that stores the first character in the selection, and another, "pSecondChar", that stores the last character. When these two properties are set to *VOID*, it means that no selection is being made at the current time.

```
property pWordSource -- text member with words
property pWordList -- assembled word list
property pMatrix -- list containing all letters
property pMatrixSize -- width and height of matrix
property pEndGameFrame
property pFirstChar -- first char position of selection
property pLastChar -- last char position of selection
```

The on *getPropertyDescriptionList* handler contains only two properties this time. The first is the member that contains the word list. The second is the frame that the game goes to when the player has found all the words. Figure 16.2 shows the Parameters dialog box.

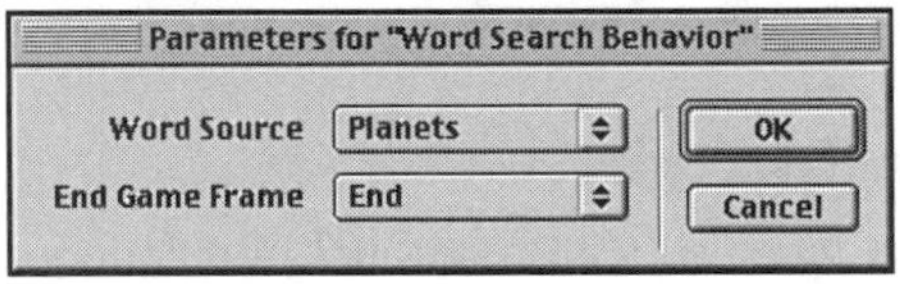

Figure 16.2

The Parameters dialog box is shown here for the word search behavior.

```
on getPropertyDescriptionList me
  list = [:]

  -- the text member with the words in it
  addProp list, #pWordSource,¬
    [#comment: "Word Source",¬
```

```
         #format: #text,¬
         #default: VOID]

   addProp list, #pEndGameFrame,¬
     [#comment: "End Game Frame",¬
       #format: #marker,¬
       #default: #next]


   return list
end
```

The behavior starts off by building the matrix and placing it and the word list on the screen. It also initializes the selection properties.

NOTE

The property "pMatrixSize" is set to 15 in this handler. However, you could set it to some other value for a larger or smaller puzzle, or even add it to the *on getPropertyDescriptionList* handler to allow it to be set in the Parameters dialog box. However, the rest of the code is optimized for a 15×15 matrix. So, you might have to make some adjustments in your font size and selection line sizes should you decide to change this property.

```
-- initialize word list, matrix, and screen displays
on beginSprite me
  pMatrixSize = 15
  buildMatrix(me)
  showMatrix(me)
  showWordList(me)
  pFirstChar = VOID
  pLastChar = VOID
end
```

The first step in creating the game matrix is to read the list of words in the text member. Just as with the cryptogram and Hangman games, this game ensures that all the letters are in uppercase, even if they have not been typed in that way.

```
-- get words from text member
on getWords me
  text = member(pWordSource).text
  -- convert all letters to caps
  repeat with i = 1 to text.length
    put convertToCaps(me,text.char[i]) into char i of text
  end repeat

  -- populate word list
  list = []
  repeat with i = 1 to text.line.count
```

```
    -- throw away blank lines
    if text.line[i].length < 1 then next repeat
    add list, text.line[i]
  end repeat


  return list
end
```

This next handler is identical to the "on convertToCaps" handlers in the previous two chapters.

```
-- utility handler that takes a character and converts it to uppercase
on convertToCaps me, c
  ascii = chartonum(c) -- get character code
  if ascii >= chartonum("a") and ascii <= chartonum("z") then -- is it lowercase?
c = numtochar(ascii-32) -- convert to uppercase
end if
  return c
end
```

Creating a matrix from the word list is a fairly complex process. First, a list of lists is created in the property "pMartix" ①. There will be 15 lists of 15 characters. Each list is a row in the matrix. All the characters in each row start off as "*" characters.

Next, the "pWordList" property is initialized to an empty list. As words fit into the matrix, they are added to the word list as well.

Then, the program loops, trying to fit random words into the matrix. This is done by first picking a random word from the list ②. Then, it picks a random direction for the word to lie in the matrix ③. Next, a random starting spot is determined ④, with special care that the word doesn't extrude out from the sides of the matrix.

After the handler knows which word, where it will be placed, and in what direction it will lie, it tries to fit the word into the matrix ⑤. If all the characters in those positions in the matrix are "*"s, the word fits in. However, if another letter has been placed in a spot by a previous word, then the overlapping letters must be exactly the same. Otherwise, the insertion is aborted and the whole process starts over again.

As the matrix fills up with words, it becomes harder and harder to fit words in. If you have enough words, it might reach the point where some will never be able to fit. In that case, the loop repeats endlessly, trying to fit the word in. To prevent this, there is a variable called "loopCount" that counts the number of times the loop repeats. After it hits a high number, the loop exits ⑥. If all the words fit quickly into the matrix, this will never happen. However, if there are too many words, the loop is assured to end, even if it means excluding some of the words.

The last two things that the "on buildMatrix" handler does is replace any remaining "*"s with random letters, and sort the word list. The latter function is done so that the word list appears in alphabetical order on the screen.

```
-- create a matrix (list of lists) with the letters
on buildMatrix me
-- build matrix with all * characters
  pMatrix = []
  repeat with i = 1 to pMatrixSize
    temp = []
    repeat with j = 1 to pMatrixSize
      add temp, "*"
    end repeat
    add pMatrix, temp
  end repeat

  -- get list of words
  list = getWords(me)
  pWordList = []

  loopCount = 0

  -- loop until all words are used
  repeat while list.count > 0
-- get random word
    w = list[random(list.count)]

-- pick random direction
    horizPlace = random(3)-2 -- horizontal direction
    vertPlace = random(3)-2 -- vertical direction

    -- check for no direction at all
    if horizPlace = 0 and vertPlace = 0 then next repeat

-- pick a random starting spot
    x = random(pMatrixSize-abs(horizPlace)*(w.length+1))
    y = random(pMatrixSize-abs(vertPlace)*(w.length+1))

    -- add to position if the word is to be placed backwards
    if horizPlace = - 1 then x = x + w.length-1
    if vertPlace = - 1 then y = y + w.length-1

-- see if the word fits in that spot
    ok = TRUE
    repeat with i = 1 to w.length
      -- get this letter
      letter = pMatrix[y+vertPlace*(i-1)][x+horizPlace*(i-1)]
```

continues

continued

```
            -- see if this letter will overlap another
            if (letter <> "*") and (letter <> w.char[i]) then ok = FALSE
        end repeat

        -- if it will fit, then add
        if ok then
          repeat with i = 1 to w.length
            -- set letter in matrix
            pMatrix[y+vertPlace*(i-1)][x+horizPlace*(i-1)] = w.char[i]
          end repeat
          -- remove word from list
          deleteOne list, w
          -- add word to word list
          add pWordList, w
        end if

        -- limit loops to avoid words that can never fit in
        loopCount= loopCount + 1
        if loopCount > 10000 then exit repeat
      end repeat

      -- replace all *s with random letters
      repeat with y = 1 to pMatrixSize
        repeat with x = 1 to pMatrixSize
          if pMatrix[y][x] = "*" then
            pMatrix[y][x] = numtochar(64+random(26))
          end if
        end repeat
      end repeat

      -- alphabetize word list
      sort pWordList
    end
```

After the matrix is complete, it needs to be drawn on the screen. The matrix is drawn by building a string from the contents of the "pMatrix" list. A space is placed between every letter, so that the width of the matrix is doubled, which matches the height of the matrix a little closer, making it close to square.

The handler also sets the *fixedLineSpace* property of the text member to 14, and the color of all the letters to black.

NOTE

The text member property *fixedLineSpace* is a somewhat unknown and unused Lingo property. However, it's the only way to set the line spacing of a text member in Lingo. This is especially useful for ensuring that line spacing is consistent cross-platform.

```
-- take matrix list and populate text member
on showMatrix me
  text = ""
  repeat with y = 1 to pMatrixSize
    repeat with x = 1 to pMatrixSize
      put pMatrix[y][x]&SPACE after text
    end repeat
    put RETURN after text
  end repeat

  -- set member text, line spacing and color
  member("Matrix").text = text
  member("Matrix").fixedLineSpace = 14
  member("Matrix").color = rgb("000000")
end
```

Another element that needs to be shown on the screen is the word list. The following handler put the contents of the "pWordList" property into a text member. As the player finds words, this list is redrawn to show only those words that remain.

```
-- put word list into text member
on showWordList me
  text = ""
  repeat with i = 1 to pWordList.count
    put pWordList[i]&RETURN after text
  end repeat
  member("Word Display").text = text
end
```

From here on, all the handlers deal with the player's interaction with the matrix. The player's only move in this game is to select a consecutive group of letters in the matrix. To start this off, the player positions the cursor over the first letter and presses down on the mouse button.

When this happens, the *on mouseDown* handler determines which character the player has selected, and sets both the "pFirstChar" and "pLastChar" to a list that contains the horizontal and vertical position of that character.

```
-- begin selection
on mouseDown me
  c = getChar(me,the clickLoc)
```

```
  -- make sure it is a valid selection
  if c = 0 then exit
  -- activate selection process
  pFirstChar = c
  pLastChar = c
end
```

To determine which character the mouse is located over, the following handler first figures out how far apart the characters are in the matrix. The horizontal distance is calculated by getting the position of the third character in the text member. By using *charpostoloc* to do this, we can calculate the distance between the first and third characters, which is the same as the distance between any two characters. Because the characters in the matrix have a space between them, this distance is the same as the distance between letters in the matrix. The vertical position is much more simply defined by the *fixedLineSpace* property of the text member.

After we know the horizontal and vertical spacing of the letters, we can take the mouse position and return a list with the horizontal and vertical position of the letter that the user is pointing to.

NOTE

Experienced Lingo programmers will ask why I'm not using *mouseChar* or *pointToChar* here. Both of these functions return the character under the mouse, but neither returns the horizontal and vertical position of the character in the matrix without many more lines of code.

```
  -- get character position from cursor position
on getChar me, loc
  -- get width and height of letter in grid
  w = charpostoloc(sprite(me.spriteNum).member,3).locH
  h = sprite(me.spriteNum).member.fixedLineSpace
  -- remove offset of sprite
  loc = loc - sprite(me.spriteNum).loc
  -- calculate location
  x = loc.locH/w
  y = loc.locV/h
  return [x,y]
end
```

The *on exitFrame* handler has the task of determining the current selection and highlighting it. The "pFirstChar" property stays the same, but the "pLastChar" property is constantly rechecked every frame to determine the current selection. After we have a "pFirstChar" and a "pLastChar", we need to be sure the selection is valid.

The only valid selections are the ones that are completely horizontal, vertical, or diagonal. By diagonal, we mean a 45-degree angle in this case. If the selection is valid, then "on drawLine" is called to show the selection.

```
-- show selection if needed
on exitFrame me
  if not voidP(pFirstChar) then
    -- get current character under cursor
    c = getChar(me,the mouseLoc)
    -- assume a valid selection
    ok = FALSE
    -- horizontal selection
    if c[1] = pFirstChar[1] then ok = TRUE
    -- vertical selection
    if c[2] = pFirstChar[2] then ok = TRUE
    -- diagonal selection
    if abs(c[1]-pFirstChar[1]) = abs(c[2]-pFirstChar[2]) then ok = TRUE
    -- if not a valid selection, change nothing
    if not ok then exit
    -- set a new last character in selection
    pLastChar = c
    -- highlight selection
    drawLine(me)
  end if
end
```

Even though highlighting the selection is little more than a detail in this game, the following handler is the most complex. There are actually many ways that you could highlight the selection. In a word search game that I have written for my site, I use vector shapes to draw an oval around the selection. This is even more involved than the following handler, which uses a line-shape sprite.

The "on drawLine" handler first gets the horizontal and vertical spacing of the letters in the matrix in the same way that the "on getChar" handler did. It then uses these values to determine the starting and ending screen points.

The line sprite can be a horizontal, a vertical, or a diagonal line. As it turns out, a diagonal line appears to be thicker when used as a background to letters. To compensate, the line is thinner when a diagonal is needed ⑦. It is 65 percent of the size of a horizontal or vertical line, to be exact.

Adjustments also need to be made to the start and end points of the line so that it covers the letters when it is positioned at different angles ⑧. These adjustments can be determined with logic, but I used trial and error to get them just right.

Finally, the line sprite is set into place. The direction of the line is set so that the proper type of line is drawn in the proper situation. Sometimes, an upper-left to lower-right line is needed, and sometimes an upper-right to lower-left line is needed ⑨.

NOTE

Every sprite in Director is defined by the rectangle of its bounding box. In the case of rectangle shapes and bitmaps, this is easy to see. However, in the case of line shapes, the bounding box rectangle does not tell the whole picture. Two lines can share exactly the same rectangle, but one can be drawn from the upper left to the lower right and the other from the upper right to the lower left. In Lingo, this difference is indicated by the *lineDirection* property.

```
-- draw the selection line
on drawLine me
  -- get the width of the grid
  w = charpostoloc(sprite(me.spriteNum).member,3).locH
  -- get the height of the grid
  h = sprite(me.spriteNum).member.fixedLineSpace

  -- get the basic location of the two ends of the line
  p1 = point(pFirstChar[1]*w,pFirstChar[2]*h)
  p2 = point(pLastChar[1]*w,pLastChar[2]*h)

  -- add location of sprite
  p1 = p1 + sprite(me.spriteNum).loc
  p2 = p2 + sprite(me.spriteNum).loc
```

⑦➤
```
  -- smaller line size if at an angle
  if (p1.locH = p2.locH) or (p1.locV = p2.locV) then
    lineSize = w
  else
    lineSize = .65*w
  end if
```

⑧➤
```
  -- adjust the line according to the angle
  if (p2.locH >= p1.locH) and (p2.locV >= p1.locV) then
    p2 = p2 + point(w,h)
  else if (p2.locH < p1.locH) and (p2.locV >= p1.locV) then
    p1 = p1 + point(w,0)
    p2 = p2 + point(0,h)
  else if (p2.locH < p1.locH) and (p2.locV < p1.locV) then
    p1 = p1 + point(w,h)
  else if (p2.locH >= p1.locH) and (p2.locV < p1.locV) then
    p1 = p1 + point(0,h)
    p2 = p2 + point(w,0)
  end if

  -- adjust line slightly
  sprite(me.spriteNum-1).rect = rect(p1,p2) - rect(3,2,3,2)
```

⑨ →
```
-- set line direction
   if ((p1.locH < p2.locH) and (p1.locV < p2.locV)) or ((p1.locH > p2.locH) and
(p1.locV > p2.locV)) then
     sprite(me.spriteNum-1).member.lineDirection = 0
   else
     sprite(me.spriteNum-1).member.lineDirection = 1
   end if

   -- set line size
   sprite(me.spriteNum-1).lineSize = lineSize
end
```

When the player lifts up the mouse button, "pFirstChar" and "pLastChar" are used to determine what the current selection actually is. There is no need to recalculate the "pLastChar" again, because it was just updated by the last *on exitFrame* handler.

The "on compileSelection" handler is used to build a string from the selection points. Then, the "on select" handler is called to determine whether the word matches one in the list. If it does, then the "on grayLetters" handler is called to permanently color those letters in. Regardless, the selection line is removed from the screen, and "pFirstChar" and "pLastChar" are reset.

```
-- end selection
on mouseUp me
   if not voidP(pFirstChar) then
     -- get word from selection
     text = compileSelection(me,pFirstChar,pLastChar)
     -- see if it is a word in the list
     if select(me,text) then
       -- change color of letters in word
       grayLetters(me)
     end if
     -- remove selection line
     sprite(me.spriteNum-1).locV = -1000
     pFirstChar = VOID
     pLastChar = VOID
   end if
end
```

The following *on mouseUpOutside* handler is used to redirect any "mouseUp" messages to the *on mouseUp* handler regardless of whether the cursor is still over the matrix when released. This might occur if the player stretches the selection beyond the boundaries of the matrix sprite.

```
-- send ALL mouseUps to same place
on mouseUpOutside me
   mouseUp(me)
end
```

The next handler, "on compileSelection", takes two selection points and compiles a string of characters from them. It does this by determining the direction of the selection as horizontal and vertical differences. Then, the "on compileSelection" handler moves from the first to the last character and adds each letter to the list.

```
-- take a first and last character and compile word
on compileSelection me, c1, c2
  -- determine difference between start and end
  dx = c2[1] - c1[1]
  dy = c2[2] - c1[2]

  -- determine line direction
  if dx <> 0 then dx = abs(dx)/dx
  if dy <> 0 then dy = abs(dy)/dy

  text = ""
  -- loop through characters
  c = c1
  repeat while TRUE
-- see if this is past the edge of the puzzle
    if c[1] < 0 or c[1] > pMatrixSize-1¬
       or c[2] < 0 or c[2] > pMatrixSize-1 then exit repeat
    -- add character to text
    put pMatrix[c[2]+1][c[1]+1] after text
    -- see if this is the last character
    if c = c2 then exit repeat
    -- next character
    c = c + [dx,dy]
  end repeat
  return text
end
```

The "on select" handler takes a word and determines whether it is in the word list. If so, the handler removes the word from the word list, and redisplays the word list. Then, it checks to see whether all words have been found. Either way, it returns *TRUE* only if a word from the list was found.

```
-- try out a player's selection
on select me, text
  -- see if it is in the word list
  if getOne(pWordList,text) then
    -- remove from list
    deleteOne pWordList, text
    showWordList(me)
    -- see if the game is over
    if pWordList.count < 1 then
```

```
         go to frame pEndGameFrame
      else
         return TRUE
      end if
   end if
end
```

When a word is found, the letters in the text member are changed to a different color to signify that they have been used in a word. The "on grayLetters" handler actually resembles the "on compileSelection" handler quite a bit. It uses the first and last character position, determines a direction, and then loops through the characters. Instead of compiling them into a string, it turns them all gray.

```
-- change letters in selection to different color
on grayLetters me
   -- determine difference between start and end
   dx = pLastChar[1] - pFirstChar[1]
   dy = pLastChar[2] - pFirstChar[2]

   -- determine line direction
   if dx <> 0 then dx = abs(dx)/dx
   if dy <> 0 then dy = abs(dy)/dy
   -- loop through characters
   c = pFirstChar
   repeat while TRUE
      -- change color
      member("Matrix").line[c[2]+1].char[2*(c[1]+1)-1].color = rgb("999999")
      -- see if the last character has been reached
      if c = pLastChar then exit repeat
      -- next character
      c = c + [dx,dy]
   end repeat
end
```

In addition to the sprite behavior, there is a simple frame behavior used to keep the frame looping while the game is being played.

```
on exitFrame
   go to the frame
end
```

Putting It All Together

This game requires two text members. The first contains the matrix, and needs to cover a large Stage area. It should use a monospaced font so that the letters line up accordingly. Figure 16.3 shows the Stage before the program has been run.

The other sprite contains the member with a list of words. To ensure that it can contain a list of virtually any length, you might want to make it a "Scrolling" text member. However, if you feel confident that all the words will fit on the Stage, then you can make it an "Adjust to Fit" or "Fixed Width" text member.

Figure 16.3

The word search Stage just after setting up the text sprites. Notice that the text members just contain dummy text to allow the sprites to be positioned on the screen.

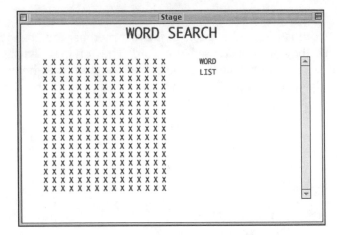

The matrix text member should be set to "Background Transparent" ink. This is to allow the line shape member to show through. This line can be created with the text tool selection in the main Director tool palette. Draw the line on the Stage and the member appears in the Cast and the sprite appears in the Score. Then, be sure that the sprite is in the channel one number lower than the matrix sprite. You should also make the color of that sprite a light gray, or something else if you prefer.

Next, make the text member that will hold the word list. Because this doesn't appear on the Stage, the font or other settings of this member do not matter.

Now, drop the game behavior onto the sprite. You are asked to specify the word list text member and the end game frame. Also, drop the simple looping frame behavior onto the frame script channel.

Game Variations

Again, we have a situation where a game contains a list of words that can be used to suggest a theme. In addition to varying the theme of the words, you can make the matrix a different size, or even adjust the difficulty of the game in a variety of ways.

Word Themes

I won't even try to list suggested word themes for this game. The truth is that almost any theme can be used. You can do a list of words that are obviously related, such as the planets in my sample movie, or you can make a list of words that vaguely suggest a theme.

Matrix Size

As mentioned during the "Making the Game" section, the matrix does not have to be 15×15. A simpler game can be created with a smaller matrix, or a harder game with an even larger matrix. A larger matrix would also allow longer words.

To change the code to accommodate a matrix of a different size, you first need to change the "pMatrixSize" property in the *on beginSprite* handler. Then, if you want to resize the letters as well, change the font size and the *fixedLineSpace* property mentioned in the code. You should also examine the game to see whether the selection line width still seems to correctly highlight the letters.

With a little trial and error, you can use this same code to present a word search game of any reasonable size.

Word Direction

Some people, including me, find it nerve-wracking to have to search for words in all eight possible directions. You can change the preceding code slightly so that words are placed only horizontally from left to right and vertically from top to bottom.

To do this, the piece of code in the "on buildMatrix" right after the "-- pick random direction" comment should be changed. Here is one way to do it.

```
-- pick random direction
   if random(2) = 1 then
     horizPlace = 1
     vertPlace = 0
   else
     horizPlace = 0
     vertPlace = 1
   end if
```

A clever programmer could even set it so that the letters can also appear diagonally, but only in the two diagonal directions that read from left to right.

Selection Methods

As mentioned earlier in the chapter, using a line-shape sprite is not the only way to highlight a selection. You could use two lines, one on each side of the selection. Or, you could use a vector shape member to create an oval around the text.

You could also eliminate the need for a separate selection sprite altogether by just using different colors for the letters. Of course, this would mean keeping track of the previous colors of the selected letters so that they can be changed back to black or gray if a selection is not fruitful.

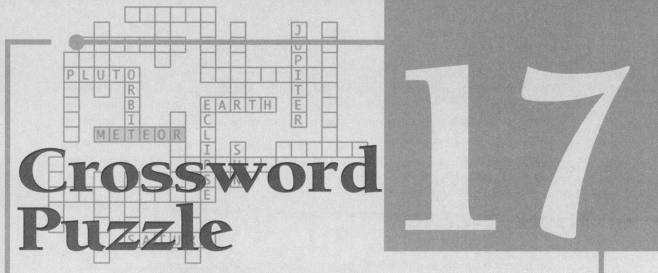

Crossword Puzzle

17

CD-ROM File: 17crossword.dir

Useful Lingo in This Chapter

- ♠ Behaviors: Using parameters
- ♠ Graphics: Using a grid of bitmaps
- ♠ Graphics: Coloring sprites with Lingo
- ♠ Input: Selecting with mouse clicks
- ♠ Input: Accepting typed input
- ♠ Lists: Using linear lists
- ♠ Lists: Using property lists
- ♠ Lists: Using lists that contain lists
- ♠ Strings: Using ASCII codes
- ♠ Strings: Converting strings to uppercase
- ♠ Strings: Parsing strings
- ♠ Strings: Replacing characters in strings
- ♠ Text Members: Using monospaced fonts to align text
- ♠ Text Members: Using text members to store data
- ♠ Text Members: Setting line spacing
- ♠ Text Members: Matching screen location and text
- ♠ Text Members: Aligning bitmaps and text

The crossword puzzle is one of the most recognizable games; in fact, the very image of a crossword puzzle grid is used to represent the idea of 'games' at times. Although primarily known as a pencil and paper game, crosswords are also great computer games.

There is no doubt that crossword puzzles are educational as well as entertaining. They require logical puzzle-solving skills, as well as vocabulary skills. Both of these skill sets are increased during play.

Game Overview

A crossword puzzle game consists of a grid of squares, as well as a list of clues. The grid can be put together in a variety of patterns, sometimes called *lattices*.

A common pattern might look like the puzzles you see in your local daily newspaper. Those grids contain between 50 and 100 words. Many of these words are short words, abbreviations, or other groups of letters. A theme is usually present, but only a handful of words will fit into this theme. These types of puzzles use a pattern of square that is almost always symmetrical.

Another type of grid is sometimes called the "crozzle" format, or educational-style puzzle. It crosses a number of words on a seemingly random pattern. All the words are related to the theme. This is the type of game that we will build.

Figure 17.1 shows the layout of the game. The left side of the screen contains the grid of squares. The right side of the screen contains the list of clues.

Figure 17.1

The crossword puzzle screen is divided between the grid and the clue list.

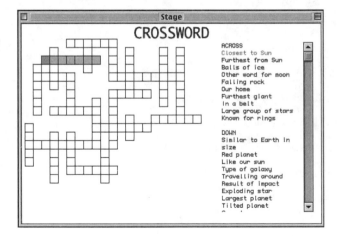

The Grid

The crossword grid actually consists of two parts. The first part is a large bank of square box bitmaps. These bitmaps are arranged in a 21×21 grid on the Stage. They are in sprites 11 through 451, with sprite 11 being the upper-right corner box, sprite 12 being the one to its right, and so on.

When the grid is drawn, all these sprites, except the ones that actually contain letters, are set to a *memberNum* of 0, thus disappearing. However, the squares that are meant to hold letters remain.

The second part of the grid is a text member that sits in a higher-numbered sprite channel, so as to appear on top of the squares. This text member starts off with only spaces, and is thus invisible to the player. However, as the player adds letters to the puzzle, this text member holds these letters.

The Clue List

The list of clues to the right of the puzzle is much simpler to create. This is a simple scrolling text member with the clues listed. The player clicks on a clue to highlight its word space in the puzzle. Likewise, the player can click on the puzzle, and the appropriate clue is highlighted in the clue list.

Building the Puzzle

To construct the puzzle, you first need a list of words and clues. This list is stored in a text member that is populated before the game runs.

The first thing the game does is take this list of words and clues and compile a list of words and their positions in the grid.

This position list needs to be compiled based on a series of rules. Word positioning is the most complex part of the game. We will have several handlers at the beginning of the code that will take care of the word positioning.

Character Entry

For the player to interact with the game, she must first click on either the puzzle or the clue list. Either action highlights a whole word in the grid, and shows a single character that represents the text cursor.

After this has been done, the player can type. The character she types is compared to the character that is supposed to be at the location of the text cursor. If they match, the character is placed in the grid and the text cursor moves to the next character. Otherwise, nothing happens.

Players can proceed to select other words in the grid or clues in the clue list. The object, of course, is to fill in every square in the grid.

Special Effects

Because this is a conversion of a pencil and paper game, no special effects are necessary. However, the colors of the word and character selection can be easily altered if need be.

Sounds are not present in the sample movie on the CD-ROM, but you can add them easily. A click can be played when the player hits a correct letter, and a more negative-sounding click when they get a letter wrong.

Making the Game

Most of the code is in one large frame behavior. This behavior deals with creating the puzzle, as well as maintaining the puzzle as play progresses. There are also small behaviors for the grid squares and the clue list.

Frame Behavior

About half of the frame behavior deals with building the grid of words. It gets the name of the text member with the words and clues from the "pWordSource" parameter and builds a list of word positions to be stored in the "pPuzzle" property. Figure 17.2 shows the Parameters dialog box for this behavior.

Figure 17.2

The Parameters dialog box is shown here for the crossword puzzle frame behavior.

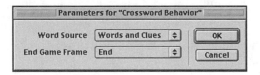

In addition, the properties that begin with "pSel" all define the location of the player's current selection: the word, character, direction, and x and y location.

```
property pWordSource -- text member with words
property pPuzzle -- words, clues and positions
property pPuzzleSize -- width and height of puzzle
property pEndGameFrame -- where the game goes when it is over
property pSelWord, pSelChar, pSelX, pSelY, pSelDirection -- defines selection

on getPropertyDescriptionList me
  list = [:]

  -- the text member with the words in it
  addProp list, #pWordSource,¬
    [#comment: "Word Source",¬
     #format: #text,¬
     #default: VOID]

  addProp list, #pEndGameFrame,¬
    [#comment: "End Game Frame",¬
     #format: #marker,¬
     #default: #next]
```

```
      return list
   end
```

The behavior begins by setting the puzzle size to 21 and then calling "on buildPuzzle" which does all the work. After that, the "on showPuzzle" handler arranges the squares on the Stage, and a call to "on selectChar" selects the first word in the puzzle.

```
-- initialize word list, and screen displays
on beginSprite me
  pPuzzleSize = 21
  buildPuzzle(me)
  showPuzzle(me)
  selectChar(me,pPuzzle[1].x,pPuzzle[1].y)
end
```

The "on getWords" handler is used by "on buildPuzzle" to extract the words and clues from the text member that holds them. The "on getWords" handler converts the words to all uppercase, but leaves the clues in mixed uppercase and lowercase just as they appear in the text member. The handler returns the entire list of words and clues as a Lingo list.

```
-- get words from text member
on getWords me
   text = member(pWordSource).text

   the itemDelimiter = ";"

   -- populate word list
   list = []
   repeat with i = 1 to text.line.count
     -- throw away blank lines
     if text.line[i].length < 1 then next repeat

     --get word and clue
     w = text.line[i].item[1]
     clue = text.line[i].item[2]

     -- convert all letters to caps
     repeat with j = 1 to w.length
       put convertToCaps(me,w.char[j]) into char j of w
     end repeat

     add list, [#word: w, #clue: clue]
   end repeat

   return list
end
```

The "on convertToCaps" handler is identical to the one used in the last few chapters.

```
-- utility handler that takes a character and converts it to uppercase
on convertToCaps me, c
  ascii = chartonum(c) -- get character code
  if ascii >= chartonum("a") and ascii <= chartonum("z") then -- is it lowercase?
c = numtochar(ascii-32) -- convert to uppercase
end if
  return c
end
```

The huge task of building the puzzle from the word list starts with a call to "on buildPuzzle". This handler first calls "on getWords" to get the list of words. The handler then initializes "pPuzzle".

```
-- create a random layout of words
on buildPuzzle me
  -- make word list
  wordList = getWords(me)

  -- start with an empty puzzle
  pPuzzle = []
```

Next, the "on buildPuzzle" handler takes the first word and adds it as a horizontal word in the grid starting at location 3, 3. This position is picked simply because the "on buildPuzzle" handler tends to add words to the right and down, so starting near the upper-left allows more words to fit. You can try playing with these numbers to see how it affects puzzle building if you want to.

```
  -- take the first word, direction, and position in upper-left corner
wordLength = wordList[1].word.length
  direction = #horiz
  x = 3
  y = 3
  add pPuzzle, [#word: wordList[1].word,¬
                #clue: wordList[1].clue,¬
                #direction: direction, #x: x, #y: y]
  deleteAt wordList, 1
```

Now that the puzzle has been seeded with a single word, we can loop through all the other words and try to add them. The following loop alternates between horizontal and vertical placements, and calls "on addToPuzzle" to see whether a word will fit in anywhere.

If the word fits, it is added to the puzzle, and removed from the initial word list. If it does not, the word is moved to the back of the word list and the next word is tried.

Because it's possible that some words might never be able to fit into the puzzle, then a limit on the number of loops is set with the "loopCount" variable. When this limit is reached, the puzzle is declared done, even if some words have not been added ①.

```
-- loop and fit words into puzzle
loopCount = wordList.count*2
repeat while wordList.count > 1 -- repeat while words are left
  if direction = #horiz then direction = #vert -- reverse direction
  else direction = #horiz
  -- see if word fits in puzzle
  if addToPuzzle(me,wordList[1].word,wordList[1].clue,direction) then
    deleteAt wordList, 1
  else
    -- put word at end of list
    add wordList, wordList[1]
    deleteAt wordList, 1
  end if
  loopCount = loopCount - 1
  if loopCount < 1 then exit repeat
  end repeat
end
```

The "on addToPuzzle" handler tries to figure out where a new word can fit into the puzzle. To do this, it loops through all the existing words in the puzzle and tries to find a character that matches a character in the new word ②.

For instance, if the first word in the puzzle is "Mercury" and the new word to be added is "Venus," then the letter "e" is the only place where the two words can cross. The position that the new word needs to be in for this cross to occur is calculated, and then "on noWordsInWay" is called to ensure that no other words in the puzzle interfere with this placement.

```
-- try to add a word to the puzzle
on addToPuzzle me, newWord, clue, direction
  -- loop through all existing words
  repeat with i = 1 to pPuzzle.count
    -- cannot cross a word if it is in the same direction
    if pPuzzle[i].direction = direction then next repeat
    -- loop through all chars in old word
    repeat with j = 1 to newWord.length
      -- loop through all words in new word
      repeat with k = 1 to pPuzzle[i].word.length
        -- see if the chars are the same
        if newWord.char[j] = pPuzzle[i].word.char[k] then{2}
          -- if they are, calculate position of new word
          if direction = #horiz then
            newy = pPuzzle[i].y + k - 1
```

```
                    newx = pPuzzle[i].x - j + 1
               else
                    newx = pPuzzle[i].x + k - 1
                    newy = pPuzzle[i].y - j + 1
               end if
               -- now check to see if any other words are in the way
               if noWordsInWay(me,newWord,newx,newy,direction) then
                    -- everything check out, so add the word
                    add pPuzzle, [#word: newWord, #clue: clue, #direction: direction,
                    #x: newx, #y: newy]
                    return TRUE
               end if
          end if
        end repeat
      end repeat
    end repeat
    -- spot for word never found
    return FALSE
end
```

The "on noWordsInWay" handler needs to run through a list of rules that could prevent a word from being added at a location in the puzzle. First, this handler determines which words that the new word legally intersects ③. If the new word "Venus" intersects the old word "Mercury" at the letter "e," then this is a legal intersection, and the word "Mercury" is not considered as in the way.

However, other words can interfere. To make a valid crossword puzzle, an old word shouldn't be immediately adjacent to the new word ④, nor should it be in the character immediately before or after the new word ⑤. This handler looks carefully for all situations that would invalidate a word placement.

```
-- see if an old word is preventing a new word from fitting it
on noWordsInWay me, newWord, newx, newy, direction
  -- loop through all the char in the new word
repeat with i = 1 to newWord.length
    -- calculate the position of the char
    if direction = #horiz then
      x = newx + i - 1
      y = newy
    else
      x = newx
      y = newy + i - 1
    end if

    -- see if it is beyond the bounds of the puzzle
    if x < 1 or y < 1 or x > pPuzzleSize or y > pPuzzleSize then return FALSE
```

```
          -- loop through all the words in the puzzle
        repeat with j = 1 to pPuzzle.count
(3)─►     intersectList = []  -- store words that intersect new one

            -- loop through all characters in old word
          repeat with k = 1 to pPuzzle[j].word.length
            -- calculate position of char in old word
            if pPuzzle[j].direction = #horiz then
              oldx = pPuzzle[j].x + k - 1
              oldy = pPuzzle[j].y
            else
              oldx = pPuzzle[j].x
              oldy = pPuzzle[j].y + k - 1
            end if

            -- if the old char is in the same spot as the new char
            if (x = oldx) and (y = oldy) then
              -- if they are in their same direction, then new word can't
fit
if (direction = pPuzzle[j].direction) then
                return FALSE
              else
                -- if they are in different direction, then chars must be identical
                if newWord.char[i] <> pPuzzle[j].word.char[k] then return FALSE
                -- add word to allowed intersections
                add intersectList, j
              end if
            end if
          end repeat

          -- loop through all the old word's chars again
          repeat with k = 1 to pPuzzle[j].word.length
            if pPuzzle[j].direction = #horiz then
              oldx = pPuzzle[j].x + k - 1
              oldy = pPuzzle[j].y
            else
              oldx = pPuzzle[j].x
              oldy = pPuzzle[j].y + k - 1
            end if

            -- see if old word occupies space just before or
(5)─►       -- after new word
            if direction = #horiz then
              if (oldx = newx-1) and (oldy = newy) then return FALSE
              if (oldx = newx+newWord.length) and (oldy = newy) then return FALSE
            end if
```

continues

continued

```
            if direction = #vert then
              if (oldy = newy-1) and (oldx = newx) then return FALSE
              if (oldy = newy+newWord.length) and (oldx = newx) then return FALSE
            end if

            -- if not an intersecting word then
            -- see if the old word is alongside the new one
            if not getOne(intersectList,j) then
              if direction = #vert then
                if (x > 1) then
                  if (x = oldx-1) and (y = oldy) then return FALSE
                end if
                if (x < pPuzzleSize) then
                  if (x = oldx+1) and (y = oldy) then return FALSE
                end if
              else
                if (y > 1) then
                  if (y = oldy-1) and (x = oldx) then return FALSE
                end if
                if (y < pPuzzleSize) then
                  if (y = oldy+1) and (x = oldx) then return FALSE
                end if
              end if
            end if

        end repeat
      end repeat
    end repeat

    -- all checks came out, so word will fit
    return TRUE
  end
```

This next handler loops through all the words and ensures the squares for the letters remain on the screen. All the other squares are removed. The handler also sets the screen text to all spaces.

```
  -- arrange sprites on screen according to puzzle
  on showPuzzle me
    -- clear out all squares
    repeat with i = 11 to 451
      sprite(i).memberNum = 0
    end repeat

    -- loop through puzzle words
    repeat with i = 1 to pPuzzle.count
```

continued

```
          -- loop through chars
      repeat with j = 1 to pPuzzle[i].word.length
          -- calculate position of letter
  if pPuzzle[i].direction = #horiz then
          x = pPuzzle[i].x + j - 1
          y = pPuzzle[i].y
      else
          x = pPuzzle[i].x
          y = pPuzzle[i].y + j - 1
      end if
      -- set that sprite to an open box
      sprite(10+(y-1)*pPuzzleSize+x).member = member("Open Block")
    end repeat
  end repeat

  -- reset text
  text = ""
  repeat with y = 1 to pPuzzleSize
    repeat with x = 1 to pPuzzleSize
      put SPACE&SPACE after text
    end repeat
    put RETURN after text
  end repeat
  member("Puzzle Text").text = text
end
```

The "on showClues" handler builds a text string of all the clues. It first gets the horizontal clues, and then the vertical ones. If a word is selected in the puzzle, it highlights the corresponding clue by coloring it red ⑥.

```
-- put list of clues, and highlight one if needed
on showClues me
  -- start text string
  text = "ACROSS"&RETURN

  -- assume no highlight
  highlight = 0

  -- loop through all clues
  repeat with i = 1 to pPuzzle.count
    -- only take horizontal clues
    if pPuzzle[i].direction = #horiz then
      -- note it if this should be highlighted
      if i = pSelWord then highlight = text.line.count
```

continues

continued

```
        put pPuzzle[i].clue&RETURN after text
      end if
  end repeat

  -- divide list
  put RETURN&"DOWN"&RETURN after text

  -- loop through all clues
  repeat with i = 1 to pPuzzle.count
    -- only take vertical clues
    if pPuzzle[i].direction = #vert then
      -- note it if this should be highlighted
      if i = pSelWord then highlight = text.line.count
      put pPuzzle[i].clue&RETURN after text
    end if
  end repeat

  -- put text into member
  member("clues").color = rgb("000000")
  member("clues").text = text

  -- color in highlight line
  if highlight > 0 then
⑥➤  member("clues").line[highlight].color = rgb("FF0000")
  end if
 end
```

When the player clicks one of the squares in the puzzle, this click is sent to the "on puzzleClicked" handler. This handler takes the sprite number and calculates the horizontal and vertical position of the square ⑦. It then calls "on selectChar" which determines which word and character are now selected.

Another function that this handler performs is to detect when the player clicks on the same spot twice ⑧. In that case, it switches "pSelDirection" in an attempt to select a word that shares the same character position, but is in the opposite orientation.

```
  -- take clicks and use to select
  on puzzleClicked me, sNum
⑦➤  -- convert sprite number into x and y
    y = (sNum-10)/21 + 1
    x = (sNum-10)-(y-1)*21

    -- if clicked the same place twice, switch directions
⑧➤  if (x = pSelX) and (y = pSelY) then
```

continues

continued

```
      if pSelDirection = #horiz then pSelDirection = #vert
      else pSelDirection = #horiz
    end if


    -- select the new character
    selectChar(me,x,y)
  end
```

The "on selectChar" handler takes an x and y position and determines which word and character are located there. It then sets all the selection properties. In addition, the handler colors in all the squares for that word ⑨, making the selected character a different color ⑩.

```
  -- when player clicks on puzzle
  on selectChar me, selx, sely
    -- assume no selection
    selWord = VOID


    -- loop through all words
    repeat with i = 1 to pPuzzle.count
      -- loop through all chars in word
      repeat with j = 1 to pPuzzle[i].word.length
        -- calculate x and y
        if pPuzzle[i].direction = #horiz then
          x = pPuzzle[i].x + j - 1
          y = pPuzzle[i].y
        else
          x = pPuzzle[i].x
          y = pPuzzle[i].y + j - 1
        end if

        -- set all squares to the default white
        sprite(10+(y-1)*pPuzzleSize+x).bgColor = rgb("FFFFFF")

        -- see if this square is the one selected
        if (x = selx) and (y = sely) then
          -- see if the word here is in the same direction as the selection
if (pPuzzle[i].direction = pSelDirection) then
            -- if same direction, it is definitely the word
            selWord = i
          else if voidP(selWord) then
            -- if different direction, then still may be the word
            selWord = i
          end if
```

continues

continued

```
        end if
      end repeat
    end repeat

    -- loop through the chars in the word and change square colors
    repeat with j = 1 to pPuzzle[selWord].word.length
      -- calculate x and y
      if pPuzzle[selWord].direction = #horiz then
        x = pPuzzle[selWord].x + j - 1
        y = pPuzzle[selWord].y
      else
        x = pPuzzle[selWord].x
        y = pPuzzle[selWord].y + j - 1
      end if

      -- see if it is the specific char selected
      if (x = selx) and (y = sely) then
        -- if the specific char, make bright red
        sprite(10+(y-1)*21+x).bgColor = rgb("FF6666")
        selChar = j
      else
        -- if another char in word, make a dull red
        sprite(10+(y-1)*21+x).bgColor = rgb("FF9999")
      end if
    end repeat

    -- set all selection properties
    pSelWord = selWord
    pSelChar = selChar
    pSelX = selx
    pSelY = sely
    pSelDirection = pPuzzle[pSelWord].direction

    -- show clues with new highlight
    showClues(me)
  end
```

The lines marked ⑨ and ⑩ point to the `sprite(10+(y-1)*21+x).bgColor` lines.

When the player presses a key on the keyboard, the character is compared to the character that is supposed to be at the selected position in the selected word ⑪ . If they match, then this character is added to the text portion of the grid on the screen ⑫ . In addition, the character selection is moved to the right or down if possible ⑬ .

```
-- take key presses and fill in squares
on keyDown me
  -- get the letter and convert to uppercase
  k = the key
  k = convertToCaps(me,k)
```

continued

```
      -- see if it matches the correct letter
⑪  if k = pPuzzle[pSelWord].word.char[pSelChar] then
        -- put char into screen text
        text  = member("Puzzle Text").text
⑫  put k into char pSelX*2 of line pSelY of text
        member("Puzzle Text").text = text

⑬  -- advance the selection one
        if pSelChar < pPuzzle[pSelWord].word.length then
          if pSelDirection = #horiz then
            selectChar(me,pSelX+1,pSelY)
          else
            selectChar(me,pSelX,pSelY+1)
          end if
        end if

        -- see if all letters have been found
        if checkDone(me) then
          go to frame pEndGameFrame
        end if
      end if
    end
```

When the player clicks on the clue list, the text of that line is sent to the "on clickClue" handler. If this text matches a clue in the "pPuzzle" list, then this clue is selected in the clue list and the corresponding word squares are selected in the grid.

```
  -- takes click on clue list and converts to selection
  on clickClue me, text
    -- loop through all clues
    repeat with i = 1 to pPuzzle.count
      -- see if the clue text matches
      if pPuzzle[i].clue = text then
        -- set new selection
        pSelDirection = pPuzzle[i].direction
        selectChar(me,pPuzzle[i].x,pPuzzle[i].y)
        -- no need to continue loop
        exit
      end if
    end repeat
  end
```

Every time a player enters a new character into the grid, the "on checkDone" handler is called to see whether all the characters have been entered. It simply loops through all the characters in all the words and checks them against the spaces in the grid. If one letter is found missing, then the puzzle is not yet complete ⑭ .

```
-- see if all letters have been filled in
on checkDone me
  -- get screen text
  text = member("Puzzle Text").text
  -- loop through all words
  repeat with i = 1 to pPuzzle.count
    -- loop through all chars
    repeat with j = 1 to pPuzzle[i].word.length
      -- get x and y
      if pPuzzle[i].direction = #horiz then
        x = pPuzzle[i].x + j - 1
        y = pPuzzle[i].y
      else
        x = pPuzzle[i].x
        y = pPuzzle[i].y + j - 1
      end if
      -- get char
      c = text.line[y].char[x*2]
      -- if it is still a space, then puzzle not done
      if c = SPACE then return FALSE
    end repeat
  end repeat
  -- no spaces found, puzzle must be done
  return TRUE
end
```

The frame behavior also has the responsibility of looping the frame.

```
-- loop on frame
on exitFrame me
  go to the frame
end
```

Grid Square Behavior

For the "on puzzleClicked" handler to get its information, the mouse clicks must be passed from the grid squares to the frame behavior. This simple behavior, attached to all the squares, takes care of this.

```
-- send clicks to frame behavior
on mouseUp me
  sendSprite(0,#puzzleClicked,me.spriteNum)
end
```

Clue List behavior

The clue list text sprite also needs a small behavior to pass along information to the frame behavior. This one-handler behavior extracts the text in the line clicked and passes it along.

```
on mouseUp me
  -- get line clicked
  clickLine = pointToLine(sprite me.spriteNum, the clickLoc)
  -- get text of that line
  clickText = sprite(me.spriteNum).member.text.line[clickLine]
  -- send to frame behavior
  sendSprite(0,#clickClue,clickText)
end
```

Putting It All Together

The preparation of the Stage and Score is much easier than the coding for this game. The hardest part is arranging the grid squares.

First, however, you need to make the list of words and clues. The code specifies the semicolon as the item delimiter that goes between each word and its clue. Every line of this text member contains a new word and clue. An example looks like this:

```
Mercury;Closest to Sun
Venus;Similar to Earth in size
Earth;Our home
Mars;Red planet
```

To make the grid of squares, create the grid square as a 15×15 pixel bitmap. Place this on the Stage near the upper-left corner, and in sprite channel 11. Then, use the Score window to copy and paste a copy of this sprite in sprite channel 12. Then, use the arrow keys to move this sprite to the right exactly 14 pixels. Do this again for sprite 13. Then, take all three sprites and copy and paste them into channels 14 to 16, moving all three over 42 pixels (14 times 3). Do this five more times to get a row of 21 squares, all 14 pixels apart, in sprites 11 through 32. Then, I copy and paste this row 20 times, placing each row of sprites 14 pixels below the row before it. When you're finished, you'll have 21 rows of 21 squares as shown in Figure 17.3.

After all the squares are present, create the "Puzzle Text" text member and place that on top of the square sprites. Use a higher-numbered sprite channel than all the squares. In the sample movie, it's in channel 460.

Type some dummy text into the grid, such as 21 rows of the letter "X" 21 times, followed by a space each time. This allows you to align the text member to the grid. A grid that has each square 14 pixels apart both horizontally and vertically should perfectly match a text member that uses "Monaco" font, 12 point, with 14-point line spacing. See the sample movie to play with a sample text member.

Figure 17.3
The Stage after 21 rows of 21 squares have been placed.

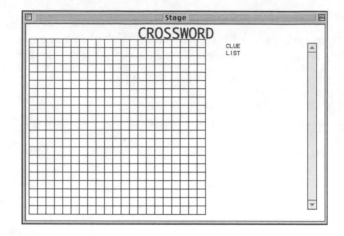

You will also need a scrolling text member for the clues. This member doesn't have to use any special font or line spacing, but it should be set to be a scrolling text member. If not, a large clue list might not fit on the screen all at once. You can place it in a low-numbered sprite channel such as 2 or 3, or a high-numbered one such as 461. It really doesn't matter in this case.

To add the behaviors, select all the square sprites in the Score and add the "Grid Square Behavior" to them all at once. Then, add the "Clue List Behavior" to the clue text sprite. Then, add the frame behavior to the frame, indicating the text member that holds the words and clues, and the frame for the movie to jump to when the puzzle is complete.

Game Variations

Again, we have a game that can use a theme to determine which words are used. In addition, the very definition of what a "word" is can be stretched in crossword puzzles.

Crossword Themes

Any topic can be used for a theme. Certainly, if you plan on using the puzzle for educational purposes, you probably had a theme in mind before even making the game.

Suggesting theme ideas makes no sense here, because they are endless. However, you should ensure that the words are all a single-word, rather than a group of words or a phrase. Crosswords don't use spaces. Sometimes, crosswords have multiple-word answers, but the player is expected to skip the spaces when writing in the answers on the puzzle.

Stretching the Definition of a Word

Crosswords traditionally use words that are not exactly words. Abbreviations and acronyms are common, and even slang. Another variation on a "word" is the use of a multiword phrase without the spaces. For instance: "Blackhole" rather than "Black Hole." Names are commonly used in some crosswords this way.

Storing Multiple Puzzles in One Game

Because the word and clue list come as a single text member, you can easily modify the code to pick up and use a different text member each time the game is played. You can have a set of dozens of theme crosswords, each with a different text member. Instead of setting "pWordSource" by the *on getPropertyDescriptionList* handler, it can be set via a list the user chooses from.

You can also have the word and clue list read in from an external file. You can use the FileIO Xtra to do this on a CD-ROM, or *getNetText* to do this on the Web. You can have a game that reads the word and clue text using *getNetText*, and then simply swap out the text file on the server every week to change the puzzle.

Skipping the Puzzle-Building Step

Building the puzzle at the beginning of the game can take a little while, especially on slower machines. You can skip this step entirely by supplying the "pPuzzle" list variable directly.

One way to do this is to use "on buildPuzzle" to create the puzzle, and then store the string of "pPuzzle" in a text member. Then, remove the "on buildPuzzle" handler call from *on beginSprite* and replace it with a command that reads in the "pPuzzle" text from the member and converts it into a list with the *value* function.

This technique allows you to tamper with the puzzle structure by reordering the word and clue list and trying each order to see how the puzzle builds. Then, when you get exactly the puzzle you want, you store the "pPuzzle" variable as a string to be used in place of the "on buildPuzzle" handler.

Part V:
Card Games

18   Video Poker   **281**

19   Blackjack   **301**

20   Solitaire   **327**

Video Poker

CD-ROM File: 18videopoker.dir

Useful Lingo in This Chapter

- ♠ Animation: Creating a delay with Lingo
- ♠ Behaviors: Using parameters
- ♠ Behaviors: Calling handlers in other behaviors
- ♠ Graphics: Using a set of bitmaps
- ♠ Interface: Having a button down state
- ♠ Lists: Using linear lists
- ♠ Lists: Using property lists
- ♠ Lists: Sorting
- ♠ Math: Using random numbers
- ♠ Members: Using a naming convention
- ♠ Output: Saving the game state
- ♠ Programming: Using a *case* statement
- ♠ Strings: Building member names
- ♠ Variables: Keeping a wallet

Video poker is one of the simplest card games you can make on a computer. In fact, it's little more than a slot machine with an extra step between the bet and the payout. Many casinos actually have video poker machines in addition to traditional slot machines.

It's important not to confuse video poker with regular poker. Regular poker is played between two or more people who make bets and bluff. Video poker uses a similar scoring system, but pays off like a slot machine.

Game Overview

In video poker, the player begins by placing a bet. Usually they take their bet from a pool of money they are given, called a wallet. Often, there is a limit to how much they can bet at any one time.

Next, they are dealt five cards. They access which cards they want to keep and which they want to replace with new cards. Then, they are dealt some new cards to replace ones that they choose not to hold.

The computer then determines how much money they win, if any, based on the five cards at the end of the game. The hand value is accessed according to standard poker rules.

Figure 18.1 shows a game in progress. The player has already placed their bet and was dealt five cards. He or she now has to decide which cards to keep. There will actually be three screens in this game. The first allows the player to make a bet. The second allows the player to choose which cards to keep. The third shows the results of the final draw. Figure 18.1 shows the second screen.

Figure 18.1

The second screen of video poker allows the player to choose which cards to keep.

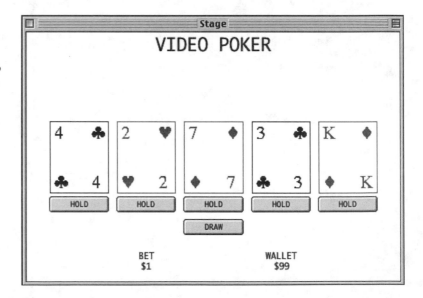

The Deck of Cards

To play this, or any card game, you first need a deck of cards. That means 52 different bitmaps. In the example movie, the cards have all been placed in a separate internal cast library. Figure 18.2 shows the Cast Window view of this library.

Figure 18.2
The "Cards" cast library used by the video poker game.

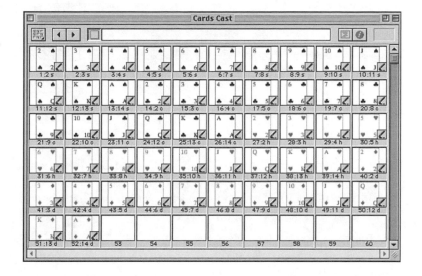

For the Lingo code to use these cards, we set the name of each cast member to something logical. Each name uses two words. The first specifies the card value, and the second the suit.

Card values are numbers from 2 to 14. The numbers 2 to 10 represent cards with those numbers. The numbers 11, 12, 13, and 14 represent the jack, queen, king, and ace. Using consecutive numbers makes it easier to write code that recognizes things such as a poker straight.

The second word of each member name signifies the suit. We'll use the letters "s," "c," "h," and "d" to represent spades, clubs, hearts, and diamonds.

A typical card member name might be "3 c" for the three of clubs, or "13 d" for the king of diamonds.

Three Screens

This game varies greatly from every previous chapter in that we will use more than one frame to represent a single segment of the game. In previous chapters, we have used frames only to represent entirely new levels.

The reason that we are using different frames is because different buttons are needed at different stages of the game. At the start of the game, we need a button to allow the player to increase his or her bet, and a button to deal the cards. Figure 18.3 shows this first screen. On this screen, all the cards are shown with a placeholder graphic.

Figure 18.3
*The first screen
that the player sees
allows him or her
to increase the bet
before the deal.*

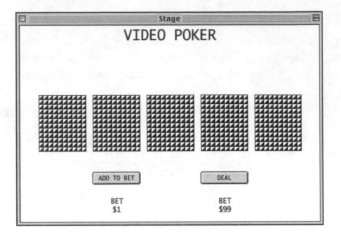

The second screen (refer to Figure 18.1) is the one that shows the player which cards have been dealt, and lets them decide which ones to keep in the upcoming draw. The "Add To Bet" and "Deal" buttons from screen one have been replaced by five "Hold" buttons and a "Draw" button.

After the player clicks "Draw," the third screen is shown (see Figure 18.4). This screen shows the results of the draw, and gives the user an indication of what the final hand is worth. The only button here is the "Next Hand" button. Clicking this takes the player back to the first screen.

Figure 18.4
*The third screen
shows the results
of the draw.*

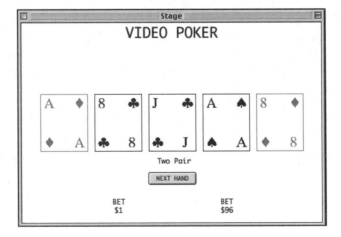

Poker Hand Values

An important part of this game is the program's capability to recognize different poker hand values. This capability is needed at the end of the game, both for display purposes and to determine the amount of money won.

The following list spells out what each hand consists of. Remember that all poker hands are arrangements of five cards. All the cards are dealt from one deck, so it's impossible to have more than one of exactly the same card in a hand. This list shows the hands in ascending value.

- **A Pair**—Two cards in the hand have the same value. For instance, the two of spades and the two of hearts, or the queen of diamonds and the queen of clubs.
- **Two Pair**—Two sets of two cards match in value. For instance, having the five of clubs, the five of diamonds, the jack of spades, and the jack of diamonds.
- **Three-of-a-Kind**—Three cards that match in value. For instance, the nine of hearts, the nine of clubs, and the nine of diamonds.
- **Straight**—All five cards are in consecutive order, regardless of their suits. For instance, the seven of clubs, the eight of diamonds, the nine of hearts, the ten of clubs, and the jack of diamonds. An ace can come either after a king or before a two.
- **Flush**—All five cards are of the same suit. For instance, a six of clubs, an eight of clubs, a jack of clubs, a king of clubs, and an ace of clubs.
- **Full House**—Having both a pair and three-of-a-kind in the same hand. For instance, a seven of clubs, a seven of diamonds, a jack of hearts, a jack of spades, and a jack of clubs.
- **Four-of-a-Kind**—Four cards that match in value. For instance, the three of hearts, the three of clubs, the three of spades, and the three of diamonds.
- **Straight Flush**—Having both a straight and a flush. For instance, a three of spades, a four of spades, a five of spades, a six of spades, and a seven of spades.
- **Royal Flush**—A Straight Flush, but with the highest possible card values. So, in other words, a straight with the values ten to ace, with all cards of the same suit. For instance, a ten of hearts, a jack of hearts, a queen of hearts, a king of hearts, and an ace of hearts.

NOTE

There are a total of 2,598,960 possible hands in poker. Out of that, here are the number of possible outcomes:

Royal Flush	4
Straight Flush	36
Four-of-a-Kind	624
Full House	3,744
Flush	5,108

continues

Straight	10,200
Three-of-a-Kind	54,912
Two Pair	123,552
Pair	1,098,240
Nothing	1,302,540

Giving Values to Hands

After the program determines which type of hand the player has, it must award the player according to the value of the hand. Obviously, a hand that has none of the previously listed values is considered a loss. As a matter of fact, most pairs are also considered a loss. Only a pair of jacks or higher are usually considered to be of any value in video poker.

Table 18.1 shows each hand and what we will award the player should he or she attain it. The award assumes that the player bet $1. If they bet more, then the award is multiplied by their bet.

Table 18.1   Money Award by Hand Value

High Pair	1
Two Pair	2
Three-of-a-Kind	3
Straight	4
Flush	5
Full House	8
Four-of-a-Kind	25
Straight Flush	50
Royal Flush	800

A high pair is considered to be a pair of jacks or higher, as stated previously. A low pair is worth nothing, as is a hand where not even a pair is achieved.

The Draw

During the game, the cards are dealt twice. The first time, five new cards are dealt. The second time, however, the number of cards dealt depends on how many cards the player chooses to hold.

The player can choose to hold all, some, or none of his or her cards. Whichever the player chooses, he or she must hit "Draw" to continue. Only then is the value of the player's hand decided.

Special Effects

Although the computer has the capability to deal cards at lightning-fast speeds, and can display a new hand of cards instantly, we will choose to animate the deal somewhat. Each card is dealt one at a time, with a slight delay in between. There is also a sound that plays when each card is dealt.

In the sample movie on the CD-ROM, the same sound is used for dealing cards as for clicking the Hold button.

Making the Game

The code for this game consists of one large frame behavior and several smaller button behaviors. Most button behaviors are one line of code that passes the click on to the frame behavior. However, the hold button behavior is a little more complex, so we can use the same behavior for all five buttons.

Frame Behavior

The frame behavior has the responsibility of keeping track of all the elements of the game. It deals the cards, determines the value of the hand, and maintains the player's wallet.

We start off by declaring the properties, which include lists that hold the deck of cards, the current hand, and which cards the player wants to keep in the draw. There is also a property for the player's wallet and his current bet.

```
property pDeck -- deck of cards
property pHand -- current hand displayed
property pHoldList -- cards the player wants held
property pBet -- current bet
property pWallet -- players total wallet
```

The *on beginSprite* handler sets the player's wallet to 100 dollars, and calls "on startHand", which begins the first round of play.

```
-- start wallet, clear hand
on beginSprite me
  pWallet = 100
  startHand(me)
end
```

The "on startHand" handler has many responsibilities. First, it ensures that the player hasn't gone broke. If he has, it sends the player to the "Game Over" screen. If not, it continues.

It resets the bet to 1, and subtracts that from the player's wallet. Then, it updates both the bet and wallet text members. Next, it ensures that the movie is positioned at frame "bet", which is the first screen. Finally, it replaces all the cards on the screen with the "Card Back" member.

```
-- clear hand, bet, show all
on startHand me
-- see if the game is over
  if pWallet < 1 then
    go to frame "Game Over"
    exit
  end if

  -- start bet at 1
  pBet = 1
  pWallet = pWallet - 1

  -- update text
  showBet(me)
  showWallet(me)

  -- go to bet frame
  go to frame "Bet"

  -- clear all cards
  repeat with i = 1 to 5
    sprite(2+i).member = member("Card Back")
  end repeat
end
```

The "on initialDeal" handler is called when the player presses the "Deal" button. It creates an ordered deck as a Lingo list. The list contains the names of all the cards in the deck. Then, one by one, five cards are picked at random ①. Each card is placed in a sprite on the Stage ②, a sound is played, and then a *repeat* loop pauses the program for 20 ticks.

The "on initialDeal" handler also clears the "pHoldList" property and advances the movie to the second screen, frame "draw".

```
-- deal five cards
on initialDeal me
  -- create an ordered deck
  pDeck = []
  repeat with suit in ["s","c","h","d"]
    repeat with num = 2 to 14
      add pDeck, num&&suit
    end repeat
  end repeat
```

```
       -- deal five random cards to hand
       pHand = []
       repeat with i = 1 to 5
         -- pick random card
①➤     r = random(pDeck.count) -- random card
       add pHand, pDeck[r] -- add to hand
       deleteAt pDeck, r -- remove from deck

       -- place card on stage
②➤     sprite(2+i).member = member(pHand[i])
       updateStage
       -- play sound
       puppetSound 1, "card sound"
       -- force delay
       t = the ticks + 20
       repeat while the ticks < t
       end repeat
     end repeat

     -- initialize hold list
     pHoldList = []

     -- go to draw frame
     go to frame "Draw"
   end
```

The "on showBet" and "on showWallet" handlers update the text members on the Stage. They place a dollar sign in front of the numbers for added effect.

```
 -- update bet text
 on showBet me
   member("Bet").text = "BET"&RETURN&"$"&pBet
 end

 -- update wallet text
 on showWallet me
   member("Wallet").text = "WALLET"&RETURN&"$"&pWallet
 end
```

The "on addToBet" handler subtracts one dollar from the player's wallet and adds it to the bet. It ensures that the player has some money in his wallet first, and also ensures that the bet is $5 or less.

```
 -- add one dollar to bet and subtract from wallet
 on addToBet me
   -- make sure there is money left in the wallet
   if pWallet < 1 then exit
```

```
       -- make sure that the bet is $5 or less
   if pBet >= 5 then exit
      -- add to bet
      pBet = pBet + 1
      -- subtract from wallet
      pWallet = pWallet - 1
      -- update screen
      showBet(me)
      showWallet(me)
   end
```

After the player reaches the "Draw" frame, he must choose which cards, if any, to hold during the upcoming draw. When he clicks a "Hold" button, a "holdCard" message is sent to the frame behavior. This handler takes the message and adds the card position to the "pHoldList" property. If the card is already in the list, it removes it instead.

The handler returns a *TRUE* if the card was added to the list and a *FALSE* if it was removed. This way, the button behavior can know whether to set the button in an up state or a down state. We will look at that behavior in the next section.

```
   -- mark a card for holding
   on holdCard me, cardNum
      -- get card
      card = pHand[cardNum]

      -- see if it is already being held
      if not getOne(pHoldList,card) then
         -- if not alresdy being held, add to list
   add pHoldList, card
         return TRUE
      else
         -- if already being held, remove from list
   deleteOne pHoldList, card
         return FALSE
      end if
   end
```

The "on draw" handler replaces cards in the hand with new ones. It checks "pHoldList" to ensure it doesn't replace a card that the player has decided to keep ③. The "on draw" handler uses the same technique as the "on initialDeal" handler to play a sound and pause the program briefly after each card is dealt.

When the new cards are in place, the "handValue" variable is set by a call to the "on calcValue" function. This string is placed in the text member "Results" so that the player sees it. Then, the variable is used to calculate the winnings, which are added to the player's wallet.

```
-- draw new cards
on draw me
  -- loop through all cards
  repeat with i = 1 to 5
    -- make sure the card is not being held
③→  if not getOne(pHoldList,pHand[i]) then
      -- pick random card
      r = random(pDeck.count) -- random card
      pHand[i] = pDeck[r] -- set card in hand
      deleteAt pDeck, r -- remove from deck

      -- show this new card
      sprite(2+i).member = member(pHand[i])
      updateStage
      -- play sound
      puppetSound 1, "card sound"
      -- force delay
      t = the ticks + 20
      repeat while the ticks < t
      end repeat
    end if
  end repeat

  -- calculate hand value
  handValue = calcValue(me)
  member("Results").text = handValue

  -- calculate winnings
  winnings = calcWinnings(me,handValue)

  -- add winnings to wallet
  pWallet = pWallet + winnings*pBet
  showWallet(me)

  -- advance to last frame
  go to frame "Done"
end
```

The "on calcValue" handler takes the "pHand" property and determines what type of hand it is. It does this by first determining whether there is a flush ④. Then, it creates a new list that just contains card numerical values ⑤ and sorts them ⑥. It uses this to determine whether there is a straight.

Then, the "on calcValue" handler uses the numbers-only list again to build a property list of card values and the number of times that they appear in the hand ⑦.

For instance, if the hand is this:

["4 h", "4 d", "2 c", "12 s", "12 d"]

The "on calcValue" handler converts the hand to a sorted numerical value list that looks like this:

[2, 4, 4, 12, 12]

Then, it converts it to a property list that looks like this:

[2: 1, 4: 2, 12: 2]

This property list reflects the fact that the hand has one 2, two 4s, and two 12s. It can use this list to determine combinations such as a pair or three-of-a-kind.

```
  -- calculate the poker value of pHand
 on calcValue me
    -- compare second word of each card to
    -- see if all match and there is a flush
    flush = TRUE
    repeat with i = 2 to 5
      if pHand[i].word[2] <> pHand[1].word[2] then
        flush = FALSE
        exit repeat
      end if
    end repeat


    -- convert hand to a list of just card numbers
    numList = []
    repeat with i = 1 to 5
      add numList, integer(pHand[i].word[1])
    end repeat


    -- sort the number list
    sort numList


    -- see if the number list is consecutive
    -- if so, there is a straight
    straight = TRUE
    repeat with i = 1 to 4
      if (numList[i] + 1) <> numList[i+1] then
        straight = FALSE
        exit repeat
      end if
    end repeat


    -- special straight with ace before a two
    if numlist = [2,3,4,5,14] then straight = TRUE
```

⑦➤ ```
    -- compile property list of values and
    -- the number of times they appear
    matchList = [:]
    repeat with i = 1 to 5
      if voidP(getAProp(matchList,numList[i])) then
        -- first time value has appeared
        addProp matchList, numList[i], 1
      else
        -- 2nd, 3rd or 4th time value has appeared
        setProp matchList, numList[i], getProp(matchList,numList[i])+1
      end if
    end repeat

    -- use info gathered above to determine the poker value
    if straight and flush and numList[1] = 10 then
      -- straight, flush, and lowest number is a 10
      return "Royal Flush"

    else if straight and flush then
      -- straight and a flush
      return "Straight Flush"

    else if getOne(matchList,4) then
      -- 4 of the same card
      return "Four-Of-A-Kind"

    else if getOne(matchList,3) and getOne(matchList,2) then
      -- 3 of one card and 2 of another
      return "Full House"

    else if flush then
      -- plain flush
      return "Flush"

    else if straight then
      -- plain straight
      return "Straight"

    else if getOne(matchList,3) then
      -- thee of one card
      return "Three-Of-A-Kind"

    else if matchList.count = 3 then
      -- exactly 3 types of values, so must be 2 pair
return "Two Pair"
```

*continues*
```

continued

```
    else if matchList.count = 4 and getOne(matchList,2) > 10 then
      -- exactly four types of values,
      -- with one pair that is jack or better
      return "High Pair"

    else if matchList.count = 4 then
      -- exactly four types of values, must be a pair
      return "Low Pair"

    else
      -- everything else
      return ""
    end if
  end
```

After a string with the hand description is obtained, it is passed into the "on calcWinnings" handler, which returns the amount won, per dollar bet.

```
-- take poker description and return winnings
on calcWinnings me, text
  case text of
    "Royal Flush": return 800
    "Straight Flush": return 50
    "Four-Of-A-Kind": return 25
    "Full House": return 8
    "Flush": return 5
    "Straight": return 4
    "Three-Of-A-Kind": return 3
    "Two Pair": return 2
    "High Pair": return 1
    "Low Pair": return 0
    "": return 0
  end case
end
```

Finally, the *on exitFrame* handler takes care of the frame looping.

```
-- loop on frame
on exitFrame
  go to the frame
end
```

Hold Button Behavior

Each of the five hold buttons on the second screen must send the "holdCard" message to the frame behavior. However, it must also send the position of the card that the button is under. To do this, we use the *on getPropertyDescriptionList* handler to allow the number to be set when the behavior is dragged onto each of the buttons. Figure 18.5 shows the Parameters dialog box.

Figure 18.5

The Parameters dialog box is shown here for the hold button behavior.

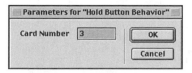

```
property pCardNum -- which card this button affects

on getPropertyDescriptionList me
  list = [:]
  addProp list, #pCardNum,¬
    [#comment: "Card Number",¬
     #format: #integer,¬
     #default: 1]
  return list
end
```

Another function that the hold button behavior must perform is to change appearance when the card has been marked for holding. The "on holdCard" handler returns a *TRUE* if the hold button should show that the card is being held, and a *FALSE* otherwise. The member of the button's sprite is set according to this returned value.

```
on mouseUp me
  -- make sound
  puppetSound 1, "card sound"
  -- send hold message
  if sendSprite(0,#holdCard,pCardNum) then
    -- if TRUE returned, then button is down
    sprite(me.spriteNum).member = member("Hold Down")
  else
    -- if FALSE returned, then button is up
    sprite(me.spriteNum).member = member("Hold Normal")
  end if
end
```

NOTE

We could have avoided the *on getPropertyDescriptionList* handler and simply cut and pasted the same code five times to make five button scripts. The difference between the five scripts would have been the "pCardNum" value passed into "on holdCard". However, making "pCardNum" a parameter and using the same behavior five times, each with different values, is a powerful feature of behavior parameters.

Other Button Behaviors

There are also four small behaviors that are needed to link up buttons with the frame behavior. The first is the button for the "Add To Bet" action.

```
on mouseUp
  sendSprite(0,#addToBet)
end
```

Next, we have the "Deal" button.

```
on mouseUp
  sendSprite(0,#initialDeal)
end
```

Then, we have the "Draw" button for the second screen.

```
on mouseUp
  sendSprite(0,#draw)
end
```

Finally, we have the "Next Hand" button for the last screen.

```
on mouseUp
  sendSprite(0,#startHand)
end
```

Putting It All Together

Because this game requires three screens, the Score setup is a little more involved than the previous games. But first, you need to prepare your deck of cards.

Take a close look at the deck used in the sample movie. The cards are pretty basic. I haven't even used colorful images for the face cards. The cards are all the same size, however, which is important because they must be interchangeable.

 NOTE

If you plan to make your own deck of cards, complete with nice drawings on face cards, note that there are standard ways of drawing the jack, queen, and king, depending on the suit. For instance, some of the jacks are "one-eyed," meaning that they have their head turned to one side. Also, one king is a "suicide king," meaning that the sword is being poked through his own head or heart. Get an ordinary deck of cards to check out exactly which features you can find in each face card.

In addition to the 52 cards, you should have a bitmap called "Card Back" in your main Cast. This should be exactly the same size as the rest of the cards. However, it should be either blank, or have some design or pattern on it.

NOTE

The sample movie on the CD-ROM uses bitmaps for the 52 cards. However, Flash members might be the best way to go. Don't underestimate the time it will take to make 52 Flash cards, however, especially if you plan to have detailed face cards.

You need three text members, one called "Bet", one called "Wallet", and one called "Results". The first two contain the current bet and player's wallet, as shown earlier in Figure 18.1. The last contains the value of the hand (refer to Figure 18.4).

You also need five buttons: "Hold", "Deal", "Add to Bet", "Draw", and "Next Hand". The "Hold" button needs two states. In the code, they are referred to by their names: "Hold Normal" and "Hold Down".

The code also refers to the sound "card sound", so you need that in the Cast as well.

After you have all the members ready, you can create three named frames in the Score: "Bet", "Draw", and "Done". Stretch the frame behavior through all of them as a single sprite. Do not break it up into three individual sprites. See Figure 18.6 to see how the "Video Poker Behavior" does this.

Figure 18.6

The Score set up for the Video Poker game.

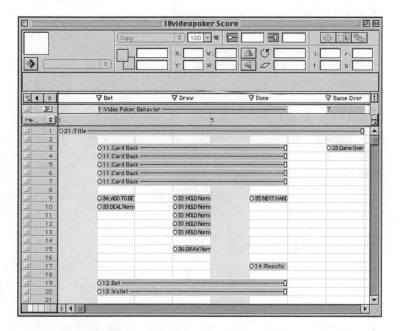

Now, you need to add the five "Card Back" sprites just like they are shown in Figure 18.6. They should also stretch across all three frames. The "Bet" and "Wallet" text members also need to be on all frames.

Next, you need to add the buttons to each screen. All three screens have different buttons. The first screen has the "Add to Bet" button and the "Deal" button. You can see those in sprite channels 9 and 10 in Figure 18.6.

The second frame has five hold buttons, each placed directly under a card on the Stage, as shown earlier in Figure 18.1. You also need a "Draw" button on this frame.

The last frame needs only the "Next Hand" button. In addition, you must place the "Results" text member in a sprite on this frame. Refer to Figure 18.3 to see how this is positioned.

Finally, you just need to add the behaviors to the buttons. The only behavior that has parameters which need to be set are the hold buttons. Drop the "Hold Button Behavior" onto each of these separately, and set them to numbers 1 through 5.

Game Variations

After you have the game basics working, there is a lot you can do to make the game more exciting. Some ideas require changes only to the bitmaps, although others require working with the code.

Colorful Background

A game like this really cries out for a more colorful background. Any space outside the cards and buttons can be colored in. A casino theme is the first that comes to mind. Another idea is to use the background to make it look more like a machine, with metallic textures and such.

Better Cards

You should definitely use more interesting cards than the ones supplied with the sample movie on the CD-ROM. Place the typical pictures on the jack, queen, and king for starters.

The "Card Back" member can also be customized with the name of your company or your client's logo.

No Card Backs

Another option would be to have no "Card Back" member at all. Just take that bitmap and place a single pixel in it. You can set the registration point of that bitmap so that the pixel doesn't even appear on the Stage.

With this option, the first screen appears to have no cards at all, a more realistic setup than having the back of cards showing.

Win Sounds

You can easily add win sounds for various hands by placing *puppetSound* commands in the "on calcValue" handler just before each *return* command. Place a ringing bell sound with every result better than a flush, and a buzzing sound for a losing hand. Or, place a different sound for every single combination.

Progressive Scoring

The "pWallet" property is set to 100 in the *on beginSprite* handler. However, you can have the code use *getPref* instead to read a text file with this value. If the text file is not present, then you can use 100. Otherwise, you can pick up the value of the user's previous wallet.

```
text = getPref("pokerwallet.txt")
if voidP(text) then wallet = 100
else pWallet = value(text)
```

To save the wallet, place a "Leave Game" button on the "Done" frame. This button calls an "on endGame" handler in the frame behavior that saves the player's wallet.

```
on endGame me
  setPref("pokerwallet.txt",string(pWallet))
  halt
end
```

You might also want to have a "Reset Wallet" button on the "Bet" screen that resets a wallet to $100 any time the user wants it to. This comes in handy when the player loses all of his or her money.

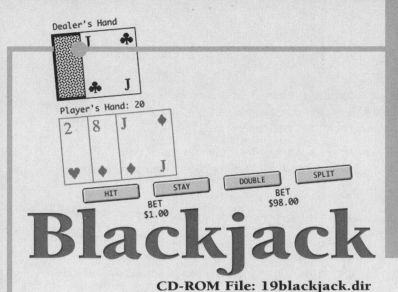

Blackjack

19

CD-ROM File: 19blackjack.dir

Useful Lingo in This Chapter

- ♠ Animation: Creating a delay with Lingo
- ♠ Graphics: Using a set of bitmaps
- ♠ Graphics: Using registration points
- ♠ Lists: Randomizing a list
- ♠ Lists: Using linear lists
- ♠ Lists: Lists that contain lists
- ♠ Math: Using random numbers
- ♠ Members: Using a naming convention
- ♠ Strings: Building member names
- ♠ Variables: Keeping a wallet
- ♠ Variables: Setting the number of decimal places

The game of blackjack is possibly the most popular card gambling game. The game has two distinct variations. The first is the game that people can play among groups of friends, and the second is the game played in casinos.

Although both variations have the same basic rules, the casino game features a dealer who deals the cards and plays the house's hand. Most computer versions of blackjack simulate this casino version.

Game Overview

Blackjack is also called Twenty-One, which makes sense because the whole game revolves around that number. A simple game consists of two hands: the dealer's hand and the player's hand.

First, the player makes a bet. Then, the dealer and the player are both dealt two cards. The first card given to the dealer is face down, so as to be hidden from the player.

Next, the player has the chance to add cards to his or her hand. The goal is to get as close to a total of 21 as possible, without going over 21. If the player has a total of more than 21, then the player loses.

After the player is done, the dealer takes extra cards, if necessary, to ensure that the dealer's hand is at least 17. If the dealer has a total of more than 21, then the player wins. Otherwise, the player only wins if he or she has a higher total than the dealer. If there's a tie, then it's called a "push" and the player gets his or her bet back, but no winnings.

Figure 19.1 shows a typical game. The dealer's hand is the one on top, with the first card hidden. The player's hand is below it. The player now has the opportunity to add another card, or "stay." If they do, it ends the player's turn and forces the dealer to complete the game. There are some other options for the player as well, which you'll learn about shortly.

This explanation of the game is, of course, oversimplified. In fact, if the game were this simple, the code would be a lot shorter. However, there are many extra rules to the game that complicate things. Most notably, the "split" rule adds a great deal to the code. These intricacies of blackjack are discussed later in the game overview.

Let's look at all the aspects of the game and decide how to implement them in the program.

The Shoe

A shoe is a set of several decks of cards. Casino blackjack is usually played with a shoe of six or eight decks. We'll use six decks for this game.

Figure 19.1

A typical blackjack screen—it's the player's turn to decide whether to hit or stay.

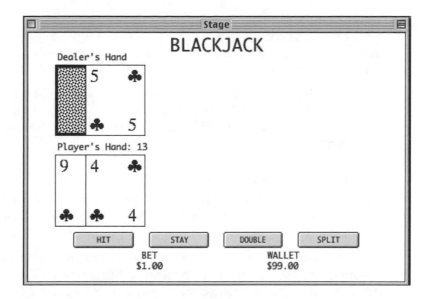

The decks are stored in a list property called "pDeck." We use the same card notation as in the previous chapter, where the two-word card name contains first the card number, and then the suit. So, the nine of diamonds is "9 d" and the king of spades is "13 s." Again, a 14 is used to represent an ace.

The movie also uses a second cast library with bitmaps of each of the 52 cards. The member names match the card notation discussed previously.

The shoe is created as a temporary list of six decks, with each deck in perfect order. Then, we use a shuffle routine to move each card, at random, into the "pDeck" property. The result is a completely random shoe.

We also need to watch the shoe during the game to ensure that there are enough cards left. When the shoe is almost empty, we have to create a new one. The proper time to do this is just before a deal. However, we also need a new shoe if we happen to completely run out of cards during play.

The Cards As Sprites

In the poker game, we knew that there would always be exactly five cards displayed at any time. However, in blackjack, you can have anywhere from 1 to 11 cards in each hand. We get the number 11 from the unlikely case where the player draws only 2s. In that case, the eleventh card would bust their hand at 22.

NOTE

Technically, the player can draw 21 aces, but when the player has 11 aces, they have 21, so they would have no reason to hit again.

To accommodate these 11 cards, we set up two banks of 11 sprites in the Score. The sprites are close enough so that the cards overlap (refer to Figure 19.1). The sprites are already positioned on the Stage in precisely the location where the cards will appear, so we never have to deal with sprite locations in our code at all.

The sprite channels actually contain placeholder members. These placeholder members are one-pixel bitmaps that have their registration points set so far away from the pixel that it doesn't appear on the Stage at all. However, when this member is swapped for a card member, it appears in the right location.

Displaying Hands

We use a single handler to display the dealer's hand and the player's hand. Because they use different sprite banks, we need to specify the first sprite in the bank when calling this handler.

We also want to pass a list of the cards in the hand into this handler. In addition, a third parameter indicates whether the first card in the hand should be shown, or the "Card Back" member should be substituted instead. This parameter enables us to use this same handler for both the player and dealer.

Hand Values

Another utility handler in our game takes any list of cards and returns its blackjack value. It isn't as simple as just adding up the value of each card. First, the jack, queen, and king must be recognized as a value of 10.

Then, any aces have to be dealt with. In blackjack, an ace can be worth either one or eleven. It turns out that it works if you simply count aces as a 1, but note that an ace is in the hand. Then, when all the cards have been added, if an ace was found, try adding 10 to the value. If this puts the total over 21, then don't add the 10.

This works even if there is more than one ace in a hand. This is because you can never have more than one ace worth 11, because the two aces alone would equal 22. So, only one ace can possibly be worth 11.

Insurance

The first odd rule of blackjack that complicates our code is insurance. If a dealer is showing an ace, the player should be offered a chance to buy insurance. This is sort of like a side bet. The player pays an additional amount of half of his or her initial bet. Then, if the dealer is hiding a card of value 10, thus giving the dealer a blackjack, the player wins twice the insurance. This exactly covers the player's initial bet, which is usually lost to the dealer's blackjack.

NOTE
Although insurance is offered in just about every casino in the world, it never pays off for the player in the long run. Expert gamblers never consider taking insurance for this reason.

To add insurance to the game, we need to have an entire frame that deals with it. The movie jumps to this frame if the dealer is showing an ace. The frame contains a "Buy Insurance" button as well as a "Continue" button.

Double

Another rule is the "Double" or "Double Down." The player's opportunity to do this is immediately after the initial deal. If the player chooses to double, he doubles their initial bet and receives one, and only one, additional card.

The double doesn't actually complicate our program too much. It's the exact equivalent of doubling the bet, doing a "hit," and then immediately doing a "stay."

Splits

Making a blackjack game without the split option would be a much simpler task. Even though the rule is not used very often, and almost never used by beginners, it's an important part of blackjack.

The player is allowed to split a hand when they have two cards of identical value. For instance, if they are dealt two fives, or two aces, or a king and a jack, they can choose to split. They dish out another bet, of the same value as their original bet, to support this second hand.

Then, they have two hands. They play out the first hand as normal, and then proceed to play out the second hand. This means that instead of having a single list of cards as the player's hand, we need to have a list of lists.

To further complicate things, the player is allowed to split again if they draw another matching card. Although some casinos limit the number of times you can split, some do not. Computer games frequently limit splits to just one, but we will go all the way here and allow the player to keep splitting as many times as he or she can.

Not only does this mean that we have to maintain a list of lists that hold the player's hands, but we also have to calculate the results of each and every hand at the end of a turn. Quite often, when the user splits, they can win some, lose some, and push some.

Multiple Screens

Although the poker game used three frames to represent the three different stages of the game, the blackjack game needs six frames.

The first allows the player to place their bet. The movie goes to the second screen to deal the initial cards out. Then, it advances to either the third screen to offer insurance, or the fourth screen to allow the player to draw more cards.

The fifth screen is used to allow the dealer to complete the dealer's hand. Then, the last screen shows the results of the hand, and allows the player to pause before going back to the first screen again.

Special Effects

In addition to a sound for each card that is dealt, we will also have a sound that plays each time a new shoe is created. This "shuffle" sound actually serves a minor function. It lets the player know when a new shoe is being used. If the player is trying to use the blackjack technique of counting cards, then this is very important. Card counting is when the player keeps track of which cards have been played in their head, and tries to use this information to figure out the probability of a card being drawn when the shoe is almost empty.

This game also uses a text member to display miscellaneous messages to the user. This comes in handy when we want to relay information such as the fact that the player does not have enough money to double, or that they cannot split.

Making the Game

All the code for this game is in one single frame behavior. The only other scripts are one-line *on mouseUp* handlers that call handlers in the frame behavior. Because the scripts are all one line, we don't need to mention them here. They all send a single message using the *sendSprite* command, such as the Buy Insurance button, which sends a #buyInsurance message. They are all in the sample movie on the CD-ROM if you want to see them.

For a complex game, blackjack has surprisingly few properties. We need one to hold the deck—one for the dealer's hand, and one for the player's hands. Because the player can have more than one hand, we need a property to indicate which hand is currently being played. We also need to store the current bet and the user's wallet.

```
property pDeck -- deck of cards
property pDealerHand -- dealer's Hand
property pPlayerHands -- player's hands
property pPlayerHandNum -- player's current hand
property pBet -- current bet
property pWallet -- player's total wallet
```

A game starts the player with $100. We set the "pWallet" property to 100.0, instead of just 100, so that it is always a floating-point number. We need it to be a float because when a player wins with a blackjack, they win one and half times their initial bet. This means that if they bet $1, they win $1.50. That 50 cents requires us to use decimal values rather than just integers.

To ensure that the player's bet and wallet are displayed as numbers such as "1.50" and not "1.5000," we set the Lingo property *the floatPrecision* to 2. This displays all floating point values with two decimal places.

```
-- set up the game
on beginSprite me
  -- use two decimal places for $
  the floatPrecision = 2

  -- start wallet at $100
  pWallet = 100.0

  -- create the shoe
  shuffleDeck(me)

  -- reset all elements
  clearScreen(me)
end
```

The "on shuffleDeck" handler creates a list containing each of the 52 cards a total of six times. Then, it picks cards out at random, one by one, and places them in "pDeck" to create a shuffled shoe of cards.

```
-- create a shoe of 6 decks
on shuffleDeck me
  -- play shuffle sound to indicate shuffle
  puppetSound 1, "shuffle sound"

  -- create an ordered shoe
  temp = []
  repeat with i = 1 to 6
    repeat with suit in ["s","h","c","d"]
      repeat with num = 2 to 14
        add temp, num&&suit
      end repeat
    end repeat
  end repeat

  -- pick random cards to create shuffled deck
  pDeck = []
  repeat while temp.count > 0
    r = random(temp.count)
    add pDeck, temp[r]
    deleteAt temp, r
  end repeat
end
```

To begin each turn of the game, many properties and text members need to be reset. But first, the handler checks to be sure that the player has at least one dollar left in their wallet ①. If not, the move goes to a frame named "Game Over".

Next, the shoe is examined to ensure there is least half a deck, or 26 cards, left. If not, a new shoe is created. ②

The two properties that hold the hands are reset. The dealer's hand is a single list, so it's set to []. However, the player can have multiple hands with a split, so the "pPlayerHands" property is really a list of lists, each list a hand. We initialize it by setting it to [[]].

All the card sprites on the Stage are set to display text that reflects the fact that the turn is just beginning.

Finally, the minimum bet of $1 is placed and subtracted from the player's wallet.

```
-- begin a hand
on clearScreen me
  -- see if the player is broke
  if pWallet < 1 then
    member("Results").text = "Out of money!"
    go to frame "Game Over"
    exit
  end if

  -- if less than half a deck left, get new shoe
  if pDeck.count < 26 then shuffleDeck(me)
  -- clear hands
  pDealerHand = []
  pPlayerHands = [[]]

  -- set all sprites to placeholder
  repeat with i = 1 to 11
    sprite(15+i).member = member("Card Placeholder")
    sprite(27+i).member = member("Card Placeholder")
  end repeat

  -- set all text on screen
  member("Results").text = "Place Your Bet"
  member("Player Text").text = "Player's Hand"
  member("Dealer Text").text = "Dealer's Hand"

  -- set up initial bet
  pBet = 0.0 -- start at $0
  addToBet(me) -- add first $1

  go to frame "Bet"
end
```

① → member("Results").text = "Out of money!"

② → if pDeck.count < 26 then shuffleDeck(me)

The "on addToBet" handler is the first of many handlers in this behavior to respond to a button click. In this case, it's the button that allows the player to increase his bet. It ensures they have the money in their wallet, and also imposes a $5 limit on bets.

```
-- add a dollar to the bet
on addToBet me
  -- make sure player has money
  if pWallet < 1 then exit

  -- only add to bet if bet is less than $5
  if pBet >= 5 then exit

  pBet = pBet + 1 -- add bet
  pWallet = pWallet - 1 -- subtract from wallet
showBet(me)
  showWallet(me)
end
```

The next two handlers update the bet and wallet text members any time that it's needed. They are used by many of the other handlers in this behavior.

```
-- update bet text
on showBet me
  member("Bet").text = "BET"&RETURN&"$"&pBet
end

-- update wallet text
on showWallet me
  member("Wallet").text = "WALLET"&RETURN&"$"&pWallet
end
```

After the player is satisfied with the bet amount, he or she clicks the "Deal" button. This action calls the "on initialDeal" handler.

This handler deals out the first two cards to the dealer and the player one at a time. It calls "on showHand" to update the sprites on the Stage each time, and "on cardSound" to play the sound and pause the program for an instant.

When all the cards are dealt, what happens next depends on whether the dealer has an ace showing. If so, then the game moves on to ask the player whether he or she wants to buy insurance ③.

```
-- deal out first two cards for dealer and player
on initialDeal me
  -- jump to frame with no buttons
  go to frame "Deal"
```

continues

continued

```
          -- remove text
          member("Results").text = ""

          -- deal out dealer's first card
          add pDealerHand, getCard(me)
          showHand(me,15,pDealerHand,TRUE)
          cardSound(me)

          -- deal out player's first card
          add pPlayerHands[1], getCard(me)
          showHand(me,27,pPlayerHands[1],FALSE)
          cardSound(me)

          -- deal out dealer's second card
          add pDealerHand, getCard(me)
          showHand(me,15,pDealerHand,TRUE)
          cardSound(me)

          -- deal out player's second card
          add pPlayerHands[1], getCard(me)
          showHand(me,27,pPlayerHands[1],FALSE)
          cardSound(me)

          -- player is using one and only hand
          pPlayerHandNum = 1

          -- see if the dealer is showing an ace
   ③→   if pDealerHand[2].word[1] = "14" then
            -- ask player for insurance
            go to frame "Insurance"
          else
            -- go right to the action
            startDraw(me)
          end if
        end
```

The "on getCard" handler is a utility handler used by "on initialDeal", "on hit", and "on dealerTurn". Its simple task is to pick the next card from the deck. Before it does that, the handler ensures that there is at least one card left in the shoe. In the unlikely case that there are no cards left, the "on getCard" handler starts a new shoe.

```
  -- deals out the next card from the deck
  on getCard me
    -- if deck is empty, do an emergency shuffle
    if pDeck.count < 1 then shuffleDeck(me)
```

```
      -- get next card
      card = pDeck[1]

      --remove from deck
      deleteAt pDeck, 1

      return card
    end
```

The "on showHand" handler takes a sprite number and a list of cards and sets the sprites to the cards in the list. If the last parameter, "hideFirst", is *TRUE*, then it displays a "Card Back" member instead of the first card in the list.

This handler is used to display both the player's hand and the dealer's hand. It is sometimes called with 15 as "startSprite", which would be the dealer's hand, and sometimes with 27, which would be the player's hand. These numbers refer to the starting sprite in the bank of sprites used for each hand on the Stage. If you were to move the sprites around in the Score, you would have to adjust these numbers.

```
    -- display a hand, using a set of sprites
    -- startSprite = first sprite in group of sprites to be used
    -- hand = list containing cards
    -- hideFirst = if TRUE, will show first card face-down
  on showHand me, startSprite, hand, hideFirst
    -- loop through all 11 sprites in group
    repeat with i = 1 to 11
      if i > hand.count then
        -- ran out of cards, make sure sprite uses placeholder
        sprite(startSprite+i-1).member = member("Card Placeholder")
      else if i = 1 and hideFirst then
        -- show back of card
        sprite(startSprite+i-1).member = member("Card Back")
      else
        -- show card
        sprite(startSprite+i-1).member = member(hand[i])
      end if
    end repeat
  end
```

This next handler does several things, all cosmetic to the game. First, it uses *updateStage* to force the sprites on the screen to update, thus showing any changes made since the frame loop began. Then, it plays the "card sound." Finally, it freezes the computer for 20 ticks, or one third of a second.

This method of freezing the computer is not the best way to create a pause in game play. However, it's an easy method that doesn't complicate our code, so I'm using it here. It is also somewhat acceptable because there is no other animation taking place on the screen, and the delay is very short. A better way would be to deal out each card based on a timer as the frame loops. But that would require a great deal more code and explanatory text, and not make much difference to the game in the long run.

```
-- force the new card to be shown, play sound, wait
on cardSound me
  -- force update
  updateStage


  -- play sound
  puppetSound 1, "card sound"

  -- delay a bit
  t = the ticks + 20
  repeat while the ticks < t
  end repeat
end
```

The "on handValue" handler is a function that takes a list of cards and returns its black-jack value. This means that face cards are given the value of 10, and aces are counted as a 1 or an 11, depending on whether a value of 11 will bust the hand or not.

```
-- determine hand value from list of cards
on handValue me, hand
  -- start with 0, no ace
  total = 0
  ace = FALSE

  -- loop through cards
  repeat with i = 1 to hand.count
    -- get card value
    n = integer(hand[i].word[1])

    if n = 14 then
      -- a 14 is an ace
      ace = TRUE -- remember an ace is present
      total = total + 1 -- add only 1 for now

    else if n > 9 then
      -- 10, jack, queen, king all equal 10
      total = total + 10

    else
      -- other cards equal face value
      total = total + n
    end if
  end repeat
```

```
        -- if an ace is present, see if it can be worth 10 more
        -- and yet still not bust the hand
        if ace and total+10 <= 21 then
          total = total + 10
        end if


        return total
      end
```

Now we begin to handle the actual game play. The first choice a player might have to make in a turn is whether or not to buy insurance. The following handler takes care of the case where they have been offered insurance because the dealer is showing an ace, but they have declined by clicking the "Continue" button rather than the "Buy Insurance" button.

This handler checks to see whether the dealer does, in fact, have blackjack ④. If so, it checks to see whether the player also has blackjack. In that case, it is a push, and the player gets his or her bet back.

If the player does not have blackjack, then the turn immediately ends ⑤. However, if the dealer doesn't have blackjack to begin with, then play proceeds as if insurance never were an issue.

```
    -- player chooses no insurance
    on noInsurance me
      -- see if dealer had blackjack
      if handValue(me,pDealerHand) = 21 then
        -- see if player also had blackjack
④➤    if handValue(me,pPlayerHands[1]) = 21 then
          -- return money to wallet
          pWallet = pWallet + pBet
          showWallet(me)
          member("Results").text = "You both have Blackjack!"
          -- show dealer's card
          showHand(me,15,pDealerHand,FALSE)
⑤➤      go to frame "Done"
        else
          -- dealer wins
          member("Results").text = "Dealer has Blackjack!"
          -- show dealer's card
          showHand(me,15,pDealerHand,FALSE)
          go to frame "Done"
        end if
      else
        -- no blackjack, play hand normally
        startDraw(me)
      end if
    end
```

The "on buyInsurance" handler reacts to the player clicking the "Buy Insurance" button. It first subtracts the cost of insurance from the player's wallet. Then, it sees whether the dealer actually has blackjack ⑥.

In the event that the dealer has blackjack and the player has blackjack, the player wins the insurance bet, and also gets his or her money back from the original bet ⑦. If only the dealer has blackjack, then the player still wins the insurance bet, but loses the original bet ⑧. If the dealer does not have blackjack, then play continues as normal.

```
-- player chooses insurance
on buyInsurance me
  -- make sure player can afford it first
  if pWallet < pBet/2 then
    member("Results").text = "You can't afford it."
    exit
  end if


  -- subtract insurance from wallet
  pWallet = pWallet - pBet/2


  -- see if the dealer had blackjack
  if handValue(me,pDealerHand) = 21 then
    -- see if player also had blackjack
    if handValue(me,pPlayerHands[1]) = 21 then
      -- pay off push
      pWallet = pWallet + pBet
      -- pay off insurance
      pWallet = pWallet + pBet*1.5
      showWallet(me)
      member("Results").text = "You both have Blackjack! Insurance paid off."
      -- show dealer's card
      showHand(me,15,pDealerHand,FALSE)
      go to frame "Done"
    else
      -- pay off insurance
      pWallet = pWallet + pBet*1.5
      showWallet(me)
      member("Results").text = "Dealer has Blackjack! Insurance paid off."
      -- show dealer's card
      showHand(me,15,pDealerHand,FALSE)
      go to frame "Done"
    end if
  else
    -- no blackjack, play hand normally
    startDraw(me)
  end if
end
```

If no insurance check was needed, or one was needed but the dealer did not have black-jack, we end up getting to the "on startDraw" handler. The first thing this does is get the current values of the player's hand and the dealer's hand. The "on startDraw" handler displays the value of the player's hand in the "Player Text" member, which appears just above the player's hand (refer to Figure 19.1).

Then, it checks for blackjack in either hand. If both dealer and player have blackjack, then it is a push ⑨. If just the player has blackjack, then the player wins the bet, plus another 50 percent of the bet ⑩.

Otherwise, the movie continues to the "Draw" frame, which shows the "Hit," "Stay," "Double," and "Split" buttons.

```
-- before allowing player to draw, check for blackjack
on startDraw me
  -- get value of hands
  playerVal = handValue(me,pPlayerHands[pPlayerHandNum])
  dealerVal = handValue(me,pDealerHand)

  -- show value of player's hand
  member("Player Text").text = "Player's Hand:"&&playerVal

  -- see if both player and dealer have blackjack
  if playerVal = 21 and dealerVal = 21 then
    -- return bet
    pWallet = pWallet + pBet
    member("Results").text = "You both have Blackjack! Push."
    -- show dealer's card
    showHand(me,15,pDealerHand,FALSE)
    go to frame "Done"
  else if playerVal = 21 then
    -- award player 3 to 2
    pWallet = pWallet + pBet*2.5
    member("Results").text = "Blackjack! You win."
    -- show dealer's card anyway
    showHand(me,15,pDealerHand,FALSE)
    go to frame "Done"
  else
    -- no blackjack, allow player to draw
    go to frame "Draw"
  end if
end
```

The "on hit" handler does little more than call "on addCardToHand". That handler does the actual work for both the "on hit" handler and the "on double" handler. However, in "on hit", we also need to check to see whether the player has busted after getting the new card.

```
-- player asks for card
on hit me
  -- get card
  addCardToHand(me)

  -- see if player busts
  if handValue(me,pPlayerHands[pPlayerHandNum]) > 21 then
    doneHand(me)
  end if
end
```

The "on addCardToHand" handler adds the next card in the deck to the player's current hand. It also updates the sprites on the screen and makes the card sound. Finally, it updates the text on the screen to show the value of the hand.

```
-- add a card to player's hand
on addCardToHand me
  -- add card
  add pPlayerHands[pPlayerHandNum], getCard(me)

  -- update screen
  showHand(me,27,pPlayerHands[pPlayerHandNum],FALSE)
  cardSound(me)

  -- show value of hand
  playerVal = handValue(me,pPlayerHands[pPlayerHandNum])
  if pPlayerHands.count = 1 then
    -- single hand
    member("Player Text").text = "Player's Hand:"&&playerVal
  else
    -- split hands
    member("Player Text").text = "Player's Hand Number"&&pPlayerHandNum&":"&&playerVal
  end if
end
```

When the player doubles, it's like a hit, but with a stay immediately afterward. Before that can happen, the handler ensures that a double is possible. This means that the player must not have split, must have exactly two cards in their hand, and has enough money in their wallet to double the bet.

```
-- player doubles
on double me
  if pPlayerHands.count > 1 then
    -- not allowed if already split
    member("Results").text = "You cannot double."
    exit
  else if pPlayerHands[pPlayerHandNum].count > 2 then
```

```
    -- not allowed if already hit
    member("Results").text = "You cannot double."
    exit
  else if pWallet < pBet then
    -- not enough money
    member("Results").text = "You don't have enough money to double."
    exit
  end if

  -- double bet
  pWallet = pWallet - pBet
  pBet = pBet*2
  showBet(me)
  showWallet(me)

  -- add card
  addCardToHand(me)

  -- immediately end hand
  doneHand(me)
end
```

A split is the most complex move that we need a handler for. First, the handler determines whether a split is allowed. The player must have exactly two cards in his or her hand, and those cards must have identical values. To determine if the values of the cards are the same, we use the "on handValue" function with a list of only one card. We send both cards to "on handValue" and if the returned number is the same, then we have a match and the split is allowed.

If a split is allowed, then money is removed from the player's wallet. Next, two new hands are created in the "pPlayerHands" list ⑪. Each new hand contains one card from the original hand. This original hand is then deleted.

Because the original hand is removed, there is no need to advance the "pPlayerHandNum" variable. If it was a 1 before, and the two new hands are created and the original deleted, then 1 would be the proper number to point to the first of the new hands.

NOTE

Some blackjack games automatically deal out a second card to any hand created by a split. This makes sense, because you can improve a hand only by adding a second card. If you want to add this feature, the "on split" handler would be the place to deal a second card to each hand as it is created.

```
-- player splits hand
on split me
  if pPlayerHands[pPlayerHandNum].count <> 2 then
    -- not allowed if already hit
    member("Results").text = "You can't split."
  else if handValue(me,[pPlayerHands[pPlayerHandNum][1]]) <>¬
         handValue(me,[pPlayerHands[pPlayerHandNum][2]]) then
    -- cards must be same value to split
    member("Results").text = "You can't split."
  else if pWallet < pBet then
    -- not enough money
    member("Results").text = "You don't have enough money to split."
  else
    -- remove money from wallet
    pWallet = pWallet - pBet
    showWallet(me)

    -- create two new hands
    add pPlayerHands, [pPlayerHands[pPlayerHandNum][1]]
    add pPlayerHands, [pPlayerHands[pPlayerHandNum][2]]

    -- remove original hand
    deleteAt pPlayerHands, pPlayerHandNum

    -- show first split hand
    member("Player Text").text = "Player's Hand Number"&&pPlayerHandNum
    showHand(me,27,pPlayerHands[pPlayerHandNum],FALSE)
  end if
end
```

⑪

When the player clicks the "Stay" button, the following handler simply passes the command on to the "on doneHand" handler.

```
-- player stands
on stay me
  doneHand(me)
end
```

The "on doneHand" handler checks to see whether this is the last hand in a player's list of hands. This is the case all the time, unless the player has split.

If the hand is not the last, then the "pPlayerHandNum" variable is increased and the next hand is displayed. If this is the last, or only, hand, then "on dealerTurn" is called.

```
-- player done with hand
on doneHand me
  if pPlayerHandNum = pPlayerHands.count then
```

```
      -- final hand, now dealer's turn
      dealerTurn(me)
    else
      -- on to player's next hand
      pPlayerHandNum = pPlayerHandNum + 1
      member("Player Text").text = "Player's Hand Number"&&pPlayerHandNum
      showHand(me,27,pPlayerHands[pPlayerHandNum],FALSE)
    end if
  end
```

The "on dealerTurn" handler plays out the dealer's hand. First, it calls "on showHand" with a *FALSE* as the last parameter, which reveals the dealer's hidden first card. Then, the handler loops, adding cards to the dealer's hand, until the total is 17 or greater.

NOTE

Some versions of blackjack have the dealer hit on a "soft 17." This is when the dealer has 17, but only because an ace has been counted as an 11. If you want to make your game like this, you need to create a new handler, much like "on handValue" that returns a TRUE if a hand value is "soft." Then, if the dealer gets a 17, test to see whether it is soft and then hit just as if the dealer had less than 17.

```
  -- deal out cards to dealer
on dealerTurn me
  -- show dealer's face-down card
  showHand(me,15,pDealerHand,FALSE)
  -- show dealer's hand value
  member("Dealer Text").text = "Dealer's Hand:"&&handValue(me,pDealerHand)
  cardSound(me)

  -- add cards until hard or soft 17
  repeat while handValue(me,pDealerHand) < 17
    add pDealerHand, getCard(me)
    showHand(me,15,pDealerHand,FALSE)
    member("Dealer Text").text = "Dealer's Hand:"&&handValue(me,pDealerHand)
    cardSound(me)
  end repeat

  -- determine winnings
  calculateResults(me)
end
```

The "on dealerTurn" handler ends with a call to "on calculateResults". This handler determines whether the player won. It uses three variables to store the number of times the player won, the number of times the player lost, and the number of times the player pushed. If the player has only one hand, as is the case most of the time, then only one of these variables will have a value of 1, and the rest will be 0.

A loop is used to go through each of the player's hands. ⑫ The value of each is compared to the value of the dealer's hand. Whether the player or dealer busted is also taken into account. The player's wallet is adjusted with each win or push at this time.

Then, if there was only one hand, one of three messages is displayed: "You win," "Push," or "You Lose." ⑬ If there is more than one hand, then a message is composed of the number of times the player has won, lost, and pushed ⑭ .

Finally, the player's wallet is updated on the screen, and the movie ends up at frame "Done" where the player can contemplate the hand, and click the "Next Hand" button when ready.

```
-- determine results of player's hands
on calculateResults me
  -- variables to keep track of win/loss/push
  numWon = 0
  numLost = 0
  numPush = 0

  -- get value of dealer's hand
  dealerVal = handValue(me,pDealerHand)

  -- loop through player's hands
  repeat with i = 1 to pPlayerHands.count
    -- get value of hand
    playerVal = handValue(me,pPlayerHands[i])

    if playerVal > 21 then
      -- player busted
      numLost = numLost + 1
    else if dealerVal > 21 then
      -- dealer busted
      pWallet = pwallet + pBet*2
      numWon = numWon + 1
    else if playerVal = dealerVal then
      -- push
      pWallet = pwallet + pBet
      numPush = numPush + 1
    else if playerVal > dealerVal then
      -- player wins
      pWallet = pwallet + pBet*2
      numWon = numWon + 1
    else
      -- player lost
      numLost = numLost + 1
```

⑫ points to the line `repeat with i = 1 to pPlayerHands.count`

```
          end if
       end repeat
```

⑬→ `-- display results as text`
```
    if pPlayerHands.count = 1 then
       -- player only had one hand
       if numWon then
         member("Results").text = "You win."
       else if numPush then
         member("Results").text = "Push."
       else if numLost then
         member("Results").text = "You lose."
       end if

    else
```
⑭→ `-- player had more than one hand`
```
       text = "You won"&&numWon&", you lost"&&numLost&", and you pushed"&&numPush&"."
       member("Results").text = text
    end if

    -- update wallet
    showWallet(me)

    go to frame "Done"
  end
```

Last, but not least, we have the *on exitFrame* handler, which creates the frame loop.

```
  -- loop on frame
 on exitFrame
   go to the frame
 end
```

Putting It All Together

This game uses six labeled frames, not including the "Game Over" frame. The frames differ mostly in which buttons are present. However, the first frame, "Bet", doesn't contain the cards, or some text sprites.

Figure 19.2 shows the top of the Score for blackjack. The "Bet" frame contains the "Bet", "Wallet", and "Results" text sprites, which are also present on all the other frames.

Figure 19.2

The top of the Score for blackjack shows you how to lay out the six game frames.

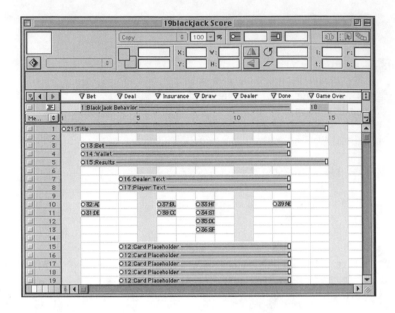

The two buttons present on the "Bet" frame are "Add to Bet" and "Deal", in sprites 10 and 11.

The frames "Deal" through "Done" contain two banks of 11 sprites—one bank for the dealer and one for the player. You can use any one card to help you lay out these 22 sprites on the Stage, and then swap them all for the single-pixel placeholder later. Figure 19.3 shows the screen setup just before the temporary card is replaced with the pixel.

Figure 19.3

Using a normal card can help you lay out the screen. When the cards are in place, just swap out the card bitmap with the place-holder bitmap.

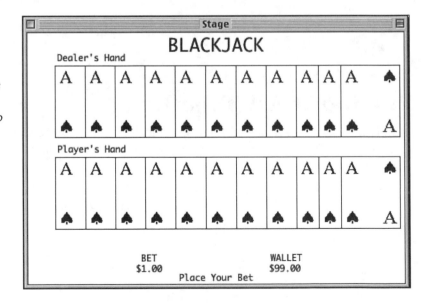

The next frame is the "Deal" frame. There are no buttons here because the game is on this frame only temporarily, as the cards are dealt. The "Dealer Text" and "Player Text" sprites that appear above each hand are present, as well as all the card sprites, starting in channel 15.

The next frame is the "Insurance" frame. The movie goes here only if the dealer is showing an ace after the deal is complete. The two buttons in sprites 10 and 11 are the "Buy Insurance" and "Continue" buttons. Figure 19.4 shows the Stage for this frame.

Figure 19.4

The "Insurance" frame for blackjack is shown here.

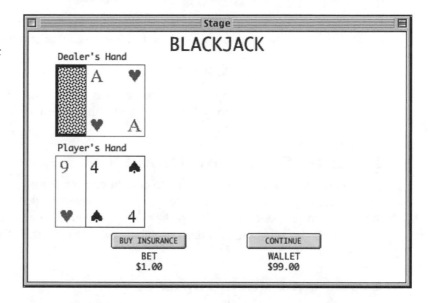

If the dealer is not showing an ace, then the movie goes to the "Draw" frame. This is where the "Hit," "Stay," "Split," and "Double" buttons appear, and the player must play out his or her hand. Figure 19.1 showed this screen earlier in the chapter.

After the player is finished, the movie goes to the "Dealer" frame. Just like the "Deal" frame, this is a screen that the movie displays only while more cards are dealt. The player never has to do anything here except watch and wait. The dealer finishes dealing out the dealer's hand, and the results of the game are calculated.

No matter which path the movie took from the "Bet" frame, a turn always ends up at the "Done" screen. The card sprites remain on the Stage so that the player can contemplate them; otherwise, the only action possible here is to click the "Next Hand" button.

You also need to set up a "Game Over" frame for when the player runs out of money.

After all the buttons and cards are in place, you need to stretch the "Blackjack Behavior" over all six frames as a single script sprite. You also need to place the single-line behaviors on all the buttons. Each one is an *on mouseUp* handler with a *sendSprite* command to send the frame behavior the right message.

Of course, there is also the detail of creating the 52-card set, plus the "Card Back" member. See Chapter 18, "Video Poker," for more details on those members.

Game Variations

You really can't make any major changes to this game before it ceases to be blackjack. The rules are so well defined that any player wanting to play your blackjack game will quickly become upset if certain rules are not followed.

However, there are many variable rules and limitations that can be added to the game to make it resemble how the game is played in one casino or another.

Dealer Hits on Soft 17

As mentioned during the code listing, you can add another handler to the behavior to check to see whether a hand is "hard" or "soft," the latter meaning that the hand contains an ace with a value of 11.

Limiting Splits and Doubles

Some casinos limit doubles and splits to certain combinations of cards. For instance, some casinos don't allow two aces to be split because the odds are too far in favor of the player. Implementing restrictions like this just requires the addition of a new handler to check for the situation, and then prohibiting the "Split" and "Double" buttons when they are clicked.

Cards and Background

Just as with the previous chapter, you can improve this game greatly over the example on the CD-ROM by making more colorful cards and a nice casino background. A dark green background color is pretty standard, because it matches the look of an actual casino table. Many tables also include payoff amounts written on them, such as "Insurance Pays 2 To 1."

Bets and the Wallet

Most casinos have a minimum and maximum bet. The code you've seen here just has a maximum bet of $5. However, you can raise this to something like $25, and then maybe have a minimum as well. You can even have the bet increments be $5 or something else, rather than $1.

Of course, if you are going to have higher bets, you will also want to have a higher starting wallet. You might even want to allow the player to go into debt, by allowing negative wallet amounts.

Chips

A clever Lingo programmer will be able to modify this game to use drag-and-drop casino chips rather than an "Add to Bet" button. You can have the player's chips appear as a stack on one side of the screen, and then they click on the chips to place a bet.

You can do this by simply making the stack of chips a button, and representing the player's bet as another stack. If the view is top-down, a stack with one chip looks just like a stack with many chips. That being the case, you will want to still show the player's bet and wallet as text in addition.

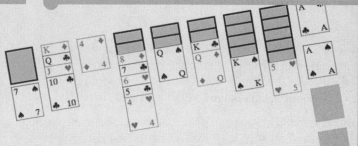

Solitaire

CD-ROM Movie: 20solitaire.dir

Useful Lingo in This Chapter

- ♠ Animation: Creating a delay with Lingo
- ♠ Behaviors: Calling handlers in other behaviors
- ♠ Graphics: Using a set of bitmaps
- ♠ Graphics: Using registration points
- ♠ Interface: Dragging and dropping
- ♠ Lists: Randomizing a list
- ♠ Lists: Using linear lists
- ♠ Lists: Lists that contain lists
- ♠ Math: Using random numbers
- ♠ Members: Using a naming convention
- ♠ Strings: Building member names

This game goes by many names. In the United States, it's usually referred to as just plain "solitaire." However, there are actually many forms of solitaire played with cards. This particular game is usually singled out with the name "Klondike." However, in other parts of the world, particularly Great Britain, this game is known as "patience."

The game is one of both skill and chance. The player's decisions throughout the game can greatly affect the results, but the random shuffle of the deck of cards determines whether it's even possible to win at all.

Played with a real deck of cards, solitaire has been around for a long time. With the advent of computer versions of the game, it is now much easier to play because the computer shuffles the cards and sets up the playing area for you.

Game Overview

Solitaire is a card game played with a standard deck of 52 cards. The cards are shuffled and then many of them are dealt out in a special pattern. The pattern is to have seven "stacks" of cards. The first stack contains one card, face-up. The second contains one card face-down and a card face-up on top of it. Then, each of the rest of the stacks has an additional face-down card until the seventh stack has six face-down cards and one face-up card.

Figure 20.1 shows an example of how these seven stacks look at the beginning of the game. You can also see the other elements, which are spaces for four "piles" of cards, the remainder of the deck at the upper left, and a space below that to put cards.

Figure 20.1

The solitaire game screen is shown here at the beginning of a game.

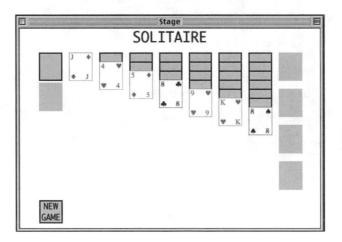

After the seven stacks are dealt, the remainder of the cards are placed face-down, at the upper left. Then, play begins. The player can choose from several different things to do. Any face-up card from any stack can be removed from the stack and added to another stack, providing that the card is the next lowest in value, and that it is of the opposite color. So, a six of spades can be added to a stack that has the seven of hearts on top.

The value of the cards goes from an ace as the lowest, to a king as the highest. So, a red jack can go on top of a black queen, and a black 10 can go on top of a red jack, and so on. As the player shifts the cards around from stack to stack, the stacks will grow.

The player can also move around several cards from a stack, as long as they remain together. So, imagine a stack showing a red ten, a black nine, a red eight, and a black seven. The player can grab the black nine, and the nine, eight, and seven will all move as one. Then, the player can place those three cards, together, on another red ten.

Another move that the player can make is to move an ace to one of the four spaces on the right. After an ace is in one of those spaces, the placer can move a two onto that ace. However, the two must be the same suit as the ace. Moving all the cards, from ace to king, onto those four stacks is the goal of the game. It sounds easy, but it isn't.

The player can also draw three cards from the deck at the upper left. These three cards are then placed, face-up in the space just below the deck. Only the third card is then showing. The player can take this card and move it to a stack or pile, providing the normal conditions are met. The player can always move groups of three cards from the deck to the space below it. If fewer than three cards are left in the deck, then just the remaining one or two cards are moved. When the deck is empty, the face-up cards in the space below are turned back over to become the deck again.

One last move that is available to the player is the ability to move any king onto a spot left open by a stack that has had all of its cards moved. If the king has a queen on top of it, as well as any other cards, they come with it, as usual.

If you are not familiar with this game, I strongly suggest you reread the rules described previously, and then play the sample movie on the CD-ROM several times before proceeding.

NOTE

Solitaire is an odd game in that you rarely win—that is, get all your cards into the piles to the right. A good solitaire player might be able to pull off several wins out of dozens of games, although a novice might play for hours without winning. The game is addictive because most losses seem close to being wins, so you feel like trying again and again.

Deck of Cards

The deck of cards we use for this game is similar, but not the same, as the decks used for poker and blackjack. For one thing, the cards have to be much smaller because solitaire takes up a lot more screen space than the previous two games.

Another difference is that the names of the ace members use a "1" rather than a "14" as their numerical value. So, an ace of spades is named "1 s" rather than "14 s." In solitaire, an ace is always counted as a 1, and always comes before a 2—never after a king.

Naming Conventions

In solitaire, the cards are always placed in little groups. We need to create list variables to hold the cards in these groups, and these variables must have names. So, it's useful to choose names now for each of the groups of cards on the screen. Here is a list of names for the groups:

- **Face-Down Deck**—The deck of cards at the upper-left side of the screen that has all cards face-down.
- **Face-Up Deck**—The face-up deck of cards just below the face-down deck. This starts off as empty.
- **Stacks**—The seven groups of cards in the middle of the screen that the player continuously rearranges during play. At the start of the game, all but the top card is face-down. Each card, however, is partially visible as the cards cascade down the screen rather than being piled directly on top of one another.
- **Piles**—The four spaces at the right side of the screen. The player starts by placing aces in each pile, and then builds up cards of the same suit from there.

Sprite Arrangement

The two decks, and four piles of cards, all just need one sprite each to represent them. This is because only the top card of each will be showing. However, the stacks need whole sets of sprites to represent them.

The first stack of cards starts with one face-up card. If that were, by chance, a king, then it could have a queen placed on top of it, and then a jack on top of that, and so on up to an ace, for a total of 13 cards in the first stack. So, we need 13 sprites for that stack.

The next stack can have the same thing, except that there is a possibility that the face-down card that the stack starts with could still be present. In that case, there could be 14 sprites needed. The seventh stack, then, could need a total of 19 sprites, to represent the six face-down cards and a king-through-ace run of 13 cards.

The chances that each stack will need the maximum number of sprites is unlikely, but we have to account for it. So, we need to arrange seven groups of sprites, with 13 to 19 sprites in each stack.

Card Movement

We use basic drag-and-drop Lingo to move the cards. However, we also have to take into account that the player might want to move several cards in a stack at once. To do this, the player clicks on the bottom card in the sequence. So, a player might want to move an eight, seven, and six at once. They would click and drag the eight and the seven and six on top of it will move along with the eight.

This is actually easy to do. The actual card being dragged just sends a message to the very next sprite when the dragging starts. This next sprite then acts as if it were being dragged as well. The message gets passed to the next sprite as well, and so on down the line, until an empty or unused sprite channel doesn't allow the message to be passed. So, we have to be sure that the groups of sprites for each stack are separated by one empty channel.

Special Effects

The only special effect in the sample movie on the CD-ROM is a standard card sound for the completion of any action. So, when the player drops a card onto a new stack or pile, they hear a "click." This same sound is played three times when the player hits the deck and turns over three cards.

Making the Game

Most of the code is in one large frame behavior. However, there is also an important behavior for the cards in the stacks and the deck up that allow the player to drag and drop the cards. In addition, there are a few very small scripts for special sprites.

Frame Behavior

The frame behavior controls the entire game state. All the principal data structures, such as the cards in the decks, stacks, and piles, are properties of the frame behavior.

In addition, other properties keep track of the sprites used by the cards, as well as the stack and number of the card currently being dragged, if any.

```
property pDeckDown -- cards in the face-down deck
property pDeckUp -- cards in the face-up deck
property pStacks -- list of lists of cards in stacks
property pPiles -- list of lists of cards in piles
property pStackSprites -- seven sprites that start stacks
property pDeckDownSprite, pDeckUpSprite -- sprites used for deck
property pPileSprites -- four sprites used for piles
property pDragStack, pDragCardNum -- used to define current card being dragged
```

When the frame begins, a new game starts. Before that, however, all the sprite channel numbers need to be defined. These numbers come from the Score, after arranging the sprites is completed. If you change the location of anything in the Score, you need to update the *on beginSprite* handler to reflect it.

```
-- set up sprites
on beginSprite me
  pStackSprites = [8,22,37,53,70,88,107]
  pDeckDownSprite = 5
  pDeckUpSprite = 6
  pPileSprites = [127,128,129,130]

  startGame(me)
end
```

The *on beginSprite* handler ends by calling the "on startGame" handler. Here, all things that must precede the first player move occur.

First, the deck is created and shuffled ①. Then, cards are dealt out to each of the seven stacks ②. The rest of the cards go into the "pDeckDown" property ③. The rest of the card lists, such as the "pPiles" property and the "pDeckUp" property, are set to empty lists ④.

Finally, three different handlers are called as many times as necessary to set up all the sprites ⑤. These are the "on showDeck", "on showStack", and "on showPile" handlers.

```
-- clear everything and start new
on startGame me
  -- create an ordered deck
  temp = []
  repeat with suit in ["s","h","c","d"]
    repeat with num = 1 to 13
      add temp, num&&suit
    end repeat
  end repeat
```

①➤
```
  -- pick random cards to create shuffled deck
  deck = []
  repeat while temp.count > 0
    r = random(temp.count)
    add deck, temp[r]
    deleteAt temp, r
  end repeat
```

②➤
```
  -- deal cards out to stacks
  pStacks = []
  repeat with stack = 1 to 7
    -- create stack
    add pStacks, []
    repeat with i = 1 to stack
      if i = stack then
        -- deal last card face-up
        add pStacks[stack], [#card: deck[1], #up: TRUE]
      else
        -- deal card face-down
        add pStacks[stack], [#card: deck[1], #up: FALSE]
      end if
      -- remove card from deck
      deleteAt deck, 1
    end repeat
  end repeat
```

```
                  -- put rest of the cards in face-down deck
③→ pDeckDown = deck
                  -- start with empty face-up deck
     pDeckUp = []
                  -- start with empty piles
④→ pPiles = [[],[],[],[]]

⑤→ -- show all stacks
     repeat with stack = 1 to 7
       showStack(me,stack)
     end repeat
     -- show decks
     showDeck(me)
     -- show all piles
     repeat with pile = 1 to 4
       showPile(me,pile)
     end repeat
   end
```

The following handler updates the sprites for a single stack of cards. It gets the sprite number from the "pStackSprites" property. It checks for the special case of a stack being empty, and places a "Card Outline" member there instead ⑥ .

It also checks to see whether the card in the stack is face-up or face-down. Each card in the "pStacks" property is represented by a small property list, with the first property, #card, being the card name, and the second property, #up, being whether the card is face-up or not. If the card is face-up, then the card's member is placed in the sprite; otherwise, the "Card Back" member is placed there ⑦ .

The loop in the handler continues past the number of cards in the stack. When the sprite is farther down the stack, and there is no card needed to be shown, then the "Card Placeholder" is shown instead. This is a bitmap of a single pixel, with the registration point set so far off that the pixel never appears on the Stage at all.

```
  -- update a stack's sprites
 on showStack me, stack
   -- loop through all sprites
   repeat with i = 1 to 13+stack
     -- see if the sprite should contain a card
     if i <= pStacks[stack].count then
       -- see if the card is face-up
       if pStacks[stack][i].up then
         -- set sprite to card
         sprite(pStackSprites[stack]+i-1).member = member(pStacks[stack][i].card)
       else
```

continues

continued

```
                    -- set sprite to back of card
⑦➤      sprite(pStackSprites[stack]+i-1).member = member("Card Back")
           end if
        else if i = 1 then
           -- first sprite is not a card, stack is empty
           -- so place an outline in first sprite
⑥➤      sprite(pStackSprites[stack]).member = member("Card Outline")
        else
           -- no card, place a placeholder member in sprite
           sprite(pStackSprites[stack]+i-1).member = member("Card Placeholder")
        end if
     end repeat
  end
```

The "on showDeck" handler updates the two sprites that show the face-up and face-down decks. The face-down deck is always a "Card Back" except for when the deck is empty. In this case, a "Card Outline" is shown.

The face-up deck is always the last card in the face-up deck, except for when no cards are face-up at all. In this case, the "Card Outline" is also shown.

```
  -- update the deck sprites
  on showDeck me
     -- face-down deck
     if pDeckDown.count = 0 then
        -- deck empty, so place outline instead
        sprite(pDeckDownSprite).member = member("Card Outline")
     else
        -- place back of card
        sprite(pDeckDownSprite).member = member("Card Back")
     end if

     -- face-up deck
     if pDeckUp.count = 0 then
        -- deck empty, so place outline instead
        sprite(pDeckUpSprite).member = member("Card Outline")
     else
        -- place last card in sprite
        sprite(pDeckUpSprite).member = member(getLast(pDeckUp))
     end if
  end
```

The "on showPile" handler updates a single pile sprite. It places either a "Card Outline" there if the deck is pile is empty or it places the last card in the pile there.

```
-- update a pile sprite
on showPile me, pile
  -- see if pile is empty
  if pPiles[pile].count = 0 then
    -- empty pile, so use outline
    sprite(pPileSprites[pile]).member = member("Card Outline")
  else
    -- use last card in pile
    sprite(pPileSprites[pile]).member = member(getLast(pPiles[pile]))
  end if
end
```

When the player clicks on the face-down deck, they are dealt three more cards to the face-up deck. The "deckClick" handler does this, provided there are cards in the face-down deck. If not, it takes the entire face-up deck and moves it to the face-down deck.

Also, if the player asks for the three cards, but only one or two are in the face-down deck, then only those cards are dealt, leaving the face-down deck empty in either case.

```
-- player clicks on face-down deck
on deckClick me
  if pDeckDown.count = 0 then
    -- if deck is empty, then take all cards from face-up deck
  -- and place in face-down deck
pDeckDown = pDeckUp
    pDeckUp = []
    showDeck(me)
  else
    -- draw three cards from face-down deck
    repeat with i = 1 to 3
      -- see if no more cards are left
      if pDeckDown.count = 0 then exit repeat
      -- deal a single card
      add pDeckUp, pDeckDown[1]
      deleteAt pDeckDown, 1
      -- update sprites
      showDeck(me)
      -- play sound and pause
      puppetSound 1, "Card Sound"
      updateStage
      t = the ticks + 5
      repeat while the ticks < t
      end repeat
    end repeat
  end if
end
```

Most of the game logic is in the "on dropCard" handler. This handler determines whether a player's drag action results in the cards changing positions. Let's look at this handler bit by bit.

First, the handler tries to determine which card is being dragged. This can either be the top card on the face-up deck, or a card from one of the stacks. In the first case, "pDragStack" is set to 0. In the second case, both the "pDragStack" and "pDragCardNum" properties are set. These show the stack number of the card, and the card number as its position in that stack. So, if the player drags the fourth card from the seventh stack, then "pDragStack" is 7 and "pDragCardNum" is 4.

Either way, the card's numerical value is taken from its name, and stored in "dragCardValue".

```
-- determine what happens when a player drops a card
on dropCard me, thisSprite, thisLoc
  -- get info on card being dragged
  if thisSprite = pDeckUpSprite then
    -- dragging a card from the deck
    pDragStack = 0
    dragCardValue = value(getLast(pDeckUp).word[1])
  else
    -- dragging a card from a stack
    getCardFromSprite(me,thisSprite)
    dragCardValue = value(pStacks[pDragStack][pDragCardNum].card.word[1])
  end if
```

Next, a message is sent back to the sprite to return it to its original position. This negates the player's drag action, but this won't be seen until the handler is complete, and cards have been shifted around into new stacks or piles.

```
-- sprite must return to original location
sendSprite(thisSprite,#returnToOrigLoc)
```

The "dropStack" variable is set using the "on getStackUnderLoc" function. This function tells the handler which stack the player has moved the card to. If the result is *VOID*, then the player has either moved the card to a pile, or they have moved it somewhere else on the screen that is not a valid resting place for a card.

```
-- get the stack that the card is dropped on
dropStack = getStackUnderLoc(me,thisLoc)
```

If the card is being dropped onto a new stack, then the numerical value of the card presently at the top of the stack is computed. If the stack is empty, then a value of 14 is used, which allows for a king, which has a value of 13, to be placed into the pile.

```
-- card is being dropped onto a stack
if not voidP(dropStack) then
```

```
-- get the value of the last card on the stack
if pStacks[dropStack].count = 0 then
  -- if stack empty, use a value of 14
  dropStackValue = 14
else
  dropStackValue = value(getLast(pStacks[dropStack]).card.word[1])
end if
```

The next step is to determine whether the card being dragged and the card it is being dragged onto have different colors. Only cards with different colors are allowed to be placed on top of each other in stacks.

The following lines of code get the suit of the two cards from their names, and then convert the suits to colors ⑧ . They then compare them and store that value in "colorsDiffer".

```
-- see if the colors of the stack and the drag card are different
if  dropStackValue = 14 then
  -- if stack empty, then colors don't matter
  colorsDiffer = TRUE
else
  -- get the suit of the last card on stack
  suit1 = getLast(pStacks[dropStack]).card.word[2]

  -- get the suit of the drag being dragged
  if thisSprite = pDeckUpSprite then
    -- card from deck
    suit2 = getLast(pDeckUp).word[2]
  else
    -- card from another stack
    suit2 = pStacks[pDragStack][pDragCardNum].card.word[2]
  end if
```

⑧➤
```
  -- get color of cards from suit
  if suit1 = "s" or suit1 = "c" then color1 = "black"
  else color1 = "white"
  if suit2 = "s" or suit2 = "c" then color2 = "black"
  else color2 = "white"

  -- see if colors differ
  colorsDiffer = (color1 <> color2)
end if
```

Now that the handler knows the number and color difference between the two cards, it can determine whether the new cards are allowed in the stack. If so, the new card is added. If the card came from the face-up deck, then the process is simple ⑨ . However, if the card came from another stack, then the handler must move that card, as well as any others that were being dragged along with it ⑩ .

```
      -- only allow drop if card is next value, and different color
      if (dragCardValue = dropStackValue-1) and colorsDiffer then
        if thisSprite = pDeckUpSprite then
⑨→      -- add card taken from deck
          add pStacks[dropStack], [#card: getLast(pDeckUp), #up: TRUE]
          deleteAt pDeckUp, pDeckUp.count
          showDeck(me)
        else -- add all cards taken from other stack
          -- get number of cards in stack
          n = pStacks[pDragStack].count
⑩→      -- loop from card being dragged to end of stack
          repeat with i = pDragCardNum to n
            -- add card to new stack, remove from old
            add pStacks[dropStack], pStacks[pDragStack][pDragCardNum]
            deleteAt pStacks[pDragStack], pDragCardNum
          end repeat
          -- update original stack
          showStack(me,pDragStack)
        end if

        -- update new stack
        showStack(me,dropStack)
        puppetSound 1, "Card Sound"
      end if
```

The other possibility for a card drop is that the player is dropping a new card onto one of the four piles. The function "on getPileUnderLoc" is called to determine which of the four piles. It then stores the numerical value of the last card in that pile in "pileCardValue". If the pile is empty, then a 0 is used, which allows the ace, a 1, to be placed in the pile.

```
    else -- card is being dropped onto pile
      -- get pile under card
      pile = getPileUnderLoc(me,thisLoc)
      if not voidP(pile) then
        -- get value of card on top of pile
        if pPiles[pile].count > 0 then
          pileCardValue = value(getLast(pPiles[pile]).word[1])
        else
          -- if pile is empty, use 0 as value
          pileCardValue = 0
        end if
```

The suit of both the card and the pile need to be compared to determine whether both match.

```
                  -- see if the suit of the pile and the suit of the card match
              if  pileCardValue = 0 then
                  -- suit doesn't matter if pile is empty
         suitsMatch = TRUE
              else
                  -- get suit of pile
                  suit1 = getLast(pPiles[pile]).word[2]
                  -- get suit of card
                  if thisSprite = pDeckUpSprite then
                     -- card is from deck
                     suit2 = getLast(pDeckUp).word[2]
                  else
                     -- card is from stack
                     suit2 = pStacks[pDragStack][pDragCardNum].card.word[2]
                  end if
                  -- determine is suits match
         suitsMatch = (suit1 = suit2)
              end if
```

If the cards match suits, and the new card is the next in line, then the drop is allowed and the new card is added to the pile. Because only one card can be added to the pile at a time, we do not have to consider whole stacks of cards being dragged in this case. In fact, the situation in which the player is dragging more than one card is looked for, and the whole process is aborted if it is true. ⑪

```
                  -- see if card is next value and suits match
              if (dragCardValue = pileCardValue + 1) and suitsMatch then
                  -- see if card is from deck or stack
                  if thisSprite = pDeckUpSprite then
                     -- add card to pile, remove from deck
                     add pPiles[pile], getLast(pDeckUp)
                     deleteAt pDeckUp, pDeckUp.count
                     showDeck(me)
                  else
⑪ ➤            -- if player dragging more than one card, abort
                     if pStacks[pDragStack].count <> pDragCardNum then exit

                     -- add card to pile, remove from stack
                     add pPiles[pile], pStacks[pDragStack][pDragCardNum].card
                     deleteAt pStacks[pDragStack], pDragCardNum
                     showStack(me,pDragStack)
                  end if

                  -- update pile
                  showPile(me,pile)
                  puppetSound 1, "Card Sound"
```

A game is won when the player moves the last king onto the last pile. Because it can end only with a move to a pile, here would be the perfect place to call our "on gameOver" function to see whether the player has won.

```
        if gameOver(me) then
          go to frame "Game Over"
        end if
      end if
    end if
  end if
end
```

The next few handlers perform some tasks needed by the "on dropCard" handler. This first one takes the sprite number of the card being dragged, and determines which stack number and card number is being dragged. It stores these two values in "pDragStack" and "pDragCardNum".

```
-- determine which card is being dragged
on getCardFromSprite me, thisSprite
  -- loop through all stacks
  repeat with stack = 1 to 7
    -- loop through all cards in stack
    repeat with card = 1 to pStacks[stack].count
      -- get sprite used by card
      s = pStackSprites[stack]+card-1
      -- see if this matches
      if s = thisSprite then
        -- note card number and stack
        pDragStack = stack
        pDragCardNum = card
        exit
      end if
    end repeat
  end repeat
end
```

The "on getStackUnderLoc" handler loops through all the sprites used by stack cards and determines whether any stacks are at a Stage location. It returns the stack number.

```
-- determine which stack the card is dropped on
on getStackUnderLoc me, thisLoc
  -- loop through stacks
  repeat with stack = 1 to 7
    -- see if this is same as original stack
    if stack = pDragStack then next repeat
    -- loop through cards in stack
    repeat with i = 1 to max(pStacks[stack].count,1)
      -- get sprite used by card
```

```
        s = pStackSprites[stack]+i-1
        -- if location is inside sprite's rect then this must be the stack
        if inside(thisLoc, sprite(s).rect) then
          return stack
        end if
      end repeat
    end repeat
  end
```

The "on getPileUnderLoc" handler performs a similar task to the last handler, but looks at the four pile sprites instead. It returns the pile number.

```
-- determine which pile the card is dropped on
on getPileUnderLoc me, thisLoc
  -- loop through piles
  repeat with pile = 1 to 4
    -- get sprite use by pile
    s = pPileSprites[pile]
    -- if location is inside sprite's rect then this must be the pile
    if inside(thisLoc, sprite(s).rect) then
      return pile
    end if
  end repeat
end
```

Another player move to account for is when the player clicks on the face-down deck to get three more cards. This handler takes care of this action by taking three cards, one at a time, from the face-down deck and adding them to the face-up deck. A sound and a slight delay are added as special effects.

```
-- player clicks on face-down card in stack
on turnCardOver me, thisSprite
  -- loop through stacks
  repeat with stack = 1 to 7
    -- get last card in stack
    card = pStacks[stack].count
    -- determine sprite used by card
    s = pStackSprites[stack]+card-1
    -- see if this is the sprite
    if s = thisSprite then
      -- turn card over
      pStacks[stack][card].up = TRUE
      -- update stack
      showStack(me,stack)
      puppetSound 1, "Card Sound"
      exit repeat
    end if
  end repeat
end
```

The game is won if the player has moved all the cards onto the piles. To determine whether this has happened, all we need to do is check each pile for a total of 13 cards.

```
-- determine if game is over
on gameover me
  repeat with i = 1 to 4
    if pPiles[i].count <> 13 then
      return FALSE
    end if
  end repeat
  return TRUE
end
```

The frame behavior must also create the frame loop.

```
-- loop on frame
on exitFrame
  go to the frame
end
```

Finally, a hook is put in the frame behavior for a "New Game" button. All this really needs to do is call the "on startGame" handler, but it's a good idea to have a separate "on newGame" handler in case other functionality is desired in the future.

```
-- get signal from button to start a new game
on newGame me
  startGame(me)
end
```

Card Drag Behavior

This behavior is for any sprite that can possibly contain a movable card. That includes all the cards in the stack and the one sprite used as the face-up deck.

The behavior uses techniques similar to other drag behaviors from earlier chapters, such as Chapter 3, "Matching Game." The "pDrag" property is *TRUE* only if the sprite is currently being dragged. The "pOffset" property is the offset between the mouse and the center of the sprite. It is used to keep the cursor and the sprite at the same relative position as the drag goes on.

```
property pDrag -- is this sprite being dragged
property pOrigLoc -- starting loc of sprite
property pOffset -- mouse drag offset
```

The original location of the sprite is recorded so that the sprite can return there after any drag is over.

```
-- record original location
on beginSprite me
```

```
      pOrigLoc = sprite(me.spriteNum).loc
  end
```

The dragging starts when the user clicks down on the sprite. First, the card is checked to see whether it is a face-down card on top of a stack. If so, a "turnCardOver" message is sent to the frame behavior. Otherwise, if the card sprite is a "Card Outline" or "Card Placeholder" member, the click is ignored.

If the card is a normal, face-up card from a stack or the face-up deck, then "pDrag" is set to *TRUE* and the offset is recorded ⑫ . The *locZ* property of the sprite is set to its current sprite number, plus 1000, which places it above all other sprites. Then, the "startFollow" message is sent to the next sprite, in case the player is trying to drag several cards at once.

NOTE

The locZ property overrides the sprite channel number. So, a sprite in channel 6 would normally be drawn under a sprite in channel 7. However, if you set the locZ of sprite 6 to 8, then it would be drawn on top.

```
  -- start drag
  on mouseDown me
     -- see if the card is face-down or an outline
     if sprite(me.spriteNum).member = member("Card Back") then
        -- face down, so just turn over
        sendSprite(0,#turnCardOver,me.spriteNum)
     else if sprite(me.spriteNum).member = member("Card Outline") then
        -- outline, so ignore click
        nothing
     else if sprite(me.spriteNum).member = member("Card Placeholder") then
        -- no card, so ignore click
        nothing
     else
⑫ ➤    -- start drag
        pDrag = TRUE
        pOffset = the clickLoc - pOrigLoc
        -- move to front
        sprite(me.spriteNum).locZ = me.spriteNum + 1000
        -- tell cards in rest of stack to follow
        sendSprite(me.spriteNum+1,#startFollow)
     end if
  end
```

When the player lifts up the mouse button, the drag ends and the "dropCard" message is sent to the frame behavior. In addition, the "endFollow" message is sent to the next sprite.

```
-- end drag
on mouseUp me
  if pDrag then
    pDrag = FALSE
    -- send message to frame behavior to drop card(s)
    sendSprite(0,#dropCard,me.spriteNum,sprite(me.spriteNum).loc)
    -- tell rest of cards in stack to stop following
    sendSprite(me.spriteNum+1,#endFollow)
  end if
end
```

We also need a handler to pass along a "mouseUp" message if the cursor has moved away from the sprite. This could happen if the player tries to drag a card off the screen. All the handler needs to do is pass the message on to the *on mouseUp* handler.

```
on mouseUpOutside me
  mouseUp(me)
end
```

After the frame behavior determines which stack or pile the card has been dragged to, it can return the sprite to its original location. This is important so that the next time the sprite is used, it's in its original location.

```
-- return card to original location and layer
on returnToOrigLoc me
  sprite(me.spriteNum).locZ = me.spriteNum
  sprite(me.spriteNum).loc = pOrigLoc
end
```

The "on exitFrame" handler positions the sprite under the cursor while a drag action is taking place.

```
-- card follows mouse
on exitFrame me
  if pDrag then
    sprite(me.spriteNum).loc = the mouseLoc - pOffset
  end if
end
```

When a card begins a drag, it sends the "startFollow" message to the next sprite. That message ends up at the next handler, which simply calls *on mouseDown*, which contains exactly the right code to have the sprite follow the original. In addition, *on mouseDown* sends the "startFollow" to the next sprite as well. This continues until all the cards on top of the current one are moving.

```
-- card gets message to follow mouse
on startFollow me
  -- perform the same as a mouseDown
  mouseDown(me)
end
```

Finally, the "on endFollow" handler responds to a message sent by the original sprite when it is finished being dragged. It stops the other sprites from being dragged and passes the message down the line so that all sprites being dragged will stop.

```
-- card gets message to stop following
on endFollow me
  pDrag = FALSE
  returnToOrigLoc(me)
  -- pass the message along
  sendSprite(me.spriteNum+1,#endFollow)
end
```

Other Behaviors

There are just two more behaviors that are needed for the game to be complete. The first is placed on the face-down deck, and sends the "deckClick" message to the frame script.

```
on mouseUp
  sendSprite(0,#deckClick)
end
```

The other handler is for a "NewGame" button and also just passes a simple message on to the frame behavior.

```
on mouseUp
  sendSprite(0,#newGame)
end
```

Putting It All Together

The first order of business should be making the deck of cards. Remember that the deck used in this game needs to have smaller cards than the deck used in the poker and blackjack games. Also, you need to name the aces with a "1," rather than a "14." See the movie on the CD-ROM for an example.

After you have the deck of cards, you also need to create a "Card Back" member and a "Card Outline" member. In the sample movie, the "Card Back" member has a dark outline and a gray interior. The "Card Outline" member is just a gray rectangle.

You also need a "Card Placeholder" exactly like the one in the blackjack game. It is a single pixel with the registration point set so far off that the pixel won't appear on the Stage.

Now that you have the members, arrange them on the Stage and in the Score. Start by placing the cards on the Stage in the groups needed to form the stacks. You can use the "Card Back" graphic to help arrange them. Figure 20.2 shows what this would look like.

Figure 20.2
*The "Card Back"
member is used to
arrange the sprites
on the Stage.*

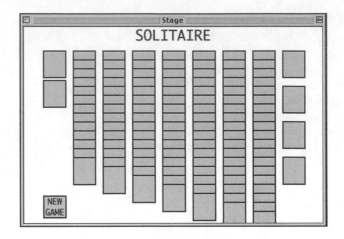

The first stack should have 13 sprites in it, and each sprite should be a little lower on the Stage. The next stack should be 14 sprites, and so on until the seventh stack has 19 sprites. You can see these stacks clearly in Figure 20.2.

Next, you need to place six more sprites: the four piles to the right, and the face-up deck and the face-down deck to the left. You can see these in Figure 20.2 as well.

In the Score, all the stacks need to occupy their own group of sprites. In the sample movie, the first stack starts at sprite 8 and goes to sprite 20. Then, the second stack goes from 22 to 35. This continues until the last stack uses sprites 107 to 125. This Score is much too long to be shown in a figure here, but you can check the sample movie on the CD-ROM if you need to.

The sprites that represent the piles are in channels 127 and 130, and the face-up and face-down decks are in sprite channels 5 and 6, respectively.

When you have finished with sprite placement, add the "Card Drag Behavior" to all the stack card sprites, as well as the face-up deck sprite. Then, add the "Face-Down Deck" behavior to the face-down deck sprite.

After you add the frame behavior to the frame script channel, the game is playable. However, you still need to make a "New Game" button and attach the "New Game Button" behavior to it as well.

Game Variations

There are many ways to create unique versions of solitaire to be used on Web sites and CD-ROMs. In fact, there are also many other types of solitaire games that you can make.

Las Vegas Rules

This is a common variation of solitaire that is just like the version in this chapter, but with scoring. The way the scoring works is that you get -52 points every time you start a new game. Then, you get 5 points for every card that you place on the piles.

This is a little odd at first, because you start out at -52 points. However, it makes sense as you play. You don't even have to win a game to do well. You can often find ways to put 10 or 20 cards on the piles before reaching the point where you can't go any further.

One other change that is required for this game is that you are able to convert the face-up deck to the face-down deck only three times. After that, the face-up deck remains and the face-down deck is forever empty. This helps put the odds back in favor of the house, but a good solitaire player can still always come out ahead in the end.

Animated Cards

I have to mention this as an option for any card game, because it is something that I have done and had great success with. CleverMedia has a game called "Not-So-Solitaire" that tries to live up to its name in two ways.

First, it uses the "Las Vegas Rules" and has a high score board. This fosters competition, which means that it isn't really "solitaire" anymore.

The second way that the game is "Not-So-Solitaire" is that the cards seem to be alive. All the face cards have animations and sounds. So, the queen of diamonds occasionally sneezes, and so on. Figure 20.3 shows the animation sequence for one of these cards.

Figure 20.3
An animated sequence that is used for a face card rather than a static graphic.

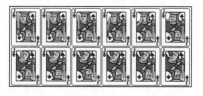

Other Solitaire Games

There are dozens of other card games named "solitaire." Although this game is referred to as "Klondike," the other games have different names and rules. Although all are one-player games, some bear little likeness to the game in this chapter. Here is a list of some of the most popular:

- **Pyramid**—In this game, the cards are arranged in a pyramid, with cards in each row overlapping the cards in the row before it. The player must use the uncovered cards, plus ones from the deck, to make matches that add up to a total of 13.

- **Poker**—In this game, cards are arranged in a five-by-five grid by the player. Each row and each column is then assigned a point value depending on the poker hand it represents.

- **Canfield**—This game is similar to Klondike, but instead of using four aces, the four piles use a random foundation card. There are only four stacks instead of seven.

- **Maze**—Instead of piling cards on top of each other, this game features the deck laid out in a grid with several spaces empty. Then, the player must rearrange them to put the deck in order.

- **Accordion**—The cards are all dealt out in a long row. The player must then match cards, by value or suit, to the card to the left, or the card three to the left. A player wins if he or she is able to build one large pile.

- **Calculation**—An ace, two, three, and four are placed face-up. There are also three "waste heap" piles. The player must place the cards in order on the ace, or every second card on the two, or every third card on the three, or every fourth card on the four, until each pile contains 13 cards. If a card cannot be placed on a pile, it can be placed on a waste heap instead. The top card on any waste heap can be played at any time.

If you are interested in creating more solitaire games, you should buy a book on the subject. You can find many at your local bookstore. A book on my shelf, *The Little Giant Encyclopedia of Card Games*, lists 31 solitaire card games.

This list is here to inspire you. Some of the code in this chapter will help you make these additional solitaire games, but it will definitely take a Lingo expert to execute most of them.

Part VI:
Adventure and Strategy Games

●●●●

21   Adventure Game   **351**

22   Maze Game   **377**

23   Strategy Game   **389**

Adventure Game

21

550

CD-ROM Movie: 21adventure.dir

Useful Lingo in This Chapter

♠ Behaviors: Calling handlers in other behaviors

♠ Behaviors: Using parameters

♠ Graphics: Changing sprite members with Lingo

♠ Graphics: Making sprites disappear

♠ Graphics: Using a rectangle shape member

♠ Graphics: Using film loops

♠ Graphics: Using a rectangle shape member

♠ Input: Accepting arrow keys

♠ Lists: Using linear lists

♠ Lists: Using property lists

♠ Lists: Lists that contain lists

♠ Math: Using random numbers

♠ Members: Using a naming convention

♠ Programming: Creating a random maze

♠ Strings: Building member names

♠ Variables: Keeping score

Adventure games have always been popular computer games. From the beginning, when they were text-based, to the present day, in which elaborate three-dimensional graphics take the place of text, adventures games have been a major genre in the computer world.

Game Overview

The term "adventure game" really describes a whole genre of games, not a specific game. I could write an entire book on different types of adventure games. However, we will have to settle on a specific game to proceed.

Making adventure games with Director can be done in many different ways. This chapter looks at a two-dimensional top-down view adventure game. We'll combine code for character movement, collision detection, and other techniques.

Rooms

Most adventure games are based on *rooms*. A room can be an actual room, perhaps in a castle, haunted house, dungeon, or space station. It also can be a section of forest or a street corner. The term *room* defines a geographic location in the game.

In text-based adventures, a room would be a sentence or two describing the location. In graphic adventures, a room would be a drawing or rendering. In our game, a room is a Director frame showing a top-down view of the area, with walls and objects. Figure 21.1 shows the first room in this game.

Figure 21.1
The first room in our adventure game shows four walls, two doors, a dagger, and the character in the center.

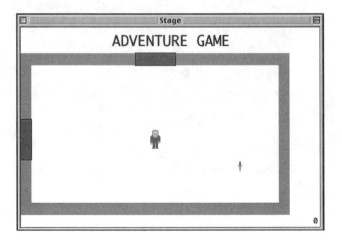

There are a total of 11 rooms in the sample movie on the CD-ROM. However, the game code supports as many rooms as you need. Each room is a different frame, with a unique frame marker name. This first room is simply known as "Room 1." We will number each room this way, but you could just as easily use names such as "Foyer" and "Dining Room."

Movement

The *character* is the personification of the player in the game. In some adventure games, the character is never seen, as the player is seeing the action through the character's eyes. In our game, the character is a sprite on the Stage.

Figure 21.2 shows the character's bitmap members. We use nine bitmaps for the character. The first simply shows the character standing. The others are four two-member animations to show the character walking in four directions.

Figure 21.2

The nine bitmaps that make up the character.

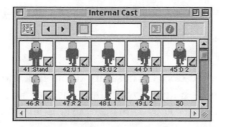

The player uses the arrow keys to control the character. When an arrow key is pressed, the character moves in one of four directions. The character also animates using the two bitmaps provided for each direction.

When the character stops, it should revert to the "Stand" bitmap. We use a timer to do this. After the player stops moving, the timer determines how long it has been since the character stopped. Then, the character's sprite reverts to the "Stand" bitmap after a set time.

Walls

Each room needs walls. A wall is simply an object that the character cannot walk through. In Figure 21.1, we see four walls, one on each side of the screen. They are just gray rectangles in this movie, but in your game they can be elaborate bitmaps of bricks, stones, or wood.

A wall doesn't have to be a "wall," either. It can be a hedge of bushes or a row of trees. Anything that a player cannot pass through is a wall. Even a stream or chasm would be considered a wall according to the game code.

Walls have a behavior attached to them that looks for instances in which the character collides with the wall. In that case, the code has to take steps to ensure that the move is not allowed.

Objects

As the player moves through the game, he or she should come upon objects. An object is an item that the player can pick up and add to his or her *inventory*.

Inventory is a common word used in adventure games to describe the list of objects that a player is carrying with them. Each time the character's sprite collides with an object, it is picked up and added to the player's inventory.

The inventory itself is shown by a collection of sprites on one side of the screen. As the player picks up objects, they disappear from the rooms and are added to the inventory.

Doors

A door is a portal to another room. In this game, and in most others, doors are placed on top of walls. When the character collides with a door, they change rooms.

For a door to work, each door must be assigned a property that tells the code which room the player is being transferred to.

In addition, we also have locked doors. These are doors that the players cannot use until they have an object that acts as a key. To facilitate this, each door also has a property that determines which object is its key. If this property is left blank, then the door is unlocked and no key is needed.

Just as with walls, a door doesn't necessarily need to be a door. It can be stairs, an entryway, a cave opening, or even a magic portal. You can even have a door that is invisible, meaning that it blends in with the background. This could allow you to have long areas where the left and right sides of each room are completely open to the next room.

Monsters

Most adventures include some sort of living creatures, usually hostile. They don't have to be, but because this is how they are commonly used, we created hostile creatures for this sample game.

Our monsters have a simple behavior in this game. When you enter a room that contains a monster, that monster comes right at you and kills you if it catches you. However, if you have the item that can kill the monster, then you kill it instead.

This game has two monsters. The first is a bat. That monster kills you unless you have the "dagger" object. Later in the game, you encounter the dragon, which kills you unless you have the "sword" item.

We also build in to our monster behavior the ability to have objects that protect you from a monster. There is a "ring" object that makes you invisible to the dragon.

Each monster needs at least three properties. The first is the speed at which the monster comes toward you. The second is the object that kills the monster. The third is the object, if any, that protects you from the monster.

Signs

Another element in the game is signs. These are objects that you do not pick up, but rather simply touch. When you touch them, some text appears on the screen. The effect is that you are reading the object.

I call these "signs" for lack of a more general description. In this sample game, we use a bitmap of a signpost. However, you could use anything that can relay words: a book, a plaque, scroll, a computer screen, a piece of paper, or even a talking parrot.

Containers

Sometimes, objects are inside containers. These are things such as chests, barrels, lockers, cans, boxes, vaults, and so on. These almost always require a key object to open them.

Our container objects have two primary properties. The first is the name of the key object that is required to open them. The second is the name of the object inside.

When the player collides with a container, we check to see whether they have the key. If they do, they are given the object that is inside.

Points

Many adventure games have both a goal and a point system. Points are a way of keeping score. As the player gets objects or kills monsters, they are awarded points.

We assign a point value to all objects, monsters, and containers. As the player gets, kills, or opens these, their score increases.

There also is a "points" object type. This is an object that the player picks up, but instead of having the object added to their inventory, they are just awarded points. In the sample movie, a pile of coins is used in several rooms as a "points" object. You also could use similar treasures scattered about your adventure.

The Puzzle

Think of an adventure game as one large puzzle. The player needs to do certain things before they can complete the puzzle. For instance, if the goal of the game is to get the treasure, but the treasure is in a locked chest, then the player needs to find the key to that chest first. The chest might be guarded by a dragon, which can be killed only by the sword. So, the player has to find the sword first, kill the dragon, and then open the chest with the key.

Constructing puzzles like this is what makes an adventure game interesting. Games can contain many smaller puzzles, all of which end up adding to the player's inventory or knowledge. Then, these completed puzzles can end up helping to solve future puzzles.

Special Effects

One room in this game corresponds to one frame in the movie. You can add anything you want to that frame, including graphics and sounds. Our sample movie is not complicated with such things, but it is easy for you to further decorate each room just by playing with the Score.

Making the Game

We build this game using very object-oriented methods. This means that each type of object has its own behavior, including the player's character.

Character Behavior

The character behavior is the primary object in the game. It contains all the properties that persist throughout play, such as the player's inventory and score. It also accepts keyboard input and controls the character animation.

The properties of the character include three lists: "pInventory", "pHaveKilled", and "pPointsList". The first is the player's inventory and determines which items are shown on the screen as being owned by the player, and also is used to prevent those items from being shown in the rooms where they were originally placed. The other two lists fill only that second function. They are used to ensure that the monsters and the points objects are no longer shown in a room when the player enters it.

```
property pInventory -- list of items owned
property pHaveKilled -- list of monsters killed
property pPoints -- number of points
property pPointsList -- list of points object gathered
property pSpeed -- speed of movement
property pAnimNum -- animation number
property pLastMove -- time of last move
```

When the behavior begins, the player's speed is set, and the two properties used to determine which member to draw on the screen are set. The inventory and the other lists are cleared.

A call is made to sprite 21, which contains a text member and a behavior that controls it. This text member is used to display information to the player. The only parameter it takes is which message to display. In this case, an empty string is passed in, which clears any previous text from the member.

```
on beginSprite me
  -- set animation properties
  pSpeed = 5
  pAnimNum = 1
  pLastMove = 0
```

```
   -- set character properties
   pInventory = []
   pHaveKilled = []
   pPointsList = []
   pPoints = 0

   -- clear screen
   showPoints(me)
   sendSprite(21,#message,"")
end
```

On each frame loop, the keyboard is checked to see whether the player is pressing an arrow key. If any arrow key has been pressed, the "on move" handler is called with the horizontal and vertical movement amount.

The *on exitFrame* handler also checks to see whether 10 ticks have passed since the last move. If so, the character sprite reverts to the "Stand" bitmap ①.

```
on exitFrame me
   -- keyboard input
   if keyPressed(123) then
     move(me,-1,0) -- left
   else if keyPressed(124) then
     move(me,1,0) -- right
   else if keyPressed(125) then
     move(me,0,1) -- down
   else if keyPressed(126) then
     move(me,0,-1) -- up
   end if

   -- if standing still, reset character
   if the ticks > pLastMove + 10 then
①→ sprite(me.spriteNum).member = member("Stand")
   end if
end
```

When the character is told to move, checks must be made to be sure that the character is not hitting a wall. At the same time, we must check to see whether some other action is needed, such as picking up an object or slaying a monster.

The "on move" handler starts off by getting the location of the character's sprite. It forms a rectangle by figuring out the maximum width and height of the current sprite member and the "Stand" member. It needs to do this because if the player stops moving, the character reverts to the "Stand" member, which might be larger than the current member. In that case, the "Stand" member might overlap an object in the room, such as a door.

As a safety precaution, the rectangle is examined to see whether the character is positioned off screen. That, of course, is not allowed.

Next, sprites 31 through 80 are told about the movement. These sprites are the ones that contain any screen object, including walls, monsters, objects, signs, and so on. The message #detectCollision is sent, complete with the new rectangle and the movement amount.

If any of the calls to "on detectCollision" returns a value of *TRUE*, then the movement is aborted ②. Otherwise, the location of the sprite is updated and the character animation is performed.

NOTE

Another reason to store the *rect* of a sprite in a variable and change that independently, instead of moving the sprite and then getting the new *rect*, is that the *rect* property of a sprite does not update until the screen is refreshed inside an *on exitFrame* handler. Therefore, moving the sprite, and then getting the *rect* returns only the old *rect*, not the new one. Because we want to get the new *rect* before the player sees a change on the screen, we make the change in a variable instead of onscreen.

```
-- move character
on move me, dx, dy
  -- get current loc
  loc = sprite(me.spriteNum).loc

  -- determine largest rect needed
  w = max(member("Stand").rect.width, sprite(me.spriteNum).rect.width)
  h = max(member("Stand").rect.height, sprite(me.spriteNum).rect.height)
  rect = rect(loc.locH-w/2-1,loc.locV-h/2-1,loc.locH+w/2+1,loc.locV+h/2+1)

  -- move loc and rect
  loc = loc + point(dx,dy)*pSpeed
  rect = rect + rect(dx*pSpeed,dy*pSpeed,dx*pSpeed,dy*pSpeed)

  -- safety check to make sure character stays on screen
  if rect.left < 0 then exit
  if rect.top < 0 then exit
  if rect.right > (the stage).rect.width then exit
  if rect.bottom > (the stage).rect.height then exit

  -- check all objects for collisions
  repeat with i = 80 down to 31
    -- all "detectCollision"s return TRUE if character should not move
    if sendSprite(i,#detectCollision,rect,dx,dy) then exit
  end repeat
```

②➤ (points to `if sendSprite(i,#detectCollision,rect,dx,dy) then exit`)

```
-- set new character location
sprite(me.spriteNum).loc = loc

-- advance animation
pAnimNum = pAnimNum + 1
if pAnimNum > 2 then pAnimNum = 1

-- set character direction
if dx > 0 then anim = "R"
else if dx < 0 then anim = "L"
else if dy > 0 then anim = "D"
else if dy < 0 then anim = "U"

-- set character member
sprite(me.spriteNum).member = member(anim&&pAnimNum)

-- remember this time as time of last move
pLastMove = the ticks
end
```

The "on takeObject" handler adds an object to the player's inventory and updates the items shown. It also puts up a message about the new acquisition. This handler, like many in this behavior, is called by the objects on the Stage when they need to alter the character's properties.

```
-- add object to inventory
on takeObject me, objectName
  add pInventory, objectName -- add
  showInventory(me) -- update screen
  sendSprite(21,#message,objectName&&"Taken!") -- show message
end
```

When a player encounters a container, the "on openObject" handler is called and the object is opened, provided the player has the proper key. When the object is opened, the item inside is added to the inventory ③ .

```
-- open a container
on openObject me, objectName, contents, key
  -- see if the container is open, or player has a key
  if key = "" or getOne(pInventory,key) then
③▶ add pInventory, contents - add
    showInventory(me) -- update screen
    sendSprite(21,#message,objectName&&"Opened."&&contents&&"Taken!") -- show message
    return TRUE -- make sure behavior removes object from screen
```

continues

continued

```
      else -- player doesn't have key
        sendSprite(21,#message,"You can't open the"&&objectName&".") -- show message
        return FALSE -- behavior keeps object on screen
      end if
    end
```

A set of seven sprites is reserved to display the player's inventory. Every time the inventory changes, the sprites are updated to show the new items. If you have more than seven objects in the game, you want to have a larger set of sprites to accommodate them.

```
  -- place objects in inventory sprites
  on showInventory me
    -- seven spots available
    repeat with i = 1 to 7
      if i > pInventory.count then -- past end of list
        sprite(10+i).memberNum = 0 -- remove sprite
      else
        sprite(10+i).member = member(pInventory[i]) -- show object
      end if
    end repeat
  end
```

When a new room is entered, the different objects use the "on haveItem" handler to inquire whether they have already been picked up on a previous visit to the room.

```
  -- utility will return TRUE if player has an item
  on haveItem me, objectName
    return getOne(pInventory,objectName)
  end
```

When a monster is killed, a call to "on killedMonster" adds it to the "pHaveKilled" list. This then is referenced by the "on haveKilled" handler every time the room is re-entered later.

```
  -- add monster to killed list
  on killedMonster me, monsterName
    sendSprite(21,#message,"You Killed the"&&monsterName&"!")
    add pHaveKilled, monsterName
  end
```

```
  -- utility will return TRUE if player has killed a specific monster
  on haveKilled me, monsterName
    return getOne(pHaveKilled,monsterName)
  end
```

When a player touches a door they should be transported to another room in the game. The "on enterDoor" handler takes care of this.

First, the door is checked to see whether it either does not require a key, or whether the player has the key. Then, the player is taken to the next room. This new room is searched for the opposite door, the one that takes the player back to the previous room. This door is used as a basis for where the character should appear in the new room.

For instance, if the player enters a door on the right side of the screen, then they should appear as if they are coming out of the door on the left side of the screen in the new room.

```
-- when player encounters door
on enterDoor me, key, path, offset
   -- remember the current frame
   lastFrame = the frameLabel

   -- see if no key is needed or the player has the key
   if key = "" or getOne(pInventory,key) then
      -- go to the new frame
      go to frame path
      -- look for opposite door
      repeat with i = 80 down to 31
         -- see if door will send you back to the previous room
if sendSprite(i,#getDoorPath) = lastFrame then
            -- this is the opposite door
            -- position player on other side of it
            sprite(6).loc = sprite(i).loc - offset
            -- make sure player is in the right position
            updateStage
            exit repeat
         end if
      end repeat

      -- show message if door was unlocked
      if key <> "" then
         sendSprite(21,#message,"You opened the door with the"&&key&".")
      end if
   else
      -- show a message because door is locked
      sendSprite(21,#message,"The door is locked and you don't have the key.")
   end if
end
```

The next handler adds points to the player's score when that is required.

```
-- add points
on addPoints me, points
  pPoints = pPoints + points -- add
  showPoints(me) -- update screen
end
```

When a player encounters an item that is meant to award points, but not to be picked up and added to the inventory, this next handler is used. It adds the frame's marker label and the sprite number to the "pPointsList". This list is then checked in "on gotPoints" when the room is re-entered, so that the item does not appear a second time.

```
-- remember that points are already taken
on getPoints me, spriteNum
  -- remember that this object has already given points
  add pPointsList, [the frameLabel,spriteNum]
end
```

```
-- check to see if points have already been taken
on gotPoints me, spriteNum
  return getOne(pPointsList,[the frameLabel,spriteNum])
end
```

The next handler takes care of the simple task of displaying the player's score on the screen.

```
-- display points on screen
on showPoints me
  member("Score").text = string(pPoints)
end
```

Finally, the "on die" handler takes care of the case where a monster kills the character.

```
-- game over
on die me
  sendSprite(21,#message,"You've been killed!")
  go to frame "Game Over"
end
```

Wall Behavior

Every object on the screen has a behavior that contains a "on detectCollision" handler. This handler is called by the "on move" handler in the character behavior.

In all cases, the *intersect* function is used to determine whether this object and the character are touching. Then, it determines what action, if any, is needed.

In the case of a wall, the value *TRUE* is returned, which simply stops the movement from taking place.

```
  -- respond to #detectCollision
on detectCollision me, rect
  -- see if there is an overlap
  if intersect(rect,sprite(me.spriteNum).rect) <> rect(0,0,0,0) then
    -- tell user why
    sendSprite(21,#message,"Blocked!")
    -- stop movement
    return TRUE
  else
    -- allow movement
    return FALSE
  end if
end
```

Object Behavior

An object is something that the player simply touches and adds to his or her inventory. When the player does this, he also is awarded a number of points.

The number of points that each object is worth is determined by a parameter through the *on getPropertyDescriptionList* handler.

```
property pPoints

on getPropertyDescriptionList me
  list = [:]

  -- points to add to score
  addProp list, #pPoints,¬
    [#comment: "Points",¬
     #format: #integer,¬
     #default: 0]

  return list
end
```

When an object sprite appears, it asks the character behavior whether the object has already been obtained by the user. If so, the object is removed from the visible screen. This prevents the player from picking up an object, leaving the room, returning, and getting a second copy of the object.

```
on beginSprite me
  -- if object already picked up
  if sendSprite(6,#haveItem,sprite(me.spriteNum).member.name) then
    -- remove from screen before it is seen
    sprite(me.spriteNum).locH = -1000
  end if
end
```

The "on detectCollision" handler sends a #takeObject message to the character behavior if the character and the object are touching. It also sends an #addPoints message to increase the player's score.

```
-- respond to #detectCollision
on detectCollision me, rect
  -- see if there is an overlap
  if intersect(rect,sprite(me.spriteNum).rect) <> rect(0,0,0,0) then
    -- add object to inventory
    sendSprite(6,#takeObject,sprite(me.spriteNum).member.name)
    -- score points
    sendSprite(6,#addPoints,pPoints)
    -- remove object
    sprite(me.spriteNum).locH = -1000
  end if
end
```

Door Behavior

The behavior to handle the door takes two parameters. The first is the name of the frame that the door takes the player to. The second is the key that the player needs to open the door. If the key parameter is empty, then the door is considered unlocked.

```
property pDoorPath
property pDoorKey

on getPropertyDescriptionList me
  list = [:]

  -- frame that door leads to
  addProp list, #pDoorPath,¬
    [#comment: "Door Path",¬
     #format: #string,¬
     #default: ""]

  -- key needed to open door
  addProp list, #pDoorKey,¬
    [#comment: "Door Key",¬
     #format: #string,¬
     #default: ""]

  return list
end
```

When the player collides with a door, the character's position relative to the door is noted. This is used to compute the location of the character in the next room.

This information is then sent to the character behavior through the "on enterDoor" handler.

The only other function that "on detectCollision" takes care of is to return a *TRUE*. This prevents the "on move" handler from looking for more sprites than the player is touching. This way, a door can be placed on top of a wall sprite, but only the door has an effect on the game play.

```
-- respond to #detectCollision
on detectCollision me, rect,dx,dy
  -- see if there is an overlap
  if intersect(rect,sprite(me.spriteNum).rect) <> rect(0,0,0,0) then

    -- where to position character around opposite door
    offset = sprite(6).loc - sprite(me.spriteNum).loc
    if dx <> 0 then offset.locV = 0
    else if dy <> 0 then offset.locH = 0

    -- let character behavior change rooms
    sendSprite(6,#enterDoor,pDoorKey,pDoorPath,offset)

    -- stop movement
    return TRUE
  end if
end
```

When the character behavior tries to compute the position of the player in the next room, it needs to check all the objects in the room to find the door that the player just came through. It uses the "on getDoorPath" to poll all the objects for this information.

```
-- when asked, return where door leads to
on getDoorPath me
  return pDoorPath
end
```

Monster Behavior

The most complex out of all the object behaviors in this game is the monster behavior. This is because the monster is actually a "living" object. It moves, rather than just stay stationary.

The monster behavior has several properties and parameters. The parameters are used to set the monster speed and the objects that kill it and protect the player from the monster.

```
property pMonsterSpeed -- how fast it moves
property pMonsterKiller -- which object will kill it
property pMonsterTricker -- which object will make it ignore player
```

continues

continued

```
property pMonsterActive -- whether the monster can move
property pPoints -- points the monster is worth

on getPropertyDescriptionList me
  list = [:]

  -- how much monster moves each frame
  addProp list, #pMonsterSpeed,¬
    [#comment: "Monster Speed",¬
     #format: #integer,¬
     #default: 3]

  -- what object can kill the monster
  addProp list, #pMonsterKiller,¬
    [#comment: "Monster Killer",¬
     #format: #string,¬
     #default: ""]

  -- what object makes you invisible to monster
  addProp list, #pMonsterTricker,¬
    [#comment: "Monster Tricker",¬
     #format: #string,¬
     #default: ""]

  -- how many points scored when monster killed
  addProp list, #pPoints,¬
    [#comment: "Points",¬
     #format: #integer,¬
     #default: 0]

  return list
end
```

When the monster behavior begins, the *on beginSprite* handler asks the character behavior whether the monster has already been killed by the player. If so, the monster is removed from the screen.

```
on beginSprite me
  -- if monster already dead, remove from screen
  if sendSprite(6,#haveKilled,sprite(me.spriteNum).member.name) then
    sprite(me.spriteNum).locH = -1000
    pMonsterActive = FALSE
  else
    pMonsterActive = TRUE
  end if
end
```

The monster behavior uses the *on exitFrame* behavior to move the monster closer to the player. If the two are touching, then a decision is made as to which is killed.

The movement is achieved by simply determining the horizontal and vertical difference between the player and the monster. Then, the monster's speed is applied to these directions ④ and the monster is moved.

```
on exitFrame me
  if pMonsterActive then
    -- if monster is touching character
    if sprite me.spriteNum  intersects 6 then
      -- player has object to kill monster
      if (pMonsterKiller <> "") and sendSprite(6,#haveItem,pMonsterKiller) then
        -- remove sprite
        sprite(me.spriteNum).locH = -1000
        -- make monster inactive
        pMonsterActive = FALSE
        -- tell frame behavior about it
        sendSprite(6,#killedMonster,sprite(me.spriteNum).member.name)
        -- score points
        sendSprite(6,#addPoints,pPoints)
      else
        -- monster kills player
        sendSprite(6,#die)
      end if

    else if (pMonsterTricker = "") or not sendSprite(6,#haveItem,pMonsterTricker) then
      -- determine distance
      dx = sprite(6).locH - sprite(me.spriteNum).locH
      dy = sprite(6).locV - sprite(me.spriteNum).locV

      -- determine direction
      if dx < 0 then dx = -1
      else if dx > 0 then dx = 1
      if dy < 0 then dy = -1
      else if dy > 0 then dy = 1

      -- detemine movement
④ ➤  dloc = point(dx,dy)*pMonsterSpeed

      -- move
      sprite(me.spriteNum).loc = sprite(me.spriteNum).loc + dloc
    end if
  end if
end
```

Sign Behavior

A sign is a fairly simple object. The player touches a sign, and another text sprite is moved into position just below the sign. It displays the text specified by the "pText" parameter.

```
property pText

on getPropertyDescriptionList me
  list = [:]

  -- text to display
  addProp list, #pText,¬
    [#comment: "Text",¬
      #format: #string,¬
      #default: ""]

  return list
end
```

The *on exitFrame* handler simply looks for the character to be touching the sign. If it is, then the text is set and moved into position. Otherwise, the text sprite is moved safely offscreen.

```
on exitFrame me
  -- if the character is over the sign
  if intersect(sprite(6).rect,sprite(me.spriteNum).rect) <> rect(0,0,0,0) then
    -- set the text
    sprite(20).member.text = pText
    -- position the text sprite
    loc = sprite(me.spriteNum).loc
    loc = loc + point(-75,20)
    sprite(20).loc = loc
  else
    -- move the text away
    sprite(20).locH = -1000
  end if
end if
```

Container Behavior

The contained behavior combines the check-for-a-key of the door behavior, and the add-to-the-inventory code of the object behavior. A parameter of the behavior specifies which item is hidden inside, and another specifies which key is needed to open the container.

```
property pContents
property pContainerKey
property pPoints
```

```
on getPropertyDescriptionList me
  list = [:]

  -- name of object inside
  addProp list, #pContents,¬
    [#comment: "Contents",¬
     #format: #string,¬
     #default: ""]

  -- which object is needed to open
  addProp list, #pContainerKey,¬
    [#comment: "Key",¬
     #format: #string,¬
     #default: ""]

  -- how many points to award
  addProp list, #pPoints,¬
    [#comment: "Points",¬
     #format: #integer,¬
     #default: 0]

  return list
end
```

After the character touches the container, and it is determined that they can open it, the contents of the container are added to the player's inventory. Points also might be awarded.

```
on detectCollision me, rect
  -- if the character is over the sign
  if intersect(rect,sprite(me.spriteNum).rect) <> rect(0,0,0,0) then
    -- contents already taken
    if sendSprite(6,#haveItem,pContents) then return FALSE

    -- see if character can open the object
    if sendSprite(6,#openObject,sprite(me.spriteNum).member.name,¬
                  pContents,pContainerKey) then
      -- award points
      sendSprite(6,#addPoints,pPoints)
    end if
  end if
end
```

Points Behavior

If an object is meant only to award points, but should not be added to the inventory, then this behavior is used. It has a single parameter: the number of points it is worth.

```
property pPoints

on getPropertyDescriptionList me
  list = [:]

  -- how many points to award
  addProp list, #pPoints,¬
    [#comment: "Points",¬
     #format: #integer,¬
     #default: 0]

  return list
end
```

When the sprite begins, the character behavior is asked to check to see whether this particular points object has already been taken.

```
on beginSprite me
  -- remove item if it has already been taken
  if sendSprite(6,#gotPoints,me.spriteNum) then
    sprite(me.spriteNum).locH = -1000
  end if
end
```

When a collision happens, the player is given his or her points and the item is added to the character behavior list so that it does not appear again.

```
on detectCollision me, rect
  -- if the character is over the sign
  if intersect(rect,sprite(me.spriteNum).rect) <> rect(0,0,0,0) then
    -- award points
    sendSprite(6,#addPoints,pPoints)
    -- remove points from game
    sendSprite(6,#getPoints,me.spriteNum)
    -- display message
    sendSprite(21,#message,pPoints&&"Points.")
    -- remove item
    sprite(me.spriteNum).locH = -1000
  end if
end
```

Message Behavior

One last behavior needed is the one that controls the message text on the screen. In addition to simply placing any piece of text into the text member, it also keeps track of when the text was placed there, and removes it when two seconds have passed. This way, old messages do not hang around to confuse the player later on.

```
property pLastMessageTime -- last time a message was dislayed

on beginSprite me
  pLastMessageTime = VOID -- no message at start
end

on exitFrame me
  -- if a message is present
  if not voidP(pLastMessageTime) then
    -- how long has it been there?
    if the ticks > pLastMessageTime + 120 then
      -- remove message
      member("Screen Message").text = ""
      pLastMessageTime = VOID
    end if
  end if
end
```

The "on message" handler is what other behaviors call to get their message shown.

```
-- new message
on message me, text
  -- set text
  member("Screen Message").text = text
  -- remember time
  pLastMessageTime = the ticks
end
```

Putting It All Together

In the case of this game, writing the scripts is only half the work needed to complete the game. After you have all the behaviors, you need to construct an adventure that uses them.

We do this in three stages. First, we create a diagram that shows the complete adventure. Then, we create each room of the adventure as a frame in the movie. Finally, we attach the behaviors to the sprites on the screen and set all the parameters.

The Game Diagram

You can use our game behaviors to create all sorts of different adventures. For this example, we try to use every behavior and option at least once.

Figure 21.3 shows a diagram with 11 rooms and how they are connected. Each room in the diagram is labeled with its name and also shows which items are contained in it.

Figure 21.3
The diagram shows all the rooms and how they fit together.

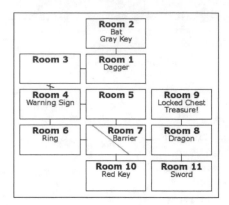

Look at the diagram and understand how to read it. Room 1, which is the room shown in Figure 21.1, contains a dagger and has doors to the north and west. Room 2, which is north of Room 1, has a door to the south and contains both a bat and a key.

It is important to plan out the game like this or it will be very difficult to create each room in the next step. You should have some idea of how all the items fit together to make the game work.

In Figure 21.3, we have a dagger, a gray key, a ring, a sword, a red key, and a chest. We also have a bat, a dragon, and a locked door between rooms 3 and 4. In the game, the player needs to get the dagger, kill the bat, get the gray key, move through the door to room 4, get the ring, get the red key, move past the dragon by using the ring, get the sword, kill the dragon, and then open the chest with the red key.

There also are stacks of coins lying about the dungeon here and there that add to the player's score.

Creating the Rooms

Each room is one frame in the movie. First, you need to create bitmaps for all the objects. Figure 21.4 shows the section of the cast with all the objects.

Figure 21.4
The Cast includes a bitmap for each of the objects in the game.

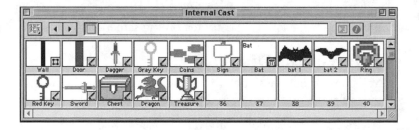

NOTE

Notice that the bat is actually a film loop that contains two bitmaps, "bat 1" and "bat 2". Both members were placed in the Score, right next to each other. Those sprites were then copied and pasted into the Cast to make the film loop. The resulting member, "bat," now flaps its wings by going between the two members. It will animate at the same tempo as the movie.

After you have all the bitmaps ready, you can start making the frames for the game. Figure 21.5 shows the layout of these frames, which looks more like a presentation done in Director than a game.

Figure 21.5

The Score shows the layout of all the frames for the adventure game.

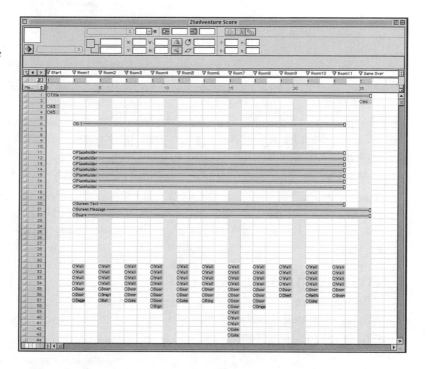

There are many sprites that stretch across all the frames in the movie—the most important of which is the character sprite, in channel 6. Channels 11 through 17 contain the inventory sprites, and are positioned on the right side of the Stage, one above the other. Channels 20, 21, and 22 are the sign text, the message text, and the score text, respectively.

Sprite channels 31 and above are for room elements. The first four in every room are the four walls. In the case of this game, they are all exactly the same. After those, the rooms begin to differ. They contain between one and four doors, different objects, and room 7 even contains additional walls.

Room 7 demands a closer look. Figure 21.6 shows the Stage setup for this room. It has the typical four walls, but also has some additional ones dividing the room in two.

Figure 21.6

Room 7 is divided into two sections by walls.

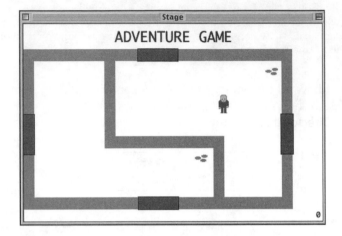

The purpose of this division is to allow the player to enter from the west, but be able to go only south from that point. Then, they have to go around the dungeon from another direction to enter from the north, which allows them to go east. The player gains some knowledge about the paths in the adventure, but does not gain access.

The room might make more sense if you think of the dividing wall not as a wall, but as an underground stream, or a deep chasm. If you wanted, you could make several rooms like this, and further complicate things. Pretty soon, the player is in a maze-like environment, able to see only a part of the maze at a time.

Attaching the Behaviors

After all the rooms look like the rooms you have designed, you still have to attach the behaviors to make them functional. First, drop the character behavior on sprite 6. This requires no parameters.

Take care of all the doors first. Drop the door behavior on each door in each room, and assign it the name of the frame where it leads. In the case of the door between rooms 3 and 4, assign it the name of the key required. I have required that key for the door both as it exists in room 3, and as it exists in room 4.

Next, assign the proper object behavior to all the objects in the rooms. Remember to make the bat so it can be killed by the dagger, and the dragon so it can be killed by the sword. Also, make the dragon's "pMonsterTricker" the ring.

Assign the container behavior to the chest. Make its key the red key, and make its contents the treasure. You don't need to place the treasure anywhere, because it is inside the chest.

Drop a lot of little point objects—in this case, a stack of coins, in different rooms. Also, don't forget to plant a signpost in room 4 and place some sort of message on it, such as "Beware!"

This movie has a pretty complex Score with a lot of behaviors and a lot of behavior interaction. I definitely recommend that you open the sample movie on the CD-ROM and examine it carefully.

Game Variations

The behaviors in this movie are very powerful because they are very general. You can use them in ways that might not seem obvious, and come up with very different results.

Scenarios

Adventure games are traditionally dungeon adventures in search of treasure. But they don't have to be. Consider a science-fiction adventure where the "dungeon" is a spaceship and the monsters are robots. You need to find the self-destruct button to destroy the ship before it crashes into Earth. Here are some other suggestions:

- Searching through a cave inhabited by giant spiders.
- Exploring a haunted house.
- Running through abandoned city streets chased by the undead.
- A mouse collecting cheese and running from the cat and dog.
- A Secret Service agent exploring an enemy military base.
- A little girl in the forest trying to find her way home, chased by wolves, bears, and a witch.
- Exploring an abandoned amusement park.

Multiple Monsters

What if you ventured into a room and found not one, but two bats? How about 30? The monster behavior in this game can be applied to more than one sprite without any modification.

Keys That Open Containers That Have Keys

What if you needed a key to open a container or a door, but that key was nowhere to be found? It could be inside a container that requires another key to open it. You can create a complex puzzle this way that requires the player to explore every bit of your scenario to solve it.

Secret Doors

What if a door looked just like a wall? It would blend in perfectly, but if the player ever thought to bump against the wall, then they would get a surprise. It certainly would increase the amount of time it takes to complete the game.

More Behaviors

Think of something that you want to add to the game that isn't covered by the behaviors here? Just write a new behavior to handle that new type of object.

For instance, it might be interesting to have living creatures that don't attack the player, but instead speak with them. This would require a whole interface where the player can type words and the creature would respond. It would be difficult but possible for an expert programmer.

The Aftermath

In this sample game, monsters that have been killed are simply removed from the game. However, you might want to change that so you can see their dead carcasses lying around in the room after their demise. Just create an additional bitmap for this, and then have that bitmap shown, rather than taking the monster completely off of the screen when the player returns to that room.

Game Over

The game in this chapter has no "You've won!" screen. You can add one easily by determining exactly when the player wins, and searching for that condition. For instance, if you want to make it so that the player wins after they get the treasure and bring it back to "Room 1," you could just test for those two conditions every time the player changes rooms.

Maze Game

CD-ROM File: 22maze.dir

Useful Lingo in this Chapter

♠ Interface: Accepting arrow key input

♠ Lists: Using linear lists

♠ Lists: Using property lists

♠ Lists: Lists that contain lists

♠ Math: Using random numbers

♠ Members: Using a naming convention

♠ Programming: Creating a random maze

♠ Programming: Using a case statement

♠ Strings: Building member names

I often see maze games made in Director. Just about every single one of these falls short of my expectations in one major way: The maze is always the same, no matter how many times you play the game.

When I created my first maze game, I looked at the option of having a static maze built in to the game and rejected it immediately. The whole appeal to playing a computer maze game, to me, is the computer's capability to generate random mazes.

Game Overview

The maze game in this chapter is a simple one. However, the fact that the maze is randomly generated each time the game is played puts this game way above almost all the Shockwave maze games out there.

Figure 22.1 shows a random maze created by this game. It is a 20 by 10 maze, which offers more than a billion possible mazes.

Figure 22.1
One randomly generated maze created by the game in this chapter.

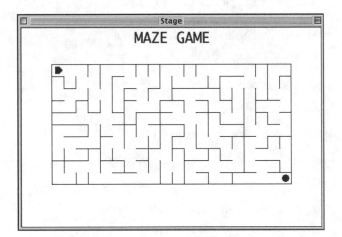

Generating a Random Maze

Creating a random maze takes some true computer science and mathematical skills. I will try to explain the process step-by-step.

First, let us define some terms. A maze is a grid of *cells*. The maze in Figure 22.1 shows 20 cells across and 10 cells down. There are a total of 200 cells in the maze.

We refer to each cell by its position in the maze. So, cell 1, 1 is the one in the upper-left (northeast) corner. The next one to the right (west) is cell 2, 1 and the cell below (south) is 1, 2, and so on.

Each cell has four walls: west, north, east, and south. Each of these walls can be opened or closed. When one cell wall is open, the opposite wall in the adjacent cell needs to be open as well. So, if the east wall in cell 5, 7 is open, then the west wall in cell 6, 7 must be open to match it.

The way we create a random maze is by arranging the cells in *sets*. A set is a group of items—in this case, cells—that are related. We start with 200 sets, each of which contains one cell. Each of these cells has four closed walls. This is essentially 200 individual mazes, all 1 by 1.

Next, we pick a random set, and a random cell in that set, and then a random wall in that cell. We open that wall. We also open the opposite wall in the cell that is adjacent and shares the wall. So, if the east wall of cell 5, 7 is picked, then the west wall of cell 6, 7 also is set to open.

After the wall and its opposite counterpart are opened, we take both sets and combine them. So, the set that contains 5, 7 and the set that contains 6, 7 is merged. Instead of 200 sets of one cell apiece, we now have 198 sets of one cell and 1 set of two cells.

This entire process is repeated, picking a random set, cell, and wall each time. The one rule that must be followed is that the cell, and the one it shares the wall with, must be in *different* sets. If they are in the same set, that means that there is already a path from one cell to the other. Adding an additional open wall simply creates a loop around in that set of cells.

After some time, the entire maze goes from 200 sets of one cell to 1 set of 200 cells. When this happens, the maze is complete. This could take a few seconds if the computer is slow and/or the maze is large.

In fact, a maze built this way has some interesting properties. There is exactly one path from one cell to any other cell in the maze. There is only one path. You can never go around in circles in the maze, and you can never end up with a maze in which there is a cell that is unreachable.

Moving Around in the Maze

In addition to the maze-creation Lingo, we have a behavior that controls the position and movement of the player's representation in the game. This is a pretty simple behavior except for its interaction with the maze data.

While we are creating the maze, we store the cells in a list. Each item in the list contains the horizontal and vertical position of the cell, as well as information about each wall of that cell. By referring to this data, we can determine whether a move is possible.

Graphics

Because the main purpose of this chapter is to teach the method for making random mazes, we shall keep the graphics and sounds to a minimum. In fact, there are no sounds at all.

The graphics are simply lines that represent the walls of the maze. Because the west wall of a cell is the same as the east wall of the next cell, and the south wall is the same as the north wall of the cell under it, there is the need for only two walls to be drawn per cell.

There are only four graphics needed to make up the maze. The first is a bitmap with both a north and west wall. The second is just a north wall. The third is just a west wall, and the fourth is no walls at all. We also want to surround the entire maze with a border.

A Goal

The goal in this game is to get to the opposite corner of the maze. To clarify this goal, we place a marker at the cell in that corner. Think of the player as the mouse and the goal as the cheese.

Special Effects

There are no sounds in this game, but we include one special effect. The character in the game has four bitmaps: one for each direction of movement. This way, when the player moves it around the screen, it appears to point in the direction of movement.

Making the Game

We have two scripts in this movie. The first is a movie script that contains handlers used to make the random maze and draw it. The second is a behavior that controls the game frame.

Maze Movie Script

The maze movie script contains a handler to create the maze, two supporting handlers, and a handler to draw the maze.

These scripts reference three global variables. The first is the list that contains the maze data. The other two are the maze height and width.

```
global gMaze -- list containing maze
global gMazeH, gMazeW -- maze size
```

The "on createMaze" handler is essentially one big loop that combines sets of cells until a maze has been generated. Before this loop can begin, the maze size is set and the 200 sets of individual cells are created.

Each cell is a property and value. The property is a short list that contains the x and y location of the cell. The value is another list, containing the north, south, east, and west wall conditions. A wall is either open or closed.

```
on createMaze
  -- set maze size
```

```
gMazeW = 20
gMazeH = 10

-- create maze with all closed cells
set gMaze = []
repeat with x = 1 to gMazeW
  repeat with y = 1 to gMazeH
    -- create cell
    prop = [#x:x, #y:y]
    val = [#n:0, #s:0, #e:0, #w:0]
    temp = [:]
    addProp temp, prop, val
    -- add cell to maze
    add gMaze, temp
  end repeat
end repeat
```

The following code is the loop. It picks a random set ① , cell ② , and wall ③ . Then, it ensures that the wall is closed and that it is not on the border of the maze. Next, it finds out which cell is on the other side of the wall, and ensures that the two cells are not already in the same set.

If all these conditions are met, then the wall is opened ④ , as well as the opposite wall in the other cell ⑤ . The two sets are combined to make one set. This continues until there is only one set left.

```
      repeat while TRUE
①➤    -- pick random set
      setNum = random(gMaze.count)
②➤    -- pick random cell
      cellNum = random(gMaze[setNum].count)
③➤    -- pick random wall
      wall = random(4)

      -- see if wall is already open
      if gMaze[setNum][cellNum][wall] <> 0 then next repeat

      -- get x and y location of cell
      x = getPropAt(gMaze[setNum],cellNum).x
      y = getPropAt(gMaze[setNum],cellNum).y

      -- don't open wall on border
      if wall = 1 and y = 1 then next repeat
      if wall = 2 and y = gMazeH then next repeat
      if wall = 3 and x = gMazeW then next repeat
      if wall = 4 and x = 1 then next repeat
```

continues

continued

```
      -- find opposite side of wall
      if wall = 1 then oppSide = findCell(x,y-1)
      else if wall = 2 then oppSide = findCell(x,y+1)
      else if wall = 3 then oppSide = findCell(x+1,y)
      else if wall = 4 then oppSide = findCell(x-1,y)

      -- already in same set, don't want a loop
      if oppSide[1] = setNum then next repeat

      -- find opposite wall
      if wall = 1 then oppWall = 2
      else if wall = 2 then oppWall = 1
      else if wall = 3 then oppWall = 4
      else if wall = 4 then oppWall = 3
```

④ ➤
```
      -- open cell wall
      gMaze[setNum][cellNum][wall] = 1
```
⑤ ➤
```
      -- open opposite cell wall
      gMaze[oppSide[1]][oppSide[2]][oppWall] = 1

      -- combine both sets
      unionSets(setNum,oppSide[1])

      -- if all one set, maze done
      if gMaze.count = 1 then exit repeat
    end repeat

    -- extract single set from list
    gMaze = getAt(gMaze,1)
    drawMaze
  end
```

One utility handler that the "on createMaze" handler uses is one that finds a cell inside the sets of cells available. It simply loops through all sets, checks their x and y values, and finds the match. The handler then returns a list with both the set number and the cell number.

```
-- search sets for which one contains cell
on findCell x, y
  -- loop through all sets
  repeat with setNum = 1 to gMaze.count
    -- loop through all cells
    repeat with cellNum = 1 to gMaze[setNum].count
      -- see if this cell is the one we are looking for
      if getPropAt(gMaze[setNum],cellNum) = [#x:x, #y:y] then
```

```
         -- return list with set and cell
         return [setNum,cellNum]
      end if
   end repeat
   end repeat
end
```

Another utility handler is one that combines two sets in the maze list. It simply takes each item from the second set and adds it to the first. Then, it removes the second set.

```
-- take two sets and combine
on unionSets firstSet, secondSet
   -- loop through cells in second set
   repeat with cellNum = 1 to gMaze[secondSet].count
      -- add each cell to first set
      addProp gMaze[firstSet], getPropAt(gMaze[secondSet],cellNum),¬
            gMaze[secondSet][cellNum]
   end repeat

   -- remove second set
   deleteAt gMaze, secondSet
end
```

After the maze is complete, the "on drawMaze" handler is called to translate it to the sprite on the screen. All the x and y values are looped through and each cell is examined to see what the values of its north and west walls are. Then, the proper bitmap is used in the proper location.

The handler uses the sprite in channel 20 to determine the location of the maze. It uses the same sprite as a bounding box, stretching it to the size of the finished maze ⑥ .

Sprite 11 is used to mark the maze destination, which is the bottom-right cell ⑦ .

```
-- draw maze on screen
on drawMaze
   --loop through all cells
   repeat with y = 1 to gMazeH
     repeat with x = 1 to gMazeW
        -- get sprite number to use
        s = (y-1)*gMazeW+(x-1)+21

        -- north wall in place?
        north = not getProp(gMaze,[#x:x,#y:y]).n
        -- west wall in place?
        west = not getProp(gMaze,[#x:x,#y:y]).w
```

continues

continued

```
                -- determine member to use from walls in place
                if north and west then set mem = "nw"
                else if north then set mem = "n"
                else if west then set mem = "w"
                else set mem = "0"

                -- set sprite member and location
                sprite(s).member = mem
                sprite(s).loc = point((x-1)*20,(y-1)*20) + sprite(20).loc
            end repeat
        end repeat

⑥➤ -- set bordering rectangle{6}
        r = rect(sprite(20).loc,point(0,0))
        r.right = r.left + gMazeW*20
        r.bottom = r.top + gMazeH*20
        sprite(20).rect = r

⑦➤ -- set end point{7}
        loc = point((gMazeW-1)*20,(gMazeH-1)*20)
        loc = loc + sprite(20).loc
        loc = loc + point(10,10)
        sprite(11).loc = loc
    end
```

Unlike behaviors, a movie script is not attached to any sprite, nor does it appear in the Score at all. The handlers are available for a behavior to call, however. The "on createMaze" handler is called by our maze frame behavior.

Maze Frame Behavior

The maze frame behavior controls the character in the game. It uses the same globals as the movie script so it knows the layout of the maze without referring to the sprites on the Stage.

```
global gMaze -- maze data
global gMazeW, gMazeH -- maze size
property pX, pY -- character location
```

When the frame begins, "on createMaze" is called to build the maze. The player's location is set to the upper-left corner as well.

```
on beginSprite me
  -- make maze
  createMaze
```

```
    -- set location
    pX = 1
    pY = 1

    -- draw character
    drawChar(me,#e)
  end
```

When the player presses an arrow key, a message is sent to "on move" with the direction of movement.

```
-- take keyboard input
on keyDown me
  case the keyCode of
    123: move(me,#w)
    124: move(me,#e)
    125: move(me,#s)
    126: move(me,#n)
  end case
end
```

The "on move" handler checks to be sure that the player is moving through an open wall. If so, it changes the "pX" and "pY" properties of the character and redraws it. It also checks to see whether the player has reached the end.

```
-- try to move character
on move me, direction
  -- get current cell
  cell = getProp(gMaze,[#x:pX,#y:pY])

  -- see if that wall is open
  if getProp(cell,direction) then
    -- move in right direction
    case direction of
      #w: pX = pX - 1
      #e: pX = pX + 1
      #s: pY = pY + 1
      #n: pY = pY - 1
    end case
  end if

  -- draw character in new spot
  drawChar(me,direction)

  -- check to see if the end was reached
  checkGameOver
end
```

Setting the location of the character sprite is easy. All that is needed is to use "pX" and "pY" to set the relative location, add the location of the maze, and then add a little bit so that the character is centered in the cell.

The member used by the character is determined by the direction of movement. This way, the character always appears to be facing the direction that it is moving.

```
-- set character location and member
on drawChar me, direction
  -- location relative to corner of maze
  loc = point((pX-1)*20,(pY-1)*20)
  -- add maze position
  loc = loc + sprite(20).loc
  -- add enough to center character in cell
  loc = loc + point(10,10)
  -- set location
  sprite(10).loc = loc

  -- set member according to direction travelled
  sprite(10).member = member("char"&&string(direction))
end
```

The game is over if the "pX" and "pY" properties show that that player has reached the bottom-right corner of the maze.

```
-- see if player has reached opposite corner
on checkGameOver
  if pX = gMazeW and pY = gMazeH then
    go to frame "Game Over"
  end if
end
```

The frame loop is needed to keep the movie on the game frame.

```
-- loop on the frame
on exitFrame me
  go to the frame
end
```

Putting It All Together

The first thing that you will need to do is to create the four bitmaps that represent the cells in the maze. Figure 22.2 shows these four members.

The registration points are set to the upper-left corner of each bitmap so that they all line up properly.

Figure 22.2

Only four bitmaps are needed to build the maze. The last bitmap is a single pixel, but the Cast Window thumbnail automatically expands that to fill the space.

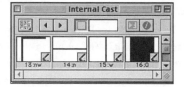

Next, you need four bitmaps to represent the four directions that the character can face. Figure 22.3 shows these. Call these names that start with "char" and end with a direction letter, for instance, "char e".

Figure 22.3

Four bitmaps represent the character.

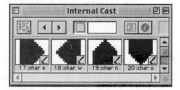

You also need a marker to show the destination cell in the maze. Put this in sprite 11 and a character bitmap sprite 10.

The maze needs some placeholder sprites in channels 21 through 220. You also want to draw a rectangle shape in sprite 20. Position it so that the upper-left corner is the location where you want to upper-left corner of the maze. The size of the rectangle is unimportant, because the script sets it.

The movie script does not need to be added to the Score at all, but the frame script needs to be placed in the frame script channel.

Game Variations

This chapter presents a very simple maze game to show you how to create random mazes. From this starting point, you can create complex puzzle and adventure games.

Better Walls

The walls in this game are simple black lines. However, they can be textured bitmaps to represent different materials. They can have any thickness, as long as the character has enough room to move around between them.

Different Size Maze

The 20-by-10 maze in the sample movie fits well into a Shockwave-sized applet. However, you can make it any size you want. Just change the "gMazeH" and "gMazeW" variable values in "on createMovie". Be forewarned that the larger you make the maze, the more time it takes to generate at the beginning of the game.

Different Maze Shape

The algorithm to make the maze relies on the short loop at the beginning of "on createMaze" to define the size and shape of the maze. If you want to use something different from this loop, you can create a maze shape that is not rectangular. The rest of the "on createMaze" doesn't really care about the shape that the cells form.

Imagine a maze that was an L-shape rather than a rectangle. You can even make odd shapes to represent different scenarios, such as a doughnut-shape for a space station. I'll leave it up to the clever Lingo programmer to determine how to make the cell arragements.

Objects in the Maze

Rather than just having the player try to get to the other end of the maze, why not have multiple goals? You can scatter markers throughout the maze to represent different things. So, a player can collect treasure as they run around the maze.

An Enemy in the Maze

What if there were another living creature in the maze with you? You could be trying to capture it, or avoid it. A behavior similar to the frame behavior in this movie could move a sprite in random directions throughout the maze. Or, a clever Lingo programmer can figure out how to have the enemy come right at you.

NOTE

For the enemy character to seek out and find a place in the maze, either the player or a treasure, you need to use *recursion*. This is an advanced programming technique in which a handler calls itself.

Strategy Game

23

CD-ROM File: 23strategy.dir

Useful Lingo in This Chapter

- ♠ Behaviors: Calling handlers in other behaviors
- ♠ Graphics: Coloring sprites with Lingo
- ♠ Graphics: Using a set of bitmaps
- ♠ Graphics: Using registration points
- ♠ Graphics: Adjusting sprite layers
- ♠ Input: Selecting with mouse clicks
- ♠ Lists: Using linear lists
- ♠ Lists: Using property lists
- ♠ Lists: Lists that contain lists
- ♠ Lists: Sorting
- ♠ Math: Using random numbers
- ♠ Members: Using a naming convention
- ♠ Programming: Using artificial intelligence
- ♠ Strings: Building member names

The last full game that we look at in this book is a strategy game. Like the term "adventure game," a "strategy game" can mean different things.

Typically, a strategy game is a war game. The strategy involved is battlefield strategy. We'll build a game that uses one of the oldest known game goals: conquest.

The game we create uses a map of the world divided into a number of countries. There are two players: the human player and a computer player. This means that we need to create a game that deals not only with the game state and interface, but also with artificial intelligence.

Game Overview

First, we need to define the rules of the game, just as if it were being played between two players on a board. We have 24 countries that connect to one another in a variety of ways. Any country that borders another is considered connected. In addition, there are a number of countries connected by sea routes. Figure 23.1 shows this map.

Figure 23.1
The Stage shows the layout of the game: 24 countries spread out over a map of the world. The numbers show the number of armies in each country.

Countries and Connections

If a country is connected to another country, then it can attack that country, or be attacked from it. Each country is occupied by one player or the other. To be occupied, it must have at least one army on it. However, a country can have many more armies, as long as they all belong to one player.

At the start of the game each player occupies 12 countries. The specific countries are decided by a random method.

Start of Play

The game begins by each player automatically getting at least one army on each country he or she owns. Then, the players take turns adding one army to any country he or she owns. The two players get to add eight armies each.

Now, each player has 12 countries and a total of 20 armies on the board. At this point, it is the first player's turn. The first player is always the human in this version of the game.

Start of a Turn

At the beginning of a turn, the player is given a certain number of armies to place on any of his or her countries. This number is determined by taking the total number of countries that the player owns and dividing by two. So, if the player owns 10 countries, he or she gets 5 armies to place.

The only exception is if the player has only one country. In that case, a single army is given to the player, even though they technically should get none.

Attacking

The main part of a player's turn is the attack. A player can attack from any country he or she owns, any country the other player owns, as long as the two countries are connected.

To attack, the player first selects his or her country. Then, the player chooses the country to attack.

The attack is basically a flip of the coin. There is a 50 percent chance that the attacking player will win, and a 50 percent chance that the defending player will win.

If the attacker wins, the defender loses an army from the country being attacked. If the defender wins, the attacker loses an army from the attacking country.

If the attacker is attacking a country that has only one army defending it, and the attacker wins, then he or she conquers that country. In that case, the attacker must move at least one of his or her armies on to this country. The attacker can move more armies, provided that at least one is left on the original country. Because this would require that the attacker have at least two armies to spread across the two countries, then the attacker cannot attack with only one army.

Victory

The goal of the game is to conquer the world. This happens when either player owns all 24 countries.

Artificial Intelligence

This game sounds pretty easy to play. It is in fact much simpler than most strategy war games. However, programming a convincing artificial intelligence can be quite difficult.

Artificial intelligence experts whom I know say that it is not important that an AI in a game is smart, but rather that it provides entertaining game play. This is a very important point. You don't have to reconstruct a human brain for a game like this. You just have to make the computer opponent seem as though it knows what it is doing. After all, in the game world, an AI that is so good that it never loses is just as bad, if not worse, than an AI that always loses.

The AI in this game follows a very simple algorithm. When it is time to place armies at the beginning of each turn, it starts by finding its strongest point and places an army there. Then, it finds its weakest point and places an army there. It repeats this until all its armies are placed.

The AI attacks by simply finding its strongest front and attacking from there. It continues to attack from its strongest front, although the location of that front might change, until it determines that it does not have a strong enough force to continue attacking.

This simple AI is actually pretty effective. You can see it in action by playing the game on the CD-ROM.

The Map

Another important element of this game is the map. It is divided into 24 countries. Each of these is different bitmaps that we color in on the Stage as the country's owner changes.

There also need to be 24 different text members that are positioned over the countries on the Stage. These show the number of armies in the country.

Another thing to consider is that the program needs to know which countries are connected. To do this, we build a large list of such connections into our code.

Special Effects

Although sounds can easily be added, we keep things simple by not having them in this sample movie. However, we use the *color* and *bgColor* properties of the country sprites to highlight the country that the player is attacking from. We use a red outline for an attacking country, and then a blue outline for a conquered country that the player can move more armies to.

To help a new player learn how to play the game, we have a text member at the bottom of the screen that constantly is telling the player what is going on in the game. It prompts them to make a move and it shows them what the computer is doing during its turn.

Making the Game

This game follows a repeated sequence. There are six steps in the game. Here is a list of these steps:

1. First, the board is set up. Countries are randomly assigned to each player and one army is placed on each country.

2. Second, the players place their initial armies. They each get eight armies to place.

3. Next, the human player places the new pieces for the beginning of his or her turn.

4. The player attacks the computer until the player decides that he or she is finished or cannot attack anymore.

5. The computer player places its pieces for the beginning of its turn.

6. The computer player attacks the player until the computer decides that it is finished or cannot attack anymore.

When the sequence of steps is complete, the game returns to step three. Steps three through six are repeated until one of the two players wins.

For each of these six steps, we have a frame behavior. In addition, there is a long movie script that contains handlers used to set global variables and utility handlers used by several of the frame behaviors.

The Movie Script

The movie handler starts by setting the "gLinks" global. This is the property list that contains all the countries and the countries that they connect to. It is used to determine which countries can be attacked from where.

Each country is referred to by a name. These names correspond to the member names of the bitmaps used to represent them in the Score and on the Stage. They could just as easily have been called "1," "2," "3," and so on. By naming them things that I recognize, I found it much easier to build the list.

```
global gLinks -- which countries border each other
global gCountries -- game state

-- make a list that has all countries and their neighbors
on getLinks
  gLinks = [:]
  addProp gLinks, "Northern Islands", ["Canada","Great Britain"]
  addProp gLinks, "Canada", ["Northern Islands","United States","Siberia"]
  addProp gLinks, "United States", ["Canada","Mexico"]
  addProp gLinks, "Mexico", ["United States", "Colombia"]
```

```
    addProp gLinks, "Colombia", ["Mexico","Argentina","Brazil"]
    addProp gLinks, "Argentina", ["Colombia","Brazil"]
    addProp gLinks, "Brazil", ["Colombia","Argentina","West Africa"]
    addProp gLinks, "Great Britain", ["Northern Islands","Western Europe",¬
    "Eastern Europe","Scandinavia"]
    addProp gLinks, "Western Europe", ["Great Britain","Eastern Europe",¬
    "West Africa","North Africa"]
    addProp gLinks, "Eastern Europe", ["Western Europe","Great Britain",¬
    "Scandinavia","North Africa","Russia","Egypt"]
    addProp gLinks, "Scandinavia", ["Great Britain","Eastern Europe","Russia"]
    addProp gLinks, "Russia", ["Scandinavia","Eastern Europe","Middle East","India",¬
    "Siberia"]
    addProp gLinks, "Siberia", ["Russia","India","China","Japan","Canada"]
    addProp gLinks, "Japan", ["Siberia","China"]
    addProp gLinks, "Middle East", ["Russia","India","Egypt"]
    addProp gLinks, "India", ["Middle East","Russia","Siberia","China"]
    addProp gLinks, "China", ["Japan","Siberia","India","Indonesia"]
    addProp gLinks, "Indonesia", ["China","Australia"]
    addProp gLinks, "Australia", ["Indonesia"]
    addProp gLinks, "West Africa", ["Brazil","Western Europe","North Africa"]
    addProp gLinks, "North Africa", ["West Africa", "Eastern Europe","Western Europe",¬
    "Egypt","Central Africa"]
    addProp gLinks, "Egypt", ["Eastern Europe","North Africa","Central Africa",¬
    "Middle East"]
    addProp gLinks, "Central Africa", ["North Africa","Egypt","South Africa"]
    addProp gLinks, "South Africa", ["Central Africa"]
  end
```

The next handler initializes the "gCountries" global. It creates a property list from the properties in "gLinks" and assigns a smaller property list with #owner and #armies as the two properties.

We use this list to keep track of who owns which country and how many armies are there.

```
-- start world with no owners and no armies
on initCountries
  gCountries = [:]
  repeat with i = 1 to gLinks.count
    addProp gCountries, getPropAt(gLinks,i), [#owner: VOID, #armies: 0]
  end repeat
end
```

This next handler is used once at the beginning of the game. It randomly assigns each country, one by one, to the two players. It also seeds these countries with a single army ①.

```
-- randomly divide countries between player and computer
on divideCountries
```

```
who = #player -- first country goes to player
repeat with i = 1 to gCountries.count
  repeat while TRUE
    r = random(gCountries.count) -- pick random country

    -- make sure it isn't already owned
    if gCountries[r].owner = VOID then

      -- assign owner
      gCountries[r].owner = who
①→   gCountries[r].armies = 1

      -- next country has different owner
      if who = #player then who = #computer
      else who = #player

      -- next country
      exit repeat
    end if
  end repeat
end repeat
end
```

The next two handlers are used to update the sprites and text on the Stage. The "on colorCountries" handler looks at each country and sets the *bgColor* according to the owner of that country.

It also sets the *locZ* of each country to its initial value, which is equal to the value of its sprite number. This is needed because we are setting the *locZ* of some sprites to a higher number to bring them to the front in other sprites. A call to "on colorCountries" not only updates the country colors, but also resets the *locZ* of each country sprite.

```
-- color all sprites according to owner
on colorCountries
  -- loop through countries
  repeat with i = 1 to gCountries.count
    -- get sprite number
    s = 10+i

    -- get owner
    owner = getProp(gCountries,sprite(s).member.name).owner

    -- color
    if owner = #player then
      -- red for player
      sprite(s).bgcolor = rgb("FF9999")
    else
```

continues

continued

```
          -- blue for computer
          sprite(s).bgcolor = rgb("9999FF")
      end if

      -- outline is black
      sprite(s).color = rgb("000000")

      -- move to default layer
      sprite(s).locZ = s
    end repeat
  end
```

The "on showArmies" handler places the number of armies on each country into the text member that corresponds to the country. These text members appear as sprites on the Stage on top of, or near, the countries they represent.

```
  -- place army amounts in text members
on showArmies
  -- loop through countries
  repeat with i = 1 to gCountries.count

      -- get country name
      country = getPropAt(gCountries,i)

      -- get army count
      armies = gCountries[i].armies

      -- only replace text if it differs
      if member(country&&"Number").text <> string(armies) then
        member(country&&"Number").text = string(armies)
      end if

  end repeat
end
```

The tiny "on message" handler sets the "Message" text member any time it is called. We use this text member to display messages to the player throughout the game.

```
  -- place a message in the text member
on message text
  member("Message").text = text
end
```

The utility handler "on checkGameOver" checks to see whether one player has conquered the whole board. It does this by taking the owner of the first country and comparing it to the owner of every other country. If all the countries match, then the board has been conquered.

```
      -- see if one has conquered all
on checkGameOver
   -- assume owner of first country is winner
   winner = gCountries[1].owner

   -- loop through all countries
   repeat with i = 2 to gCountries.count
      -- if country owner is different, then game not over
      if gCountries[i].owner <> winner then return FALSE
   end repeat

   -- game over, show who won
   if winner = #computer then
      message("Game Over. Computer Wins.")
   else
      message("Game Over. You Win.")
   end if

   go to frame "Game Over"

   -- stop all Lingo
   return TRUE
end
```

Initialization Behavior

The first frame of the game is named "Initialize" and contains the following frame behavior. It is a short behavior that calls some of the handlers in the movie script. Working together, they set up the board and all the global variables.

```
on beginSprite me
   getLinks -- set gLinks global
   initCountries -- start game state
   divideCountries -- assign countries
   colorCountries -- color map
   showArmies -- set text members
end
```

Country Behaviors

To allow the player to communicate with the game code, we need a simple behavior attached to every country on the screen. It will simply send the name of the member, which is the same as the name of the country, on to the frame behavior through the "on countryClick" handler. Several of our frame behaviors have this "on countryClick" behavior to receive this message.

```
-- pass along click to frame behavior
on mouseDown me
  country = sprite(me.spriteNum).member.name
  sendSprite(0,#countryClick,country,me.spriteNum)
end
```

Initial Place Behavior

The purpose of the "Initial Place Behavior" is to allow the player and the computer to place their first eight armies. It uses only one property, which is the number of armies that each player can place. This is set to eight in the *on beginSprite* handler.

```
global gCountries
property pToPlace -- how many armies left to place

on beginSprite me
  pToPlace = 8 -- game default is 8
  message("You are red. Begin placing your eight additional armies.")
end
```

The behavior then waits for the player to click on a country. When he or she does, the "on countryClick" handler gets the message.

It first checks to be sure that the player owns this country. Then, it adds one army to that country.

Next, "on computerPlace" is called to allow the computer to add an army to the board. Then, the "pToPlace" property is decreased by one ②, and if all the armies have been placed, the movie moves on to the next frame.

```
-- player clicks country
on countryClick me, country
  -- make sure player owns the country
  if getProp(gCountries,country).owner = #player then

    -- get number of armies
    numArmies = getProp(gCountries,country).armies

    -- increase by 1
    numArmies = numArmies + 1

    -- change game data
    setProp(getProp(gCountries,country),#armies,numArmies)

    -- update text
    showArmies
```

```
        -- computer places its army
        computerPlace(me)

        -- one less to place
②→      pToPlace = pToPlace - 1

        -- is placement done?
        if pToPlace = 0 then
          go to frame "Player Place"
        else
          message(pToPlace&&"armies left to place.")
        end if
      end if
    end
```

The computer's strategy for placing armies is a very simple one: totally random. Later in the game, the computer uses a specific strategy to place armies. But, for this part of the game, a simple random placement works satisfactorily.

```
-- computer places army
on computerPlace me
  repeat while TRUE
    -- pick a random country
    country = random(gCountries.count)
    -- make sure it is owned by the computer
    if gCountries[country].owner <> #computer then next repeat
    exit repeat
  end repeat

  -- get number of armies
  numArmies = gCountries[country].armies

  -- increase by 1
  numArmies = numArmies + 1

  -- change game data
  gCountries[country].armies = numArmies

  -- update text
  showArmies
end
```

This behavior also creates a frame loop, as do all the frame behaviors in this chapter.

```
-- loop on the frame
on exitFrame me
  go to the frame
end
```

Player Place Behavior

The next behavior is similar to the last. This one is used at the beginning of each player's turn to allow them to place their armies for the turn.

It begins by calculating how many armies the player gets. This is derived by simply adding up the total number of countries that the player has and dividing by two.

```
global gCountries
property pToPlace -- how many armies left to place

on beginSprite me
  -- determine how many armies player has to place
  pToPlace = 0 -- start with 0
  repeat with i = 1 to gCountries.count
    if gCountries[i].owner = #player then
      -- add one army for every country owned
      pToPlace = pToPlace + 1
    end if
  end repeat
  -- divide total by 2
  pToPlace = pToPlace/2
  -- make sure there is at least one army
  if pToPlace < 1 then pToPlace = 1

  message("Your turn. You have"&&pToPlace&&"armies to place.")
end
```

When the player selects a country, an army is placed there. If this is the last army to be placed, then the movie moves on to the next frame.

```
-- player clicks country
on countryClick me, country
  -- make sure player owns the countryt
  if getProp(gCountries,country).owner = #player then

    -- get number of armies
    numArmies = getProp(gCountries,country).armies

    -- increase by 1
    numArmies = numArmies + 1

    -- change game data
    setProp(getProp(gCountries,country),#armies,numArmies)

    -- update text
    showArmies
```

```
      -- one less to place
      pToPlace = pToPlace - 1

      -- is placement done?
      if pToPlace = 0 then
        go to frame "Player Attack"
      else
        message("You have"&&pToPlace&&"armies left to place.")
      end if
    end if
  end

  -- loop on the frame
  on exitFrame me
    go to the frame
  end
```

Player Attack Behavior

A player attacks by making two mouse clicks. The first would be on the country that the player is attacking from, and the second would be on the country that the player is attacking.

This behavior stores the names of these two countries in "pAttackFrom" and "pAttackTo".

After an attack has successfully conquered a country, the player then must move armies, one by one, on to the new country. The names of these countries are put in to "pMoveTo" and "pMoveFrom".

So, this behavior can be handling user input in several different modes:

- The player is selecting a country to attack from
- The player is selecting a country to attack
- The player is moving an army from the victorious country to the conquered one

```
global gCountries
global gLinks

property pAttackFrom -- country with attacking armies
property pAttackTo -- country being attacked
property pMoveTo -- country conquered
property pMoveFrom -- country where final attack was launched

-- initialize all properties
on beginSprite me
```

continues

continued

```
    pAttackFrom = VOID
    pAttackTo = VOID
    pMoveTo = VOID
    pMoveFrom = VOID
    message("Your turn to attack. Click on the country you wish to attack from.")
  end
```

When the player clicks on a country, what happens is determined by which of the three modes the behavior is in. If "pMoveFrom" is equal to the name of the country clicked, then the player must be moving an army.

However, if the player is clicking on a country they already own, then they must be selecting that country as the next one they want to attack from.

The only other possibility is that the player is clicking a country that they want to attack.

In each of these three cases, several checks are performed to ensure that the move is a valid one. In the case of an attack, the decision is made as to who won the battle, and the appropriate action is taken.

If the player attacks and then conquers a country, then the owner of that country is changed ③, a single army is moved, and "pMoveFrom" and "pMoveTo" are set so that the next click can move another army from one country to another.

```
-- player clicks on country
on countryClick me, country, spriteNum
  -- click to move armies after a conquest
  if not voidP(pMoveFrom) and country = pMoveTo then
    -- number of armies on original country
    attackArmies = getProp(gCountries,pMoveFrom).armies
    -- number of armies on occupied country
    occupyArmies = getProp(gCountries,pMoveTo).armies
    -- don't allow movement if only one army remains
    if attackArmies < 2 then
      pMoveTo = VOID
      pMoveFrom = VOID
      exit
    end if
    -- add one army to new country and subtract one from old
    setProp(getProp(gCountries,pMoveFrom),#armies,attackArmies-1)
    setProp(getProp(gCountries,pMoveTo),#armies,occupyArmies+1)
    showArmies

    -- click to select an attacking country
  else if getProp(gCountries,country).owner = #player then
    -- reset country outlines
    colorCountries
```

```
  -- record name of country
  pAttackFrom = country
  -- set this country's outline
  sprite(spriteNum).color = rgb("FF0000")
  -- move it in front of others, but still behind text
  sprite(spriteNum).locZ = 50
  -- reset move properties
  pMoveTo = VOID
  pMoveFrom = VOID
  message("Attacking from"&&country&".")

  -- click to attack
else if not voidP(pAttackFrom) then
  -- record name of country being attacked
  pAttackTo = country

  -- make sure it borders attacking country
  if not getOne(getProp(gLinks,pAttackFrom),pAttackTo) then exit

  -- get army amounts
  attackArmies = getProp(gCountries,pAttackFrom).armies
  defendArmies = getProp(gCountries,pAttackTo).armies

  -- can only attack if there are 2 armies or more
  if attackArmies < 2 then
    message("Not enough armies in"&&pAttackFrom&&"to attack.")
    exit
  end if

  -- 50% chance of winning the battle
  if random(2) = 1 then -- battle lost
    -- army destroyed
    attackArmies = attackArmies - 1
    -- set new army amount
    setProp(getProp(gCountries,pAttackFrom),#armies,attackArmies)
    showArmies
    message("Battle lost!")
  else -- battle won
    -- army destroyed
    defendArmies = defendArmies - 1
    -- see if the country has been conquered
    if defendArmies < 1 then -- country conquered
      -- move one army to new country
      setProp(getProp(gCountries,pAttackFrom),#armies,attackArmies-1)
      setProp(getProp(gCountries,pAttackTo),#armies,1)
```

continues

continued

```
                      -- set owner of new country
   ③ →  setProp(getProp(gCountries,pAttackTo),#owner,#player)
                      -- redraw country colors
                      colorCountries
                      -- set border of new country to blue
                      sprite(spriteNum).color = rgb("0000FF")
                      -- update army count text
                      showArmies
                      -- see if the game is over
                      if checkGameOver() then exit
                      message("You took"&&pAttackTo&&¬
                          "! Move armies there or choose another country to attack from.")
                      -- set up properties to move armies
                      pMoveTo = pAttackTo
                      pMoveFrom = pAttackFrom
                      pAttackTo = VOID
                      pAttackFrom = VOID
                  else -- country not yet conquered
                      -- set new army amount
                      setProp(getProp(gCountries,pAttackTo),#armies,defendArmies)
                      showArmies
                      message("Battle won!")
                  end if
              end if
          end if
      end

      -- loop on the frame
      on exitFrame me
        go to the frame
      end
```

Computer Place Behavior

When it is time for the computer to place its armies, it uses two different strategies to determine where each army goes. The first available army goes to the country that has the strongest advantage against a neighbor. The next army goes to the country that is most vulnerable to takeover. Then, the process repeats.

This behavior starts in a similar way to the player's place behavior. It determines how many armies the computer has available for placement.

```
global gCountries
global gLinks
```

```
property pToPlace -- how many armies left to place
property pPlaceType -- what type of strategy to use for placement

on beginSprite me
  -- determine how many armies player has to place
  pToPlace = 0 -- start with 0
  repeat with i = 1 to gCountries.count
    if gCountries[i].owner = #computer then
      -- add one army for every country owned
      pToPlace = pToPlace + 1
    end if
  end repeat
  -- divide total by 2
  pToPlace = pToPlace/2
  -- make sure there is at least one army
  if pToPlace < 1 then pToPlace = 1

  pPlaceType = #strongest -- first army goes to strongest
end
```

At the end of the *on beginSprite* handler, the property "pPlaceType" is set to #strongest. This means that the first army to be placed is on the country in the strongest position to attack.

The *on exitFrame* handler first checks to be sure there is at least one army left to place. Then, it calls "on placeArmy" to place a single army. The frame then loops until all armies have been placed.

NOTE

The computer places one army on each frame loop. This means that the rate of placement is controlled by the tempo. In the sample movie, the tempo is set to two frames per second. However, you can speed this up or slow it down to allow the player to see each individual placement as it happens.

```
on exitFrame me
  if pToPlace < 1 then
    -- no more armies to place, time to attack
    go to frame "Computer Attack"
  else
    -- place one army
    message("The computer has"&&pToPlace&&"armies left to place.")
    placeArmy(me)
    pToPlace = pToPlace - 1
    -- loop on frame until all armies are placed
    go to the frame
  end if
end
```

The "on placeArmy" handler uses the "pPlaceType" to determine which strategy to use in placing the army. It then calls either "on findStrongestCountry" or "on findWeakestCountry". It changes the value of "pPlaceType" ④ so that the next time an army is placed, it uses the opposite strategy.

```
on placeArmy me
  if pPlaceType = #strongest then
    -- find strongest country and place an army there
    strongest = findStrongestCountry(me)
    setProp(getProp(gCountries,strongest),#armies,¬
         getProp(gCountries,strongest).armies+1)
    -- next time, place one on weakest
    pPlaceType = #weakest

  else if pPlaceType = #weakest then
    -- get weakest country and place an army there
    weakest = findWeakestCountry(me)
    setProp(getProp(gCountries,weakest),#armies,¬
         getProp(gCountries,weakest).armies+1)
    -- next time, place one on strongest
    pPlaceType = #strongest
  end if
  showArmies
end
```

The "on findWeakestCountry" handler loops through each country owned by the computer and compares the number of armies on it to the total number of armies on each neighbor. It will then find the weakest country, or all the countries that tie for weakest. In the latter case, a random country out of all the weakest is chosen.

```
on findWeakestCountry me
  -- initialize search variables
  weakestNum = the maxInteger
  weakestCountryList = []

  -- look through all countries
  repeat with i = 1 to gLinks.count
    computerCountry = getPropAt(gLinks,i)
    -- see if it is owned by the computer
    if getProp(gCountries,computerCountry).owner <> #computer then next repeat
    -- get the number of armies on this country
    computerArmies = getProp(gCountries,computerCountry).armies
    -- count the enemy armies on the neighboring countries
    playerArmies = 0
    repeat with playerCountry in getProp(gLinks,computerCountry)
      if getProp(gCountries,playerCountry).owner <> #player then next repeat
      playerArmies = playerArmies + getProp(gCountries,playerCountry).armies
```

```
      end repeat
      -- determine difference between armies
      n = computerArmies - playerArmies
      -- see if this is weaker than the previously found weakest country
      if n < weakestNum then
        -- set search variables to this new country
        weakestNum = n
        weakestCountryList = [computerCountry]
      else if n = weakestNum then
        -- when the country ties for weakest, just add to list
        add weakestCountryList, computerCountry
      end if
    end repeat

    -- get a random country from those that tie for weakest
    weakestCountry = weakestCountryList[random(weakestCountryList.count)]
    return weakestCountry
  end
```

The "on findStrongestCountry" handler loops through each country owned by the computer and compares the number of armies on it to the number of armies on each neighbor, one at a time. It then finds the strongest country based on the difference between armies from one country to another. If more than one country has the same difference, then it puts them together in a list and that list is used to pick a random country.

```
on findStrongestCountry me
  -- initialize search variables
  strongestNum = -the maxInteger
  strongestCountryList = []

  -- look through all countries
  repeat with i = 1 to gLinks.count
    computerCountry = getPropAt(gLinks,i)
    -- see if it is owned by the computer
    if getProp(gCountries,computerCountry).owner <> #computer then next repeat
    -- get the number of armies on this country
    computerArmies = getProp(gCountries,computerCountry).armies
    -- loop through all neightbors
    repeat with playerCountry in getProp(gLinks,computerCountry)
      -- if neighbor is owned by an enemy, then compare armies
      if getProp(gCountries,playerCountry).owner <> #player then next repeat
      playerArmies = getProp(gCountries,playerCountry).armies
      -- get difference in armies
      n = computerArmies - playerArmies
      -- see if this is stronger than any other country found so far
      if n > strongestNum then
```

continues

continued

```
            -- set search variables to this new country
            strongestNum = n
            strongestCountryList = [computerCountry]
          else if n = strongestNum then
            -- when the country ties for strongest, just add to list
            add strongestCountryList, computerCountry
          end if
      end repeat
    end repeat

    -- get a random country from those that tie for strongest
    strongestCountry = strongestCountryList[random(strongestCountryList.count)]
    return strongestCountry
  end
```

Computer Attack Behavior

To decide if and where to attack, the computer searches for its strongest attack on the board. Both the placement and attack sequences are done on a frame-by-frame basis, so the command to attack is contained in the *on exitFrame* handler.

Actually, the command to attack is broken into two parts. The first part is the determination of where to attack from and which country to attack. The second part is the actual attack. So, it takes two frames to complete an attack.

The *on exitFrame* handler checks to see whether the "pAttackFrom" property is *VOID* ⑤ . If it is, then it knows the computer needs to perform the first step and find the location of the attack.

Then, on the next frame loop around, it attacks using the values of "pAttackFrom" and pAttackTo".

```
  global gCountries
  global gLinks

  property pAttackFrom -- country the computer is attacking from
  property pAttackTo -- country the computer is attacking to

  on exitFrame me
⑤➤  if voidP(pAttackFrom) then
      -- find strongest country to attack from
      findAttack(me)
      if voidP(pAttackFrom) then
        -- nothing returned, turn is over
        go to frame "Player Place"
      else
```

```
        -- show where attack is coming from
        message("The computer is attacking"&&pAttackTo&&"from"&&pAttackFrom&".")
        go to the frame
      end if

    else
      -- know where we are attacking from, now need to attack
      if attack(me) then exit -- TRUE = victory
      -- need to decide where attacking from all over again
      pAttackFrom = VOID
      go to the frame
    end if
  end
```

To find an attack, the computer performs a search similar to the one in the previous behavior that looked for the strongest country. It compares the number of armies in every computer-owned country to the number of armies in its player-owned neighbors. The highest difference between these two is determined, and these countries are stored in "pAttackFrom" and "pAttackTo".

During this search, the computer ignores any of its countries that have only one army ⑥ . This speeds up the search. It also checks to ensure that a possible attack has at least a difference of two armies. So, it does not attack from a country with three armies a country with two, for instance.

```
  -- set pAttackFrom property
on findAttack me
  -- initialize search variables
  attackNum = -the maxInteger
  attackList = []

  -- loop through all countries
  repeat with i = 1 to gLinks.count
    -- get country
    computerCountry = getPropAt(gLinks,i)
    -- see if it is owned by the computer
    if getProp(gCountries,computerCountry).owner <> #computer then next repeat
    -- get the number of armies
    computerArmies = getProp(gCountries,computerCountry).armies
    -- only consider attack if there are 2 armies or more
⑥→  if computerArmies < 2 then next repeat
    -- loop through all neighbors
    repeat with playerCountry in getProp(gLinks,computerCountry)
      -- make sure neighbor is owned by player
      if getProp(gCountries,playerCountry).owner <> #player then next repeat
```

continues

continued

```
        -- get player's armies
        playerArmies = getProp(gCountries,playerCountry).armies
        -- determine army difference
        n = computerArmies - playerArmies
        -- see if this beats the previously found strongest attack
        if n > attackNum then
          -- set search variables for new attack
          attackNum = n
          attackList = [[computerCountry,playerCountry]]
        else if n = attackNum then
          -- attack strength same as last, so just add to list
          add attackList, [computerCountry,playerCountry]
        end if
      end repeat
    end repeat

    -- make sure that the computer has at least 2 more armies than the player
    if attackNum < 2 then
      pAttackFrom = VOID
      pAttackTo = VOID
      exit
    end if

    -- get a random attack from those that tied for best
    attack = attackList[random(attackList.count)]

    -- set attack properties
    pAttackFrom = attack[1]
    pAttackTo = attack[2]
  end
```

The computer's attack is almost identical to the player's attack. There is a 50 percent chance of either side winning. The losing side loses an army. If the computer wipes out the last army in the defending country, it automatically moves all its armies there, except for one ⑦ . Although that might not be the best strategy, it works well most of the time.

```
  -- make attack
  on attack me
    -- get number of armies on both sides
    attackArmies = getProp(gCountries,pAttackFrom).armies
    defendArmies = getProp(gCountries,pAttackTo).armies

    -- see who won battle
    if random(2) = 1 then
      -- computer lost, reduce armies
```

```
      attackArmies = attackArmies - 1
      setProp(getProp(gCountries,pAttackFrom),#armies,attackArmies)
      showArmies
      message("The computer loses the battle.")
  else
    -- computer wins
    defendArmies = defendArmies - 1

    -- see if country is conquered
    if defendArmies < 1 then
      -- set country owner
      setProp(getProp(gCountries,pAttackTo),#owner,#computer)
      -- move all armies except one to new country
      setProp(getProp(gCountries,pAttackFrom),#armies,1)
      setProp(getProp(gCountries,pAttackTo),#armies,attackArmies-1)

      -- update screen
      colorCountries
      showArmies
      message("The computer took"&&pAttackTo&".")

      -- see if the computer has conquered all
      if checkGameOver() then return TRUE

    else
      -- no conquest, just update new army counts
      setProp(getProp(gCountries,pAttackTo),#armies,defendArmies)
      showArmies
      message("The computer wins the battle.")
    end if
  end if
  return FALSE
end
```

Putting It All Together

To take these scripts and make a game out of them, you first need to build the map. Figure 23.1 shows this map, but does not show how it is stored in the Cast.

Each country needs to be an individual cast member. You can see them all in Figure 23.2. There are 24 countries, so there are 24 members.

In addition to these bitmaps, there are 24 text members. Each member should be named the same as its country bitmap, but with the word "Number" following it. So, the text member for "Brazil" would be "Brazil Number".

Figure 23.2
*The Cast contains
the 24 bitmap
images that make
up the map.*

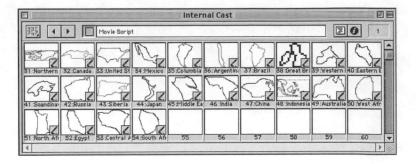

I created the bitmaps in the sample movie by first taking a map of the world. Then, I drew lines to divide the countries up. Next, I copied and pasted this map 24 times. I edited each of the 24 bitmaps until it contained only one country. The registration points, however, remained at the virtual center of the map.

NOTE

If you edit a bitmap in Director 7 while it is set to 32-bit, it will reset the registration point to the center of the bitmap. However, if you edit it in 8-bit, then it will not move the registration point.

After all the bitmaps and text members are ready, drag them to the Stage and stretch them across many frames. We need this map to exist throughout each of the frames in the movie.

Figure 23.3 shows the top of the Score for this movie. There are six primary game frames, plus the "Start" and "Game Over" frames.

The first and last frames contain only a simple looping frame script. However, the six primary frames contain the six frame behaviors. These behaviors refer to each frame by name, so be sure to name the frames properly.

In addition to the countries and text members, you also need to place the "Message" text member on every frame. Then, on frame "Player Attack", you need a "Done Turn" button for the player to be able to signal that he or she is done attacking.

This button calls the handler "colorCountries" to update the screen and it also goes to frame "Computer Place."

Figure 23.3
The top of the Score for the strategy game.

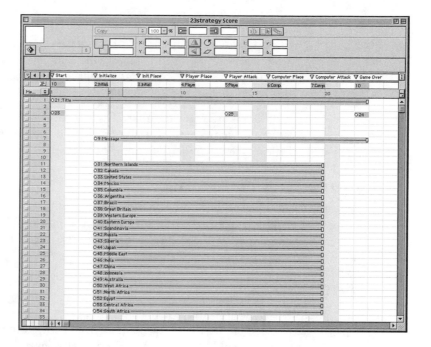

Game Variations

Strategy games are one of the largest genres of computer games. This is partially because there are so many variations on the theme.

Even with this simple framework, you can create many different types of games. Here are some suggestions as to how you can change and improve the game in this chapter.

Better AI

Your first task should be improving the artificial intelligence in this game. Right now, it plays like a novice human player. However, with the computer's capability to quickly analyze the board and sort possibilities, it can become almost unbeatable.

AI for games is not as mysterious as it sounds. You simply have to come up with algorithms for examining the board and finding the right move.

Think about how you play this game. What strategies are you using? How can you write handlers to mimic these strategies?

Creating a better AI can take a lot of time and effort, but you are rewarded in the end by a challenging game.

Some simple ways to make the opponent more challenging would be to simply give the computer more armies each turn. Then, the player becomes the underdog, which can make for a fun game.

Different Maps

Most of the game code here is independent of the actual map and make-up of the countries. But by creating new bitmaps and changing the "on getLinks" handler, you can come up with a map that has more countries. Realistically, a game like this should have 30 to 50 countries to be challenging.

You also can use different areas for the map. For instance, instead of the entire world, you can just show the United States as it was during the Civil War, or Europe during World War II. You can even change the countries to planets for a science-fiction game.

Victory Determinants

Instead of using the 50/50 method of determining who is victorious in a battle, you might want to make the algorithm more complex. For instance, you might want to weight the battles in favor of the defender. Or, you might want to make the chances of victory dependent on the size of the armies.

Fortifications

In this game, the only way to move armies from one country to another is by battle. You might want to add another step in the game that allows the players to move armies from one country to a neighbor after they are done attacking.

This would prevent armies from getting left behind after the front shifts to another part of the board. The players can slowly move masses of troops from the back to the front over a series of turns.

Extra Armies

Board games similar to this game often offer many other ways to get extra troops other than simply owning more countries. For instance, if you own all the countries in a continent, you might get a few bonus troops in your next turn. Or, there can be a random system, such as a deck of cards that awards extra armies to the owner of certain countries.

More Players

This game works well as a two-player game. However, you might want to consider allowing more than one computer player. This can complicate the game in interesting ways as the computer players attack one another as well as the human player.

If you are experimenting with different AIs, you can assign a different one to each computer player. This not only keeps the player on his or her toes as he or she fights off different strategies, but also shows you which AI strategy is dominant.

Part VII:
Multiplayer Games

24 High Score Boards   **417**

25 Multiplayer Game   **431**

High Score Boards

24

CD-ROM File: 24highscorefolder

Useful Lingo in This Chapter

- ♠ Input: Accepting typed input
- ♠ Output: Saving high scores
- ♠ Strings: Parsing strings
- ♠ Strings: Using items
- ♠ Text Members: Adjusting tabs with Lingo
- ♠ Variables: Keeping score

Most Shockwave games, even though they are on the Internet, use very little of the Internet's potential for communication between players. They are simply single-player games that are housed inside Web pages. The players are not really connected to others or to the site.

One easy way to connect players is to use high score boards. These have existed since the dawn of the video game. In those days, as today, each machine had its own high score board where players could compare their score against someone else's who had played on the same machine.

With the Internet, you can have worldwide high score boards with scores from everyone who plays the game. This is not only a nice feature, but helps drive return traffic to the game as players try to beat other scores.

Basic Method

Shockwave games can easily be connected to high score systems. To do this, Lingo sends information through the Web browser back to the server. On the server, a program takes this information and records it.

HTML Forms

The Web uses two methods to send information back to the server. They are known as GET and POST. Both use HTML forms to allow the Web user to type or select information. You see these forms all over the Internet, from e-commerce order pages, to free Web email services, to Web forums.

When an HTML form sends information back to the server, it uses either the GET method or the POST method. The GET method simply sends a long string of characters to the server. It is then up to the server to take this long string and extract information from it.

The POST method, on the other hand, sends back one or many pieces of information. Each piece of information has a label. This is much like the property lists in Director.

In Director 4, 5, and 6, only the GET method was possible. This is because you can implement a GET without using an HTML form at all. You can simply put the string of information after a question mark in a regular URL. So, for instance, you could use `getNetText("highscore.cgi?gary&56")` to report a score of 56.

Because Shockwave would just pass the *getNetText* URL directly to the browser as a request for a Web page, it didn't matter whether it was a real Web page, or a call to a server program. So, even though Director 4, 5, and 6 did not support calls to server programs, you could use *getNetText* to make one anyway.

On the other hand, the POST method is a supported feature of Director 7. Using the Lingo command *postNetText*, you can send a property list to a server program. This list would resemble the fields and options in an HTML form.

We use POST as the method for sending scores to our high score board server program.

 NOTE
In the HTML world, the difference between GET and POST is significant. As compared to Lingo, GET is like using a linear list and POST is like using a property list. As a further restriction, GET calls are limited in size, usually to 4K.

CGI Scripts

For scores to be recorded and shared, we must have something on the server that accepts new high scores, records them, and sends out a list of top scores when asked. To do this, we use a CGI script.

CGI stands for *Common Gateway Interface*. It is a catchall term to describe any program that runs on a server and handles information coming in to and going out of Web sites.

CGI programs are most frequently written in a language called Perl. However, they also can be written in C, C++, Java, or just about anything else as long as the server supports it.

We use Perl because it is supported on just about any server, and it is an accepted standard for CGI programs. Perl also is an easy language to learn, although we will not be doing much with it.

Implementations

There are many ways to implement a high score board for your game. Although this chapter presents a common method, let us review some of the different methods used from time to time.

HTML High Score Board

All high score boards get their score from the Shockwave game, and most also ask the player for his or her name inside the game. However, after the score has been submitted to the server, the task of displaying the top scores is another matter.

One way to do this is not to bother the game with displaying high scores at all. Instead, use another CGI script to create an HTML page that shows the high scores in a table.

This high scores page can be accessed separately from the game. The advantages are that the game doesn't have to worry about an area to display the scores, the high score board is a separate page and therefore a separate ad banner impression, and players don't have to load the entire game just to see the scores.

Built-In High Score Board

A nicer way to show a high score board is to have it built right into the game. This closely resembles how a video arcade game works.

When the game starts, the first screen or introduction sequence shows the high scores. When the player completes a game, they are given the chance to add their score to the list. Then, the game returns to the starting screen to display the high scores again.

The advantages here are that no player can miss the high score board, as it is always there at the beginning of the game. Also, you don't have to build or maintain a separate HTML page for the high scores. Another advantage is that you can process the high scores in Lingo, so the CGI script needs to return only some raw data, rather than building an HTML table. This simplifies the CGI script, and because we are Lingo programmers and not HTML programmers, this is the method we use in this chapter.

Score Rotation

If you have a popular site, a high score board can fill up pretty fast. If you show only the top ten high scores, and you have 10,000 people playing a game in a few days, only a few will get to see their name on the board. In addition, if some player gets a really good score, he or she can end up staying on top of the board forever.

One thing I like to do with the high score boards that I make is to record the date that each score was submitted. Then, after the score gets to be a few days, a week, or a month old, I delete it. This means that the high score board is then really only the high score board for the past *n* number of days, and not for all-time.

This method actually gets people to play the game more often. If they are the top scorer, they want to return in a few days to claim that title again. If they are not that good, they might keep trying, in hopes that their score makes the board after the best player's scores have been retired.

Making the High Score Board

The high score board is not a movie in itself, but rather part of a larger movie that includes a game. As an example, I have put together a very simple "whack-a-mole" game for the CD-ROM. However, the game itself is unimportant for this example. It populates a global variable called "gScore" with the game score. Other than that, I will not go in to the game any further.

High score code is present in two places. The first is when the game starts. At this point, the server is asked for a list of high scores to display. We have a Lingo behavior that calls the server, and a Perl script that sits on the server and handles the call.

The second part of a high score system comes in when a new score needs to be sent to the server. There is a behavior and a Perl script for this as well. Because that is the simpler step, we start by examining that first.

Submitting a High Score

The Lingo part of submitting a score is very simple. The behavior sits on its own frame at the end of the movie. It relies on two values: the score and the player's name. The first is taken from the "gScore" global. The second is from a text field that the player has filled in on the "Game Over" screen. This screen can be seen in Figure 24.1.

Figure 24.1

The "Game Over" frame allows the player to type their name and press the "Submit Score" button to start the submission process.

The behavior assumes that the "player name" field is already filled in. It places that value in a variable and makes a property list containing that value and the score. This property list is used by *postNetText* to mimic an HTML form.

```
global gScore -- game score
property pNetID -- network connection ID number

on beginSprite me
  -- set the URL of the CGI script
  saveScoreCGI = "http://clevermedia.com/resources/gamesbook/highscore/savescore.cgi"

  -- get the player's name from the text member
  playerName = member("player name").text

  -- make list to post
  postList = ["name":playerName, "score":string(gScore)]

  -- post data to server
  pNetID = postNetText(saveScoreCGI,postList)
end
```

The *postNetText* command is not one that can be executed and forgotten about. A network function such as this has two parts: the initial call, and the receipt of the response.

The call to *postNetText* returned a number that we stored in "pNetID". This number is Lingo's way of identifying the connection made to the network.

In the *on exitFrame* handler, we use *netDone* to check whether this connection is complete. When it is, we use *netTextResult* to take the response from the buffer where Lingo has been holding it. We do this to complete the network operation, even though we aren't using this value for anything in this particular case. This completes the network circuit and we can move back to the beginning of the movie to allow the player to play again.

```
on exitFrame me
  -- see if the net connection is done
  if netDone(pNetID) then

     -- get text, even though it is not used
     text = netTextResult(pNetID)

     -- jump to the first frame
     go to frame "Start"

  else
     -- loop until net connection is done
 go to the frame
  end if
end
```

Recording a High Score

The Lingo for saving a score is very simple. This is because the server does most of the hard work. Here, we have a Perl program that handles adding the score to a database file.

Perl is a language similar to Lingo. You can have subroutines and arrange your code in a variety of fashions. However, because the two scripts we are writing here are fairly simple, we stick to a command-after-command style of programming, rather than getting into using subroutines.

NOTE

Perl is an interpreted language. This means that there is actually a program called "Perl" on the server. It opens your Perl program, reads it, and executes its commands. Some servers have a Perl program that runs constantly and handles any Perl scripts that need to be run.

Because it is not my intention here to teach Perl, I show each line of code here and comment on it. However, I try not to get too much into how Perl works or what the commands do. This information can be found in many other books.

Comments in Perl start with a # character. The first line, which looks like a comment, is actually used by the server to determine the path of the Perl program. The path given here is a very commonly used path and might work on your server as well. If not, consult your server's documentation or ask your Internet service provider.

```
#!/usr/bin/perl
```

The first line of code defines the type of output that the Perl script creates. In this case, it is plain text, which, in server language, is defined by "text/html".

```
# create header for text document to return
print "Content-type: text/html\n\n";
```

The next line gets the physical length of the posted information.

```
# get size of post data
$size_of_data = $ENV{'CONTENT_LENGTH'};
```

The length of the posted information is then used to get the information itself. This is stored in the Perl variable "$post_data".

```
# get post data
read (STDIN, $post_data, $size_of_data);
```

The next two lines have the task of taking the posted text and converting it to normal text. This is necessary because your browser and the server communicate in such a way that any nonalphanumeric characters are converted to their ASCII codes, and spaces are converted to plus symbols. This line converts it to normal text.

```
# convert escape characters
$post_data =~ s/%([\dA-Fa-f][\dA-Fa-f])/pack ("C",hex($1))/eg;
$post_data =~ tr/\+/ /;
```

When we save the scores to the database we add the time to each one. This is UNIX server time, which is measured in seconds, so it is just a plain integer.

```
# get the server time in seconds
$server_time = time();
```

The next few lines loop through the items in the posted data and create a Perl array. We are able to access each of the items in this array by name, in a similar way that we were able to do so in Lingo.

```
# take post data and create an array of data
@split_data = split("&",$post_data);
foreach $data_item (@split_data)
  {
  ($key, $value) = split("=",$data_item);
  $info{$key} = $value;
  }
```

This line puts the name of the database file into a variable. The database is actually just an ordinary text file, with each line a score record.

```
# set filename for highscore database
$filename = "highscore.txt";
```

A line of text is returned at this point to signify that the Perl program made it okay to this point. If we wanted, we could have checked the returned text to see whether there was an error when the Perl script ran.

```
# signify data receieved ok
print "Data Received.\n";
```

Now the program opens the database file. The ">>" means that the file is being opened for appending. The two barlike characters are the same as an *or* in Lingo. In this case, they are used to perform the "exit" command if the "open" command is not successful.

```
# open the database
open(OUTFILE,">>$filename") || exit;
```

The next line writes the score, the time, and the player's name to a new line in the database file. It uses an ampersand (&) as the item delimiter between these. The "\n" at the end is a return character.

```
# append the data to the database
print OUTFILE "$info{'score'}&$server_time&$info{'name'}&\n";
```

All that is left is to close the file, send along a message that the script was successful, and end the script properly with an "exit".

```
# close the database
close(OUTFILE);

# signify data written ok
print "Data written.\n";

# end this script
exit;
```

A Perl script is just a simple text file. To get it to run on your server, you need to upload it. Then, you need to set its permissions properly. As an example, Figure 24.2 shows the Permissions setting dialog box for the popular Macintosh program "Fetch," which is used to upload files to a Web server.

You need to set the permissions for the Perl script according to how your server is set up. Try giving the script all nine permissions first. However, some servers do not allow a script to run like this, as it could be considered a security weakness. Consult your server documentation or Internet service provider.

You also need to upload a blank text file called "highscore.txt" to be used as a starting point for the database. You need to set the permissions for this file as well. Try all nine permissions first, although you shouldn't need any of the "Search/Execute" permissions shown in Figure 24.2.

Figure 24.2
The Fetch window allows you to set the permissions for a file on your Web server.

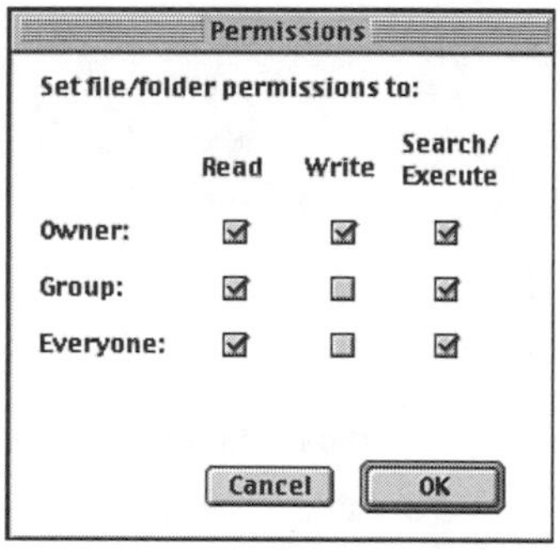

Getting the High Score Board

The Perl script to save a score is only one side of the picture. The other is a Perl script that takes the score database and returns the top scores.

It starts off like the previous script. The first line points to the server's Perl program. Then, the returned information is set up as text.

```
#!/usr/bin/perl

# create header for text document to return
print "Content-type: text/html\n\n";
```

The filename of the database is stored in a variable. Then, the file is opened and the complete contents are read into a Perl array "@score".

```
# set filename for highscore database
$filename = "highscore.txt";

# read high score data
open(DATABASE,$filename) || exit;
@score_text = <DATABASE>;
close(DATABASE);
```

The server time is recorded, as well as the number of seconds in seven days. This is used to determine the time seven days ago, which is the cutoff time for saving a score. Anything older than seven days is removed from the file, making room for new scores.

```
# get the server time
$server_time = time();

# how long to keep the scores
# (7 days * 24 hours * 60 minutes * 60 seconds)
$keep_time = 7*(24*60*60);
```

The next lines reopen the file and write out each line one by one. However, they will write only lines that have a time of less than seven days old.

```
# open database file for writing
open(DATABASE,">" . $filename) || exit;

# loop through each score
foreach $score_line (@score_text) {
  # get score data
  @score_item = split(/&/,$score_line);
  # get score time
  $score_time = $score_item[1];
  # if the score is not old, write it back out again
  if ($score_time > ($server_time-$keep_time)) {
    print DATABASE "$score_line";
  }
}

#close database
close(DATABASE);
```

The only thing left for the script to do is to return the top ten scores. First, it sorts the scores. Because each line of the database starts with the score, we can just sort the database as an array of lines.

```
# sort scores
@score_text = sort { $b <=> $a } @score_text;
```

The following lines loop through each of the lines in the now-sorted array. The code then outputs the first ten of these.

```
# determine number of scores to send
$num_scores = 10;
$score_count = 0;

# loop through first scores and send the data
foreach $score_line (@score_text) {
    print $score_line;
    $score_count = $score_count + 1;
    if ($score_count >= $num_scores) { last; }
}

#exit script
exit;
```

This Perl script is called "getscores.cgi". The previous script was called "savescore.cgi". I am using the ".cgi" at the end of the filename because many servers require this to make the script executable. However, some servers accept, or even require, a ".pl" to identify the file as a Perl script.

Displaying the High Score Board

Our Director movie starts by calling the "getscores.cgi" script on the server. It does this with a *getNetText* command. The *postNetText* command is not used because no data is required to be sent.

```
property pNetID -- network connection ID number

on beginSprite me
  -- set the URL of the CGI script
  getScoreCGI = "http://clevermedia.com/resources/gamesbook/highscore/getscores.cgi"

  -- initiate the connection
  pNetID = getNetText(getScoreCGI)
end
```

The behavior then loops on the frame until data is returned. When that happens, the text is taken and parsed into something that can be displayed in a text member.

```
on exitFrame me
  -- see if still connecting
  if pNetID <> VOID then
    -- see if connection done
    if netDone(pNetID) then
      -- get the text returned
      scoretext = netTextResult(pNetID)
      -- remember connection is done
      pNetID = VOID

      -- set up to parse text
      text = ""
      the itemDelimiter = "&"

      -- parse text
      repeat with i = 1 to scoretext.line.count
        -- get each name and score
        name = scoretext.line[i].item[3]
        score = scoretext.line[i].item[1]
        -- put into new text
        put name&TAB&score&RETURN after text
      end repeat

      -- place text into text member
      member("highscores").text = text
      member("highscores").tabs = [[#type: #left, #position: 100]]
      member("highscores").alignment = #left
    end if
  end if
```

continues

continued

```
     -- always loop on the frame
   go to the frame
end
```

Using the High Score Board

If you have never set up a high score board like this before, please note that it takes some patience. You will probably have to work for a while to learn how to set the permissions for the Perl program and database file according to how your server is set up.

If you are having problems, start using debugging techniques to determine where the problems are. For instance, be sure that the call to *getNetText* and *postNettext* are returning valid numbers. Then, examine what text value is returned through *netTextResult*. You can use *put* commands to place these values into the message window.

Most problems that people have in setting up high score boards can be fixed with some debugging and lots of patience.

Setup

The basic steps to using the code in this chapter to make a high score board start by uploading your two Perl scripts and your blank text file to the server. Then, set the permissions.

Next, create your Director movie, or use the sample one from the CD-ROM. You want to change the location of the CGI programs first. In the sample movie, they are set to a location on my server, which is not the appropriate place for you.

NOTE

If the Shockwave movie and the CGI script are not on the same server, you can still call the CGI script by using a full path URL in *getNetText* and *postNetText*. However, this is considered a security risk in most browsers. As a result, the player sees a message stating the location of your high score program and asking him or her whether it is okay that the server be contacted. Having a message like this appear is considered highly unprofessional and not appropriate for a commercial Web site. So, you should be sure that your movie and your CGI script are on the same server.

The behavior to get the scores goes on the first frame of the movie. Then, the behavior to submit the scores goes on its own frame elsewhere in the movie—in this case, at the end.

You will need to add an editable text member or field for the player to be able to enter his or her name. Do this on the frame *before* the submission frame. This way, when the submission frame is reached, the player's name is already in place.

I encourage you to study the sample movie on the CD-ROM before trying this on your own. Also, be prepared for some frustrating moments as you get this to work for the first time.

Other Uses for High Score Boards

The technology in this chapter can be used for a number of things in addition to, or instead of, high score boards. Here are a few ideas.

Contests

Because you have people submitting high scores anyway, you might as well give them something for it. You can award prizes, for instance.

In this case, you want the player to give more than just his or her name. You at least need an email address. Then, when you pick the winner, you are able to email him or her and ask for a mailing address to send the prize to.

NOTE

High score contests are a good idea, but they are dangerous. Hackers easily are able to change their score in their local computer's memory and send in huge scores that they don't deserve. Some hackers can even intercept the high score submission data and figure out how to send in false scores. It's like a casino allowing people to take their slot machines home and tinker with them.

Surveys

You can use high score boards to collect information about the people who play your game. Instead of just asking them for a name, you can ask them for some demographic information, or even survey-like questions. Then, you can record these along with the score.

Replacing HTML Forms

Why not just forget the game altogether? You can use this same technique to send information other than high scores. So, instead of using an HTML form, you could use a Shockwave movie.

High Scores from a Projector

Do you know how much you have to change to make this work from a Projector instead of Shockwave? Absolutely nothing. The *postNetText* and *getNetText* commands work from Director and Projectors, as long as there is an Internet connection.

Multiplayer Game

CD-ROM File: 25multiplayer.dir

Useful Lingo in This Chapter

- ♠ Behaviors: Calling handlers in other behaviors
- ♠ Graphics: Changing sprite members with Lingo
- ♠ Graphics: Using a grid of bitmaps
- ♠ Input: Accepting typed input
- ♠ Input: Clicking on text as input
- ♠ Input: Selecting with mouse clicks
- ♠ Lists: Using linear lists
- ♠ Lists: Lists that contain lists
- ♠ Programming: Using a case statement
- ♠ Programming: Using an Xtra

For a while, the multiplayer game was the holy grail of Internet gaming. Most developers couldn't figure out how to do it, and those who did found their efforts hindered by network security, firewalls, and users with bad connections.

In 2000, multiplayer games are all over the Internet. Most are done with Java applets. However, with Macromedia's multiuser server, it is fairly easy to create a multiplayer game in Shockwave.

Game Overview

As an example, we create a simple tic-tac-toe game. However, because it is a multiplayer game, there needs to be a lot of code committed to just hooking the players up over the Internet. It is assumed that this game is a Shockwave game, not one that runs as a Projector, although that would work, too.

What You Will Need

To get this game running, even for a test, you need at least two computers hooked up to the Internet. Ideally, you should have three computers: one to run the Multiuser Server, and one for each player. However, you should be able to run the server on the same computer as one of the players.

The Multiuser Server is a small program that comes with Macromedia Director Internet Studio. It came with Director 7, and, at the time of this writing, also should be shipping with Director 8. People who purchased Director as a standalone application might not have it.

NOTE

The Multiuser Server that comes with Director 7 supports up to 50 simultaneous users. This is certainly enough for testing and small- to medium-sized sites. However, if you need more users, you can purchase a larger license from Macromedia from their Web site.

The three computers also must be hooked up to the Internet. This can be done through a modem or a permanent line. However, each computer should have its own Internet address (IP address). So, situations where several computers are hooked up through a single modem and they all share an IP address probably will not work.

The three computers also should not be behind a restrictive firewall. Some companies have firewalls that protect their computers from hackers, but still allow communication such as the type used by Macromedia's server. Other firewalls do not. If you are having trouble, contact your network administrator. If he or she asks, we are using "port 1626." This information might allow your network administrator to adjust the firewall for you.

NOTE

Don't have what it takes to set up a multiuser server in the office? As of the time of this writing, Macromedia is offering a free area to test your multiuser Shockwave applets. Go to `http://www.macromedia.com/support/director/ts/documents/trialserver.htm` and find out what you need to do to access a server owned by Macromedia.

Running the Multiuser Server

Setting up the Multiuser Server is very easy. Just install it from the Director installer CD-ROM on to the computer that you are using as the server. Then, run it.

The result is a screen as in Figure 25.1. The Multiuser Server can be run on either a Macintosh or Windows, and both screens look basically the same.

Figure 25.1

The Multiuser Server program being run.

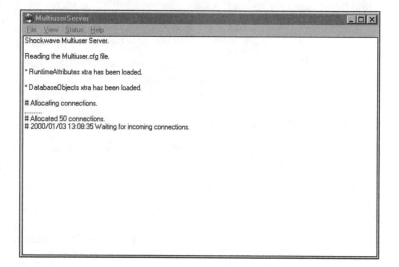

The only extra step that you need to take is to select the Status, Server menu item. This adds information to the window. One of these pieces of information is the "Server IP address." This is a series of four numbers separated by periods. You need this number to create the game.

Making a Game Lobby

Multiuser games would be much easier to make if people knew one another by the IP address of their computers, rather than their names. However, because people don't even know their own IP address, and often these addresses change every time a modem user dials in, we need a game lobby.

The sole purpose of a game lobby is to allow two or more people to start a multiplayer game. To facilitate this, we list the players in the lobby and allow them to chat. Then, when any player clicks on another player's name, it takes both players to another screen.

The player being challenged is asked whether he or she wants to play the challenger. A "Yes" and "No" button allows the player to make this decision. The challenger, meanwhile, waits for this decision on another screen.

The chat in the lobby is fairly simple. The player is allowed to type one line of text at a time and send it to the chat room. A text member then lists all the chat lines submitted by any user. This allows players the chance to get to know one another before starting a game.

Game Play

After the game begins, only one player is allowed to move at a time. There needs to be a message area where players are told the status of the game. It will have text such as "Your turn" or "Your opponent's turn."

The two players also are allowed to chat with each other. This is a private chat, and not connected to the chat going on in the lobby.

Making the Game

Most of the code in this game has to do with the multiuser communication. This is in a large movie script. There are a few supporting behaviors as well. Finally, there is a frame behavior that controls the tic-tac-toe game.

Movie Script

The movie script uses a variety of global variables. The comments after each declaration explain its use.

```
global gServerIP -- address of server
global gXtra -- Xtra object
global gUserName -- name user typed
global gUserList -- list of all users on server
global gOpponentName -- name of opponent
global gMode -- #none, #lobby or #game
global gTurn -- TRUE if it is this player's turn
```

When the movie starts, some of the globals are set. In particular, the IP address of the Multiuser Server is stored in "gServerIP". Don't use the number shown next, but use the number of your own server.

```
on startMovie
  -- initialize globals
```

```
    gMode = #none
    gUserList = []
    gServerIP = "216.160.156.91" -- use your own IP address here

    -- clear text
    member("Chat Type").text = ""
    member("Chat Text").text = ""
    member("Name").text = ""

    go to frame "register"
 end
```

The first frame the player sees is one that asks them to type their name and press the
"Continue" button. Figure 25.2 shows this screen from the example movie. After they
do this, the "on startGameLobby" handler takes things from there. It creates the
instance of the Shockwave Multiuser Xtra, sets the message handler, and connects to
the server.

Figure 25.2

*The first screen of
the multiplayer
game asks the user
to enter a name.*

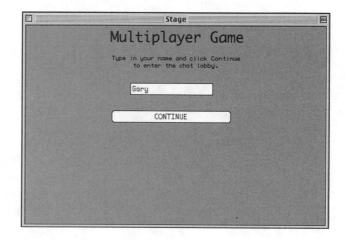

```
on startGameLobby
  -- get name from field
  gUserName = member("Name").text

  -- start Xtra
  gXtra = new(xtra "Multiuser")
  SetNetMessageHandler(gXtra, #messageHandler, script "Movie Script")

-- start connection
  ConnectToNetServer(gXtra, gUserName, "password", gServerIP, 1626, "gamelobby")
end
```

The *SetNetMessageHandler* command tells the Multiuser Xtra object how to communicate with the movie. When the multiuser object has something to report, such as an incoming message, it calls the handler stated, in this case "on messageHandler".

Here is that handler. It checks the number of waiting messages, which is usually just one, and then gets the message or messages.

Each message is a short property list with at least a #subject and a #content property. These two properties are extracted into their own variables. Then, a case statement performs the appropriate action according to the subject.

Each part of the case statement is well commented, and I will let the comments speak for themselves. Most of the cases call other handlers.

```
-- this handler is called when the server contacts the player
on messageHandler
  -- count the number of messages
  n = GetNumberWaitingNetMessages(gXtra)

  -- loop through each message
  repeat with i = 1 to n
    -- get message
    list = GetNetMessage(gXtra)

    -- get subject and content from message
    subject = getAProp(list,#subject)
    content = getAProp(list,#content)

    -- handle each type of message
    case subject of
      "ConnectToNetServer": -- initial connection successful
        enterLobby

      "getGroupMembers": -- server returns list of members
        -- set user list
        gUserList = content.groupMembers
        -- show users on screen
        showUsers

      "enterLobby": -- another user has entered lobby
        addUser(content)

      "leaveLobby": -- another user has left the lobby
        removeUser(content)

      "chatLobby": -- a user sends a chat message
        addChat(content)
```

```
    "challenge": -- another user challenges this one
      -- get opponent's name
      gOpponentName = content
      -- set screen text
      member("Challenge Message").text =¬
          content&&"has challenged you to a game. Do you accept?"
      -- go to frame with Yes and No buttons
      go to frame "ask"

    "decline": -- user that was challenged responded with a No
      alert "Your challenge has been declined."
      -- return to lobby
      go to frame "lobby"

    "accept": -- user that was challenged responded with a Yes
      -- leave lobby group
      leaveLobby
      -- other player goes first
      gTurn = FALSE
      -- clear chat
      member("Chat Text").text = ""
      member("Chat Type").text = ""
      -- start game
      gMode = #game
      go to frame "game"

    "turnDone": -- a turn in the game is over
      -- send message to game behavior
      sendSprite(0,#opponentMove,content)

    "chatGame": -- chat message sent from opponent
      addGameChat(content)

    "newGame": -- restart the game with the same player
      -- your turn
      gTurn = TRUE
      -- start game
      go to frame "game"

    "leaveGame": -- other player bailed
      alert "Your opponent has left."
      -- restart at lobby
      enterLobby

  end case
end repeat
end
```

After the code gets a message back from the server that a connection has been established, the next step is for the player to establish his or her presence in the game lobby. This is done by first sending a message to the server to join a group called "@GameLobby".

A group is just a list of users on a server that can be referred to by a single name, rather than a whole list. Anyone who is part of the "@GameLobby" group receives messages sent to the group.

After the user is part of the group, the code then requests a list of the other people in the group. In addition, a message is sent to the others in the group so that they know someone new has entered.

```
on enterLobby
  -- join lobby group
  sendNetMessage(gXtra,"System","joinGroup","@GameLobby")

  -- see who's here
  sendNetMessage(gXtra,"System","getGroupMembers","@GameLobby")

  -- send message to all other in lobby
  sendNetMessage(gXtra,"@GameLobby","enterLobby",gUserName)

  -- set mode and go to proper frame
  gMode = #lobby
  go to frame "lobby"
end
```

When a new user enters the lobby, they announce their presence by sending an "enterLobby" message. This, in turn, triggers the "on addUser" handler for everyone else in the lobby. The purpose of this handler is to add a name to the list of people present in the room. Figure 25.3 shows the game lobby. You can see the list of users at the upper right.

Figure 25.3
The game lobby shows the chat area and a list of users present.

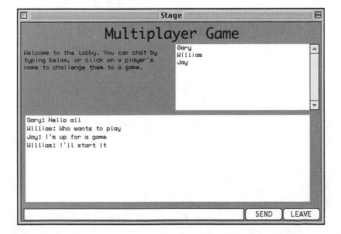

```
-- add a new user to the list when they come in to the lobby
on addUser newUser
  if not getOne(gUserList,newUser) then
    add gUserList, newUser
  end if
  showUsers
end
```

Likewise, when a player leaves the lobby, their name must be removed from the list. This happens when the player starts a game, or when they quit.

```
-- remove a user from the list when they leave
on removeUser user
  deleteOne(gUserList,user)
  showUsers
end
```

The next handler takes the list of users in the lobby and places it in a text member on the screen.

```
-- take whole list and place on screen
on showUsers
  text = ""
  repeat with i = 1 to gUserList.count
    put gUserList[i]&RETURN after text
  end repeat
  member("User List").text = text
end
```

The most common action in the game lobby is to send a chat message to the others in the lobby. This is done by sending a message with the subject "chatLobby" and contents that include the username and the chat text.

```
-- player pressed button to send chat line
on sendChat
  sendNetMessage(gXtra,"@GameLobby","chatLobby",¬
      [#userName: gUserName, #chatText: member("Chat Type").text])
  member("Chat Type").text = ""
end
```

When a new line of chat is received, it is simply appended to the end of a text member. If that member already has too many lines, then one line is removed from the top.

```
-- add a line of chat to the text member
on addChat content
  text = member("Chat Text").text
  put content.userName&":"&&content.chatText&RETURN after text
  if text.line.count > 11 then delete line 1 of text
  member("Chat Text").text = text
end
```

When the player leaves the lobby to go play a game, they send a "leaveLobby" message to all others there, which removes their name from the list of users. They also leave the server group.

```
-- leave the lobby to play a game or when user quits
on leaveLobby
  if objectP(gXtra) then
    -- send message to others in lobby
    sendNetMessage(gXtra,"@GameLobby","leaveLobby",gUserName)
    -- leave lobby group
    sendNetMessage(gXtra,"System","leaveGroup","@GameLobby")
    -- go to last frame and change mode
    go to frame "Done"
    gMode = #none
  end if
end
```

Similarly, when a player leaves a game, a message is sent to the opponent.

```
-- leave a game in progress
on leaveGame
  if objectP(gXtra) then
    -- send message to opponent
    sendNetMessage(gXtra,gOpponentName,"leaveGame","")
    -- go to last frame and change mode
    go to frame "Done"
    gMode = #none
  end if
end
```

When a player clicks on another player's name in the list, a message is sent to that player to alert them of the challenge. Then, the first player is sent to a wait screen where they await the other player's reply. Figure 25.4 shows this wait screen.

Figure 25.4
The player who makes the challenge must wait for the other player to respond.

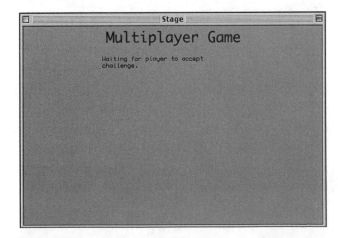

```
-- click on a user's name in the list
on challengeUser n
  -- make sure it is a valid list item
  if n < 1 or n > gUserList.count then exit

  -- make sure the user didn't click on his or herself!
  if gUserList[n] = gUserName then exit

  -- get the opponent's name
  gOpponentName = gUserList[n]

  -- send the challenge
  sendNetMessage(gXtra,gOpponentName,"challenge",gUserName)

  -- wait
  member("Challenge Message").text = "Waiting for player to accept challenge."
  go to frame "wait"
end
```

The player being challenged goes to a frame with a "Yes" and a "No" button. You can see this frame in Figure 25.5. If they press "Yes," then they leave the lobby and signal the other player that the game has begun.

Figure 25.5

The player being challenged needs to respond in one of two ways to the challenge.

```
-- respond Yes to a challenge
on acceptChallenge
  -- leave lobby
  leaveLobby

  -- tell opponent
  sendNetMessage(gXtra,gOpponentName,"accept","")
```

continues

continued

```
       -- go first
       gTurn = TRUE

       -- start game
       gMode = #game
       member("Chat Text").text = ""
       member("Chat Type").text = ""
       go to frame "game"
     end
```

On the other hand, if the challenge is declined, then both players are sent back to the lobby.

```
  -- respond No to a challenge
  on declineChallenge
    -- respond to challenger
    sendNetMessage(gXtra,gOpponentName,"decline","")

    -- return to lobby
    go to frame "lobby"
  end
```

While the two players play the game, they can chat with each other. We use the same text members for this chat, but we need to use different handlers for sending and receiving the chat. You can see in Figure 25.6 that the chat takes up more of the screen than the game itself.

Figure 25.6

The game screen shows the game board and the chat elements.

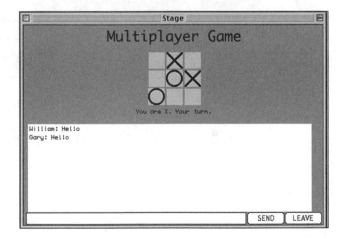

```
on sendGameChat text
  -- get text
  chatText = member("Chat Type").text
  content = [#userName: gUserName, #chatText: chatText]
  -- send to other player
  sendNetMessage(gXtra,gOpponentName,"chatGame",¬
      content)
  -- also put in chat text here
  addGameChat(content)
  -- clear chat line
  member("Chat Type").text = ""
end

on addGameChat content
  text = member("Chat Text").text
  put content.userName&":"&&content.chatText&RETURN after text
  if text.line.count > 11 then delete line 1 of text
  member("Chat Text").text = text
end
```

After a game is over, one of the two players can press a "New Game" button to start
over again. This needs to signal the other player to let him or her know that the game is
starting again.

```
-- new game with same opponent
on newGame
  -- tell opponent to start over
  sendNetMessage(gXtra,gOpponentName,"newGame","")

  -- begin game again
  gMode = #game
  gTurn = FALSE
  go to frame "game"
end
```

When a player completes a turn, a "turnDone" message is sent to the other player. This
includes an entire new game state, which has the most recent move. This new game
state is taken by the other player and used to update the screen.

```
-- player finishes turn in game
on gameTurnOver newMatrix
  -- send new game state to opponent
  sendNetMessage(gXtra,gOpponentName,"turnDone",newMatrix)
end
```

The *on stopMovie* handler gets executed if the player closes the browser window or
otherwise quits the game. We use this handler to have the player gracefully leave the
game or the lobby.

```
-- catch it when the user quits
on stopMovie
  -- use proper handler to close down connection
  if objectP(gXtra) then
    if gMode = #lobby then
      leaveLobby
    else if gMode = #game then
      leaveGame
    end if

    -- close connection to server
    gXtra = VOID
  end if
end
```

User List Behavior

One small behavior that is needed is the one that attaches to the user list in the game lobby. This allows the player to click on a name in the list and challenge the player. All that this behavior needs to do is pass on the line number that was clicked.

```
-- get the lin clicked and return that number
on mouseUp me
  l = pointToLine(sprite me.spriteNum, the clickLoc)
  challengeUser(l)
end
```

Tic-Tac-Toe Behavior

The game behavior is a rather simple one, complicated only by the fact that it is part of a multiplayer scenario. It uses the global "gTurn", which is set to *FALSE* if the player is the challenger, and *TRUE* if the player is the one being challenged.

The property "pPlayerSymbol" contains the symbol, either an "X" or an "O", that this player uses in the game. The property "pMatrix" is the small 3-by-3 tic-tac-toe matrix.

```
global gTurn -- TRUE if it is this player's turn
property pPlayerSymbol -- X or O
property pMatrix -- tic tac toe matrix


on beginSprite me
  -- set up tic tac toe board
  pMatrix = []
  repeat with i = 1 to 3
    add pMatrix, [0,0,0]
  end repeat
```

```
-- if player goes first, then make him or her X
if gTurn then
  pPlayerSymbol = "X"
  message(me,"You are X. Your turn.")
else
  pPlayerSymbol = "O"
  message(me,"You are O. Your opponent's turn.")
end if

showBoard
end
```

When the player clicks on a square, the message is sent from a small behavior on those sprites to this next handler. It sets the square in the matrix and calls the "on gameTurnOver" handler in the movie script. This then contacts the other player and tells them about the move.

```
-- player clicked on square
on clickSprite me, x, y
  -- make sure it is player's turn
  if not gTurn then exit

  -- see if the spot is already taken
  if pMatrix[x][y] <> 0 then exit

  -- set square to symbol
  pMatrix[x][y] = pPlayerSymbol
  showBoard

  -- end turn
  gTurn = FALSE

  -- tell opponent
  gameTurnOver(pMatrix)

  -- see if game is over
  if checkGameOver(me) then
    message(me,"Game Over.")
  else
    message(me,"Waiting for your opponent to move.")
  end if
end
```

When a message is received that the other player has moved, the new game state is set in the "on opponentMove" handler.

```
-- get message of opponent's move
on opponentMove me, newMatrix
  -- set squares
  pMatrix = newMatrix
  showBoard


  -- see if game is over
  if checkGameOver(me) then
    message(me,"Game Over.")
  else
    gTurn = TRUE
    message(me,"Your turn.")
  end if
end
```

This next handler draws the board according to the current game state.

```
-- draw squares matrix
on showBoard me
  -- loop through all squares
  repeat with y = 1 to 3
    repeat with x = 1 to 3
      -- get sprite number
      s = (y-1)*3+x+10
      -- set each square
      case pMatrix[x][y] of
        0: sprite(s).memberNum = member("Blank")
        "X": sprite(s).member = member("X")
        "O": sprite(s).member = member("O")
      end case
    end repeat
  end repeat
end
```

Whenever a move is complete, this next handler checks to see whether the game is over. This happens if one player gets three in a row, or if all the squares on the board are filled.

```
-- see if game is won, lost or a draw
on checkGameOver me
  -- three in a row down
  repeat with x = 1 to 3
    if (pMatrix[x][1] = 0) or (pMatrix[x][2] = 0) or (pMatrix[x][3] = 0) then next ¬
    repeat
    if (pMatrix[x][1] = pMatrix[x][2]) and (pMatrix[x][2] = pMatrix[x][3]) then ¬
    return TRUE
  end repeat
```

```
  -- three in a row across
  repeat with y = 1 to 3
    if (pMatrix[1][y] = 0) or (pMatrix[2][y] = 0) or (pMatrix[3][y] = 0) then next ¬
    repeat
    if (pMatrix[1][y] = pMatrix[2][y]) and (pMatrix[2][y] = pMatrix[3][y]) then ¬
    return TRUE
  end repeat

  -- diagonals
  if (pMatrix[1][1] <> 0) and (pMatrix[2][2] <> 0) and (pMatrix[3][3] <> 0) then
    if (pMatrix[1][1] = pMatrix[2][2]) and (pMatrix[2][2] = pMatrix[3][3]) then ¬
    return TRUE
  end if
  if (pMatrix[3][1] <> 0) and (pMatrix[2][2] <> 0) and (pMatrix[1][3] <> 0) then
    if (pMatrix[3][1] = pMatrix[2][2]) and (pMatrix[2][2] = pMatrix[1][3]) then ¬
    return TRUE
  end if

  -- see if all squares used
  repeat with x = 1 to 3
    repeat with y = 1 to 3
      -- if one still open, game not over
      if pMatrix[x][y] = 0 then return FALSE
    end repeat
  end repeat

  -- all filled, game is a draw
  return TRUE
end
```

The "on message" handler was used throughout this behavior to update the text on the screen.

```
-- update message text
on message me, text
  member("Message").text = text
end
```

Finally, we have the frame loop.

```
-- loop on frame
on exitFrame me
  go to the frame
end
```

Game Sprite Behavior

This short behavior is used on the nine squares in the tic-tac-toe board. It determines the x and y position of the square when it is clicked, and passes that on to the frame behavior.

```
on mouseUp me
  -- get sprite
  s = me.spriteNum - 11
  -- determine the x and y position
  y = s/3
  x = s-y*3
  -- tell frame behavior
  sendSprite(0,#clickSprite,x+1,y+1)
end
```

Putting It All Together

This sample movie needs a total of seven frames. Figures 25.2 to 25.6 showed five of them. The sixth frame is a "Game Over" state for the tic-tac-toe game. This is similar to the game frame, but with a "New Game" button. Figure 25.7 shows this frame.

Figure 25.7
The "Game Over" frame is the same as the game frame, with chat elements and all, except for the "Game Over" text and the "New Game" button.

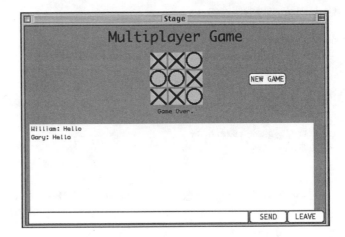

The last frame simply is one that displays a "Good Bye" message. This is used when the player leaves the game lobby. You can place a "Start Again" button here if you want, although I just left the frame in the example blank.

All the frames except the game frame have a simple *go to the frame* script on them. The game frame, of course, has the game frame behavior instead.

In addition to the behavior on the user list in the lobby, and the behavior on the square sprites in the game, there are a lot of one-line button behaviors that call the various handlers in the movie script. You can see all these in the sample movie.

Game Variations

This game is only the tip of the iceberg for multiplayer games. Think of *every* two-or-more-player game you have *ever* played in your life and how it can be adapted as a multiplayer game like this one. Also, think of the possibilities for original games.

To close this chapter, I would be remiss if I didn't go in to the many ways in which this game can be improved.

Input Validation

Right now, the game doesn't check the player's name or chat lines for valid input. You probably want to be sure that the player entered some sort of name, at least two characters, before letting them join the lobby. You also want to restrict the length of their name, perhaps to 16 characters.

In addition, you also might want to check to be sure the player does not send a blank line of text to the chat room, nor can they send a line of text that is too long. On the other hand, you might want to allow multiple lines of text, in which case you want to be sure the chat text member can handle text lines that wrap.

You also might want to filter the chat text to take out curse words or such. If the site is for children, you might even want to prevent the player from typing text of their own, but instead have them pick from a list of lines such as "Hello," "Anyone want to play?," and so on.

Cancellation

One improvement that you can add is to allow the challenging player to cancel the challenge. Just include a "Cancel" button on the "wait" frame that returns this player to the lobby. It also has to send a new message to the player being challenged to let them know that they missed their chance.

Multiple Challenges

The way the game is set up now, more than one person can challenge a single player. You probably want to put a stop to this by noting when a player is being challenged, and when the second challenge message arrives by automatically sending back a "busy" message.

Better User Identification

Right now, each user is identified by the name they give. What happens if there are two "Bob"s in the room? You want to avoid this at all costs.

One way to do it is to not allow a second person on the server who uses the same name. You could check the server for someone with that name, and then alert the player to pick another name instead.

A better way to handle this would be to use something besides the player's name as their identification on the server. You could use that player's IP address, as obtained by the *getNetAddressCookie* function. In this case, you want to send along the player's chosen name to the other players, so that this can be listed in the lobby user list. However, you want to store the IP addresses of each user in a hidden list and refer to the players by IP address rather than their username. This can get tricky, but it is the best route for an expert Lingo programmer.

Part VIII:
Appendixes

A Useful Lingo Index **453**

B Useful Internet
Resources **457**

Useful Lingo Index

At the beginning of each chapter is a list of Lingo topics that can be found inside the chapter. These are topics that can be used in all sorts of Director projects—not just games. Here's an index of these topics so that you can quickly find the chapters dealing with a topic you might need more information about.

Feature	Task	Chapters
Animation	Creating a delay with Lingo	4, 10, 18, 19, 20
Behaviors	Calling handlers in other behaviors	4, 5, 7, 10, 11, 12, 18, 20, 21, 23, 25
	Using parameters	3, 4, 5, 6, 8, 9, 10, 11, 12, 13, 14, 15, 16, 17, 18, 21
	Using a ranged parameter	4, 8, 9, 12, 14, 15
Graphics	Adjusting sprite layers	5, 23
	Changing sprite members with Lingo	3, 4, 7, 8, 10, 11, 15, 21, 25
	Coloring sprites with Lingo	12, 17, 23
	Making sprites disappear	4, 7, 9, 10, 11, 12, 13, 21
	Moving sprites	3, 5, 6, 7, 8, 9, 10, 11, 12
	Rotating sprites	11
	Using a grid of bitmaps	4, 7, 17, 25
	Using a rectangle shape member	12, 21
	Using a "reverse" ink sprite as a text cursor	14
	Using a set of bitmaps	3, 4, 5, 8, 18, 19, 20, 23
	Using film loops	21
	Using line shape members	16
	Using points	5, 6, 8, 9, 10, 11
	Using registration points	3, 5, 8, 19, 20, 23
Input	Accepting arrow keys	7, 10, 11, 14, 21, 22
	Accepting typed input	14, 17, 24, 25
	Clicking on text as input	15, 25
	Dragging with the mouse	5, 8, 12, 16
	Selecting with mouse clicks	4, 9, 17, 23, 25

Feature	Task	Chapters
Interface	Dragging and dropping	3, 20
	Using button-down states	13, 18
	Using custom cursors	9
Lists	Randomizing a list	19, 20
	Using linear lists	5, 6, 7, 8, 14, 16, 17, 18, 19, 20, 21, 22, 23, 25
	Using lists that contain lists	5, 7, 16, 17, 19, 20, 22, 23, 25
	Using property lists	5, 7, 14, 17, 18, 21, 22, 23
	Sorting	18, 23
Math	Using random numbers	4, 5, 6, 7, 8, 10, 11, 13, 18, 19, 20, 21, 22, 23
Members	Using a naming convention	3, 4, 18, 19, 20, 21, 22, 23
	Using Cast libraries	8
Output	Saving high scores	24
	Saving the game state	18
Programming	Bouncing objects off walls	12
	Collision detection	3, 7, 8, 10, 11, 12
	Creating a random maze	22
	Creating a timer	4
	Using artificial intelligence	23
	Using a case statement	3, 18, 22, 25
	Using an Xtra	25

continues

continued

Feature	Task	Chapters
Strings	Building member names	11, 18, 19, 20, 21, 22, 23
	Comparing strings	13, 15
	Converting strings to uppercase	14, 15, 16, 17
	Parsing strings	14, 15, 16, 17, 24
	Replacing characters in strings	14, 15, 16, 17
	Using ASCII codes	14, 15, 16, 17
	Using items	13, 24
Text Members	Adjusting tabs with Lingo	24
	Aligning bitmaps and text	17
	Coloring text	16
	Matching screen location and text	16, 17
	Setting line spacing	16, 17
	Using monospaced fonts to align text	14, 16, 17
	Using text members to store data	13, 14, 15, 16, 17
Variables	Keeping a wallet	18, 19
	Keeping score	8, 9, 10, 11, 12, 13, 21, 24
	Setting the number of decimal places	19

Useful Internet Resources

A wealth of Lingo and game development knowledge is at your fingertips on the World Wide Web. This is by no means a complete list of resources, but it should help you get started if you want to seek out more information.

Director and Lingo

The following sites have information about Macromedia Director and Lingo. There are literally hundreds of such sites, and most of these provide links that will help you find just about anything you want to know.

Director Web

`http://www.mcli.dist.maricopa.edu/director/`

Tips and tricks, lists of known bugs, links to other resources on the Web, and a huge list of Shockwave sites.

Macromedia

`http://www.macromedia.com`

The official site. Developer pages, technotes, developer locator, newsgroups, and a list of Xtras.

CleverMedia Developer Resources

`http://clevermedia.com/resources/`

Links, tips, and the Director Community Resource forum.

Director Online Users Group (DOUG)

`http://www.director-online.com/`

The best source for the latest news about Director and Director-related products. It also has a lot of interviews and articles written by developers.

UpdateStage

`http://www.updatestage.com`

Articles and resources.

Behaviors.com

`http://behaviors.com`

A repository for behaviors and some Xtras.

DirectOregon

`http://www.moshplant.com/direct-or/`

Snippets of useful information, including many open source code examples.

Grommett.com

`http://www.grommett.com/`

Useful tips and techniques, as well as articles on multimedia production.

Shockwave Game Sites

In addition to developer resources, the Web can offer inspiration. Here is a list of sites that have games developed in Macromedia Director:

- The CleverMedia Shockwave Arcade—`http://clevermedia.com`
- GameScene—`http://gamescene.com`
- GamesPark—`http://gamespark.com`
- Shockwave.com—`http://www.shockwave.com`
- Aftershock's Arcade Alley—`http://www.onShore.com/main/multimedia/games.shtml`
- At the Crossroads—`http://www.at-the-crossroads.com/asp/home.asp`
- Bunko—`http://www.bunko.com/`
- Online Shockwave Games—`http://onlinemediagroup.com/goldrake/shock.shtml`
- ShockBlitz—`http://www.shockblitz.com/`
- Adveractive—`http://www.adveract.com/games/games.htm`
- Ezone—`http://www.ezone.com/`
- Blip—`http://www.fringenet.com/blip/`
- Headbone Zone—`http://hbz.yahooligans.com/zone/shock_games.html`
- Shockade—`http://www.sito.org/~horn/shockidx.htm`
- Candystand—`http://www.candystand.com/home.htm`

Game Design

The following sites have information about designing games. They are not geared toward Director, or any authoring tool in particular, but talk about game design in general.

Game Design: The Essence of Computer Games

`http://www.lupinegames.com/articles/essgames.htm`

An article about how to design a game.

The Art of Computer Game Design

`http://www.vancouver.wsu.edu/fac/peabody/game-book/Coverpage.html`

An entire online book about game design.

Realism Versus Playability in Simulation Game Design

http://aragorn.uio.no/nanvaent/creator_info/realism_playability.html

An article on game design.

Game Theory—The Myth of Reality

http://members.home.net/yankeeap/THEORY.HTM

Realism in war games.

Addictive Games

http://www-cs-students.stanford.edu/~amitp/Articles/AddictiveGames.html

An article on designing addictive games.

Space Game Design Tips

http://www.game-developer.com/ezine/issue1/design.shtml

An article on designing space games.

The Focus of Gameplay

http://www.lupinegames.com/articles/focus_gameplay.html

An article about game design.

Scott Kim, Puzzle Master

http://www.scottkim.com/

Information and links to puzzle games.

Game Design 101

http://www.gamecenter.com/Features/Exclusives/Design/

A C|NET article about game design.

Game Development Central

http://www.gdcentral.com/

Information on game design, programming, and the industry.

Balance

http://www.obsession.se/balance/index2.html

A site of articles on game design.

36 Dramatic Situations

`http://bricolage.bel-epa.com/etc/drawer/polti.html`

Some ideas for elements in adventure games.

Medieval Price List

`http://www.gamedev.net/reference/design/archive/gmedieval.htm`

Accurate prices for objects in an adventure game.

Objects in a Medieval City

`http://www.funet.fi/~vesanto/citydes/city.contents.html`

A list of potential objects for your adventure game.

I Have No Words & I Must Design

`http://www.crossover.com/~costik/nowords.html`

An article on game design.

Game Programming

These sites have information about game programming, but not Lingo game programming. A clever programmer will be able to adapt interesting pieces of code to be used in their Lingo programs.

David's Game Programming

`http://www.geocities.com/SiliconValley/Haven/5613/`

One programmer shares some of his C/C++/Visual Basic code.

The Getting Started Guide to Game Development FAQ

`http://www.strangecreations.com/library/games/gamfaq.txt`

A hodgepodge of information about programming games.

Allegro

`http://www.talula.demon.co.uk/allegro/`

A library of functions for use in computer games, written for the djgpp compiler in a mixture of C and assembly language.

3D Coding

`http://www.geocities.com/SiliconValley/Horizon/6933/3d.html`

Some 3D basics, in C.

Amit's Game Programming Information

`http://www-cs-students.stanford.edu/~amitp/gameprog.html`

Many links to game programming information of all types.

Artificial Intelligence

The topic of artificial intelligence is particularly popular among game design and programming sites. Here is a list of some sites that have good information, plus links to other sites.

Steven Woodcock's AI Site

`http://www.gameai.com/`

A great site with information and links about artificial intelligence in games.

Artificial Intelligence, and Robot Wisdom

`http://www.robotwisdom.com/ai/`

General information about AI.

AI on the Web

`http://www.cs.berkeley.edu/~russell/ai.html`

A huge list of links to sites and people in the artificial intelligence community.

Campaign for Real AI in Games

`http://www.gamesdomain.com/gdreview/gdr.cgi?zones/strategy/craig/craig.html`

A site for discussion of the improvement of AI in games.

Artificial Intelligence FAQs

`http://www.faqs.org/faqs/ai-faq/`

A list of FAQs that deal with AI.

Strategy and Tactics: DreamWeaver's Thoughts

`http://www-cs-students.stanford.edu/~amitp/Articles/StrategyAndTactics.html`

An article on AI in war games.

Computer Attacks Archive

`http://theory.stanford.edu/~amitp/Archives/ComputerAttacks.html`

Transcript of a game AI discussion.

Empire Games

`http://www-cs-students.stanford.edu/~amitp/Articles/EmpireGames.html`

Use of AI in strategy games.

COMP.AI.GAMES FAQ

`http://intranet.ca/~sshah/cagfaq.html`

FAQs from a newsgroup.

The Art of Computer Game Design

`http://Mark.Baldwin.net/tacgd.htm`

Articles on game design and AI.

Classic Video Games

One great source of inspiration for Director game development can be game emulators. These are programs that enable you to play classic arcade and console games on your computer. Here are some sites that have more information.

Emulation.net

`http://www.emulation.net/`

Macintosh game emulations software.

Multiple Arcade Machine Emulator

`http://www.mame.net/`

Enables you to play classic games on your PC.

Dave's Video Game Classics

`http://www.vintagegaming.com`

Links and news about emulators.

General Game Information

These sites contain general information about games and game development.

Computer Gaming World

http://www.gamespot.com/cgw/index.html

News and reviews of PC games.

GameSpot

http://www.gamespot.com/

News, reviews, and downloads.

Gamasutra

http://www.gamasutra.com/

A magazine for game developers.

GameDev.net

http://www.gamedev.net/gamedev.asp

An online magazine with an emphasis on information exchange.

Game Dictionary

http://www.gamedev.net/dict/

An online dictionary of computer game terms.

Happy Puppy Game Developer Den

http://www.happypuppy.com/biz/biz_dev.html

A lot of links to game development sites.

Game Development Search Engine

http://www.game-developer.com/

A Yahoo!-like directory of game information on the Web.

Why Being a Computer Game Developer Sucks

http://slashdot.org/features/99/08/20/143215.shtml

A firsthand account of the game-development world.

The Computer Game Developers Association

http://www.cgda.org/

An association established to foster the creation of a worldwide game-development community.

Game Developer Magazine

http://www.gdmag.com/

A magazine for game developers.

Amateur Game Developer

http://www.gamedeveloper.cwc.net/

Articles and resources.

Index

SYMBOLS

3D Coding Web site, 462
3D graphics, quality in Director environment, 13

A

Accordion, solitaire variation, 348
adventure games
behaviors, attaching, 374-375
building, 356-371
CD-ROM directory, 352
characters
behavior, 356-362
movement, 353
containers, 355
behavior, 368-369
diagramming, 371-372
door behavior, 354, 364
game over screens, 376
handlers
on beginSprite, 366
on detectCollision, 362-365
on enterDoor, 361
on exitFrame, 367-368
on getDoorPath, 365
on getPoints, 362
on getPropertyDescriptionList, 363-365, 368-371
on killedMonster, 360
on move, 358-359
on onDie, 362
on openObject, 359
on showInventory, 360
on takeObject, 359
message behavior, 370-371

monster behavior, 365-367
multiple puzzle completion, 355
objects
behavior, 363-365
inventory, 353-354
overview, 352
points, 355
behavior, 369-370
rooms, 352
creating, 372-374
scenarios, 375
sign behavior, 368
text-based computer game, 30
variations
multiple monsters, 375
secret doors, 376
secret keys, 375
walls, 353
behavior, 362-363
Aftershock's Arcade Alley Web site, 459
Allegro Web site, 461
alpha testing, 24
Amateur Game Developer Web site, 465
Amit's Game Programming Web site, 462
ammunition
Space Rocks game, 169
sprite invaders game, 151-152
targets in shooting gallery game, 134
animation
falling objects game, 130
shooting gallery game
hits, 148
targets, 133
sliding puzzle games, piece motion, 89
solitaire cards, 347

answers (trivia games)
disappearing, 204
mechanisms, 203
penalties for wrong answers,
203
varied numbers, 212
arcades, 1980's statistics, 32
armies (strategy games)
attacking, 391
extra troops, 414
fortifications, 414
victory, 391
**arranging grid in crossword
puzzles, 275-276**
**arrays versus list termino-
logy, 17**
artificial intelligence
strategy games, 392, 413
Web site resources, 462-463
**Artificial Intelligence FAQ Web
site, 462**
**Asteroids, arcade popularity,
30-31**
**At the Crossroads Web site,
459**
Atari, 30-31

B

backgrounds
falling blocks game, 112
falling objects game, 130
shooting gallery game, environ-
mental variations, 147-148
video poker game, 298
backstory screens, 19
balls
falling objects game
catch determination, 117
game over options, 118
good versus bad, 118
penalties, 118
special effects, 119
timing drops, 117
paddle bricks game
behavior, 190-195
difficulty levels, 187
movement, 186-187
multiple, 198
special effects, 187

behaviors
adventure games, attaching,
374-375
defined, 16
OOP, 15-16
parameters
getPropertyDescriptionList
handler, 16-17
setting, 16
Behaviors.com Web site, 458
beta testing, 24
**betting screen (video poker
game), 283**
between level screens, 20
bitmaps
card deck value (video poker
game), 283
maze cells, 386-387
blackjack (Twenty-One), 302
building, 306-321
cards, sprite channels, 303-304
CD-ROM directory, 302
double down rule, 305
frame behavior, 306-321
frames
Bet, 321
Deal, 322
Game Over, 323
Insurance, 323
Results, 321
Wallet, 321
handlers
on addCardToHand, 316
on addToBet, 309
on beginSprite, 306-307
on buyInsurance, 314
on calculateResults, 320-321
on cardSound, 311
on clearScreen, 308
on dealerTurn, 319
on doneHand, 318-319
on doubleMe, 316-317
on getCard, 310
on handValue, 312-313
on Hit, 315
on initialDeal, 309-310
on noInsurance, 313
on showBet, 309
on showHand, 311
on shuffleDeck, 307-308
on splitMe, 317-318
on startDraw, 315

hands
displaying, 304
values, 304
insurance, 304-305
overview, 302
shoes, deck storage, 302-303
special effects, 306
split option, 305
variations
card backgrounds, 324
chips, 325
dealer hits, 324
limiting splits and doubles,
324
minimum/maximum bets,
324
**blast sprites, behavior in
shooting gallery game,
145-146**
blocks (falling blocks game)
colors, 112
drop rates, 101
keyboard movement, 101
positioning, 100-101
special effects, 101
speed, 112
varied shapes, 111
board games
companies, 29
evolution, 28-29
Hoyle, Sir Edmund, 29
**bombs (falling objects game),
130**
**bounding box sprites (match-
ing games), 41**
**Breakout, home marketing
of, 31**
bricks (paddle bricks game)
appearance, 187
behavior, 195-196
colors, 197
special effects, 187
built-in high score boards, 420
bullets
Space Rocks game, sprite
behavior, 182-183
sprite invaders game, 162-163
**Bushnell, Nolan, Atari video
games, 30**
buttons
behavior in trivia games,
208-210
video poker game, 297-298

C

C++ versus Lingo programming, 12

Calculation, solitaire variation, 348

Canfield, solitaire variation, 348

capital letters usage (cryptograms), 216

card decks
blackjack
card backgrounds, 324
hands, displaying, 304
hands, values, 304
sprite channels, 303-304
memory games
appearance, 58
cast library, 65-66
game over condition, 58
hidden pictures, 57
pause times, 57
shuffling, 57
solitaire, 329
animated cards, 347
drag behavior, 342-345
individual movements, 330-331
outline member, 345-346
placeholder member, 345-346
sprite arrangements, 330
stack groupings, 330
video poker
back design, 296-298
betting screen, 283
bitmap values, 283
dealing, 286
faces, 296
hand values, 284-286
money values, 286
results screen, 284
special effects, 287

cartridges, video game evolution, 32

cast library
cards, memory games, 58, 65-66
falling objects game, 128
jigsaw puzzle game, 84
sliding puzzle pieces, 88-89

catches (falling objects game)
balls, 117
game over options, 118
penalties, 118
special effects, 119

cells (mazes), 386-387

CGI forms, high score boards, 419

challenges in multiplayer Internet games, 449

chances, number of (Hangman), 238-239

characters
adventure games, 353
behavior, 356-362
entry in crossword puzzles, 261

chess, board game evolution, 29

classic video games, Web site resources, 463

CleverMedia Developer Resources Web site, 458

clicking and dragging matching games, see matching games

clock tick effect (trivia games), 212

clue list (crossword puzzles), 261, 275

code continuation characters ¬, 45

coding high score boards, 420

computer attack behavior (strategy games), 408-411

Computer Attacks Web site, 463

Computer Game Developers Association (CGDA) Web site, 465

computer games
evolution, 30
MIT development, 30
reference books, 34-36

Computer Gaming World Web site, 464

configuring
high score boards, 428
Multiuser Server for Internet gaming, 433

container behaviors (adventure games), 355, 368-369

contests (high score boards), 429

countries (strategy games)
armies, 391
attacking, 391
extra armies, 414
fortifications, 414
maps, 392
occupation of, 390
outline boundaries, 392
victory, 391

creating rooms (adventure games), 372-374

crossword puzzles
building, 262-275
with pPuzzle list variable, 277
CD-ROM directory, 260
character entry, 261
clue list, 261, 275
construction prerequisites, 261
frame behavior, 262-274
grid, 260-261
arranging, 275-276
grid square behavior, 274
handlers
on addToPuzzle, 265-266
on buildPuzzle, 264-265
on checkDone, 274
on clickClue, 273-274
on convertToCaps, 264
on getPropertyDescriptionList, 262-263
on getWords, 263
on keyDown, 272-273
on mouseUp, 274-275
on noWordsInWay, 266-268
on puzzleClicked, 270
on selectChar, 271-272
on showClues, 269-270
on showPuzzle, 268-269
lattices, 260
multiple, storing, 277
overview, 260
variations
themes, 276
word types, 276

cryptograms
building, 216-224
CD-ROM directory, 214
difficulty levels, 226
frame behavior, 216-224
handlers
on convertToCaps, 220-221
on getPhrases, 218

on
getPropertyDescriptionList,
216-218
on keyUp, 222-223
on mouseUp, 221
on phraseSolved, 224
on setUpPhrase, 219-220
on showCursor, 221
hints, 226
overview, 214
phrases
capital letters, 216
encoding, 214-215
solution displays, 215
storage, 215-216
text cursors, 215
scoring setup, 225
solutions, displaying, 226
text
colors, 224
fonts, 224
text cursors, shape, 225
timers, adding, 226
variations, 225
cursors (cryptograms)
shape, 225
text, 215

D

David's Game Programming
Web site, 461
dealing card deck (video poker
game), 286
debugging
development phase, 23
high score boards, 428
demographic information (high
score boards), 429
designing games, Web site
resources, 459-461
development
debugging phase, 23
planning phase, 22
preparation phase, 22
start phase, 22
troubleshooting phase, 23
user testing phase, 24
diagrams in adventure games,
371-372
difficulty levels (Space Rocks
game), 170

Director (Macromedia)
as game development tool, 12
evolution, 33-34
educational games development, 33
Internet Studio, 432-433
Shockwave, 34
strengths, 12
versions, 12
weaknesses, 13
Web site resources, 458-459
Director Online Users Group
(DOUG) Web site, 458
DirectOregon Web site, 458
disappearing answers (trivia
games), 204
displaying
scores on high score boards,
427-428
solutions for cryptograms, 215
distribution
Projectors, 25
Shockwave, 25
Doom, PC popularity, 33
doors (adventure games), 354
behavior, 364
secret, 376
double down rule (blackjack),
305
dragging pieces in jigsaw
puzzles, 72
drop rates in falling blocks
game, 101
Dungeons & Dragons, seminal
role playing game, 29-30

E - F

Empire Games Web site, 463
Emulation.net Web site, 463
encoding phrases (cryp-
tograms), 214-215
end game screens, 20
extra armies (strategy games),
414
faces (video poker card decks),
296
falling blocks game
blocks
drop rates, 101
keyboard input, 101

positioning, 100-101
special effects, 101
building, 102-111
CD-ROM directory, 100
frame behavior, 102-111
handlers
on beginSprite, 102-103
on checkGameEnd,
108-109
on checkRows, 107-108
on dropNewPiece, 104-106
on fallOnPiece, 107
on getPieceList, 103-104
on hitBottom, 106
on hitOtherPiece, 110
on movePiece, 111
on pushAwayFromEdges,
109
overview, 100
variations, 112
falling objects game
balls
catch determination, 117
good versus bad, 118
timed drops, 117
building, 119-128
cast library, 128
CD-ROM directory, 116
difficulty levels, 118
frame behavior, 119-128
game over options, 118
handlers
on beginSprite, 123
on checkCaught, 125-127
on checkEndGame,
127-128
on dropObject, 125
on exitFrame, 123
on
getPropertyDescriptionList,
119-123
on letObjectsFall, 124
on showScore, 127
overview, 116
penalties, 118
special effects, 119
variations
animation effects, 130
background perspective, 130
bombs, 130
difficulty levels, 130
educational variants, 129
fan testing, 24

finger cursor (sliding puzzle games), 95-96
firewalls, multiplayer Internet games, 432
flying saucers (Space Rocks games), 184
focus group testing, 24
fonts
    cryptograms, 224
    Hangman, text members, 238
    word search games, 243
fortifications (strategy games), 414
frames
    behavior
        blackjack, 306-321
        crossword puzzles, 262-274
        cryptograms, 216-224
        falling blocks game, 102-111
        falling objects game, 117-128
        Hangman, 230-237
        jigsaw puzzle game, 75-77
        mazes, 384-386
        paddle bricks game, 188-190
        shooting gallery game, 141-144
        sliding puzzle games, 90-95
        solitaire, 331-342
        Space Rocks game, 170-177
        sprite invaders game, 158-161
        trivia games, 204-207
        video poker game, 287-294
        word search games, 244-255
    blackjack
        Bet, 321
        Deal, 322
        Game Over, 323
        Insurance, 323
        Results, 321
        Wallet, 321
    multiplayer Internet games, 448
    sprites, length of, 15
    strategy games, 412

G

Gamasutra Web site, 464
game background screens, 20
***Game Developer Magazine* Web site, 465**
Game Development Central Web site, 460
game over conditions
    matching game, 43
    memory games, 58
    sliding puzzle games, 89
game over screens, 376
game screens
    backstory, 19
    between level, 20
    end game, 20
    game background, 20
    high score display, 21
    instruction, 19
    introduction, 18-19
    payoff, 21
game sprite behavior, multiplayer Internet games, 447
GameDev.net Web site, 464
games
    adventures
        behavior attachment, 374-375
        CD-ROM directory, 352
        character behavior, 356-362
        character movement, 353
        container behavior, 368-369
        diagramming, 371-372
        door behavior, 354, 364
        game over screens, 376
        message behavior, 370-371
        monster behavior, 354, 365-367
        multiple monsters, 375
        multiple puzzle completion, 355
        object behavior, 363-365
        object inventory, 353-354
        overview, 352
        points behavior, 369-370
        rooms, creating, 372-374
        scenarios, 375
        secret doors, 376
        secret keys, 375
        sign behavior, 355, 368
        wall behavior, 355, 362-363

        artificial intelligence resources, 462-463
    blackjack
        card backgrounds, 324
        cards as sprites, 303-304
        CD-ROM directory, 302
        chips, 325
        dealer hits, 324
        double down rule, 305
        frame behavior, 306-321
        hands, displaying, 304
        hands, values, 304
        insurance, 304-305
        limits on splits and doubles, 324
        minimum/maximum bets, 324
        overview, 302
        shoes, 302-303
        special effects, 306
        split option, 305
    board
        chess, 29
        companies, 29
        evolution, 28-29
        Nine Men's Morris, 28
        Senet, 28
    computers
        Adventure, 30
        Lunar Lander, 30
        MIT development, 30
    creation overview, 18-21
    crossword puzzles
        CD-ROM directory, 260
        character entry, 261
        clue list, 261, 275
        construction prerequisites, 261
        frame behavior, 262-274
        grid, 260-261, 274
        overview, 260
        themes, 276
        word types, 276
    cryptograms
        capital letters, 216
        CD-ROM directory, 214
        difficulty levels, 226
        frame behavior, 216-224
        hints, 226
        overview, 214
        phrase encoding, 214-215
        phrase ideas, 225
        phrase storage, 215-216

solution displays, 215
text cursors, 215
timing, 226
design resources, 459-461
development, 22-23
distribution
  Projectors, 25
  Shockwave, 25
falling blocks
  backgrounds, 112
  block colors, 112
  block positioning, 100-101
  block shapes, 111
  CD-ROM directory, 100
  drop rates, 101
  frame behavior, 102-111
  keyboard input, 101
  overview, 100
  scoring, 112
  special effects, 101
  speed, 112
falling objects
  animation effects, 130
  background perspective, 130
  balls, catch determination,
    117
  balls, good versus bad, 118
  balls, timed drops, 117
  bombs, 130
  cast library, 128
  CD-ROM directory, 116
  difficulty levels, 118, 130
  educational variants, 129
  frame behavior, 117-128
  game over options, 118
  overview, 116
  penalties, 118
  special effects, 119
Hangman
  CD-ROM directory, 228
  frame behavior, 230-237,
    244-255
  graphics, 229
  keyboard input, 239
  letter behavior, 237
  letter guesses, 228
  message area, 229
  next phrase button, 229,
    237
  overview, 228
  phrase sources, 239-240
  phrases, 230

replacement of traditional
    Hangman graphic, 240
  sounds, 230
high score boards
  built-in, 420
  CD-ROM directory, 418
  CGI scripts, 419
  code, 420
  contests, 429
  debugging, 428
  demographic information,
    429
  HTML forms, 418-419
  overview, 418
  score displays, 427-428
  score retrieval, 425-426
  score rotation, 420
  score saving, 422-425
  score submission, 421-422
  setup, 428
home video
  cartridge, 32
  evolution, 32-33
  Nintendo N64, 33
  Sony PlayStation, 33
jigsaw puzzle
  CD-ROM directory, 72
  completion, 74
  cursor effects, 74
  frame behavior, 75-77
  hints, 85
  overview, 72
  piece shapes, 86
  pieces, building, 73-74
  pieces, dragging, 72
  pieces, random place-
    ment, 74
  ship sprite behavior, 77-84
matching
  behavior scripts, 44-50
  CD-ROM directory, 40
  correct match determination,
    41-42
  creative screen layout, 53
  game over condition, 43
  lengthening, 51
  movie frame looping, 51
  overview, 40
  randomizing behavior, 53-54
  scoring, 51-52
  sound effects, 43
  sprites, 40-41
  sprites, locking, 42-43

timing, 52-53
  uses, 40
mazes
  CD-ROM directory, 378
  end goal, 380
  enemy characters, 388
  frame behavior, 384-386
  movie script, 380-384
  overview, 378
  player movement, 379
  random, 378-379
  shapes, 388
  sizes, 388
  wall variations, 387
memory
  behavior scripts, 59-65
  card appearance, 58
  card shuffling, 57
  CD-ROM directory, 56
  game over condition, 58
  hidden pictures, 57
  overview, 56
  pause times, 57
  scoring, 66-67
  sound effects, 59
  timing, 67-68
  two-player, 69-70
multiplayer Internet
  CD-ROM directory, 432
  firewalls, 432
  frames, 448
  game sprite behavior, 447
  input validation, 449
  IP addresses, 432
  lobbies, building, 433-434
  movie script, 434-443
  multiple challenges, 449
  Multiuser Server, 432-433
  overview, 432
  player turns, 434
  Shockwave applet tests, 433
  system requirements, 432
  tic-tac-toe behavior,
    444-447
  user identification, 449-450
paddle bricks
  ball behavior, 190-195
  ball movement, 186-187
  brick appearance, 187
  brick behavior, 195-196
  brick colors, 197
  CD-ROM directory, 186
  difficulty levels, 187

frame behavior, 188-190
horizontal/vertical orientations, 198
multiple balls, 198
overview, 186
paddle behavior, 196
paddle movement, 186
paddle size, 197
special effects, 187
PC, 33
programming resources, 461-462
reference books, 34-36
role playing, 29-30
shooting gallery
    ammunition, 134
    background environments, 147-148
    blast sprite behavior, 145-146
    CD-ROM directory, 132
    frame behavior, 141-144
    graphics, 146-147
    hit animations, 148
    less violent options, 148
    overview, 132
    point values, 134
    random timing, 133
    screen elements, 134
    special effects, 134-135
    target animation, 133
    target behavior, 135-141
    targets, adding, 146-147
    variations, 147
sliding puzzle
    behavior scripts, 90-96
    CD-ROM directory, 88
    finger cursor, 95-96
    game over conditions, 89
    numbers, 97
    overview, 88
    rectangular pieces, 97
    special effects, 89
solitaire
    Accordion, 348
    animated cards, 347
    Calculation, 348
    Canfield, 348
    card deck, 329-330
    card drag behavior, 342-345
    card movement, 330-331
    CD-ROM directory, 328
    frame behavior, 331-342

game rules, 328-329
game screen appearance, 328-329
Las Vegas rules, 347
Maze, 348
overview, 328-329
Poker, 348
Pyramid, 347
sprite arrangements, 330
Space Rocks
    ammunition limits, 169
    bullet sprite behavior, 182-183
    CD-ROM directory, 168
    difficulty levels, 170
    flying saucers, 184
    frame behavior, 170-177
    overview, 168
    rock disintegration, 169
    rock graphics, 170
    rock movement, 168
    rock sizes, 184
    rock sprite behavior, 180-182
    screen wrap, 169
    shields, 184
    ship movement, 168
    ship sprite behavior, 177-180
    thruster graphics, 184
    vector shaped rocks, 184
sprite invaders
    ammunition effects, 152
    bullet behavior, 162-163
    bullets, 151
    CD-ROM directory, 150
    difficulty levels, 152
    frame behavior, 158-161
    invader behavior, 155-157
    invader bullet behavior, 164-165
    invader movement, 151
    number of lives, 152
    overview, 150
    ship behavior, 152-154
    ship movement, 150-151
    variations, 166
strategy
    artificial intelligence, 392, 413
    CD-ROM directory, 390
    computer attack behavior, 408-411

computer place behavior, 404-408
countries, 390-391
extra armies, 414
fortifications, 414
initial place behaviors, 398-399
map variations, 414
movie script, 393-397
overview, 390
player attack behavior, 401-404
primary frames, 412
step sequence, 393
victory, 391, 414
trivia
    answering mechanisms, 203
    behavior scripts, 204-210
    CD-ROM directory, 202
    clock tick effect, 212
    disappearing answers, 204
    levels of play, 212
    number of answers, 212
    overview, 202
    penalties, 203
    question database, 202-203
    question randomizer, 212
    screen layout, 203
    sound effects, 204
    timing elements, 203
video, 30-32
    Web site resources, 463
video poker
    background design, 298
    betting screen, 283
    card deck, 283
    CD-ROM directory, 282
    dealing, 286
    frame behavior, 287-294
    hand values, 284-286
    hold button behavior, 294-296
    money values, 286
    overview, 282
    progressive scoring, 299
    results screen, 284
    sound, 299
    special effects, 287
war
    evolution, 29
    original purpose, 29
    Wells, H.G., 29

word search
  CD-ROM directory, 242
  highlighted selections, 257
  matrix, populating, 243-244
  matrix, sizes, 257
  overview, 242
  themes, 256
  word direction, 257
  word list, 243
  word markups, 243
Gamespot Web site, 464
GET method, high score boards, processing, 418-419
getPropertyDescriptionList handler, 16-17
graphics
  Hangman
    bitmap images, 229
    constructing, 238-239
    replacement of traditional Hangman graphic, 240
  maze walls, 379
  shooting gallery game, 146-147
grid (crossword puzzles), 260-261
  arranging, 275-276
Grommett.com Web site, 459
guessing letters (Hangman), 228

H

hand values (video poker game), 284-286
handlers
  getPropertyDescriptionList, 16-17
  on acceptChallenge (multiplayer Internet games), 441
  on addCardToHand (blackjack), 316
  on addChat (multiplayer Internet games), 439
  on addNewUser (multiplayer Internet games), 439
  on addScore (shooting gallery game), 144
  on addToBet
    blackjack, 309
    video poker, 289-290

on addToPuzzle (crossword puzzles), 265-266
on allowAnimation (shooting gallery game), 141
on askQuestion (trivia games), 205-206
on attack (strategy games), 410-411
on beginSprite
  adventure games, 366
  falling blocks game, 102-103
  falling objects game, 123
  jigsaw puzzle game, 76-77
  matching games, 46-47
  mazes, 384
  memory games, 61-62
  multiplayer Internet games, 444-445
  shooting gallery game, 138
  Space Rocks game, 173-174
  sprite invaders game, 159
  strategy games, 397
on buildMatrix (word search games), 246-248
on buildPuzzle (crossword puzzles), 264-265
on buyInsurance (blackjack), 314
on calculateResults (blackjack), 320-321
on calcValue (video poker), 291-294
on calcWinnings (video poker), 294
on cardSound (blackjack), 311
on challengeUser (multiplayer Internet games), 441
on changeDirection (sprite invaders game), 157
on checkAllMatched (memory games), 63-65
on checkCaught (falling objects game), 125-127
on checkDone (crossword puzzles), 274
on checkEndGame
  falling objects game, 127-128
  shooting gallery game, 144
on checkForAllMatch (matching games), 50

on checkForGameOver (sliding puzzle games), 94-95
on checkGameEnd (falling blocks game), 108-109
on checkGameOver
  mazes, 386
  multiplayer Internet games, 446-447
  strategy games, 396-397
on checkHitBricks (paddle bricks game), 194-195
on checkRows (falling blocks game), 107-108
on checkSidesHit (paddle bricks game), 193
on clearScreen (blackjack), 308
on clickAnswer (trivia games), 206
on clickClue (crossword puzzles), 273-274
on clickPuzzle (sliding puzzle games), 92-93
on colorCountries (strategy games), 395-396
on compileSelection (word search games), 253-254
on computerPlace (strategy games), 399
on convertToCaps
  crossword puzzles, 264
  cryptograms, 220-221
  Hangman, 235
  word search games, 246
on countryClick (strategy games), 398-404
on createMaze (mazes), 380-383
on dealerHand (blackjack), 319
on deckClick (solitaire), 335
on declineChallenge (multiplayer Internet games), 442
on detectCollision (adventure games), 362-365
on didIHit (sprite invaders game), 163
on divideCountries (strategy games), 394
on doneHand (blackjack), 318-319
on doubleMe (blackjack), 316-317
on draw (video poker), 290-291
on drawChar (mazes), 386

on drawLine (word search games), 251-253

on drawMaze (mazes), 383-384

on dropCard (solitaire), 336-340

on dropNewPiece (falling blocks game), 104-106

on dropObject (falling objects game), 125

on endLife (paddle bricks game), 189-190, 194

on endTurn (memory games), 69-70

on enterDoor (adventure games), 361

on enterFrame (sprite invaders game), 159-160

on enterLobby (multiplayer Internet games), 438

on exitFrame, 15, 51
adventure games, 367-368
falling objects game, 123
matching games, 48
paddle bricks game, 192
shooting gallery game, 138-140
sprite invaders game, 163
trivia games, 207
word search games, 251

on fallOnPiece (falling blocks game), 107

on findAttack (strategy games), 408-410

on findStrongestCountry (strategy games), 407-408

on findWeakestCountry (strategy games), 406

on fireBullet (Space Rocks game), 174-176

on gameTurnOver (multiplayer Internet games), 443

on getBehaviorDescription (matching games), 44-46

on getCard (blackjack), 310

on getCardFromSprite (solitaire), 340

on getDoorPath (adventure games), 365

on getLinks (strategy games), 393-394

on getMatch (matching games), 50

on getPhrases (cryptograms), 218

on getPieceList (falling blocks game), 103-104

on getPileUnderLoc (solitaire), 341

on getPoints (adventure games), 362

on getPropertyDescriptionList
adventure games, 363-365, 368-371
crossword puzzles, 262-263
cryptograms, 216-218
falling objects game, 119-123
Hangman, 230-232
jigsaw puzzle game, 75
matching games, 44-46
paddle bricks game, 188-196
shooting gallery game, 135-137, 141-143
sliding puzzle games, 90-91
Space Rocks game, 170-173
sprite invaders game, 152-158, 162-163
trivia games, 208-209
video poker, 294-295
word search games, 244-245

on getScore, 51-52

on getStackUnderLoc (solitaire), 340

on getWords
crossword puzzles, 263
word search games, 245

on grayLetters (word search games), 255

on handValue (blackjack), 312-313

on Hit (blackjack), 315

on hitBottom (falling blocks game), 106

on hitOtherPiece (falling blocks game), 110

on holdCard (video poker), 290

on initCountries (strategy games), 394

on initialDeal
blackjack, 309-310
video poker, 288-289

on invaderAlive (sprite invaders game), 157

on keyDown (crossword puzzles), 272-273

on keyHit (trivia games), 210

on keyUp (cryptograms), 222-223

on killedMonster (adventure games), 360

on leaveGame (multiplayer Internet games), 440

on leaveLobby (multiplayer Internet games), 440

on letObjectsFall (falling objects game), 124

on lockInPlace (matching games), 49

on messageHandler (multiplayer Internet games), 436-437

on mouseDown
matching games, 47
shooting gallery game, 141, 144
strategy games, 397
word search games, 249-250

on mouseLeave, 15

on mouseUp
crossword puzzles, 274-275
cryptograms, 221
Hangman, 237
matching games, 48
multiplayer Internet games, 447
trivia games, 209
video poker, 295-296

on move
adventure games, 358-359
mazes, 385

on movePiece (falling blocks game), 111

on newGame
multiplayer Internet games, 443
solitaire, 342

on nextQuestion (trivia games), 207

on noInsurance (blackjack), 313

on noWordsInWay (crossword puzzles), 266-268

on onBeginSprite
blackjack, 306-307
solitaire, 331
video poker, 287

on onDie (adventure games), 362

on openObject (adventure games), 359

on opponentMove (multiplayer Internet games), 445

on phraseSolved (cryptograms), 224

on placeArmy (strategy games), 404-406

on pushAwayFromEdges (falling blocks game), 109

on puzzleClicked (crossword puzzles), 270

on randomizePieces (sliding puzzle games), 91-92

on removeUser (multiplayer Internet games), 439

on returnCards (memory games), 63

on selectChar (crossword puzzles), 271-272

on sendChat (multiplayer Internet games), 439

on sendGameChat (multiplayer Internet games), 443

on setUpPhrase
  cryptograms, 219-220
  Hangman, 233-234

on shipHit (sprite invaders game), 161

on showArmies (strategy games), 396

on showBet
  blackjack, 309
  video poker, 289

on showBoard (multiplayer Internet games), 446

on showClues (crossword puzzles) 269-270

on showCursor (cryptograms), 221

on showDeck (solitaire), 334

on showHand (blackjack), 311

on showHangman (Hangman), 235

on showInventory (adventure games), 360

on showLetters (Hangman), 234-235

on showMatrix (word search games), 249

on showPile (solitaire), 334

on showPossiblePoints (trivia games), 206

on showPuzzle (crossword puzzles), 268-269

on showScore
  falling objects game, 127
  memory games, 67
  Space Rocks game, 177
  sprite invaders game, 160

on showStack (solitaire), 333-334

on showTimer (memory games), 68

on showTurn (memory games), 69-70

on showWallet (video poker), 289

on showWordList (word search games), 249

on showWorkspace (Hangman), 233

on shuffleDeck (blackjack), 307-308

on splitMe (blackjack), 317-318

on startDraw (blackjack), 315

on startGame (solitaire), 332-333

on startGameLobby (multiplayer Internet games), 435

on startHand (video poker), 287-288

on startMovie (multiplayer Internet games), 434-435

on startTimer, 52-53

on stopMovie (multiplayer Internet games), 443

on takeObject (adventure games), 359

on tryLetter (Hangman), 236-237

on turnCardOver (solitaire), 341-342

recursion, 388

hands (blackjack), display values, 304

Hangman
building, 230-237
CD-ROM directory, 228
chances, number of, 238-239
frame behavior, 230-237
graphics, 229
  constructing, 238-239
handlers
  on convertToCaps, 235
  on getPropertyDescriptionList, 230-232
  on mouseUp, 237
  on setUpPhrase, 233-234
  on showHangman, 235
  on showLetters, 234-235
  on showWorkspace, 233
  on tryLetter, 236-237
letters
  behavior, 237
  guessing, 228
message area, 229
next phrase button, 229, 237
overview, 228
phrases, 230
sounds, 230
text members
  font selection, 238
  loading, 238-239
variations
  graphics, 240
  keyboard input versus mouse clicks, 239
  themes, 239-240

Happy Puppy Game Developer Den Web site, 464

hidden pictures, memory games, 57

high score boards
built-in, 420
CD-ROM directory, 418
CGI scripts, building, 419
coding, 420
getNetText command, 427-428
HTML forms, building, 418-419
overview, 418
scores
  debugging, 428
  displaying, 427-428
  retrieving, 425-426
  rotation, 420
  saving, 422-425
  submitting, 421-422
screens, 21
setup, 428
variations
  contests, 429
  demographic information, 429

hints
cryptograms, 226
jigsaw puzzle game, 85

hold button (video poker game), 294-296

home video games, 32-33
horizontal momentum, 168
Hoyle, Sir Edmund, game rules codification, 29
HTML forms, high score boards, 418-419

I – K

identifying players (Internet gaming), 449-450
initial place behavior (strategy games), 397-399
input validation (multiplayer Internet games), 449
instruction screens, 19
insurance (blackjack), 304-305
Internet, multiplayer games
    CD-ROM directory, 432
    firewalls, 432
    IP addresses, 432
    lobbies, building, 433-434
    Multiuser Server, 432-433
    overview, 432
    player turns, 434
    Shockwave applets testing, 433
    system requirements, 432
introduction screens, 18-19
invaders (sprite invaders game)
    behavior, 155-157
    bullet behavior, 164-165
    movement, 151
IP addresses, multiplayer Internet games, 432

Java versus Lingo programming, 12
jigsaw puzzle game
    building, 75-84
    cast library, 84
    CD-ROM directory, 72
    completion, 74
    frame behavior, 75-77
    handlers
        on beginSprite, 76-77
        on getPropertyDescriptionList, 75
    overview, 72
    pieces
        building, 73-74
        cursor effects, 74
        dragging, 72
        random placement, 74
        registration points, 73-74
    variations
        hints, 85
        piece shapes, 86
Jobs, Stephen, Atari Breakout designer, 31

keyboard input
    falling blocks game, 101
    Hangman, 239

L

Las Vegas rules (solitaire), 347
lattices in crossword puzzles, 260
letters (Hangman)
    behavior, 237
    guessing, 228
linear lists, 17
Lingo
    index, 453-456
    lists
        handling, 18
        uses, 18
        versus array terminology, 17
    programming overview, 14-15
    reference resources, 14
    versus
        C++, 12
        Java, 12
    Web site resources, 458-459
lists
    defined, 17
    handling, 18
    linear, 17
    property symbols, 17
    syntax, 18
The Little Giant Encyclopedia of Card Games, 348
live testing, 24
lobbies, building (Internet gaming), 433-434
locking sprites (matching games), 42-43
Lunar Lander, text-based computer game, 30

M

Macromedia Director, *see* Director (Macromedia)
maps (strategy games)
    bitmaps, 411-412
    variations, 414
marking words (word search games), 243
Massachusetts Institute of Technology (MIT), 30
matching games
    behaviors
        on beginSprite handler, 46-47
        on checkForAllMatch handler, 50
        on exitFrame handler, 48
        on getBehaviorDescription handler, 44-46
        on getMatch handler, 50
        on getPropertyDescriptionList handler, 44-46
        on lockInPlace handler, 49
        on mouseDown handler, 47
        on mouseUp handler, 48
        setting, 44-50
    CD-ROM directory, 40
    correct matches, sprite channels, 41-42
    game over condition, 43
    movies, frame loop, 51
    on getScore handler, 51-52
    on startTimer handler, 52-53
    overview, 40
    sound effects, 43
    sprites
        bounding box, 41
        loc property, 41
        locking, 42-43
        precision, 40
        rect property, 41
        registration point, 41
    uses, 40
    variations
        creative screen layout, 53
        lengthening, 51
        randomizing behavior, 53-54
        scoring, 51-52
        timing, 52-53
matrix (word search games)
    font selection, 243
    populating, 243-244
    size of, 257

Maze, solitaire variation, 348
mazes
  building, 380-386
  CD-ROM directory, 378
  cells, 378
    bitmaps, 386-387
    sets, 379
  end goal, 380
  frame behavior, 384-386
  handlers
    on beginSprite, 384
    on checkGameOver, 386
    on createMaze, 380-383
    on drawChar, 386
    on drawMaze, 383-384
    on move, 385
  movie script, 380-384
  overview, 378
  player movement, 379
  random, creating, 378-379
  sizes, 388
  variations
    enemy characters, 388
    shapes, 388
    wall construction, 387
  wall graphics, 379
memory card handlers
  on endTurn, 69-70
  on showScore, 67
  on showTimer, 68
  on showTurn, 69-70
memory games
  behaviors, setting, 59-65
  cards
    appearance, 58
    cast library, 65-66
    hidden pictures, 57
    pause times, 57
    shuffling, 57
  CD-ROM directory, 56
  game over condition, 58
  handlers
    on beginSprite, 61-62
    on checkAllMatched, 63-65
    on getPropertyDescription,
      59-61
    on returnCards, 63
  overview, 56
  sound effects, 59
  variations
    scoring, 66-67
    timing, 67-68
    two-player, 69-70

messages
  adventure games, 370-371
  Hangman, 229
momentum
  horizontal, 168
  vertical, 168
**money values (video poker
  game), 286**
**monsters (adventure games),
  354**
  behavior, 365-367
  multiple, 375
movie scripts
  mazes, 380-384
  multiplayer Internet games,
    434-443
  strategy games, 393-397
moving
  cards in solitaire, 330-331
  in mazes, 379
multiplayer Internet games
  building, 434-447
  CD-ROM directory, 432
  firewalls, 432
  frames, 448
  game sprite behavior, 447
  handlers
    on acceptChallenge, 441
    on addChat, 439
    on addNewUser, 439
    on beginSprite, 444-445
    on challengeUser, 441
    on checkGameOver,
      446-447
    on declineChallenge, 442
    on enterLobby, 438
    on gameTurnOver, 443
    on leaveGame, 440
    on leaveLobby, 440
    on messageHandler,
      436-437
    on mouseUp, 447
    on newGame, 443
    on opponentMove, 445
    on removeUser, 439
    on sendChat, 439
    on sendGameChat, 443
    on showBoard, 446
    on startGameLobby, 435
    on startMovie, 434-435
    on stopMovie, 443
  input validation, 449
  IP addresses, 432

  lobbies, building, 433-434
  movie script, 434-443
  multiple challenges, 449
  Multiuser Server, 432-433
  overview, 432
  player turns, 434
  Shockwave applets, testing, 433
  system requirements, 432
  tic-tac-toe behavior, 444-447
  user identification, 449-450
**Multiple Arcade Machine
  Emulator Web site, 463**
**multiple levels in trivia games,
  212**
**multiple players (memory
  games), 69-70**
Multiuser Server, 433
Myst, PC game standard, 33

N - O

**naming card stack groupings
  (solitaire), 330**
**next phrase button (Hangman),
  229, 237**
**Nine Men's Morris, board
  game evolution, 28**
Nintendo N64, 33
**numbered pieces (sliding puz-
  zle pieces), 97**
**object-oriented programming,
  see OOP**
objects (adventure games)
  behavior, 363-365
  inventory, 353-354
**Odyssey, original home video
  game, 32**
**on acceptChallenge handler
  (multiplayer Internet
  games), 441**
**on addCardToHand handler
  (blackjack), 316**
**on addChat handler (multi-
  player Internet games),
  439**
**on addNewUser handler (multi-
  player Internet games), 439**
**on addScore handler (shooting
  gallery game), 144**
on addToBet handler
  blackjack, 309
  video poker, 289-290

on addToPuzzle handler (crossword puzzles), 265-266
on allowAnimation handler (shooting gallery game), 141
on askQuestion handler (trivia games), 205-206
on attack handler (strategy games), 410-411
on beginSprite handler
  adventure games, 366
  blackjack, 306-307
  falling blocks game, 102-103
  falling objects game, 123
  jigsaw puzzle game, 76-77
  matching games, 46-47
  mazes, 384
  memory games, 61-62
  multiplayer Internet games, 444-445
  shooting gallery game, 138
  solitaire, 331
  Space Rocks game, 173-174
  sprite invaders game, 159
  strategy games, 397
  video poker, 287
on buildMatrix handler (word search games), 246-248
on buildPuzzle handler (crossword puzzles), 264-265
on buyInsurance handler (blackjack), 314
on calculateResults handler (blackjack), 320-321
on calcValue handler (video poker), 291-294
on calcWinnings handler (video poker), 294
on cardSound handler (blackjack), 311
on challengeUser handler (multiplayer Internet games), 441
on changeDirection handler (sprite invaders game), 157
on checkAllMatched handler (memory games), 63-65
on checkCaught handler (falling objects game), 125-127
on checkDone handler (crossword puzzles), 274

on checkEndGame handler
  falling objects game, 127-128
  shooting gallery game, 144
on checkForAllMatch handler (matching games), 50
on checkForGameOver handler (sliding puzzle games), 94-95
on checkGameEnd handler (falling blocks game), 108-109
on checkGameOver handler
  mazes, 386
  multiplayer Internet games, 446-447
  strategy games, 396-397
on checkHitBricks handler (paddle bricks game), 194-195
on checkRows handler (falling blocks game), 107-108
on checkSidesHit handler (paddle bricks game), 193
on clearScreen handler (blackjack), 308
on clickAnswer handler (trivia games), 206
on clickClue handler (crossword puzzles), 273-274
on clickPuzzle handler (sliding puzzle games), 92-93
on colorCountries handler (strategy games), 395-396
on compileSelection handler (word search games), 253-254
on computerPlace handler (strategy games), 399
on convertToCaps handler
  crossword puzzles, 264
  cryptograms, 220-221
  Hangman, 235
  word search games, 246
on countryClick handler (strategy games), 398-404
on createMaze handler (mazes), 380-383
on dealerHand handler (blackjack), 319
on deckClick handler (solitaire), 335
on declineChallenge handler (multiplayer Internet games), 442

on detectCollision handler (adventure games), 362-365
on didIHit handler (sprite invaders game), 163
on divideCountries handler (strategy games), 394
on doneHand handler (blackjack), 318-319
on doubleMe handler (blackjack), 316-317
on draw handler (video poker), 290-291
on drawChar handler (mazes), 386
on drawLine handler (word search games), 251-253
on drawMaze handler (mazes), 383-384
on dropCard handler (solitaire), 336-340
on dropNewPiece handler (falling blocks game), 104-106
on dropObject handler (falling objects game), 125
on endLife handler (paddle bricks game), 189-190, 194
on endTurn handler (memory games), 69-70
on enterDoor handler (adventure games), 361
on enterFrame handler (sprite invaders game), 159-160
on enterLobby handler (multiplayer Internet games), 438
on exitFrame handler, 15
  adventure games, 367-368
  falling objects game, 123
  matching games, 51
  paddle bricks game, 192
  shooting gallery game, 138-140
  sprite invaders game, 163
  trivia games, 207
  word search games, 251
on fallOnPiece handler (falling blocks game), 107
on findAttack handler (strategy games), 408-410
on findStrongestCountry handler (strategy games), 407-408

on findWeakestCountry handler (strategy games), 406

on fireBullet handler (Space Rocks game), 174-176

on gameTurnOver handler (multiplayer Internet games), 443

on getBehaviorDescription handler (matching games), 44-46

on getCard handler (blackjack), 310

on getCardFromSprite handler (solitaire), 340

on getDoorPath handler (adventure games), 365

on getLinks handler (strategy games), 393-394

on getMatch handler (matching games), 50

on getPhrases handler (cryptograms), 218

on getPieceList handler (falling blocks game), 103-104

on getPileUnderLoc handler (solitaire), 341

on getPoints handler (adventure games), 362

on getPropertyDescription handler (memory games), 59-61

on getPropertyDescriptionList handler
adventure games, 363-365, 368-371
crossword puzzles, 262-263
cryptograms, 216-18
falling objects game, 119-123
Hangman, 230-232
jigsaw puzzle game, 75
paddle bricks game, 188-192, 195-196
properties, 46
shooting gallery game, 135-137, 141-143
sliding puzzle games, 90-91
Space Rocks game, 170-173
sprite invaders game, 152-158, 162-163
trivia games, 208-209
video poker, 294-295
word search games, 244-245

on getScore handler (matching games), 51-52

on getStackUnderLoc handler (solitaire), 340

on getWords handler
crossword puzzles, 263
word search games, 245

on grayLetters handler (word search games), 255

on handValue handler (blackjack), 312-313

on Hit handler (blackjack), 315

on hitBottom handler (falling blocks game), 106

on hitOtherPiece handler (falling blocks game), 110

on holdCard handler (video poker), 290

on initCountries handler (strategy games), 394

on initialDeal handler
blackjack, 309-310
video poker, 288-289

on keyDown handler (crossword puzzles), 272-273

on keyHit handler (trivia games), 210

on keyUp handler (cryptograms), 222-223

on killedMonster handler (adventure games), 360

on leaveGame handler (multiplayer Internet games), 440

on leaveLobby handler (multiplayer Internet games), 440

on letObjectsFall handler (falling objects game), 124

on lockInPlace handler (matching games), 49

on messageHandler handler (multiplayer Internet games), 436-437

on mouseDown handler
matching games, 47
shooting gallery game, 141, 144
strategy games, 397
word search games, 249-250

on mouseLeave handler, 15

on mouseUp handler
crossword puzzles, 274-275
cryptograms, 221
Hangman, 237
matching games, 48
multiplayer Internet games, 447
trivia games, 209
video poker, 295-296

on move handler
adventure games, 358-359
mazes, 385

on movePiece handler (falling blocks game), 111

on newGame handler
multiplayer Internet games, 443
solitaire, 342

on nextQuestion handler (trivia games), 207

on noInsurance handler (blackjack), 313

on noWordsInWay handler (crossword puzzles), 266-268

on onDie handler (adventure games), 362

on onInvaderAlive handler (sprite invaders game), 157

on openObject handler (adventure games), 359

on opponentMove handler (multiplayer Internet games), 445

on phraseSolved handler (cryptograms), 224

on placeArmy handler (strategy games), 404-406

on pushAwayFromEdges handler (falling blocks game), 109

on puzzleClicked handler (crossword puzzles), 270

on randomizePieces handler (sliding puzzle games), 91-92

on removeUser handler (multiplayer Internet games), 439

on returnCards handler (memory games), 63

on selectChar handler (crossword puzzles), 271-272

on sendChat handler (multiplayer Internet games), 439

on sendGameChat handler (multiplayer Internet games), 443

on setUpPhrase handler
cryptograms, 219-220
Hangman, 233-234

on shipHit handler (sprite invaders game), 161

on showArmies handler (strategy games), 396

on showBet handler
blackjack, 309
video poker, 289

on showBoard handler (multiplayer Internet games), 446

on showClues handler (crossword puzzles), 269-270

on showCursor handler (cryptograms), 221

on showDeck handler (solitaire), 334

on showHand handler (blackjack), 311

on showHangman handler (Hangman), 235

on showInventory handler (adventure games), 360

on showLetters handler (Hangman), 234-235

on showMatrix handler (word search games), 249

on showPile handler (solitaire), 334

on showPossiblePoints handler (trivia games), 206

on showPuzzle handler (crossword puzzles), 268-269

on showScore handler
falling objects game, 127
memory games, 67
Space Rocks game, 177
sprite invaders game, 160

on showStack handler (solitaire), 333-334

on showTimer handler (memory games), 68

on showTurn handler (memory games), 69-70

on showWallet handler (video poker), 289

on showWordList handler (word search games), 249

on showWorkspace handler (Hangman), 233

on shuffleDeck handler (blackjack), 307-308

on splitMe handler (blackjack), 317-318

on startDraw handler (blackjack), 315

on startGame handler (solitaire), 332-333

on startGameLobby handler (multiplayer Internet games), 435

on startHand handler (video poker), 287-288

on startMovie handler (multiplayer Internet games), 434-435

on startTimer handler (matching games), 52-53

on stopMovie handler (multiplayer Internet games), 443

on takeObject handler (adventure games), 359

on tryLetter handler (Hangman), 236-237

on turnCardOver handler (solitaire), 341-342

one frame movies (Score), 15

Online Media Group Web site, 459

OOP (object-oriented programming), 15-16

P

Pac-Man, popularity, 32

paddle bricks game
balls
behavior, 190-195
movement, 186-187
bricks
appearance, 187
behavior, 195-196
special effects, 187
building, 188-196
CD-ROM directory, 186
difficulty levels, 187
frame behavior, 188-190
handlers
on checkHitBricks, 194-195
on checkSidesHit, 193

on endLife, 189-190, 194
on exitFrame, 192
on getPropertyDescriptionList, 188-192, 195-196
overview, 186
paddle
behavior, 196
moving, 186
size of, 197
sprite channels, 196-197
variations
brick colors, 197
horizontal/vertical orientations, 198
multiple, 198
paddle size, 197

payoff screens, 21

PC games
arcade game translation, 33
evolution, 33

penalties, falling objects game, 118

phrases
capital letters (cryptograms), 216
encoding (cryptograms), 214-215
sources
cryptograms, 225
Hangman, 239-240
storage (cryptograms), 215-216

pieces
jigsaw puzzles
building, 73-74
cast library, 84
completion, 74
dragging, 72
random placement, 74
registration points, 73-74
shapes, 86
special effects, 74
sliding puzzle games
cast library, 88-89
motion animation, 89
numbered, 97
rectangular, 97
Stage, 96

player attack behavior (strategy games), 401-404

players (multiplayer Internet games)
identification, 449-450
turns, 434

points (adventure games), 355, 369-370
Poker, solitaire variation, 348
Pong, home marketing of, 31
populating matrix (word search games), 243-244
positioning blocks (falling blocks game), 100-101
POST method, high score boards, processing, 418-419
programming games, Web site resources, 461-462
progressive scoring (video poker game), 299
Projectors, game distribution, 25
property lists, 17
Pyramid, solitaire variation, 347

Q - R

questions (trivia games)
  format, 202-203
  randomizing, 212
random mazes, creating, 378-379
randomizing
  matching games, 53-54
  questions in trivia games, 212
rect property (sprites), 41
rectangular pieces (sliding puzzle pieces), 97
recursion (handlers), 388
registration points, 41, 73-74
retrieving scores from high score boards, 425-426
Robotwisdom Web site, 462
rocks (Space Rocks game)
  disintegration, 169
  movement, 168
  special effects, 170
  sprite behavior, 180-182
  varied sizes, 184
  vector shaped, 184
role playing games, 29-30
rooms (adventure games), 352
  creating, 372-374
Russell, Steve, computer game originator, 30

S

saving scores (high score boards), 422-425
scenarios (adventure games), 375
Score, one frame movies, 15
scoring
  cryptograms, 225
  falling blocks game, 112
  matching games, 51-52
  memory games, 66-67
  shooting gallery game, 134
  trivia games, timing elements, 203
Scott Kim Puzzlemaster Web site, 460
screens
  backstory, 19
  betting, 283
  between level, 20
  game background, 20
  high score, 21
  instruction, 19
  introduction, 18
  matching games, 53
  payoff, 21
  results, 284
  shooting gallery game, 134
  trivia game layout, 203
  wrapping (Space Rocks game), 169
secret doors (adventure games), 376
secret keys (adventure games), 375
selecting words (word search games), 243, 257
Senet, board game evolution, 28
shaping mazes, 388
shields (Space Rocks games), 184
ships
  movement (Space Rocks game), 168-170
  sprite invaders game
    behavior, 152-154
    bullets, 151
    movement, 150-151
ShockMachine, 34

Shockwave, 34
  game distribution, 25
  Web site resources, 459
shoes, deck storage (soltaire), 302-303
shooting gallery game
  blast sprite behavior, 145-146
  building, 135-146
  CD-ROM directory, 132
  cursor command, 143
  frame behavior, 141-144
  graphics, 146-147
  handlers
    on addScore, 144
    on allowAnimation, 141
    on beginSprite, 138
    on checkEndGame, 144
    on exitFrame, 138-140
    on getPropertyDescriptionList, 135-137, 141-143
    on mouseDown, 141, 144
  overview, 132
  screen elements, 134
  special effects, 134-135
  targets
    adding, 146-147
    ammunition, 134
    animation, 133
    behavior, 135-141
    point values, 134
    random timing, 133
  variations
    environments, 147-148
    hit animations, 148
    less violent options, 148
shuffling cards (memory games), 57
signs (adventure games), 355, 368
sliding puzzle games
  behaviors, setting, 90-96
  CD-ROM directory, 88
  finger cursors, 95-96
  game over conditions, 89
  handlers
    on checkForGameOver, 94-95
    on clickPuzzle, 92-93
    on getPropertyDescriptionList, 90-91
    on randomizePieces, 91-92
  overview, 88

pieces
  cast library, 88-89
  motion animation, 89
  Stage, 96
special effects, 89
variations, 97
solitaire
also known as
  Klondike, 328
  patience, 328
building, 331-345
card deck
  card back member, 345-346
  card outline member, 345-346
  card placeholder member, 345-346
  stack groupings, 330
card drag behavior, 342-345
card movement, 330-331
CD-ROM directory, 328
frame behavior, 331-342
game rules, 328-329
game screen appearance, 328-329
handlers
  on beginSprite, 331
  on deckClick, 335
  on dropCard, 336-340
  on getCardFromSprite, 340
  on getPileUnderLoc, 341
  on getStackUnderLoc, 340
  on newGame, 342
  on showDeck, 334
  on showPile, 334
  on showStack, 333-334
  on startGame, 332-333
  on turnCardOver, 341-342
overview, 328-329
sprite arrangements, 330
variations
  Accordion, 348
  animated cards, 347
  Calculation, 348
  Canfield, 348
  Las Vegas rules, 347
  Maze, 348
  Poker, 348
  Pyramid, 347
solutions (cryptograms)
displaying, 226
phrases, 215
Sony PlayStation, 33

sound
Hangman, 230
matching game, 43
memory games, 59
trivia games, 204
video poker game, 299
Space Game Design Tips Web site, 460
Space Rocks game
ammunition limits, 169
building, 170-183
bullets, sprite behavior, 182-183
CD-ROM directory, 168
difficulty levels, 170
frame behavior, 170-177
handlers
  on beginSprite, 173-174
  on fireBullet, 174-176
  on getPropertyDescriptionList, 170-173
  on showScore, 177
overview, 168
rocks
  disintegration, 169
  graphics, 170
  movement, 168
  sprite behavior, 180-182
screen wrap, 169
ships
  movement, 168
  sprite behavior, 177-180
variations
  flying saucers, 184
  rock sizes, 184
  shields, 184
  thruster graphics, 184
  vector shaped rocks, 184
Special Edition Using Director 7, 14
Special Edition Using Director 8, 14
special effects
blackjack, 306
falling blocks game, 101
jigsaw puzzles, 74
shooting gallery game, 134-135
sliding puzzle games, 89
Space Rocks game, 170
strategy games, 392
video poker game, 287
split option (blackjack), 305

sprite invaders game
building, 152-165
bullets
  behavior, 162-163
  special effects, 152
CD-ROM directory, 150
frame behavior, 158-161
handlers
  on beginSprite, 159
  on change Direction, 157
  on didIHit, 163
  on enterFrame, 159-160
  on exitFrame, 163
  on getPropertyDescriptionList, 152-163
  on invaderAlive, 157
  on shipHit, 161
  on showScore, 160
invaders
  bullet behavior, 164-165
  movement, 151
overview, 150
ships
  bullets, 151
  difficulty levels, 152
  movement, 150-151
  number of lives, 152
sprite banks, 165
variations, 166
sprites
arrangements, solitaire cards, 330
banks (sprite invaders), 165
behaviors, 16
blackjack cards, 303-304
bullet behavior (Space Rocks game), 182-183
channels (paddle bricks), 196-197
frame lengths, changing, 15
matching games
  bounding box, 41
  channels, 41-42
  correct matches, 41-42
  loc property, 41
  locking, 42-43
  precision, 40
  rect property, 41
  registration point, 41
rock behavior (Space Rocks game), 180-182

ship behavior
    jigsaw puzzle game, 77-84
    Space Rocks game,
        177-180
**Stage, sliding puzzle
    pieces, 96**
**Stephen Woodcock's AI Web
    site, 462**
storing
    multiple puzzles in single cross-
        word puzzle, 277
    phrases (cryptograms), 215-216
**Strategy and Tactics Web site,
    462**
strategy games
    artificial intelligence, 392
    building, 393-411
    CD-ROM directory, 390
    computer attack behavior,
        408-411
    computer place behavior,
        404-408
    countries
        armies, 391
        attacking, 391
        occupation, 390
        victory, 391
    country behaviors, 397
    handlers
        on attack, 410-411
        on beginSprite, 397
        on checkGameOver,
            396-397
        on colorCountries, 395-396
        on computerPlace, 399
        on countryClick, 398-404
        on divideCountries, 394
        on findAttack, 408-410
        on findStrongestCountry,
            407-408
        on findWeakestCountry, 406
        on getLinks, 393-394
        on initCountries, 394
        on mouseDown, 397
        on placeArmy, 404-406
        on showArmies, 396
    initial place behaviors, 397-399
    maps, 392
        bitmap images, 411-412
    movie script, 393-397
    overview, 390
    player attack behavior, 401-404

player place behaviors,
    400-401
primary frames, 412
special effects, 392
step sequence, 393
variations
    artificial intelligence, 413
    extra armies, 414
    fortifications, 414
    maps, 414
    victory determinants, 414
**submitting scores (high score
    boards), 421-422**

T

targets (shooting gallery game)
    adding, 146-147
    ammunition, 134
    animation, 133
    point values, 134
    random timing, 133
    special effects, 134-135
text
    colors (cryptograms), 224
    font selection (Hangman), 238
**text cursors (cryptograms),
    215, 225**
**text members (word search
    games), 255-256**
themes
    crossword puzzles, 276
    Hangman sources, 239-240
    word search games, 256
**thrusters (Space Rocks
    games), 184**
**tic-tac-toe behavior (multi-
    player Internet games),
    444-447**
timing
    ball drops (falling objects game),
        117
    cards (memory games), 57
    cryptograms, 226
    dropping blocks (falling blocks
        game), 101
    matching games, 52-53
    memory games, 67-68
    targets (shooting gallery game),
        133
    trivia games
        clock tick effect, 212
        scoring structure, 203

trivia games
    answering mechanisms, 203
    behaviors, setting, 204-210
    CD-ROM directory, 202
    disappearing answers, 204
    handlers
        on askQuestion, 205-206
        on clickAnswer, 206
        on exitFrame, 207
        on
            getPropertyDescriptionList,
            208-209
        on keyHit, 210
        on mouseUp, 209
        on nextQuestion, 207
        on showPossiblePoints, 206
    overview, 202
    penalties, 203
    question database, 202-203
    screen layout, 203
    sound effects, 204
    timing elements, 203
    variations, 212
**troubleshooting development
    phase, 23**
Twenty-One, *see* blackjack

U - V

UpdateStage Web site, 458
**user testing (development
    phase), 24**

vertical momentum, 168
**victory determinants (strategy
    games), 414**
video games
    arcades, 32
    Asteroids, 31
    Breakout, 31
    Computer Space, 30
    evolution, 30-32
    Pac-Man, 32
    Pong, 31
    reference books, 34-36
    Web site resources, 463
video poker
    building, 287-296
    button design, 297-298
    card deck, 283
        back design, 296-298
        faces, 296
    CD-ROM directory, 282
    dealing, 286

frame behavior, 287-294
hand values, 284-286
handlers
    on addToBet, 289-290
    on beginSprite, 287
    on calcValue, 291-294
    on calcWinnings, 294
    on draw, 290-291
    on getPropertyDescriptionList, 294-295
    on holdCard, 290
    on initialDeal, 288-289
    on mouseUp, 295-296
    on showBet, 289
    on showWallet, 289
    on startHand, 287-288
hold button behavior, 294-296
money values, 286
overview, 282
screens
    betting, 283
    results, 284
special effects, 287
variations
    background design, 298
    progressive scoring, 299
    sounds, 299
Vintage Gaming Web site, 463
violence, friendlier variations (shooting gallery games), 148

walls
    adventure games, 353, 362-363
    mazes, 378-379
        variations, 387
war games, 29
Web
    game distribution, 25
    high score boards, implementing, 418-419
Web sites
    3D Coding, 462
    Aftershock's Arcade Alley, 459
    Allegro, 461
    Amateur Game Developer, 465

Amit's Game Programming, 462
Artificial Intelligence FAQ, 462
artificial intelligence resources, 462-463
At the Crossroads, 459
Behaviors.com, 458
CleverMedia Developer Resources, 458
Computer Attacks, 463
Computer Game Developers Association (CGDA), 465
Computer Gaming World, 464
David's Game Programming, 461
Director Online Users Group (DOUG), 458
Director resources, 458-459
DirectOregon, 458
Empire Games, 463
Emulation.net, 463
Gamasutra, 464
game design resources, 459-461
Game Developer Magazine, 465
Game Development Central, 460
game programming resources, 461-462
GameDev.net, 464
Gamespot, 464
general game resources, 464-465
Grommett.com, 459
Happy Puppy Game Developer Den, 464
Lingo resources, 458-459
Macromedia, 458
Multiple Arcade Emulator Machine, 463
Online Media Group, 459
Robotwisdom, 462
Scott Kim Puzzlemaster, 460
Shockwave resources, 459
Space Game Design Tips, 460
Stephen Woodcock's AI, 462
Strategy and Tactics, 462
UpdateStage, 458
video game resources, 463
Vintage Gaming, 463

Wells, H.G., recreational war game originator, 29
word search games
    building, 244-255
    CD-ROM directory, 242
    frame behavior, 244-255
    handlers
        on buildMatrix, 246-248
        on compileSelection, 253-254
        on convertToCaps, 246
        on drawLine, 251-253
        on exitFrame, 251
        on getPropertyDescriptionList, 244-245
        on getWords, 245
        on grayLetters, 255
        on mouseDown, 249-250
        on showMatrix, 249
        on showWordList, 249
    matrix, populating, 243-244
    overview, 242
    text members, 255-256
    variations
        highlighted selections, 257
        matrix sizes, 257
        themes, 256
        word direction, 257
    words, marking, 243
wrong answer penalties (trivia games), 203

License Agreement

This package contains one CD-ROM that includes software described in this book.

By opening this package, you are agreeing to be bound by the following: